The Rail

The Rail

What Was Really Doin' in the 60's Bronx!

Tommy Donovan *July 2016*

Ellen —
Enjoy the stories!
Love & friendship,
Tommy Donovan

Veronica Lane Books
www.veronicalanebooks.com
Books that make a difference!

 *Veronica Lane Books*

www.veronicalanebooks.com   email: etan@veronicalanebooks.com
2554 Lincoln Blvd. Ste 142, Los Angeles, CA 90291 USA
Tel: +1 (800) 651-1001

Library of Congress Cataloging-In-Publication Data
    Donovan, Tommy, 1950
    The Rail / by Tommy Donovan
    -- 1st Edition
    p. cm.

SUMMARY: The story of a young man growing up during difficult times in the Bronx, New York.

ISBN 978-09910083-9-1

I have tried to recreate events, locales and conversations from my memories of them. In order to maintain their anonymity, in some instances I have changed the names of individuals and places. I may have changed some identifying characteristics and details such as physical properties, occupations, and places of residence.

- Tommy Donovan

Cover photo: Louis Lefty

Dedication

To my mother, Helen Irene Donovan, who loved her children with unparalleled fierceness, and to my sister, Margaret Mary (Peggy) Donovan, who bore more than her share.

"When I am with a group of human beings committed to hanging in there through both the agony and the joy of community, I have a dim sense that I am participating in a phenomenon for which there is only one word . . . glory."

M. Scott Peck
The Different Drum: Community Making and Peace

Table of Contents

Acknowledgments

I hold immense love and gratitude for my life-partner, Dr. Kim C. Colvin, who every step of the way provided encouragement, cajoling (when necessary), full-spectrum support, eagle-eyed proofreading, and abiding love. I can honestly say that fashioning a book out of this story would not have been possible without her at my side. I kneel in thanks, my lover, my friend, my colleague.

To my publisher, Etan Boritzer, whose tenacity in encouraging creative people to find the ways to express themselves, and tell their story, is heartening. Thank you, Etan.

To the people who inhabited the Amalgamated, thank you for creating a community. To those who are not mentioned herein, I assure you that you are not forgotten and you live in my memory still.

To the founders of the Amalgamated, thank you for your dream and vision and your *chutzpah* in turning the hinterlands of the north Bronx into a neighborhood founded on cooperation.

To Ed Yaker, Board President of the Amalgamated Housing Corporation, thank you for sending me the *Story of a Co-op Community: The First 75 Years*, an invaluable resource for my research. Thank you also for sending me photographs of the neighborhood.

To my editor, John Bowman, who with an discerning eye and a poet's sensitivity, nurtured my manuscript so my heart could appear openly on these pages. At every turn you showed me how to make my voice more powerful, more authentic.

To Kent Davis, for the hours we spent at local coffee shops sharing our approaches to the writing process. Thank you for your laughter, your unfailing encouragement, and your friendship.

To Jane Freeburg, for her support, calm reassurances, and insights into the publishing world. Thank you for reading the early manuscript.

To the Bozeman Library I offer my thanks for a supportive staff and a quiet second-floor area with panoramic windows where I watched the seasons change over the course of my writing.

To Katie, librarian at the Carnegie Public Library in Big Timber, Montana, who allowed me, a complete stranger, to check out an important reference book under her library privileges; thank you for your trust.

To the Webber family of Big Timber, Montana, Ed, Cindy, and Robb, in whose secluded bungalow near the Boulder River, I was allowed to immerse myself in my manuscript with no distractions whatsoever. Thank you for the beauty and hospitality of your ranch.

To Carl, Cliffy, George, Howie, and Jeff – who died way too young – I thank you for the unique and wondrous ways you each shared my formative years. You are ever my Bronx Brothers, my Roundtable Knights. I hope I did you proud.

To all the people in this memoir, living or dead, thank you for all the ways you helped shape me into the human being I am today. I am, only because we were.

Introduction: Past is Prologue

There was one particular section of the fence that ran along Van Cortlandt Park South, that came to serve as each generation's true north and the epicenter for all manner of social interaction – especially for the postwar baby-boomers. Directly in front of the park, this portion of the fence stretched east from the retaining wall to the asphalt pathway leading into the playground area, approximately 60 feet in length. When we were little, it was just part of the landscape demarcating the boundary between the street and the park, claiming no particular attention during our comings and goings. At that tender age, even if we noticed the older kids hanging out there it had little impact on us and even less interest. As we found ourselves inexorably thrust into our teenage years, this spot in front of the playground began to loom larger and larger in our lives and our imaginations as the place to be. This section of fence was known to everyone as, simply, The Rail.

* * * * *

I AM THE BASTARD SON of an immigrant Irishman. For this reason, and more that you will discover in the course of this memoir, I have had a difficult time locating home, trusting family, finding safe harbor in many of my intimate relationships. Yet between the years 1956-1972 (spanning the ages between five and twenty-one), home, family, and a place of safety were located in the Bronx. I found them not in my own house, but in the homes, schoolyards, playgrounds, and streets of a tiny, modern-day *shtetl* populated predominantly by Jews. Beneath the apparent incongruity of this statement – safety in the streets of the Bronx, family among people of a completely different religion, and home within others' homes – a deep and abiding kinship revealed itself over the course of my childhood, a kinship with a place and the people who lived there that shaped decisively who I was then and who I am now.

Indeed, this sense of kindredness has informed my entire life; during these tender and impressionable years, I learned how to trust, how to share, how to stand up for what I believe, and how to love.

The soil that nurtured this unlikely, lifelong bond with this place, with Jewish culture, and with the friendships forged there – many continuing to this day – was seeded by a variety of episodes, traumatic and elegant, painful and exquisitely loving. Mine was a coming of age in a peculiar time and place. Wedged between the nightmare of World War II and the thunderous, shattering Sixties, my coming of age awoke in me, and many of us, common rhizomatic stirrings to live beneath a sun different than the one we inherited. Pulled by an indescribable draw toward a deep mutuality, there arose a desire to band together in ways that would lift us beyond what the larger world offered as the apparently irreconcilable differences of ethnicity, class, gender, religion, and race. Our sensibilities were shaped by a nascent determination to defy a history of fear and the promise of more of the same and, instead, create something we imagined would be entirely new.

The shadows of past trauma stretched toward us from below, from the hellish death camps of Europe, while the dark forebodings of a nuclear future loomed above us in the shape of mushroom clouds rising from two still-smoldering cities in Japan. Despite the postwar celebrations and the surge toward boom, prosperity, and a horizonless future innervating the entire American landscape, most of the children my age arrived in the world comprising our Bronx neighborhood already swaddled in existential gravitas.

As a psychologist I am quite aware of how experiences of trauma (often called post-traumatic stress disorder or PTSD) can affect the human spirit in complex and contradictory ways. On the one hand it can bring crushing demoralization and defeat, with their offspring of self-medication, a variety of addictions, and an entire arsenal of psycho-social defense mechanisms that protect one from reliving the past or experiencing any feeling or emotion whatsoever. On the other hand, trauma can inspire a fierce determination not to succumb, a determination that can break shackles and liberate souls, urging the human spirit to re-engage fully and dynamically with life. Lives that have experienced trauma, firsthand or inherited, are often an oscillating mixture of both these types of responses, depending on the depth and significance of the trauma and the surrounding support systems. Further, and as an important dimension of the psyche-jarring power of traumatic experiences, I am also conversant with the notion of intergenerational post-traumatic stress disorder, the idea that traumas of a certain scale and magnitude, especially those directed at or affecting entire peoples and cultures, can be passed intergenerationally

iv

and expressed in a variety of symptoms despite not being experienced directly by subsequent generations. Studies relating to the genocide against Native Americans and the impact on today's generations living on reservations and in urban centers have documented this phenomenon, as have investigations into the traumatic impact of the American slave system and Jim Crow apartheid upon subsequent generations of black people in the United States. So, too, have studies examining the impact of the Holocaust, the *Shoah*, demonstrated the intergenerational shadow that continues to be cast upon Jews throughout the diaspora.

IN MY OWN CASE there is a legacy of intergenerational trauma as well. My father, Thomas O'Donovan, was born in 1900 in the city of Cork, Ireland, amidst growing agitations for independence and nationhood. His grandparents lived *an Gorta Mór*, the Great Hunger of 1845, and as a result felt the cascading waves of departure forcibly drain the population, a scattering that continued well into the 20th century and has come to be known as the Irish diaspora. My father's lineage, since the 12th century conquest by King Henry II, labored under the terror and repression of various forms of English colonization, based on the theft of the land and the forcible proscriptions against speaking Irish and practicing the rituals and ceremonies of their culture. Without land, a language, and the symbolic rites that anchor a people in an understandable and meaningful world, the Irish suffered mightily. Against this backdrop, centuries in the making, my father, who was a teenager when the chimes of freedom were struck in Dublin with the Easter Rising of 1916, took up arms for the cause of national freedom in the West Cork countryside; he subsequently spent two years in jail and lost a sister to the conflict. Not long after, his native land now torn by civil war, he would flee to America with the last remnants of hope trailing behind him.

This familial history gives me some certainty that one thread weaving the fabric of my kinship with my Jewish neighbors was our common wrestling with intergenerational-PTSD, with all its existential anxieties, however unconscious that struggle might have been in our early childhoods. These shared, uneasy legacies of injustice, oppression, alienation, and diasporic exile transmitted deep wounds throughout our families of origin and, subsequently, from them into us. This thrust many of us into the psychologically dark and unpredictable waters between the Scylla of desperately longing for safe and loving relationships, and the Charybdis of deeply fearing them at the same time. After all, when so much can be taken away so suddenly and violently, why risk the heartbreak? Within the apparent stability of a post-World War II peacetime that we were thrown into and which was everywhere across

America giving rise to heliotropic joy and a renewed faith in the future, the terrain just beneath the asphalt sidewalks of our little piece of the Bronx remained tremulus. Regardless of one's religious or ethnic background, living in nearly an all-Jewish neighborhood we all labored to some degree under lurking stresses and potential slippages as our psycho-emotional tectonics strained under the multivalent pressures of dislocation, dissociation, and nightmare memories of the Holocaust. With Jewish culture and sensibilities providing the container and orienting compass for so much of our coming of age, how could it have been otherwise?

Curiously, another important thread in weaving this bond between me and many of those who became my dearest friends was our mutual alienation from the dominant cultures that surrounded us, various levels of outsider-ness also shaping our identities. In my situation, after my mother and father separated, my mother, sister, and I moved to the Bronx to live under the roof of my mother's parents, within a milieu of German-Dutch sensibilities. This was a house where the Protestant ethos of "children should be seen and not heard" ruled, where the punishing "Board of Education" pine-paddle hanging ominously on the kitchen window-frame martially backed up the edicts for a stern silence and rigid orderliness. Neither my inherited Irish-rebel spirit nor my innate childlike curiosities were welcomed under that roof. At the same time, being one of the very few non-Jews in the neighborhood made for some confused and agonizing identity crises over the course of my growing up.

Similarly, but on a much larger scale, my Jewish neighbors and friends were still reeling – consciously for many of the adults, and mostly unconsciously for my generation – from the Nazi genocidal effort to exterminate them while a world, for far too long, seemed to look on in silence and apathetic inaction. For Jewish people in the aftermath of World War II, a neighborhood like ours provided a sanctuary of relative homogeneity, a safe haven of familiarity where life, for most of our formative years, generally followed the seasonal rhythms of Judaism – where religious holidays meant the closure of the local schools and businesses, where Bar Mitzvahs were still a sacred rite of passage, and where Hebrew and Yiddish were familiar languages to most people's ears.

ADDED TO THE SOCIO-CULTURAL FABRIC of our upbringing were the typical strivings of children trying to make sense of their environment, inside and outside our homes. The developmental minefields embedded in growing up, in attempting to navigate the mutually intersecting, often colliding, worlds of family life, school, religious instruction and belief, friendships, burgeoning sexual desires – not to mention making sense of all the other various and sundry adults populating our compact enclave with their own idiosyncrasies and neuroses – provided a richness and depth to our daily neighborhood experiences.

Yet within our neighborhood domain there was hardly equilibrium, much less stasis. Akin to medieval legend, the neighborhood served – literally and metaphorically – as a modern alchemical vessel. We had no say in choosing where we grew up. As we came of age we co-created our identities by rubbing up against each other in ways both soothing and hurtful. It was as if the blood of our mutually inflicted wounds, and the tears of our mutually offered solaces, flowed freely into each other's' lives and onto these streets, commingling into an organismic pulse. The admixture that ignited the processes we underwent, those we were subjected to or willingly subjected ourselves to, were clearly of the times while simultaneously offering glimpses of something of our desires to reach beyond the times. Our lives were lived as initiatory moments, a thousand cuts of ritual scarification. Coming of age between the *Shoah* and the Sixties brought us all unique psycho-emotional challenges that we met in our own distinctive ways. It was never easy to distinguish lead from gold within our neighborhood vessel or within ourselves, each other, or the world at large. The ultimate beauty, though, of living the ways we did was that we realized early on that these elements couldn't be separated; we were developing a hard-won appreciation for ourselves and each other as complex, contradictory human beings.

Since I am by schooling a psychologist, I feel it is important to clarify that this memoir is not a recalling of the past in the service of therapy, especially modern, smiley-faced therapy that lusts after salvaging something positive out of life's contingencies. Neither is this remembering in the service of exorcising the bad childhood experiences by bringing light into the darkness of suffering; nor is it one of attempting to banish trauma and tragedy, making it palatable by linking it to some higher purpose or outcome. That early deaths claimed some of us and not others, the fact that some of us still limp and others soar, is beyond judgment. They are but the mysteries of life. Yet, psycho-emotional threads run through the entirety of this memoir, since I have come to understand that acts of living *are* applied psychology. I mean this in the sense that life consists primarily of desires thwarted and desires satiated, and the unpredictable fallout from those oscillating and osculating moments. I write here with more of the mind demonstrated by the poet Ranier Maria Rilke. When asked about undertaking psychotherapy with the illustrious Sigmund Freud, he replied: "No. If they take away my demons then they take away my angels too."

Herein, then, are my impressionistic remembrances of the angels and the demons encountered within this neighborhood and within myself; memories of lives touched irrevocably, lifted to ecstatic heights, wounded, broken, cut short, made stronger. No one remained unaffected; we were all touched and transformed one way or another by our very commingling betwixt and between a profound and existentially liminal field, where the raw edges of the *Shoah* and the unpredictable, shape-shifting outlines of the Sixties mysteriously and dramatically pressed tectonically against each other. In this fiery embrace the skeleton-ghosts from the crematoria, joined by the dematerialized-wraiths of nuclear annihilation, whispered the brute meaninglessness of life while, simultaneously and incongruously, there was ignited an emergent imagination within our post-war generation, causing us to openly wonder about and freely attempt to create new meanings, to enact from out of the dark rubble a glorious *what if?* It was a living moment in history when Freud's twin Titans, Death and Eros, danced and whirled wildly, so close and intertwined that choices between one or the other were neither easily distinguishable nor easily made. These were the fierce streams and roiling currents that fed our formative experiences, consciously and unconsciously, that stone-washed our bodies and remade our souls, which watered the roots of our histories in this tiny Bronx enclave. It is the same water of remembrance that I attempt to fill my pen with so as to write herein.

YET, AS WE KNOW, MEMOIR RELIES on the least reliable faculty we humans possess: memory. So much goes into remembering and our memories shift with the elasticity of childhood time and the facticity of adult time, with accumulated experience altering perspectives once held to be the final word, the truth about the past. This is one of the reasons, for example, why three siblings remember *that* Thanksgiving Day dinner with varying descriptions – often highly contentious ones – as to what happened, each peering through a slightly different retrospective lens stained and shaded by temperament, age, gender, birth order, relationship to one or the other parent and to each other, and on and on. Because of the mercurial nature of memory these same siblings will also recollect completely different scenarios as to what or who was responsible for their parents' divorce, or who spent the most time looking after their dying mother. Such is the terrain of memory.

As is the case with this memoir, gather any of the people mentioned within, people who I grew up with – three, six, ten, or twelve of them at a time – and begin talking about a certain neighborhood event and you will get three, six, ten, or twelve varying recollections. Their remembrances will also be colored by their place in the social hierarchy, their age and gender, whether or not there was tension or equanimity at home, and a host of other dynamics affecting what is considered by each of them to have been impactful and therefore important to recall. This is simply the way it is when attempting to conjure the past in any agreed upon, recognizable form, much less attempting to label one version or another as the true version.

In an important sense, the memories I've recalled and written about here are more akin to jazz great Ornette Coleman's theory of *harmolodics*: they are more free-form rather than suffering under a typical narrative arc that seeks to make linear sense of events *after* they occur. In an important sense each memory is an instrument that together creates the rhythmic patterns making up this chapter of my life. These are visceral imprintings of images, sounds, smells; felt bodily emotions registering notes upon my flesh, all occurring prior to any logical thought. In this regard they all share equal value, all improvising together to express the music of these recollections. As such these memories will shift in time and space, jump to the foreground or retreat to the background, cut away suddenly, demand center-stage, or fade completely into shadows. There may arise within what appear as redundancies, but these are my attempts at turning the gem of these precious years from facet to facet, in the hopes of offering with these new angles fresh perspectives on the person or event described. With this in mind, memories reconstructed here are not truth claims; they are, rather, experiences significant to me that occurred along the trajectory of my life during these seventeen years in the Bronx neighborhood depicted within.

Perhaps, rather than calling this a memoir, what I have attempted to convey upon this canvas is more accurately the significant and impactful *impressions* that colored my life then and, further, give it its distinctive hue now. In my efforts to write from my open heart, painting with words *en plein air*, as the saying goes, I take full responsibility for what I've laid bare, with apologies in advance to all poorly remembered people, events, times and places. All omissions, mistakes, or misunderstandings are unintended, the consequences of one man's turning to the past to recall to the best of his ability what had meaning then, what remains salient today. It has been said that one's personal experiences, shared in all their raw honesty, often have the power to create bridges to the experiences of others, by either stirring similar memories or by stimulating reverie in the service of one's own remembrance and contemplation of their particular and unique life journey. This is my intent in writing this recollection; may it also be your experience as you read along.

Chapter One
From the Heights

Jimmy Bradley was in trouble, the biggest trouble of his life, the kind of deadly trouble no bartender ever wants. A broken whiskey bottle was poised just inches from his face and throat. He could smell the fast-draining spirits – from the bottle and from his soul – and hear them both spattering on the bar. The remaining liquor seeped with agonizing slowness from the inside of the bottle, forming droplets that seemed to hang on the amber-colored glass fangs expectantly, just like the now-hushed patrons. The air in the bar was taut, like a repressed scream begging for release but fearing the outcome. Jimmy Bradley's eyes were wide, his telltale mottled-red face now gone pale, his breath caught somewhere between his lungs and his lips. The man wielding the bottle was drunk and angry. His eyes were narrow with determination and purpose. It wasn't Jimmy Bradley who was the target of his blind, flailing rage and that's what made approaching him so dangerous; on this night he was ready to gouge the life out of anyone who came near. The veins in Jimmy Bradley's neck pulsed, as if to demonstrate the hope that his life would go on regardless. The hand holding the bottle began to sway ever so slightly, the muscles in the bare forearm tensing, perhaps coiling to strike. What happened next would imprint me for a lifetime.

*****

FOR THE FIRST FIVE YEARS of my life, from wide-eyed baby-carriage passenger, to toddler, to bold neighborhood explorer, I was part of the nightly crowd at Bradley's Bar. From the outside Bradley's resembled any other bar along Amsterdam Avenue, or any other similar establishment that dotted the Washington Heights section of northern Manhattan. Yet open the door, especially in the evening, and what confronted any would-be patron was nothing less than an unpredictable blue-collar bar at the margins of middle-class America. Gathered inside were gritty dockworkers, some with their longshoreman's hook slung in their belts.

1

A phalanx of merchant seamen, many who spoke multiple languages from their travels to foreign ports-of-call, and some who had been firsthand participants in making history as crew members on supply convoys plying the oceans east and west during World War II, also were drawn to Bradley's. They all bellied to the bar, their broad backs forming an intimidating wall for anyone seeking to get the bartender's attention. A handful of women, both tethered and loose, appeared like roses amidst this brooding privet of tangled masculine protest, men press-ganged within a proletarian greyness that they hoped Bradley's Bar would blessedly disturb or at least numb into a brief submission. The scents and laughter from the women intimated these possibilities; if not, there was always the liquor. Rounding out the denizens populating Bradley's on most nights was an assortment of day laborers and petty street toughs, lean, furtive, and not planning to stay past a drink or two so as to be ready when the next hustle beckoned – legal or underhanded. Bradley's Bar had an edge to it, an edge that offered protection to the menagerie of regulars within, backed up by a tightly wound defensiveness that could easily be sprung to deter outsiders. In those days outsiders were anyone who wasn't Irish and white.

Yet Bradley's Bar was my home, first or second home depending on the time of day and, like the neighborhood streets, another arena for me to play and learn. The apartment where I lived with my father, mother, and younger sister, 502 West 168th Street, was literally around the corner from Bradley's. My father, Thomas Donovan, had emigrated from Ireland in 1927 (dropping the O' from Donovan in hopes of avoiding anti-Irish discrimination). He landed here, in Washington Heights, where a thriving Irish community had formed a decade earlier. Shortly after his arrival he joined the International Longshoreman's Association (ILA), and began working the docks. My mother, Helen Irene Scheel, met my father when she was a candy-striper volunteer at a hospital in the late-1940s and he was recuperating from a serious back injury sustained on the job. They fell in love, or at least my mother did; she left her parents' home and middle-class life in the Bronx and moved to the blue-collar part of Manhattan.

By then my father was already well into his slide into the bottle, yet it was beyond my mother's capacity to see and therefore easy to deny. She was seventeen years younger and he was her first experience with a man, both in a relationship and sexually. She was in love beyond her wildest imagination, especially for a woman whose legs and hips carried the noticeable but not crippling deformations of childhood polio. That a man would choose her at all colored her every experience with my father and fashioned him romantically into the one and only true love of her life. My father saw a companion and comfort. Perhaps in these one-sided relationships, where commitment and love hold purchase at such wildly differing depths, the offspring experience their first taste of abuse when the sperm collides with the egg.

My father was 50 and my mother was 33 when I was born on November 28, 1950; my sister, Margaret Mary (Peggy), came along unexpectedly – and unwantedly – on February 28, 1952. No fanfare or welcome greeted either one of us. While my mother adored me as her firstborn, and disparaged the arrival of my sister as "a mistake," for all intents and purposes we were just two more mouths to feed in our two-room Washington Heights apartment.

Bordering Harlem to the south along 155th Street, the Inwood district to the north along Dyckman Street, and bounded on either flank by the Harlem River to the east and the Hudson River to the west, Washington Heights was a neighborhood roiling with ethnic, religious, and racial tension. Throughout the early part of the 20th century, Washington Heights was a magnet for immigrants making their way in New York City and often a springboard onto the conveyor belt of upward mobility. It was a neighborhood of transients, a stopover to perhaps gain a temporary foothold and vantage point on the quest to embody the American Dream of a good job and home ownership, somewhere away from the claustrophobia of growing urban density. Armenians, Jews, Irish, and Greeks percolated within the social aquifers feeding the fluid demography of Washington Heights, some fleeing persecution in their homelands, others escaping the overcrowded conditions in Manhattan's Lower East Side.

By the late 1930s, German and Eastern European Jews made up the largest portion of the residents, with the Irish a close second. On the eve of America's entry into World War II, anti-Semitic groups like Father Coughlin's Christian Front, and a split-off from the Front, the Christian Mobilizers headed by Joseph McWilliams, focused their attention on New York City. They fomented "Buy Christian" boycotts of Jewish businesses and incited Irish gangs to carry out violent attacks against Jewish residents in Washington Heights. After the war and well into the 1950s, even with the dissipation of overtly fascistic organizations and despite efforts by community and social service organizations to move toward reconciliation and tolerance, the poison had been swallowed: anti-Semitic outrages continued to emanate from within the Irish community of Washington Heights. Though unbeknownst to me at the time, the formative environment of my infant life was already psycho-emotionally influenced by, and partly shaped within, a relationship to Jewish people. There was no doubt that I had been dipped in attitudes of fear, negativity, and animus toward neighborhood Jews simply by osmosis. Even at such a tender age, Jewishness as otherness was among the very first threads to be woven into my nascent awareness regarding the world around me. This would become the central through-line of my eventual coming-of-age experiences in the Bronx, fashioning a complex and vital tapestry influencing my entire life.

Yet from the lived experiences of my pre-school childhood, from my knee-high view of the surrounding environment, life in Washington Heights was vibrantly alive and ignorantly safe. The constellation of my life essentially consisted of eight luminous stars, each of which I inhabited regularly enough (usually with my mother and sometimes with my infant sister along as well) to consider them the sum total of my life-world orbit.

The first star – my sun, really – and the center of gravity from which I launched my naïve explorations was our apartment building. I recall us living on the top floor of a three-story walk-up. I would often sit on the front steps and watch the iceman deliver huge cubes of block-ice held securely in metal tongs for the iceboxes of the residents. I would track his coming and going by the widening trail of droplets, tribute exacted by the merciless summer sun.

Underneath those steps was a basement apartment where the landlord lived. My only memory of him was the day he tried to hang himself on the clothesline behind our building, his act summoning a shrieking, lights-flashing cavalcade of police cars, fire engines, and ambulances. I eventually heard my mother talking about him still being alive, though he never again returned to take up residence. The only other apartment in the building that incites a vague, opaque quality of recall is the one where Margarita, a Puerto Rican teenager, lived and acted as the building's in-house babysitter for her own siblings and for any other mother that needed to run an errand without a child along, or just needed a break in her day. I remember lots of running around, laughing and jumping on beds in that apartment, and one moment in particular etched in my childhood memory: Margarita and I standing on a bed with her hand behind my head, pressing my young mouth to suck on her naked breast while the other kids ran amok, oblivious.

Our apartment was a two-room flat with a tiny kitchen; the communal bathroom was at the end of the hallway, shared by how many others I do not remember. The door to our apartment opened to reveal one large common space with two windows that overlooked the roof of the neighborhood dry cleaning store. I loved the sweet intoxicating smells of the solvents and fluids that wafted steadily upwards from rooftop vents toward our apartment, along with the hissing sounds of the steam presses working nonstop to make wrinkles disappear and creases perfect. My parents' bed was beneath the furthest window, my sister's crib alongside. Further to the right stood a small table surrounded by some chairs and, beyond them, through a doorless frame, was the kitchen. My bed was against the same wall as the door to the apartment, close enough so that every time the door opened it struck the foot of my bed. Throughout my years living there I had a recurring nightmare in which the entry door opened, hit my bed, and a strange man would enter and cut both of my legs off at the knees. I always woke up alarmed and calling out for my mother. Looking back, perhaps this was my intuitive, precognitive sense of the pressures that were building just under the relatively placid surface of our family life, a dreamtime symbol of the turbulence that my father's alcoholism would eventually wreak upon my sense of home, stability, and safety.

Bounding down the steps of my apartment building and turning left, the sidewalks of 168th Street led westward toward the Hudson River boundary of Washington Heights. Barely five brownstone houses in this direction, on our side of the street, was the second star in my constellation which riveted my attention whenever I encountered her, which was regularly since she was constantly out on her stoop or navigating the neighborhood on her errands. This was the domain of Old Biddy. No one knew much about Old Biddy's history and she appeared to like it that way, casting a stern, impenetrable gaze on all she surveyed when she perched atop the stoop of her brownstone. She was a huge woman with a face that was round, her wrinkles undulating convolutions that made her appear like a potato too long sequestered in a dark bin, wild black hairs sprouting from her ears and from nearly every facial fold, her tiny black eyes pressed into her unhappy visage like raisins into discolored dough. Old Biddy was a widow, made clear to everyone who saw her by the fact that she always wore black – a black, short-sleeved dress, appropriate in length for a woman who must've been well beyond her 60s. The dress also served to modestly conceal the rolled-down tops of her black support hose which, unbeknownst to Old Biddy, peeked out every time she mounted the steep stairway that led up into her building. It might've been the same dress every day for all anyone knew. In wintertime a black coat struggled to wrap her girth, yet the strain, for Old Biddy and the fabric itself, forced the coat to hang open even in the harshest of weather. Her hair was held properly clamped and flattened in a black hairnet with not a wayward strand detectable. With her sad breasts enfolded in her widow's uniform and blending in with the folds of her large torso, it was only the dress and hairnet that clearly identified Old Biddy as a woman.

But the most amazing thing about her, and the thing that kept my eyes wide and unblinking, was the fact that she somehow held up her enormous body while walking on the outsides of her feet. With her stockinged feet stuffed into her black shoes, her feet rolled perpetually outwards, urged illogically in this precarious direction by the sheer force of her weight pressing on the columns of her bowed legs. The soles of her feet literally faced each other when she walked, close enough at times during her wobbly gait that one could imagine a desire concocted between them to clasp onto each other, toes entwined, and offer a petitionary prayer for relief. I stared incessantly at her feet with perplexed awe at the impossibility of what I was seeing.

Yet Old Biddy ambled her way unfailingly around the neighborhood, sometimes eliciting teasing catcalls from some of the older kids, always attracting stares and their companion whispers. Witchy in her silence and her demeanor, she might have been Italian or Greek or Irish, but Old Biddy transcended all identifications, embodying a solitary specter of mourning and death in a neighborhood bursting with its own particular expressions of renewed life-force so recently released in the victorious aftermath of the Good War. Old Biddy absolutely magnetized me by the very starkness of her difference – and her indifference – to any other person or thing in the neighborhood.

One place I often encountered Old Biddy was in Mario's grocery store, another stable star within my neighborhood trajectory. It was less than a block away from where we lived; across 168th Street and just north up Amsterdam Avenue. My mother would stop in to buy her Tareyton cigarettes, a jar of Nescafé instant coffee, a can of Carnation evaporated milk, a yellow box of Domino's sugar, and whatever other groceries we needed. Mario was always wrapped in a white apron. He was round, as if he was constructed of circles; one huge one for his body and a smaller, but no less spherical one for his head. Mario was a jovial spirit, always friendly, always welcoming, his words nearly musical in his Italian accent. After saying hello to me by name, Mario and my mother would always spend time talking about grown-up things that I had no understanding of or interest in. While they talked I busied myself at my favorite location in the store: a huge wooden barrel, at least a head taller than I was, filled with fresh, raw string beans. While my mother scolded and Mario encouraged, I would reach my hand up over the lip of the barrel and grab a handful of string beans and begin munching. They were so crisp and fresh and juicy that I could hardly get enough. Eventually my mother, revealing the German side of her upbringing, would demand I "stop *fressen*" and leave the string beans alone. Taking me by one hand and grabbing her groceries in the other, my mother always tried to pay Mario for my transgressions in the string bean barrel, knowing full well that he would never take a penny.

Bordering Old Biddy's apartment building was a vacant lot. For the kids in the immediate neighborhood this was our urban playground and the fourth marker within my universe. It was another world, a disordered landscape etched with debris-strewn hills and valleys that seemed to beg us to explore, to build forts, to wait in ambush, to play with toy soldiers. Most of what made up the lot was the broken brick and concrete rubble of whatever structures stood there previously. Nails, pieces of rusty metal, splintered wood, and broken glass taught us the importance of paying attention. Over the years people continued to toss broken or used-up items into the lot: old radios and televisions, tires, mops, brooms and buckets, headless dolls. Our imaginations ran wild as we stole over and through the rubble, strewn with the detritus of castoff commodities, fashioning fantastical worlds in which to play.

What made it even more compelling was the fact that it was strictly off-limits. Even though my mother's regularly shouted admonition, "*and stay out of the lot*," always felt more obligatory on her part than truly carrying any meaningful weight, kids caught in the lot could certainly be arrested. Even after I was captured in the lot and brought to our apartment door at the age of five by one of New York's finest out on his regular foot patrol – "arrested," my mother would exasperate from then on, feigning shame whenever she recounted this story of my childhood mischief – none of the kids ever considered the lot truly out of bounds.

In an attempt to discourage delinquent transgression, the lot had been corralled by what appeared to be hundreds of knob-less wooden doors of every conceivable color. On the inside of the fence, pieces of wood, one end rammed into the ground and angled so that the other end was nailed into the doors at the midway point, served as anchoring braces. Additionally, every door was then secured to every other door from the inside by wooden support railings nailed in parallel tracks, one track closer to the ground, the other closer to the top to further stabilize the barricade. If the police showed up these railings also made it easier to scramble out of the lot, providing as they did perfectly placed toeholds and handholds to a quick escape. Getting into the lot was even easier since the pack of neighborhood boys included kids ranging in age from four and five up to eleven and twelve, and the older boys always helped the younger ones up and over the fence when necessary.

Once over the fence and inside the lot it was like being dropped through a portal where only we existed, the barrier that was supposed to keep us out now transformed into a magical partition shielding us from adult eyes and blocking any possible entry into our world by their world. Amidst the stone-throwing tribal warfare that sprang up periodically, amidst the individual skirmishes that erupted into black eyes and bloody noses, amidst the games of tag, army, cowboys and Indians, cops and robbers, we unrelentingly imagined this vacant lot as if it were entirely new to us every day. Joyously, we scrambled within our secret domain as if it were the makings of an immaculate state-of-the-art playground, swimming over the terrain and over each other; in the vacant lot and throughout our childhood interactions we were continuously buoyed upon cascading waves of feral innocence and exploration now only tantalizingly remembered.

Moving further west along 168th Street to the corner of St. Nicholas Avenue, then turning south for less than a full block, Mitchell Square Park stood like an island. This triangular-shaped park was another star in my neighborhood ambulation, a small oasis amidst the bustle of nonstop city traffic. With its shade trees, water fountain, and benches, Mitchell Square Park was a wonderful respite for taxi-dodging pedestrians crossing traffic-laden Broadway, those waiting to catch a bus, or neighborhood residents out for a stroll. While Highbridge Park, with its public pool and green parklands above the East River, was ideal for a family outing, it was a dozen blocks away. With my sister and me both under the age of five, this meant my mother being subjected to a really tedious and burdensome bus ride even on the best of days. Two blocks from our apartment, though, Mitchell Square Park provided everything toddlers could ever want. My sister and I would spend hours feeding bread crumbs to the legions of pigeons, she from her stroller and me wandering amongst them with a cellophane bag of bread pieces. The park had numerous benches that could be turned into stage coaches or planes or police cars. An outcropping of Manhattan schist rose in the middle of this tiny park, which I clambered over tirelessly and played all kinds of imaginary games on with my toys. Mostly it was simply the scaling of what appeared to me to be mountains, often on all fours, that gave my young body a sense of exhilarating adventure.

The most arresting feature of Mitchell Square Park, though, was the World War I memorial sculpture. Created by artist, Gertrude Vanderbilt Whitney, and perhaps inspired by the unprecedented carnage and the popular slogan that this was "the war to end all wars," the images were not particularly grandiose, nor even that overtly heroic. Instead of a general on horseback, or an officer with raised sword poised to direct a military charge, or soldiers raising a flag over conquered territory, these bronze images evoked a darker visage of war, its real dangers, physical pain, and hardship. Three soldiers stood atop the memorial: one is clearly wounded; another physically supports him, while a third leans in to take a closer look at the injured soldier.

As a young boy I was often mesmerized by these images. I felt like I stared at them for hours, lost in some deep, inarticulate, preverbal reverie plucking a temperamental chord within me that was slowly being awakened to the nobility of responding to the suffering of another. Somehow these larger-than-life men, depicted in their essential battlefield rawness, were touching some nerve-root embedded within me

8

that stimulated a real sense of the importance of being loyal, of looking after those who were in a bad way, of taking care of and protecting each other. It felt like these bronze wounded warriors were giving me guidance on some of the important qualities that go into shaping a man. Little did I imagine or understand how precious this imprinting – even from inanimate statues – would be for me at this tender age. For very soon my father would simultaneously embody and reject these very qualities, sending confusing and destabilizing temblors across the fault-lines of my vulnerable heart.

Directly opposite Mitchell Square Park and across Broadway stood one of the more ominous nodes in my neighborhood constellation, a place that I frequented more than I wanted to and a place that gave me fits of anxiety and sometimes outright terror: Vanderbilt Clinic, the area's gateway into the New York City Public Health System and quite literally into the adjoining Columbia Presbyterian Hospital. It felt like so much of my early years in Washington Heights consisted of my mother and I walking those two blocks from our apartment and entering the efficient bustle of Vanderbilt Clinic for what seemed to me an endless series of childhood inoculations.

Going to the clinic was always emotionally confusing to me. On the one hand I was let loose to explore a large playroom, expressly designed to distract children from becoming anxious or impatient with waiting; once there I got to joyfully put crayons to coloring book to my heart's content. I was quickly lulled into a sense that coloring was really the only reason I was there in the first place. On the other hand and without fail, my joy would ice over with the ominous, disembodied sound emitted through the hospital intercom: "Thomas Donovan, please report to Station 9." Station 9 was where the vaccinations were dispensed. Yet somehow, despite a spreading sense of dread in the aftermath of my being beckoned, I never put the playroom and the coloring books together with the reality of why I was visiting Vanderbilt Clinic, even when my mother walked in to retrieve me as the announcement was echoing away. As we walked toward Station 9, the fact that once again I was about to receive a painful shot – usually in one of my arms, though sometimes in my rear end – only hit me when my nostrils filled with the smell of rubbing alcohol and my eyes beheld a towering nurse dressed in white, syringe poised hungrily. Inevitably, I was already crying by the time I was matter-of-factly delivered to Station 9, all remembrances of coloring books and crayons driven utterly from my terrified mind. At the moment of reckoning my mother would scoop me up and hold me fast as the nurse, for who knows how many times that morning, inflicted pain in the name of prevention upon me, her already quivering target. The only thing that helped stanch the flow of my tears, though barely and not until I was seated at the counter, was my mother's promise of a hamburger and a milkshake at the local diner as a reward for me being such a brave little boy.

The neighborhood diner, on the southeast corner of the intersection of 168th Street and Amsterdam Avenue, was close enough to our apartment that I could smell the hamburgers being grilled at lunchtime. While it wasn't, by any means, a regular stop for my mother and me, given our family's lack of income, the fact that it served to assuage my Station 9 trauma causes it to stand out as another star in my childhood world. I recall it being green and white, skirted in silvery metal, and looking like an old railcar. Inside was a counter fronted by stools that swiveled, where my mother and I always chose to sit. The smells of the hamburger and fries were so exquisitely comforting to me, the tastes so utterly soothing. My consistent choice of milkshake was vanilla which, by the end of my lunch, I was dreamily sipping through a paper straw while floating in circles on the slowly rotating stool. All pain from the shots, all smells of Station 9, and all recollections of the terrifying nurse now subsumed within this sumptuous act of eating.

While my neighborhood orbit always began and ended inside our apartment, the eighth and final locale within my constellation, despite – or, perhaps because of – its darkling quality, was where life impressed itself most vividly upon my developing mind and body. That place was Bradley's Bar.

JIMMY BRADLEY, THE OWNER AND CHIEF BARTENDER, was born in Ireland like my father, and he sure looked and sounded the part. He was short and roundish, with a jovial face mottled red, especially his puffy, veiny nose. Most evenings he was busy behind the bar, wearing a long-sleeved white shirt, wrinkled and sweaty even in winter, his waist wrapped tightly in a white apron. Periodically he would sweep through the bar, greeting patrons in his distinct Irish brogue, making the simplest names sound poetic. On his rounds Jimmy would grab empty glasses and plates, replace overflowing ashtrays, and then re-appear back behind the bar uncannily in time to field the next round of drink orders from those perched immobile on the stools. Like seagulls inhabiting the pilings at the waterfront, these hunched imbibers maintained precise equidistance from each other as if they all possessed intuitive radar that prevented their bodies from getting too close. If there was conversation at all at the bar the words were spoken into the drinks, eye contact clearly being a risk at intimacy that these rugged laborers would neither conceive nor dare.

Every night Bradley's Bar was alive with the energy of workingmen. A steady baritone hum filled the air, periodically punctuated by laughter, rising voices in debate and argument, or the few inebriated lines of an Irish freedom song. From a voice aching with longing, words would suddenly sprout as the night moved into Bradley's, enveloping the remaining drinkers like a shroud: "For they're hanging men and women there, for the Wearin' o' the Green," sung forlornly, beckoned from the deeps of a melancholy soul. The bar could've easily been lifted right out of Ireland, replicating as it did one of the pubs of the "old sod." While Bradley's was clearly a male domain populated by longshoremen, laborers, and seafarers, it wasn't unusual at all for wives, girlfriends, and single women from the neighborhood to mingle. But what brought home the Irish-pub nature of Bradley's was the sound of children; children running in and out of the front door, especially on hot summer nights; children sitting at tables with their families; and children ever-present near the shuffleboard table, watching with wide-eyed fascination as the pucks glided back and forth under the bridge of lights and through the powder, emitting their distinctive clacking as they sent an opponent into the alley.

When it wasn't too crowded I was allowed to sit at the bar nursing a Coke with a maraschino cherry floating amidst the ice cubes, courtesy of Jimmy. One of my strongest recollections was my regular encounter sitting at the bar next to a grizzled seafarer. He always looked sideways at me, from under the brim of his captain's cap. He never spoke to me, preferring to silently acknowledge me like he would a drinking buddy. He always ordered whiskey and a glass of milk – perhaps a poor man's version of *scáiltín*, or Irish milk punch – which even at my young age I found strange. Prior to lifting his glasses in tandem, milk first for a coating, then the whiskey, he explained to no one in particular that it was for his ulcers; of course I had no idea what an ulcer was, what he was talking about, or who he was talking to. Yet with all its strangeness and hubbub, for immigrants from the Emerald Isle like my father and many of the others who flocked there, the scene in Bradley's Bar served to provide familiarity and a native comfort that promised welcome and safety in a world that often seemed to have little of either to spare.

The friendship between my father and Jimmy Bradley ranked my family a regular table toward the back, near the phone booth, the cigarette machine, and close enough to the shuffleboard table as to periodically draw my gaze when people were playing. There was even room next to our table, closer to the rear wall and away from foot traffic to and from the bathroom, for my sister's carriage, as there had been for me when I was an infant. We'd all sit there together, my mother drinking Coke and my father moving from beer to whiskey as the night progressed. They would both be smoking incessantly; my mother favoring *Tareyton* cigarettes while my father drew repeatedly from his unfiltered *Camel* pack. When my father's cigarettes ran out he would take the silver lining of the pack and fold it neatly into a tiny square. This was my cue to become mesmerized. As I watched he deftly tore little bits out of the paper with his fingernails until it looked like Swiss cheese, but I knew what happened next. As he unfolded the silver paper the image that appeared, despite what originally seemed to be a series of random holes, was a Celtic cross. I was always overjoyed when he held up his magic handiwork and passed it to me to marvel over. This was also my cue to ask my father if I could get him a new pack of cigarettes. He would slide a quarter across the table to me and I would gleefully run around the shuffleboard machine straight toward the cigarette dispenser. Standing on tip-toes I would drop the coin in the slot, search the icons below for the distinctive dromedary camel, then grasp the handle above with two hands and pull with all my strength. The handle would snap back with a metallic crash and whoosh, my father's pack of cigarettes would slide down. I'd grab them and race back to our table, proud of my accomplishment.

WE WERE AT OUR TABLE the night Jimmy Bradley faced off with a drunken patron wielding a broken whiskey bottle only inches from Jimmy's face and neck. Upon the sound of the breaking bottle – so indelibly distinguishable to the ever-alert antennae of this rough-and-tumble crowd from the noise of dropped plates or glasses – an electric hush swept over the people in the bar as their eyes were drawn in the direction of the sound. Anticipation, pressing urgently against the silence, surrounded the figures of Jimmy Bradley and his assailant, framing them in a holy, numinous glow, the kind of aura that forms when the expectation of bloodshed and possible death inhabits without warning. There was one person in the bar who claimed Jimmy as a dear friend, and because that meant everything honorable to him he was ready to risk his own life to see to it that no harm befell Jimmy Bradley. That person was my father.

Before the bottle-wielding man could render Jimmy's face into bloody, raw meat, or sever his jugular vein, my father flashed across the room to the bar. Grabbing the man's arm at the wrist he twisted and sent the broken bottle shattering to the floor. A fist-fight ensued as the drunkard turned his rage toward my father. It was over quickly, the man bloodied and out cold amidst some toppled barstools. While Jimmy called the police, the crowd erupted into cheers and began slapping my father on the back. My father made his way through the relieved and rejoicing patrons and returned to our table, pulling a *Camel* from his pack and lighting up, smiling and shrugging his shoulders in gestures that seemed to say "it was nothing." Suddenly, my eyes widened with the shock of what I saw. Spreading from the top button of his shirt downward, near to his belt buckle and radiating out toward his armpits, his white shirt was stained with an enormous swath of glistening blood. I was unable to move or speak or cry; I was simultaneously captivated and frightened. Even when my mother reassured me that my father was okay, that it was not his blood, still I stared transfixed. Somehow I knew instinctively that my father did something good that night; that standing up for the underdog, stepping up for what's right even at the risk to oneself, comes wrapped in nobility and sometimes in blood. I imagined the statues of the wounded soldiers in Mitchell Square Park, aiding one another. Like them, here was my father standing heroically in front of me, the image of his bloodied shirt billowing through the chambers of my young heart. I wanted so much to be like him.

IT WAS MERE MONTHS LATER when the entire heroic edifice I had constructed and placed my father atop of, came crashing down. Already in his mid-50s and suffering relentless pain from his back injury, my father had begun working on the docks less and less. He was aimless and angry. As a result he began drinking more and more, leaving my mother at home to tend to me and my sister. As my mother explained it years later, his nightly arrival at the apartment from Bradley's Bar began to grow increasingly tense between them. When my father began physically lashing out, my mother began fearing that my sister and I would eventually become targets of his rage. At that point two of her strongest instincts collided: her deep-seated impulse to do anything to protect her children smashed headlong into the profound love that filled her for the only man she'd ever been with, the only man she ever loved. From within the wreckage of her heart, amidst the debris of a life unexpectedly overturned by capricious, inebriated fate, my mother knew what had to be done and she moved decisively.

Having left her previous job as a salesgirl at F. W. Woolworth's right before I was born –the job that she had gotten when she decided to leave home and marry my father – my mother was completely without any source of income. On the precipice of becoming a single parent with two small children there was only one place for her to turn: back to her parents' house in the Bronx, back to the family she fled in order to fall into the arms of an immigrant Irish longshoreman, and a Catholic on top of it all. My mother knew that her departure from the family fold, under such shameful circumstances, would never be forgiven or forgotten; she was well aware that there would be a heavy price to pay if she asked to return under their roof. For my mother, though, protecting my sister and me was non-negotiable, even if it meant leaving herself unprotected as a result.

It was an incongruously beautiful spring day when my mother's brother-in-law, my Uncle Chuck, appeared in front of our apartment with a small truck to take us away from my father. Just like that, without any real warning, much less understanding on the part of my sister and I, our world in Washington Heights came to a sudden and definitive end. There was no conversation to break the awkward tension, only the matter-of-fact movements of packing up one life in the hopes of finding a better one elsewhere. It was something my father did over 25 years earlier when he left Ireland. Now the legacy of leaving – of fleeing, really – was being passed to the next generation.

There was hardly anything to load into the truck: my small bed, a chest of drawers, some bags of clothes, and more bags filled with the few toys we had. It was stifling and eerily silent, as if an oxygen-deprived vacuum suddenly enveloped me. All I remember is my father standing on the sidewalk at the foot of those steep stairs that led up to the front door of our building. His black wavy hair hung just above his eyebrows, a pack of *Camels* in the pocket of his white shirt. He simply stood and stared as Uncle Chuck closed the back of the truck and we all loaded into the front seat, me against the passenger door so I could look out the window, and my sister on my mother's lap in the middle.

I watched my father as we drove away. He never moved. He didn't even light up a cigarette. As we began our five-mile sojourn to the Bronx – an oddly short distance between two vastly distinct worlds – my mind and heart were stricken with sadness, confusion, and shock. My father, my hero, was not coming with us. For the life of me I couldn't tell if we were leaving him or if he was leaving us. The answer to that question would shape-shift throughout the course of my life in the Bronx, as I wrestled the twin demons of desperately loving my father and hating him with equal passion.

Chapter Two
3987 Saxon Avenue

It was the trees that mesmerized me as we proceeded toward our new home. On both sides of Saxon Avenue enormous maple trees rose like guardians, their leafy branches crossing each other at their apex like drawn swords to form a living, protective archway high above. The motion of the truck, along with the sun dappling the windshield, gave me the distinct impression that I was entering a wonderland, a very different place from where we had only just that morning called home. I felt like I was being transported through a magical, arboreal tunnel to another world and I was scared and excited. When my uncle pulled the truck into the driveway at 3987 Saxon Avenue, I saw what looked to me like a castle. I became very quiet and very alert.

*****

MY FIRST INDELIBLE IMPRESSION of the Bronx was when my Uncle Chuck turned the truck northward onto a one-way street called Saxon Avenue. With me, my sister and mother crammed next to him in the cab of the truck, trailing the rapidly dissipating vapors of our former lives, it was visually other-worldly, magical enough to make me forget momentarily leaving my father; it was wondrous enough to turn the pained, five-mile drive from Washington Heights and all my jumbled emotions into a receding blur. On the east side of the street, running nearly the entire single block that comprised Saxon Avenue, there stood a massive building that looked like a page lifted out of a children's picture book about medieval Europe. A four-story, Tudor-style apartment complex made of brick and wood, with vines of ivy climbing skyward, sat securely, almost proudly. This, I would find out shortly, was the original structure built to start off the Amalgamated Housing project – the so-named First Building anchoring the southeast-corner boundary of the neighborhood. On that same side of the street, adjacent to the sprawling apartment complex and claiming the northeast corner and remainder of Saxon Avenue, stood the institutional edifice of St. Patrick's Home for the Aged and Infirm.

On the west side of the street, what was now my new home stood amidst a phalanx of two-family houses that ran, one after the other, nearly the entire length of Saxon Avenue. Each house was a different color, each displayed singular front-yard and front-door configurations, and each one was separated by a shared driveway that led to quintessentially American two-car garages in back. On the northwest corner, where Saxon Avenue joined Van Cortlandt Park South, the edge of Amalgamated Housing's Sixth Building – also Tudor designed – could just be discerned. The homes on the west side of Saxon Avenue, dubbed "private houses" by the neighborhood's apartment-dwellings, were built years prior to the arrival of the Amalgamated's First Building, constructed in 1927. In comparison, these proto-suburban homes seemed to exude an air of superior indifference, an impenetrable aloofness of being there first, of somehow being better, closer to the American Dream than living in apartments; these were the intangible sensibilities through which one navigated when walking along Saxon Avenue. This is what greeted us as we shakily returned to my mother's roots.

Family lore tells that my grandfather, Frederick Christian Scheel, and my grandmother, Emma Irene Scheel (nee Plangemann), were both growing tired of living in Manhattan, where their family had already burgeoned to four of their eventual seven children (including one child dying at the age of four). Despite a prosperous and comfortable life owning a successful store on 9th Avenue, featuring made-on-the-premises ice cream and candy, and collecting rents from the apartments above the store and another apartment building on West 82nd Street, living in the heart of the city was becoming cramped. Looking north toward the decidedly un-urban, spacious hinterlands of the Bronx, my grandfather bought a seven-year old house on Saxon Avenue in 1927, at the same time Amalgamated Housing was breaking ground for the First Building just across the street.

The 3,560 square-foot, three-story, two-family house was brick with yellow wooden trim and lots of windows. Standing with one's back to Saxon Avenue, and looking at the front of the house, the door on the left-hand side of the structure was marked 3985 Saxon Avenue; this led to a flat occupying the entire ground floor wherein a single tenant lived. Mrs. Cohen was a widow with a quiet, pleasant demeanor, to whom my grandparents were cordial yet never overtly friendly. Mrs. Cohen stayed mostly inside her flat, receiving periodic visits from her adult son. The door to the right, marked 3987, led into the rest of the house, encompassing the second and third floors, where my extended family resided. Our arrival swelled the inhabitants to nine, as we joined my grandparents, Uncle Chuck Drolet and his wife, Evelyn, and their two sons, Brian, the oldest, and Ned, in what was to become very close quarters.

Outside, the house was fronted by a rectangular garden space, about eight feet wide and extending another ten feet to the sidewalk, sitting between the twinned yellow front doors. Each doorway possessed an identical brick-and-concrete stoop with five granite steps inviting entrance. A metal milk box sat to the left of our door, where fresh milk in glass bottles appeared regularly. About twice a week tantalizing boxes of donuts and crumb cake were left by the Dugan's "bakers for the home" white and blue delivery truck. Just across the sidewalk, in line with each of the front doors, towered two enormous maple trees – part of the leafy arch enfolding Saxon Avenue. To the left of Mrs. Cohen's door another, narrower, garden plot created the property line in that direction. To the right of our family's entrance another garden space ran to the edge of the driveway. Each of these sections of garden was framed by a raised lip of concrete, atop which ran two-foot-tall hedges acting as a border and barrier. My grandfather's favorite pastime was carefully tending to these tiny plots. As long as he was able to make it up and down the stairs (he was 88 years old when we arrived), into and out of the house, he was a daily fixture in his garden during good weather. He was either trimming the hedges, sitting in his folding aluminum lawn chair plucking weeds to protect his azaleas, or watering in the early evening as the sun began its descent, all the while incessantly chiding me, his reluctant helper, to never water when the sun was blazing high in the sky.

On the driveway side, a slender strip of garden continued halfway down the length of the house to a side entrance. Two brick walls with flower boxes atop them embraced a small landing, with two steps leading to a door; inside this door a central staircase connected the top floor to the basement. The garden continued on past the side entrance toward the backyard; it was filled with flowering bushes and shrubs.

At the rear of the house, a white wooden door with a single-pane of glass led down two concrete steps to another door and eventually into the basement. In the space between the two doors, on both sides of the steps, were paraphernalia for gardening: a variety of specialized rakes and shovels leaning against the walls, an assortment of hand-held clippers lying in baskets along with dozens of pairs of well-used gloves. My grandfather never walked out of the basement without taking some implement with which to tend to his garden, nor walked back in without carefully replacing the cleaned tool in its proper place. Inside this rear entryway, looking toward the front of the house, the basement ran the entire length, with a very low ceiling and a latticework of water pipes clinging to it overhead. The floor was concrete. On either side, the whitewashed walls were periodically interrupted by tiny wood-framed, glass-paned windows. They were so close to the ground that only the most shadowy of light could enter, giving the basement a drab and sometimes eerie feel, even when the lights were on. Halfway down on the left was the door leading to the central stairway that ran the entire house, bottom to top. Directly across the way on the opposite wall, was a twin-basined porcelain work sink, the front of which angled sharply down and under toward the plumbing below. Gritty, pumice-laden bars of Lava soap seemed to perpetually inhabit the tiny tray that was etched into the sink's rim to the right of the faucet. A barrel-shaped washing machine stood next to the sink, complete with a state-of-the-art automatic electric wringer and a thick black hose for laundry-water runoff nosing into one of the sink basins. This was where all the household clothes began their soiled, after-use journey back to presentable. In the space between the backdoor and this approximate halfway point, just to the right as you entered, were a miscellaneous assortment of boxes, a few racks with clothes hanging on them, and two battered pedal-braking bicycles; to the left, neatly sequestered beneath one of the windows, were items that Mrs. Cohen stored. In the space from this midline toward the front of the house, was my grandfather's work area.

This part of the basement maintained an off-limits aura around it; this was not a place to play and no one ventured into it without my grandfather being there and extending an invitation. Like any sacred area it was organized around a central fire: the coal-fed furnace that my grandfather was strictly in charge of. An undersized open entryway, that required my grandfather to stoop a little to traverse, led into the small area under the very front of the house where the coal bin was situated. Directly above the bin were two small portals where the coal delivery man would insert a chute and proceed to fill the space with this dark and dusty fuel. It was in here that my grandfather would walk and dip his hand-shovel into the coal to feed the flames in the furnace. When he was in a particularly peaceable mood, he would sometimes allow me and my cousins to do the honors of tossing the coal into the maw of the roaring fire. This was always a scary, reverent, act. Within a few years of my family's arrival, the coal furnace was converted to an oil-burning one, the mysterious and enthralling task of keeping the fires stoked with shovelfuls of coal suddenly disappearing into an automated mundane.

Just in front of the coal bin, a rickety wooden wall presented an assortment of tools: hammers, files, jars of nails, nuts and bolts, and screws and screwdrivers. Propping the wall up was the larger of my grandfather's workbenches, while to the right a smaller bench, angled at 90-degrees, formed the area into an L-shaped work space. Each bench had a steel vise attached, one larger than the other. Underneath the benches, on makeshift shelves, clustered various boards of incongruous widths and lengths, along with odd pieces of linoleum and roofing shingle. Off to the side of the smaller workbench stood two wooden-handled sledge hammers of different sizes, which my cousins and I delighted in trying to heft. This subterranean place and the garden areas surrounding the house were my grandfather's sanctuaries.

Directly behind the house sat a two-car garage, the spaces rented out to neighborhood car owners seeking security and protection for their vehicles. A quince tree stood just to the left of the garage door and a cherry tree overhung the back of the garage roof; a grapevine clung to the bricks of the house like a waterfall spilling down from the metal trellis three stories above on the back roof. The cherries, the quinces, and the grapes perennially made their way into my grandmother's jam jars.

UPON THE HEAVY, YELLOW FRONT DOOR that led to our part of the house, were the greenish, oxidizing metal numbers: 3987. Once through that first door, typically unlocked during daylight hours, there stood a second, locked door filled with small glass panes from top to bottom. After looking downstairs to ascertain the identity of the caller who rang the bell, this door could then be opened by a buzzer in the kitchen. Beyond this door, a long stairway led up to a landing on the second floor. Here, beneath a narrow window, stood a small desk with a chair tucked underneath, along with a large, black rotary telephone – the only phone in the house.

Standing on this landing a visitor could enter into the main part of the house through one of two doors. The door directly ahead was solid wood, never closed, and led into the kitchen. Immediately inside the kitchen, to the left, was a thick, white, swinging door that provided entry into the dining room. Just past this door, along the same wall of the kitchen, ran an extended porcelain sink with a place for food preparation on one side of its basin and a dish-drying rack on the other (though this area was rarely used since hand-washing and drying dishes, pots and pans was a communal undertaking after each meal). The sink, supported by slender, steel-reinforced porcelain legs, had open space underneath for storage, as well as providing easy access to the exposed plumbing. Directly above the sink, pantry shelves enclosed by two glass-paneled doors protruded, holding an abundant assortment of foods in jars, bottles, and cans, along with myriad boxes of rice, pastas, cereals, cookies, plus bags of sugar and flour for my grandmother's baking. Next, partially blocking a door to the common stairway running through the center of the house, stood a refrigerator, its belly, door-shelves, and the freezer compartment above filled with a cornucopia of milk, juices, fruits, meats, and assorted other items requiring refrigeration, the likes of which never existed in the tiny icebox in our apartment in Washington

21

Heights. Against the far wall, directly opposite the landing, was a small compartment with a latching door that housed a fold-down ironing board and companion steam iron. This was often the site of early morning hustle and bustle as school and work clothes were de-wrinkled, mostly by my mother and aunt (though my uncle's stint in the Navy gave him some proficiency with ironing). Slightly to the right of this, along the same wall and commanding the corner was the four-burner gas stove. The wall opposite the sink had two large windows that overlooked the driveway and beneath which squatted a cast-iron steam radiator. A table, surrounded by three chairs, sat next to the windows, edging its way slightly into the center of the kitchen. Behind and above the chair that sat immediately to the right of the door to the landing, a built-in hutch clung; the three drawers below the serving counter held pots, pans, and an assortment of Pyrex cookware, while above, behind two glass-paned doors, were four shelves holding the day-to-day dishes.

The second possible way to enter the main quarters from the hallway landing was a glass-paneled door to the immediate left that when opened revealed the living room. A Motorola black-and-white television, atop a stand that housed my grandparents' 78-rpm records in a cabinet at the bottom, immediately grabbed the attention of anyone entering through this door, looming as it did like an altar across the room in the far corner. Circling the room to the right from where the television stood, a set of glass-paned double-doors, folded perpetually open, provided another portal that accessed the dining room. Between this doorway and the door to the hallway landing, sat my grandfather's massive, wine-colored, over-stuffed fabric armchair, perfectly positioned to give him a front-row seat to the only things he watched on television: the *CBS Evening News*, with Walter Cronkite; Friday night wrestling; *The Lawrence Welk Show*, every Saturday night without fail; and topping off the weekend, *The Ed Sullivan Show* on Sunday night. Behind his chair stood a floor lamp that illuminated his balding head whenever he sat there; in front his green, leather footstool squatted, providing respite for his weakening legs. To his right was a small table with an ashtray for his cigars and room enough to hold a shot glass for his periodic indulgences of *Schnaps*; it was a table which would soon be increasingly cluttered with his medicines as age and infirmity began to assert themselves upon the body of the Scheel family patriarch. On the left arm of his chair hung his ever-present wooden cane, which he used to raise and lower himself, navigate the stairs to tend to his garden, and shake mightily and angrily, in rhythm with his German curse words: *"Himmeldonnerwetter"* would resound throughout the house whenever one of the masked, villainous wrestlers got the best of one of his favorites, or whenever the decibel level from noisy kids got the best of him.

Behind and off the left shoulder of my grandfather's chair, against the wall opposite the television, sat an Adirondack-style couch. The couch was usually reserved for my uncle's family, with my sister and I typically relegated to the floor space in front of the television, all of us watching whatever our grandfather was watching. Directly across from the doors that led to the dining room stood another set of glass-paned, double doors that opened to reveal the sun parlor. This was a tiny room, with a black, never-played upright piano on one side and a narrow metal-framed, army-style cot directly opposite. Banks of tall, narrow windows, running from knee-level almost to the ceiling, lined the remaining three sides of the room, allowing us to look out upon Saxon Avenue from various angles. The windows and the doors in the sun parlor were all curtained, affording privacy, especially when my bachelor uncle, Walter Scheel, claimed this space when he made regular holiday visitations from his home in Washington, D.C. In the far-left corner of the living room stood an uncomfortable, rigidly upright chair, upholstered in a floral pattern. On the wall behind this chair hung an oil portrait of my grandfather when he was younger, a vital man in his forties, sporting a full head of hair and an immaculate moustache, exuding a determined, upstanding, and successful demeanor. When my grandmother was not in the kitchen, or sewing on her pedal-driven sewing machine in my grandparents' bedroom, this is the spot she wordlessly occupied in the living room, especially when Lawrence Welk was on. Between her chair and the television, the wall opposite the landing door held wide, twinned windows beneath which sat another radiator. These windows looked across into the neighbor's house and were, therefore, closed off by perpetually downcast Venetian blinds.

AS MIGHT BE EXPECTED, the dining room was the physical center of the house (though the kitchen bustled as the in-gathering hub of activity, especially during holidays). A huge, dark, walnut table, with sliding extension leaves accessible on either end for guests, sat heavily under a chandelier. Carved and etched beautifully it sat like an Old World Great Table, sanctifying family traditions, enforcing unspoken rankings, anchoring the family, and creating appropriate social spacing. The legs of the table were solid and round, thicker in the middle, thinner where they connected to the underbelly of the table and where they sat upon the floor (my mother's recurring lament and nightmare memory every time she passed this table was her being cursed as a child to have to use toothbrush and wood polish on these ornately fashioned table legs whenever cleaning day arrived). Six matching chairs with high, straight backs, circled the table. The two at either end – where our grandparents presided – were the only chairs possessed of slightly curved arms for support and a touch of austere elegance.

Except for the wall opposite the swinging kitchen door, where a steam radiator crouched below windows with the requisite shuttered Venetian blinds, dark, matching dining room furniture surrounded the table. A wall-length china cabinet sat behind my grandmother's chair, housing an assortment of the best bowls and serving platters. Against the wall that held the swinging kitchen door, stood a buffet filled with more implements for entertaining, a rectangular, gold-framed mirror just above. That same wall, on the other side of the swinging kitchen door, presented a five-foot tall polished, dark-wood bookcase with locked glass-paned doors. On the shelves old hardcover books with a variety of colored spines stood silently, untouchable due to their aged fragility. A half-dozen diorama Easter eggs beckoned intriguingly from different shelves but were ruled off limits to children, visually accessible through the glass but never to be handled. Nearest to where my grandfather sat, his back to the double doors that led into the living room, there stood a tall, narrow hutch to his left. between his chair and the windows. This structure housed the good china: plates, cups, and saucers up top; a drawer with the good silver at waist height; lower shelves filled with placemats and a variety of cloth napkins. The bookcase was the single piece of furniture in the dining room that had glass panes, but this alone could not relieve the overpowering sense of unrelenting claustrophobia brought on by the immensity of the furnishings and dark color of the wood. Heaviness pervaded this room, a respectable Protestant stolidness that brooked no laughter and little conversation; only the polite sounds of silverware barely touching the plates, wielded always with proper form and address to the food before us.

LEAVING THE DINING ROOM and moving further on toward the rear of the house, the hallway passed a tiny bathroom on the left and another door to the central staircase immediately opposite on the right. The bathroom housed a toilet, a pedestal sink with a mirrored medicine cabinet above, a bathtub, and a separate tiled shower. At the foot of the tub a copper sheath held the long, metal bathtub stopper, lowered when filling the tub, pulled up and rested on the lip of the sheath to let the water drain. The faucets and tap for the bathtub protruded stylishly from the middle of the wall forming one side of the tub rather than from the wall at the foot. This bathroom weathered the daily demands of my grandparents, my mother, my sister, and me, the five of us who inhabited the middle floor. A multi-shelved linen closet, filled with clean towels, bedding, and various and sundry ointments, liniments, and first-aid supplies was to the immediate right of the bathroom.

Just beyond the bathroom, the hallway terminated at two mirror-image bedrooms. The bedroom to the left was where my grandparents slept in separate beds. Two windows, one looking out over the narrow, shrub-laden side of the house, the other looking directly over the cherry tree and garage in the back, brought little light into their room. A walk-in closet with a full-length mirror on the inside of its door, shared the same wall as the entryway. In the other room, where my mother, sister, and I slept, the same basic layout was replicated: one window looking over the driveway, the other overlooking the space between our garage and the neighbor's garage at the rear of the house. The window facing the backyard was the only access to the clothesline that stretched from the window frame to a tall, thin pole near the fence at the property boundary. A cloth bag of wooden clothespins hung from a metal hook just below where the clothesline was attached. After the clothes had been washed in the basement they would be brought upstairs and into our bedroom where, one-by-one they would be fastened to the clothesline and slid out over the backyard.

We shared a similar walk-in closet with mirrored door, a thin wooden pole for hanging clothes, and shelves above for games and other items, Along the wall to the right of the rear window was the double bed where my mother and sister slept; at the foot of their bed, extending nearly to the closet, was my bed, the small Castro convertible that we had taken from our apartment in Washington Heights. This room, formerly my grandmother's bedroom and sewing room, was now our shared space. The arrival of our broken family had evicted my grandmother, cramming her back into cohabiting in a bedroom with her aging husband. The tensions of this forced rearrangement would become steadily more evident as time went on.

THE THIRD FLOOR, accessed via the central stairway, was where the Drolet's lived – Uncle Chuck, Aunt Evelyn, and their two sons, Brian and Ned. It consisted of two bedrooms and a bathroom, and two walk-in closets. The bedroom at the front of the house was small and made smaller by the fact that the eaves sliced off a portion of the ceiling on two sides, making it necessary to watch one's head when approaching these areas. Some additional breathing room was made possible through a wooden door that permitted access to a small rooftop patio enclosed by a wooden railing painted yellow. During the summertime a screen door provided access to the periodic breezes that broke away from the humid clutches of the typically still air. This room, where my Aunt Evelyn and Uncle Chuck slept, was plush-carpeted in white, very feminine and clearly not for kids unless specifically invited.

A short walk down the hallway, back toward the rear of the house, were two walk-in closets nestled under the eaves on the right and, on the left, my cousins' bedroom. My cousins shared a bunk-bed, with

Brian, the oldest, commandeering the top bunk and Ned relegated to the bottom. Various erector-set projects were always in some phase of construction, as were models of ships, planes, and tanks from the various belligerents of World War II. Shoeboxes filled with assorted card collections – baseball and Davey Crockett cards being my cousins' favorites – were stacked around the room along with a variety of comic books.

Just past my cousins' bedroom and also on the left, was the bathroom. Painted by my uncle with specific instructions from his wife, it was white with pink trim, giving it a distinctly feminine feel; perhaps my aunt's bid to salvage a relatively testosterone free *toilette*. It contained a tub (with a jury-rigged rubber hose running from the faucet to a shower-head hooked high on the wall), a sink (with a white metal, mirrored medicine cabinet above the porcelain basin), and a toilet (with a fuzzy pink cover). If you sat on the toilet lid and turned a quarter turn to the left, access to a vanity shelf was available. This was my aunt's mysterious cosmetic domain, complete with a two-sided round make-up mirror (one side able to magnify), and myriad creams and lotions applied with a logic known only to her. Finishing the top floor, a door led outside to another, larger, tar-papered rooftop patio at the rear. A metal trellis, entwined by a grapevine that extended down the back of the house all the way to the ground, covered fully one-third of the rooftop area offering some shade in the summer and luscious grapes in the fall. The wall that enclosed the back roof was about four feet high and topped with a series of concrete planter boxes, barren and filled only with dirt.

I sat there in the driveway, peering out from the truck cab at what was now the house we would be living in, a house that appeared easily larger than the entire apartment building where we had lived in Washington Heights. I was reeling, stunned at the radical shape-shifting my life had just undergone in the few hours it took to pack up all our belongings and drive from Washington Heights to the Bronx. I knew I was in a very different world, perhaps two worlds really: one outside, with unfamiliar streets and unknown people; the other one populated by my new extended family waiting inside 3987 Saxon Avenue – also unknown. What I would not – could not, really – know until many years later, was that there was some gut-level intuition feeding my hesitation to enter this seemingly beautiful castle rising before me.

Chapter Three
The Neighborhood – Oasis in Brick

During the years I was growing up, when people in New York City were asked where they lived, the common response was to reply with the name of your neighborhood. While loyalty to one's borough was certainly invoked at times in order to situate a particular neighborhood, or to tutor the ignorant, the more tenacious roots of identity emerged from soils nurtured within distinctive neighborhood confines. In no uncertain terms it was the neighborhood that was structured upon the living culture of its inhabitants, fed by aquifers of ethnic and racial pride while, in turn, reciprocally imbuing the lives of those clustered there with safety, meaning and character. In the Bronx, to the question "Where do you live?" you might hear answers like these: Marble Hill, Mosholu Parkway, Riverdale, Bronx River, Highbridge, Tremont, Eastchester, Hunts Point, Kingsbridge, Woodlawn, City Island, Co-op City, Morrisania, Pelham Parkway, Crotona, Fordham, Bedford Park, Castle Hill, Throggs Neck, University Heights, and so on. When even more specificity was demanded, referencing a particular street that characterized and further signified the neighborhood was common. Our neighborhood was situated in the Van Cortlandt Park area, but since the park was the fourth largest in New York City, claiming over 1,100 acres, naming our main street – Van Cortlandt Park South – immediately pinpointed where in the vast expanse of the parkland we lived.

Interestingly, to those informed and initiated about New York's demographics (as most natives were by matter of an upbringing that was keen on designating what neighborhoods were safe to traverse and what others were definitely to be avoided), not only was a geographic location conjured by naming a neighborhood or a street within it, but quite often the reference indicated to the listener the general racial, ethnic, and class characteristics of the people living there. In Manhattan, Harlem was a black neighborhood, as was Bed-Stuy in Brooklyn; Chinatown was obvious, as was Little Italy; Inwood was unmistakably Irish. Jewish neighborhoods thrived in Brooklyn, in places like Flatbush, Crown Heights, and Forest Hills. In the Bronx, for example, everyone knew that Arthur Avenue meant a littler Little Italy, while the South Bronx was another black neighborhood; East Tremont was Puerto Rican, and Woodlawn was Irish. Even closer to where we called home, regarding the contiguous neighborhoods surrounding ours, referencing Villa Avenue immediately meant working-class Italians, while the name Bailey Avenue meant working-class Irish. The section of Jerome Avenue closest to us, fanning eastward from Gunhill Road, across Bainbridge Avenue to Webster Avenue, was a mixture of Jews, Irish, and Germans. When one heard you were from Van Cortlandt Park South, it meant a neighborhood of aspiring middle-class Jews.

*****

OUR NEIGHBORHOOD AROSE UPON A VISION.

Unlike most neighborhoods in New York that simply evolved willy-nilly, where a few immigrant families established a foothold and others of similar race, religion, or ethnicity followed – only to yet again have the environment metamorphize when economic conditions shifted and another wave of different faces speaking different languages appeared – our neighborhood was truly the first *intentional* community in the five boroughs. The vision of the Amalgamated Housing Cooperative was simple and profound: create affordable housing that was cooperatively owned and democratically managed.

The post-World War I period was marked by droves of returning veterans and thousands fleeing war-ravaged Europe. These conditions impacted all of New York City, especially in the poorer neighborhoods, spawning a severe housing shortage that initiated, and was in turn fueled by, rapacious speculation. The nightmare slums of the Lower East Side, the capriciousness of avaricious landlords, and the grim impossibility of ever being able to afford the exorbitant costs of moving to a nicer neighborhood (much less buying a home of one's own), drove the mostly Jewish members of the Amalgamated Clothing Workers of America (ACWA) clustered in this area to demand a different world; they looked to their labor associations for its realization. As a result, the housing issue was a central topic at the ACWA's 1924 convention.

Led by the Secretary-Treasurer of the ACWA's credit union, Abraham E. Kazan, and supported by Sidney Hillman, President of the ACWA – as well as by people gathered around *Forverts* (*The Forward*, a Yiddish-language daily newspaper) – a sparsely populated region of the north Bronx became a living field of dreams. It seemed only fitting that the formation of the Amalgamated Housing Cooperative in 1927 (referred to simply as "The Amalgamated"), was inspired by The Rochdale Society of Equitable Pioneers in Rochdale, England, the birthplace of the modern cooperative movement in 1844. Rochdale was England's center for the burgeoning textile and weaving industry; therefore, what better models for the ACWA visionaries than these original "cooperators," these kinsmen-by-trade. Further, the spirit of the founding Rochdale Principles permeated the imaginations of these modern men, especially the visionary Abraham Kazan who led the cooperative housing revolution in New York – transforming these Bronx hinterlands into the nation's first cooperative project. It was as if simultaneous with the first groundbreaking, the seeds of a modern Rochdale were also sown, providing these earliest cooperative pioneers, now settling the Bronx, with a root system that would blossom and guide them and this nascent community across the twentieth century. Both the tangibles and intangibles within their founding principles provided the cornerstone and the scaffolding for this project: voluntary and open membership; democratic governance; surpluses belonging to cooperative members; no social or political discrimination; education of members and the public in the cooperative movement; cooperation with other cooperatives; and care for the community. It was impossible to live in our neighborhood without both touching and being touched by this progressive and communal spirit that seemed to be everywhere.

In 1927 the First Building, as it came to be known, was built. Consisting, actually, of Buildings 1-5, it covered two-thirds of the area bounded by Dickenson Avenue to the east, Sedgwick Avenue to the south, Saxon Avenue to the west, and Van Cortlandt Park South to the north. This was the beachhead for cooperative housing in the Bronx, the anchoring structure housing over 300 families that set the stage for the subsequent development of the Amalgamated. Curiously, and certainly incongruously, the remaining third of the land on that same side of Saxon Avenue, just to the north and contiguous to the First Building, eventually became home to the Carmelite Order's St. Patrick's Home for the Aged and Infirm, built four years later in 1931. Located at 66 Van Cortlandt Park South, St. Patrick's was literally a lone outpost of Catholicism on the very edge of what was to become a nearly all-Jewish neighborhood. Complete with habit-clad nuns shepherding their elderly charges, either guiding them arm-in-arm or pushing them in wheelchairs, the grounds bustled with activity and strangeness. Immersed in a cloistered world, where the hours pecked away at the lives of the aged and infirm awaiting their end, the residents of St. Patrick's seemed untouchable and only visible during their brief ambulations around the grounds. Thanks to my father's affinity for Catholic churches (he reflexively made the sign of the cross whenever he was in proximity of one), I had a passing acquaintance with nuns, which meant I was fully acquainted with fear and trepidation at the sight of them. As a child I always made sure that I stayed on my side of Saxon Avenue when playing outdoors. At mealtimes, the food odors that only institutional cooking can create assaulted any passerby who veered too close to the doors of the kitchen or the garbage containers festering out behind the building. The grounds were dotted with holy icons strategically placed; ever-present crosses rising up at every turn in the garden and near the benches. Atop the rocky outcrop at the intersection of Van Cortlandt Park South and Dickinson Avenue, stood a placidly beatific, life-sized statue of Jesus, arms raised, addressing the multitude from literally on high. St. Patrick's, even on the sunniest spring days, always evoked a mixture of solemnity and curiosity in me as to what was really going on behind those doors.

THE FIRST BUILDING was a magical, inspired landscape. There were twenty-four lettered entrances, running from A to Z (skipping "I" because it might be confused with the number "1," and "Q" because it might be confused with the letter "O"). The buildings were all five stories high, without elevators, and were oriented so every window let in light and had a view of either a park or an inner courtyard. Stone and metal staircases led upwards from small lobby areas that contained banks of mailboxes. Landings decorated with inlaid tile allowed pause for those living on the upper floors, or those that were older or were *schlepping* kids or groceries or both. The design features reflected the original, blue-collar guiding vision for the Amalgamated Cooperative: bedrooms had cross ventilation so tired workers could get better sleep; kitchens were eat-in, with a window, and crafted so the women had space to do their cooking and serving, plus room for modern appliances; high ceilings, parquet hardwood floors, and tiled bathrooms added a sense of luxuriousness completely absent in the Lower East Side.

In homage to the Rochdale forebears the First Building was constructed in Tudor style, with verdant ivy clinging stylishly to the Holland brick construction. The buildings were designed so that entrances looked inwards upon a courtyard, creating a protected enclave that seemed to foster communal interactions – no one could simply come and go without being seen or without running into a neighbor. The basements were organized with tenant-designated storage bins, filled with bicycles, baby carriages and strollers, beach chairs, folding card tables, and all manner of things that residents used only periodically or seasonally. But the real wonderland, at least to us kids, was the immense courtyard configured with a unique blending of gardens, fountains, archways, and a wide, column-guarded stairway leading to Sedgwick

Avenue. Colorful slate walkways meandered their way from entrance to entrance. In the spring tulip beds blossomed, manicured hedges marked the borders beyond which cool green lawns beckoned. The fountains burbled as goldfish swam in circles beneath gently recycling waterfalls.

We would bike ride or roller skate, clamping on our metal skates with a skate key, play tag, hide-and-seek, or red-light/green-light. We found endless joy in just jumping from red tile to red tile on the multicolored slated pathways snaking around the courtyard. The development (collectively buildings 1 through 5), was so huge that it required five different mailing addresses, one at 4015 Dickinson Avenue, two at 3965 and 3975 Sedgwick Avenue, and two at 3990 and 4010 Saxon Avenue.

On the building's Saxon Avenue side, directly across the street from my house, was a door marked "Canteen." In the early days of the First Building this was the site of the first Co-op grocery store, while other rooms held a nursery and a library. For most of my childhood the Canteen was a shared space. Two-thirds of it was commandeered in the summertime by the neighborhood children involved in the Amalgamated-run Circle Pines Day Camp; the remaining space, a medium-sized room always locked to designate it as off-limits to the uninvited, was the all-male domain the neighborhood elders used to play cards and smoke cigars, undisturbed by wives and children. By the time I became a teenager the Canteen had been turned into a coin-operated laundry room for the building's tenants. Because the First Building was across the street from where I lived, and because many of my classmates and friends lived there, I would come to know this terrain intimately over the years. In 1966, when these original structures were demolished to make way for two modern high-rise buildings, dubbed The Towers I & II, a significant part of the history and charm of the Amalgamated disappeared beneath the wrecking ball of progress, with no resultant Phoenix of comparable beauty or craft emerging from the rubble to take its place.

THE SIXTH BUILDING followed in 1928, situated on the northwest corner of Saxon Avenue directly across from St. Patrick's, bordering Van Cortlandt Park South to the north and Norman Avenue to the west (Norman Avenue would eventually be renamed Hillman Avenue in 1950, in honor of Sidney Hillman, one of the Amalgamated founding fathers). The street address was 74 Van Cortlandt Park South. This building was a five-story walk-up and also replicated the inward-facing Tudor design. It had five entrances covered with ivy. It had a much smaller garden area replete with fountain and bordered by hedges. The multicolored slate walkway led from Saxon Avenue into the courtyard area, where it met up with a beautifully columned, twin stairway that cascaded down from opposite directions, eventually blending into one staircase that guided people under an archway and out onto Van Cortlandt Park South. Within the archway was a door that led to the basement storage bins and to the garbage incinerator. At the corner of Hillman Avenue and Van Cortlandt Park South, the Sixth Building had one unusual feature: an auditorium. Within this communal space lectures, panel discussions, dance socials, and ballet classes were held. During the summer it provided an indoor venue for Circle Pines Day Camp. Originally called simply the Auditorium, it was officially named Vladeck Hall in 1938 after one of the original organizers of Amalgamated Housing, Baruch Charney Vladeck.

THE SEVENTH BUILDING (80 Van Cortlandt Park South) arrived in 1929, bounded by Van Cortlandt Park South to the north and Hillman and Gouverneur Avenues to the east and west respectively. Once again the protective, inward-facing Tudor style was chosen. An immaculate circular courtyard with a fountain in the middle and a foot-high metal fence wrapped with hedges provided a tranquil setting. Sadly, the aesthetically pleasing colorful slate walkways were replaced by concrete in a cost-cutting move. This building had eight entrances, was six stories high, but was finally equipped with elevators. Storage bins were situated in various basement locations throughout the building, along with an area designated for building facilities workers ("Porters," as we called them) to change clothes, eat lunch, and store tools.

The Seventh Building could be accessed from four directions. A main archway led into the courtyard directly across Van Cortlandt Park South from the playground. Whenever summer thunderstorms erupted the arch became the neighborhood hangout as sheets of hot rain drove kids and parents out of the playground seeking shelter. We would huddle together as the thunder rolled and lightening flashed, talking, laughing, and watching the deluge of rain pummel the sidewalks. Eventually the rain would subside while the smell of wetness evaporating off the concrete in its aftermath offered familiar and comforting scents. Another access point led from Hillman Avenue, down twin stairways and through another covered passageway into the courtyard. A half-block further down Hillman, a narrow walkway also offered entry into the Seventh Building. Finally, at the furthest end directly opposite the main archway, a narrow concrete pathway entered from the middle of Gouverneur Avenue (across the street from the *Shul* and about halfway between the playground and the Co-op Market), past a small sandy play area, and made a sharp left turn into the central courtyard.

IN 1932 THE NINTH BUILDING was completed at 100 Van Cortlandt Park South, with Gale Place to the southwest and Orloff Avenue to the east.

This structure was the final homage to the Tudor-style design. It was six stories high, with elevators. The anchoring, in-facing courtyard concept was refashioned so that there were five paired entrances with each pair sharing their own smaller garden area. The walkways to the entrances, as well as the entire circumference of the building, had a mixture of low ornamental metal chains and neatly trimmed hedges.

During the decade comprising the years 1941-1951, the remaining pieces of the neighborhood took shape according to plan: the Tenth, Eleventh, Fourteenth, Eighth, Twelfth and Thirteenth Buildings were constructed, in that order, based on the housing needs of new tenants and the financial wherewithal of the Amalgamated. These structures took a decided turn away from the Tudor-style that had marked the earlier designs. While keeping the beauty of the landscaped gardens that the previous buildings possessed, though on a smaller, less ornate scale, all the structures built after the Ninth Building were clearly claims to modern, postwar architecture: red brick exteriors, fireproof, faster elevators, replete with a variety of terraces, balconies, and penthouses.

THE TENTH BUILDING wrapped around from Hillman Avenue's west side to Gouverneur Avenue, paralleling the northern edge of both the Little and Big Schoolyards of P.S. 95. These were two-story garden apartments comprising 12 entrances at three addresses (3989 and 3995 Hillman, and 4002 Gouverneur). Behind these apartments, on Hillman Avenue, a greenhouse sat, utilized by the Amalgamated gardeners in their seasonal quest to keep the grass, plants, and flowers fresh and beautiful.

THE ELEVENTH BUILDING sat on the east side of Hillman Avenue, immediately south of the Sixth Building and directly behind my house on Saxon Avenue. It comprised the addresses 4010, 4016, and 4022 Hillman, and was known formally as the Veterans' Building. It had a basement passage that ran from one end of the building to the other, connecting all three entrances and providing a great place for us kids to rampage through, much to the chagrin of some of the older tenants who made a pastime of shooing us away whenever we noisily ventured too close. The Eleventh Building was four-stories and it and the Tenth Building held to a significantly modified style from the original Tudor inspiration. It had limited garden areas and appeared to have been built to accommodate the fit allowed by the available land, with little creative design left over.

THE FOURTEENTH BUILDING (designated 14-A and 14-B and located respectively at 92 and 98 Van Cortlandt Park South), was a brick structure, twelve stories high, had odd-even elevators, and held forth between Gouverneur and Orloff Avenues overlooking the playground and the golf course beyond.

THE EIGHTH BUILDING (collectively referred to as Gale Place since it took up the entire west side of that street) was comprised of three entrances and had odd-even elevators. Moving south to north toward the park, the addresses were, respectively, 120, 124, 130 Gale Place. This structure housed a huge boiler room that generated power for the housing complex. In addition, a beautiful roof-garden area was constructed atop the indoor parking garage, creating a space for families and kids to play and for elders to sit in the sun or stroll the grounds. These were twelve stories high with an additional penthouse crowning each address. Since the elevators only went to the twelfth floor, visitors to the penthouses had to walk up the final flight of stairs, making these apartments seem all the more private and exotic.

THE THIRTEENTH BUILDING straddled the land between Gouverneur and Orloff Avenues (with its A-entrance at 3980 Orloff and its B-entrance at 3985 Gouverneur). These topped off at 12 stories and also possessed odd-even elevators. One of the by-products of this construction was the creation of a small park across the street on the corner of Gale Place and Orloff Avenue. Originally the staging area for the construction materials for the Thirteenth Building, residents decided to transform it into a park after two children almost got hit by cars while playing in the street. In an effort to keep kids under control and make the park safe for the elders, a concrete replica of a train was built right in the middle of the area for children to play on and to serve as a baffle for playing team sports like baseball or football, or riding bikes too recklessly. A garden with two pine trees – the official Amalgamated emblem – was also added, making the area more sedate and serene. Officially dubbed Ostroff Plaza after another original cooperator, Harold Ostroff, the neighborhood residents simply referred to it as the Train Park or the Little Park.

THE TWELFTH BUILDING (on the southeast corner of Hillman Avenue where it joined Sedgwick Avenue), was nine stories, had three entrances at 3960, 3970, and 3980 Hillman, and stood like a brick phalanx directly across the street from the main entrance to P.S. 95 elementary school.

    With these new buildings' façades oriented outwards toward the streets, changed also was the concept of a central courtyard as an in-gathering space for neighbors to interact. In the aftermath of World War II, the focus, perhaps mimicking the spirit of the country, was now out into the wider world. While this was apparent with the latest architecture it was hardly true for the neighborhood at large – it still felt and acted like a tiny enclave hidden within the greater Bronx.

The bulk of the neighborhood's construction was essentially complete by the end of 1951. Between 1955-1958 three more buildings were added under the auspices of the Park Reservoir Corporation, two on Sedgwick Avenue, just southwest of our neighborhood shopping area, and one atop a hillock on Orloff Avenue overlooking Van Cortlandt Avenue West; the third apartment building was built by the Mutual Housing Association, situated on the southeast side of Sedgwick Avenue. All of these were thirteen stories high and thoroughly modern in their appointments and appearance.

By the time I moved into my new Bronx neighborhood in the spring of 1956, the dream of Rochdale had essentially been made manifest. America was moving inexorably into postwar prosperity and the Amalgamated was as well, having given birth to a thriving community. It was a place safe enough from anti-Semitism to hold the nightmares of Europe during World War II in abeyance, though for many of the survivors there would always be shadows lurking and restless nights. It was a place of verdant beauty and full of promise, especially for a new generation that seemed destined to come of age into what appeared to be a bright and boundless future.

As if to underscore the idea that there were no limits to what one could do, or be, especially if one applied themselves and got a good education, six schools were more or less within walking distance. Public School 95, built in 1933, sat on the southwest corner of Hillman Avenue, its main entrance (3961 Hillman) and the Little Schoolyard directly across the street from the Twelfth Building. Sedgwick Avenue bordered the school to the south while the Big Schoolyard took up a third of the east side of Gouverneur Avenue, the school's west border. Originally designated for grades kindergarten through eighth, it eventually became a K-6 elementary school when John Peter Tetard Junior High School 143 was built and the first middle-school classes began in fall of 1956. Tetard was less than a mile away, southeast around the reservoir at 210 West 231st Street, and housed grades 7 through 9.

Directly across Sedgwick Avenue from the First Building, at 100 West Mosholu Parkway South, stood the ominously penal-looking structure of De Witt Clinton High School. Founded in 1897 and named after the sixth governor of New York State, it eventually moved from Manhattan to the Bronx in 1929. Catering to over 6,000 students, it was the district's single-sex, all-male institution.

Meanwhile, just on the other side of the reservoir at 2780 Reservoir Avenue, typically requiring a short bus ride from our neighborhood, stood the all-girls complement, Walton High School. Clinton and Walton were examples of industrial-sized education and served in that capacity the demands of the burgeoning baby boom.

Just past Clinton, at 75 West 205th Street, was the chic and modern Bronx High School of Science, where students had to pass an exam in order to attend. Its claim to fame (besides having a difficult-to-pass entrance exam) was a massive mural highlighting many of the wonderful discoveries and their inventors over the centuries. The colorful mural, rising from the floor to the ceiling, dominated the atrium-like main entrance in homage to the power of human ingenuity and scientific inquiry.

Two blocks further on, past Bronx Science on the other side of Harris Field, sat the campus of Hunter College (later renamed Lehman College in 1968, in honor of Herbert H. Lehman, the forty-fifth Governor of New York State).

Like the postwar era generally, the aura of education as the key to unlocking a secure and prosperous future permeated our neighborhood. Not only was education the linchpin to getting a good-paying job or obtaining a profession to be proud of, it was the bulwark of being an informed citizen, of participating in the democratic process. Education was to postwar baby-boomers the beckoning door to opportunity and the cornerstone to success and greatness, both personally and as a nation.

By the time of my arrival, the neighborhood stood completely incongruous with the stereotypes of urban crowding, tenements, and endless miles of pavement that come to mind when one typically imagined the Bronx. It glowed like a pristine jewel nestled on the very boundary-edges of northern New York City. The memories of the Lower East Side that first gave urgency and impetus to the Amalgamated cooperative movement, despite being twenty-five years removed, coupled with the lamentations of the *Shoah* so vividly recent, underscored for the residents of this predominantly Jewish neighborhood that they had created a sanctuary of sorts in a terrible world. The very topography lent its features and contours to this feeling. It was a small, physically and geographically protected enclave, barely noticeable or easily accessible – except to those who belonged there.

PERHAPS LIKE MOSES' PROMISE in Deuteronomy, the physical landscape itself offered an embrace, a gentle in-gathering energy of sorts in the aftermath of the Holocaust. At the neighborhood's southern edge loomed the Jerome Park Reservoir. Built in 1906 on what was originally the Jerome Park Racetrack, site of the world's first outdoor polo competition in 1897, it squatted like an inland sea with its two-and-a-half mile circumference forming an imposing barrier to direct access from the south. Sedgwick Avenue ran alongside, circling nearly halfway round the reservoir; it was the only major thoroughfare and bus route moving directly through our neighborhood.

It was at the three-pronged intersection of Sedgwick Avenue, Gouverneur Avenue, and Van Cortlandt Avenue West that the Co-op Market sat. Built in 1951 and referred to simply as "the Co-op," it anchored the neighborhood shopping area, creating a center for endless social interactions. Slightly downhill on Van Cortlandt Avenue West, sharing part of the building that housed the Co-op, the K&R dry cleaning store was located; a bit further was Lee's Chinese laundry. Nearby, on Sedgwick, were Manna Bakery, the barber shop, EM's candy store and luncheonette, the drugstore, The Bootery & The Cobbler, and finally the Kosher Community Butcher. A few blocks further up Sedgwick, located on the ground floor of one of the non-Amalgamated apartment buildings, was housed the neighborhood public library.

Directly across the street from EM's candy store the Van Cortlandt Jewish Center arrived in 1965 at 3880 Sedgwick Avenue, replacing the tiny and rickety *Shul* on Gouverneur Avenue that had seen better days. Just past the Jewish Center, housed in the ground floor of another small, non-Amalgamated apartment building, Claire's beauty salon sat as the "hers" to the "his" barber shop right across the street.

In front of this building, as well as right in front of EM's candy store, were bus stops for the Bronx One and Bronx Two bus lines. We could take either of the buses south along the Grand Concourse when we wanted to get to Fordham Road for shopping and movies. We could also take either bus to Fort Independence Street on our way to Tetard Junior High School; but it was only the Number One bus that went all the way to 231st and Broadway for more shopping and movies. Everything anyone needed for basic sustenance was within the confines of our neighborhood, or a short hike or bus ride away.

The neighborhood's eastern border was Dickinson Avenue, a one-block street which intersected Gun Hill Road at its north end and Sedgwick Avenue at its south. Gun Hill Road ran east, passing the on-ramp for the Sawmill River Parkway and the Major Deegan Expressway, then on through the Jerome Avenue shopping area, under the elevated structure of the Number 4 Woodlawn train, past Montefiore Hospital, and finally into the heart of the East Bronx. From Dickinson, Sedgwick Avenue curved southeast past De Witt Clinton High School, eventually providing access points to Mosholu Parkway and the Grand Concourse.

The demarcation line to the west was Van Cortlandt Avenue West (commonly referred to as Snake Hill due to its serpentine curves). From the front of the Co-op Market, this street ran downhill where it branched into three arms after reaching the bottom: one continuing straight and arriving at Broadway and the elevated train of the Number 1 line; one turning left and heading onto Bailey Avenue; and the third turning right, accessing Van Cortlandt Lake and Golf Course or the on-ramp to the

Major Deegan Expressway that funneled drivers northwards out of New York City and into suburbia.

To the north, for as far as the eye could see, over 1,100 acres of Van Cortlandt Park (named after Dutch settler and land baron, Orloff Van Cortlandt), provided the neighborhood an enormous cradling greenbelt, rounding off and softening some of the urban sensibilities.

Van Cortlandt Park South, a one-way street that ran west to east, paralleled the vast expanse of parkland for the six blocks that made up the width of our neighborhood. It served as an anchoring boundary at the innermost edge between the apartment buildings and houses and the seemingly endless vista of greenery undulating northward. In fact, all of the neighborhood streets – Gale Place, Orloff Avenue, Gouverneur Avenue, Hillman Avenue, Saxon Avenue, and Dickinson Avenue – were conduits either moving people away from or toward Van Cortlandt Park South. In other words, one rarely happened upon our neighborhood by accident. If you were walking these streets you knew where you were going and everyone else knew whether you belonged there or not.

All along Van Cortlandt Park South, from Gale Place to Dickinson Avenue, six blocks in length, ran a fence. Between Gale Place and Gouverneur Avenue the two parallel fence railings ran atop a stone-and-concrete retaining wall, low at either end and higher in the middle. From Gouverneur Avenue the fence continued eastward to its termination point at Dickinson Avenue. The entire fence created a simple, functional, and ornamental marker at the northernmost edge of the neighborhood, separating the business of living from the recreation provided by the playground and expanse of park beyond.

There were four entry points that allowed access through this fence and that eventually steered people to the playground oasis at the heart of the neighborhood. At the east terminus of the fence, at Dickinson Avenue, the asphalt path ran approximately 100 yards past the fence before it branched. Going straight, the path meandered past a tree-and-brush-entangled expanse know as Ghost Town, and eventually led to Van Cortlandt Park Lake and the entrance to the public golf course. Turning left, this portion of the path would guide strollers between The Plateau and The Bushes, downhill to the playground.

At the west end of the fence, at Gale Place, the path ran slightly above and parallel to Van Cortlandt Park South. It meandered over a small hillock, running along the chain-link fence enclosing the golf course, and from that direction brought people to the entrance of the playground.

A third path breached the fence where Hillman Avenue t-boned Van Cortlandt Park South. This gave access to a grassy open space, populated with a scattering of good-sized shade trees. It was an area that was a favorite for neighborhood families since it overlooked the playground mere yards away, providing visual and physical proximity to the children below. During the spring and summer months dedicated quartets of *mahjong* players would appear like mushrooms after a rain, card tables, folding chairs, and a legion of *kibitzers* creating a joyful clamor, the air laced with Yiddish expletives lamenting defeat or celebrating triumph.

The most frequently used thoroughfare into the park, however, was the pedestrian pathway that began where Gouverneur Avenue dead-ended at Van Cortlandt Park South. Here the path led immediately and directly into our neighborhood playground.

We felt like we had it all. Verdant parkland for exploring, a fully equipped family-friendly playground, and a golf course stretching to our northern horizon as far as the eye could see. Friends and playmates populated nearly every single apartment and house in the neighborhood, courtesy of the Baby Boom. All our schools were within a stone's throw, while shops and businesses formed the commercial heart of the neighborhood, anchored by the bustling Co-op Market. There were more stores and movie theaters just a stroll to Jerome Avenue or a short bus ride to 231st and Broadway. Most of all it was safe, and everybody knew everybody else. It was our Bronx oasis and for a while we thought it would never change.

Chapter Four
The Rail

The Rail was complex terrain. The Rail was simultaneously a location, an object of desire, a destination and, alternatingly, the place to be, or get to, or get away from. The Rail was a communal heartbeat and, variously, a state of mind – all depending on one's age, one's gender, the time of day, and the season of the year. The Rail, while clearly appearing inert to an outside observer, was always a living encounter between time, space, and people. It was the stillpoint around which, unconsciously and consciously, our young lives spun centripetally, safely counterbalancing for a time the centrifugal demands of the wider world. Over time The Rail took on iconic proportions as different age groups – usually during the years consuming high school and right after – claimed it as their own, cherishing its capacity to serve as a brake, momentarily slowing the maturation process while amplifying each group's belief in the eternal bond of this time, this place, and these friends.

* * * *

THE SCENE AT THE RAIL CHANGED WITH THE SEASONS but it always remained a focal point for all manner of social intercourse. It was the place for young people of all ages to meet, to congregate, to await the arrival of friends or the arrival of an ice cream truck.

In the summertime it was a variety of ice cream trucks that would vie for customers: Bungalow Bar, Good Humor, Mr. Softie, and our sentimental favorite, Uncle John's. Originally driving a Bungalow Bar truck, with its familiar peaked and brown-shingled roof, John Soleotis was, at first glance, an unlikely ice cream man. John was always dressed in white pants, with a white t-shirt that stretched like a leotard over his protruding belly, a belly that nearly hid the coin dispenser belted to his waist. With the ever-present cigarette dangling from the corner of his mouth, he served ice cream with a distinctively curmudgeonly affection, often giving us frozen treats on credit if we promised we would get the money from our mothers later. Eventually he bought his own truck, proudly emblazoned on both sides with the words "Uncle John's Ice Cream." During the winter months John drove a fuel-oil truck, making deliveries to peoples' homes and businesses, but come spring he would be back making the rounds between many of the north Bronx neighborhoods.

Uncle John was so down to earth, so real to talk to, his competitors in the ice cream business really couldn't sway our allegiance to him, try as they might. Yet they hardly suffered. Once the ringing of the bells or the blaring of the music reached our ears in the confines of the playground, no matter which truck arrived first or whether they converged at once, what seemed like hundreds of kids would pour out into the street in front of The Rail to partake in a panoply of ice-cold delight: fudge bars, twin pops, push-ups, soft ice cream swirled into spires atop flaky cones, ice cream sandwiches and more. A universal favorite was Italian ices, especially in the heat and humidity of summer. Italian ices were a snow cone compressed into a cup, the ice infused with a variety of flavored syrups, ranging from lemon to root beer and from cola to cherry. The best way to savor this treat was to eat it halfway down into the cup and then, using the small wooden spoon shaped like a paddle, flip it over to behold a concentration of syrup saturating the remaining ice. It was an unreal assault on the taste buds as each ice-cold, syrupy mouthful slid over our tongues and brought relief to our overheated bodies.

In addition to ice cream trucks, every once in a while The Whip would make an appearance in front of the playground. This was a spinning, twirling children's ride, most often found in amusement parks but, in this case, mounted on the back of a flatbed truck. We'd line up, pay a few cents, climb the three corrugated metal steps, and clamber into one of the two-seater pods and eagerly wait for the spinning and whipping (in a variety of conflicting directions) to commence. Once the machine started, it was nonstop shrieks and laughter until it ground to a halt. We would all stumble off the steps at the back of the truck, laughing and dizzy and wanting to get back in line for another go-round.

On other days the *Fox's u-bet* truck (sometimes called the seltzer truck) would pull up and park, the driver collating beverage orders for Amalgamated residents. He would carefully pack a wooden soda case with glass seltzer bottles, complete with the silver press-handle used to squirt a stream of carbonated water when depressed, along with jars of *Fox's u-bet* chocolate syrup for delivery to the apartments.

At other times it was the horse-drawn fresh vegetable truck, complete with hanging scale and small green produce bags, which claimed a spot in front of the playground. We would be mesmerized by the old, blinkered brown horse and tentatively pat its flank, while adults haggled for a bargain on this or that pound of vegetables or fruit, calling into question its freshness, or speculating with raised eyebrows and a laugh whether the scale was really accurate.

In the winter months The Rail was a great place from which to mount a snowball fight, using the retaining wall as a fort from which to bombard kids taking up positions behind parked cars on the other side of Van Cortlandt Park South.

During the hours when school was in session, The Rail remained virtually empty and quiet. Throughout the day, though, The Rail appeared to be waiting, waiting for us. After school, especially in good weather and between the hours of three o'clock and dinnertime, the wait was over, the stillness joyously disturbed. The area suddenly bustled with activity as kids sat on The Rail waiting to meet their friends before going into the playground to engage in their favorite activity. Others sat, or stood, waiting for the arrival of the ice cream trucks.

After dinner, and especially after dark on weekends, The Rail became the exclusive domain of the older kids, ranging in age from high school to those recently graduated. Awash in the unpredictable and unmanageable ebbs and flows of their hormonal seas, this was a safe place to smoke a cigarette away from the judging eyes of parents or other adults. It was the place for pairing into exploratory boyfriend-and-girlfriend configurations under the shadows cast by the tree branches overhead. It was certainly the site of many a first kiss and the promises of more. Here they could talk about the trials and tribulations of school, of home, of going steady, of what the future after high school might hold. Talk would inevitably turn to favorite songs or bands and, as if on cue, a small group would break into a harmonious *a Capella* version of a current hit song under the nearby streetlight.

WHEN MY GROUP OF FRIENDS HIT JUNIOR HIGH SCHOOL we envied the kids who claimed The Rail and we imagined ourselves taking their places someday. It seemed inevitable, the way things worked in our part of the Bronx.

There was a fierce hierarchy guarding The Rail and determining who would possess it. For younger kids, though, especially in the evenings, The Rail was clearly a "no trespassing" zone. Most times this was made clear with unspoken energy and body language by those perched there, sitting for hours, or milling around. If necessary, a group's claim could be backed up with muscle, but this was rarely the case, so entrenched was the governing protocol. Yet time would inevitably have its way with all the groups that once laid claim to The Rail. Eventually, at the close of high school, some combination of college, making a living, military service, or marriage would fracture each group and dispatch them from The Rail and sometimes even dispatch them completely from the confines of the neighborhood. Those who left The Rail, pulled away by the vagaries of adult responsibility, would often say, with fond memories and pride, "I still have The Rail groove in my ass."

In these ways The Rail was more than a gathering place; it was about life in all its manifestations, a vortex of energies, a magnetic field alternating in direction and magnitude. Most of the time, we all just held fast and rode the whirlwinds of our adolescence. No one could possibly predict or even imagine just what the swirling tumult of the 1960s would mean for our relationship to The Rail and to each other.

When marijuana and psychedelics arrived in our world one immediate impact was that they acted as levelers, as dissolvers of hierarchy, as people of all ages came together under the rainbow of turning on, tuning in, and dropping out. Almost overnight The Rail went from one group's territory to everyone's domain as a spirit of togetherness, sharing, and loving each other replaced the former abrasive energies and sometimes hostile distancing by age group. Suddenly the old ways of The Rail seemed as silly as the old ways throughout society, the old habits and mores that drugs, music, and protests were illuminating in bold relief and trying to push aside. The desires to shed the old paradigms of male-female stereotypes, to think for oneself, and to seek alternatives to going sheep-like into the military or into corporate America were percolating. Especially the desire to experience life at an intensity that seemed to have been drained from our parents' generation drove us like a sword. Into each other's' arms we rushed, to dispense with selfishness and greed and jealousies, to experiment with free love, to seek together in realms of higher consciousness via drugs, nature, and a new spiritual awareness. The Rail would once again become the center-point for these new gatherings.

Chapter Five
Rhythms of Judaism

*M*y *first real experience indicating to me that I was in a very different world than the one I left in Washington Heights occurred immediately upon arriving in first grade. Within days after my very first class, I had to go to school on the Jewish High Holy Days, Rosh Hashana and Yom Kippur, September 5 and 14, 1956. One morning, as a brand new first-grader on my way to school, I expected to be joining the throngs of students at P. S. 95. Instead I arrived to find it almost emptied of kids. In fact, my sister, my two cousins and me, made up nearly half of the attendees. This was a Jewish holiday, I was informed; the Jewish kids did not have to come to school. I was amazed. On top of my amazement it simply felt weird for fewer than a dozen students to move from classroom to classroom, together in a pack through the eerily still hallways, and do virtually nothing all day. Odder still, was that on one of these holidays, Rosh Hashanah, the Jewish New Year, my friends feasted, especially enjoying the sweetness of honey and apples, symbolic of the wish that God would grant a year just as sweet. In contrast, on the other holiday, Yom Kippur, the holiest day of the year, they fasted and prayed – for this was the Day of Atonement where repentance and forgiveness filled the air. When I saw them after school those first days they were all dressed up, suits and dresses on prominent display. The boys were all wearing these strange skullcaps that I would learn in time were called* yarmulkes. *Everyone's demeanor was appropriate to whether they were joyously feasting or solemnly fasting. I had no way of making sense of all this. To make matters even more complicated, during the High Holy Days, all the stores in our neighborhood were closed as well. The Co-op Market, Manna Bakery, EM's, the drugstore, all of them shuttered. I wandered the halls of P.S. 95 and the streets of our neighborhood alone, feeling completely alien.*

* * * * *

THERE IS AN OLD JEWISH JOKE that goes like this: There are two Rabbis arguing over some fine points in the *Torah*. How many opinions do they have? Three, comes the answer. This goes to the heart of Jewish culture because argument and debate – most times in the quest for deeper understanding and wisdom – is the fascial matrix that builds and solidifies the Jewish community. In this quest for grasping the multifaceted nature of truth it is not only permissible, but obligatory, for each person to know enough of the issues to not only speak their opinion but be well enough versed in the opposing side as to be able to argue that as well. In fact, if you were really knowledgeable, throwing in a third opinion was a highly laudable move. In our neighborhood three opinions were rarely good enough; in our neighborhood the more opinions the better, as this made for a much more interesting conversation.

My first five years as a regular of Bradley's Bar was similar to Jewish culture in this respect: argument and debate was everywhere. It was dissimilar, though, in this respect: in Bradley's things were often taken personally because few could entertain a third opinion and polarities often devolved into physical altercations to prove who was right. In some ways I had been primed as well as any child could be to be able to verbally mix it up, yet the transition to the house on Saxon Avenue put an abrupt brake on my nascent curiosity and my even having opinions. With unspoken rules demanding strict adherence to never questioning my patriarchal grandfather and my matriarchal grandmother, and the martial enforcement that children especially should be seen (as little as possible) and not heard (ever), I reflexively began to repress my questions and opinions rather quickly as a matter of survival. What I would experience in short order was that outside my house the rhythms of Judaism called to me like a siren song, like a fresh breeze that sprung up, periodically clearing the air around me of all the Protestant inhibitions that I could not effectively fight against alone under my own roof. The difference felt radical and I wanted more of what I felt my friends had. It wasn't very long after moving to the Bronx that I began to realize intuitively that my salvation lay away from my house and in the streets of the neighborhood among my Jewish friends.

For the most part, it was the Jewish calendar and three specific holidays that marked the turning of the seasons in our neighborhood. Just as school began, with the smell of autumn crisp in the air, the High Holy Days arrived to mark Rosh Hashanah, the Jewish New Year, quickly followed by Yom Kippur, the Day of Atonement. I watched in wonder as everything pretty much came to a stop, as school became a ghost town and businesses shut their doors. I was one of the only kids in the neighborhood who was not dressed up, who could play freely and get dirty (even though some of the Jewish kids wound up playing stickball or punch-ball anyway, with their ties loosened and their sport coats in a pile nearby). But I felt weird joining in, like I was disturbing something sacred, or that since it was a Jewish holiday the playing of games was somehow reserved only for the Jewish kids. Even running into my friends later in the day, when I was finally released from the ghostly halls of P.S. 95, I stayed mostly to myself, tentative, quiet and observing the customs of this strange new world.

The winter brought the Hanukah festival, consisting of the nightly lighting of the *menorah* candles (in a special *menorah* called a *hanukkiyah*), spinning the *dreidel*, singing, and sharing Hanukah *gelt* candy amongst the children (chocolate candy wrapped in gold foil to look like coins). Of course there was food as well – especially, and indelibly, *latkes* (potato pancakes) and apple sauce. Hanukah seemed more secular in many ways and more accessible, especially since we learned about it in grade school along with the approaching Christmas holidays that would give us all more than a week off. It was a festive holiday, filled with the miraculous story of the tiny amount of ritual oil that kept the purifying lamp burning in the Temple for eight days, signifying the victory of light over darkness. Further, since Hanukah often fell close to Christmas it felt like the whole neighborhood was celebrating together. One of my strongest memories was the annual Hanukah Bazaar, held in the basement of the *Shul* on Gouverneur Avenue, and organized by the women of the Jewish Sisterhood. The Sisterhood was an auxiliary to the synagogue, composed of women who were dedicated to developing women's leadership and supporting social issues. It was here I had my first homemade *knish*. As the *knishes* were being individually crafted in the kitchen, I would stand transfixed amidst the hustle and bustle of the crowded bazaar with growing Pavlovian anticipation, watching as the magic hands of Celia Bernstein shaped each one, brushing oil on the *knishes* right before sliding a full tray into the oven. Eventually, out they came, piping hot, the smell filling the entire basement with visceral comfort and goodness. The first bite was a combination of spices and hot potato baked to perfection, a complete soothing of my body and soul – simply to die for.

In the springtime Passover (*Pesach*) arrived, celebrating the Jewish exodus from Egypt, where they were enslaved and oppressed by Pharaoh. It also commemorated the fact that when God unleashed his tenth plague against the Egyptians in an effort to convince the Pharaoh to free the Jews – slaying the first-born child of everyone in Egypt – he passed over the homes of the Jewish children whose doors had been previously identified with markings of lamb's blood. While I was never invited to a *Seder*, over time I put the pieces together of the importance of this holiday to my friends and their families. Eventually I learned about the *Haggadah* (containing the Passover story and requisite rituals); the ingredients that made up the *Seder* plate and their meanings; the four questions (especially the refrain "Why is this night different from all other nights?"); the empty seat and glass of wine for the Prophet Elijah; and the ritual of having the youngest child search for the piece of *matzo* called the *Afikoman*. It was all so strange, exotic and compelling to me, especially since I was living in a house where religious observance seemed dutiful, like a bland punishment devoid of mystery or excitement. Beyond the obligatory collection of presents under our Christmas tree there was no magic that I could find, and I longed for magic.

When my Jewish friends were celebrating their holidays I felt alone; when I was sequestered in my house during Thanksgiving, Christmas, and Easter, I felt separated even more, like I really belonged out there and not in here. Even as my extended family gathered to open presents or break bread together, depending on the holiday, in all instances I ached to be with my Jewish friends. Everything Jewish was beginning to exercise a magnetic pull on my curiosity, lifting my spirit and causing me to imagine what being Jewish might be like. It would not take long before this imagining began to turn into envy and actual yearning.

WHILE THE HOLIDAY TRADITIONS OF JUDAISM touched nearly everyone, being Jewish in our neighborhood was hardly monolithic; instead, just like the joke about the two Rabbis debating the deeper points of the *Torah* and possessing at least three perspectives between them, Judaism was approached from a variety of angles and outlooks. Given that the creation of the neighborhood was first imagined under the auspices of the Amalgamated Clothing Workers of America (ACWA), Judaism in our neighborhood had a certain progressive, labor-centric cast to it. What this often meant was that observance and participation in Jewish traditions and holidays were primarily a means to foster cultural identification rather than serving as an ongoing, devout religious practice. It was a way of straddling the post-war world of America, driven by science and progress and the image of one great secular melting pot, while never forgetting one's Jewish heritage, especially after the *Shoah*. As a result, for many families seeking a sense of assimilation, the larger holidays, like the High Holy Days, Passover, and especially Hanukah, morphed into ways of primarily maintaining Jewishness within the dominant culture rather than serving as devoted religious exercises. Even the weekly, Friday-at-sundown celebration of *Shabbat*, complete with the ritual lighting of the menorah and the sharing of fresh, braided *Challah* from

Manna Bakery, was buffeted by the pressures to identify as American first and Jewish second. And frankly, after the *Shoah*, there were some who did not want to emphasize their Jewishness in any way whatsoever for fear of stirring the ever-lurking beast of *pogrom*.

At the same time, adding more color and complexity to our neighborhood, there was an Orthodox synagogue, the *Shul*, housed on Gouverneur Avenue (before it moved in 1965 to the newly named Van Cortlandt Jewish Center on Sedgwick Avenue). The *Shul* was very traditional, with the ground floor reserved for the men and a balcony section designated for the women during services.

There was also an established Workman's Circle chapter. Founded in America in 1900, Workman's Circle (or *Der Arbeter Ring*), was a fraternal socialist organization dedicated to the promotion of an enlightened Jewish culture, social justice, and the preservation of the Yiddish language. As a result, Yiddish was heard everywhere in the neighborhood. The Workman's Circle also ran Camp Kinder Ring, the sleep-away camp many of my friends attended during the summer months.

It was fascinating to my ears to hear the Yiddish language as a matter of course throughout our neighborhood. It was everywhere, salted into conversations that were mainly in English, as well as serving as the primary language of discourse for many of the parents and elders. It wasn't unusual for some of the adults to shift from English to Yiddish upon my approach or when they caught sight of me on the street or in the aisles of the Co-op Market. Of course I couldn't tell if they were lauding me as a fine, young *mensch* (albeit of the Gentile variety), or if I was being denigrated as a *fershluninga goy*. It likely had something to do with whether I was being polite and holding open a door, or acting like a disrespectful teenager. Often, though, despite the language barrier, I got the message by virtue of the vocal tones and facial expressions that accompanied some of the utterances.

While expressions like *oy gevalt, mazel tov, ver klempt, shayna punim*, and *alter cocker* were ubiquitous, as were the daily familiar words like *klutz, bissel, bubbe* and *zeyde, yenta, tzuris*, and hundreds of others, it was the curses and putdowns that launched Yiddish into the realms of the poetic. Imagine being told that *Ale tseyn zoln bay dir aroysfaln, nor eyner zol dir blaybn oyf tsonveytung* (All your teeth should fall out except for one, so you can still have a toothache); or, *Got zol oyf ir onshikn fun di tsen makes di beste* (God should visit upon her the best of the Ten Plagues); or *Zolst vaksn vi a tzibele mitn kop in drerd* (May you grow like an onion with your head in the ground) – you'd certainly know that you were being cursed in no uncertain terms. There was never a day that went by when I didn't hear Yiddish and, as a result, didn't wonder what was being said around me and about me.

Nevertheless, while strict orthodoxy was hardly the tenor of how Judaism was practiced by most people in our neighborhood, nearly all my male friends had their Bar Mitzvah at age thirteen (and, thanks to the progressive outlook of Rabbi Sodden, so did some of the girls have a Bat Mitzvah when they reached twelve). This meant hours of after-school education at the *Shul*, learning Hebrew and learning a specific *Torah* portion to be recited at their Bar Mitzvah under the tutelage of the esteemed Rabbi, the officiant of the synagogue congregation. Other Hebrew school teachers over the years included: Abe Sodden, Mrs. Danzig, Mr. Bernstein, Mrs. Inzelbuch, Mr. Goodfriend and Rabbi Grossman. Yet, while the neighborhood was unmistakably imprinted as a Jewish one, the upheavals of the Sixties would exert a powerful push-pull on many of my friends. I would watch them oscillate between appreciating and celebrating their Judaism and distancing themselves in the spirit of breaking with the old ways that so often provided the tenor of the times.

WITHIN THIS OVERWHELMINGLY JEWISH WORLD I only experienced discrimination based on my not being Jewish a few times. The first was shortly after a couple of young representatives of *Hashomer Hatzair* (or Youth Guard) came to speak at a public meeting in the *Shul* in the early 1960s. Their focus that day was agitating for the boycott of all products made in Germany in payback for the Holocaust, everything from toys to Volkswagens. Living in a house with a German-born grandfather I was immediately self-conscious as the discussion went on, imagining, with shame rising rapidly within, everyone's eyes upon me.

The next instance was during a meeting to organize a neighborhood softball team, complete with uniforms. All the boys in the neighborhood were excited and the meeting at the *Shul* was packed with eager kids. As the details were being laid out it was mentioned that the team would be only for Jewish kids. That meant me and Gregg Kai, who was Asian, were not going to be allowed to play. Immediately the room burst out into rumbles of discontent, partly because Gregg and I were decent athletes and partly because this rattled everyone's nascent sense of fairness. As Gregg and I left the meeting together I never felt so estranged. For a moment I was thrust into exile, lost between my alienating home life and this rejection from the people I wanted to be like. It stung, and I hurt for the rest of that afternoon. Fortunately it didn't last long as the onrush of day-to-day interactions at school and in the playground with my friends quickly reassured me that I was not truly forsaken.

The other instances of being made to feel different and unwelcome because I wasn't Jewish would come a few years later when my growing maturity and my budding sexuality pushed me into the dating arena. This developmental milestone made me, in the eyes of some of the parents and grandparents, a *goy* to be watched closely when it came to dating, and potentially tainting, neighborhood Jewish girls.

As I came to realize throughout elementary school, I was navigating a very new and different terrain. I didn't like being in my house, but I liked being in my friends' apartments instead; I wasn't Jewish, but I wanted to be. I wanted so achingly bad to go beyond an attitude of "us" and "them," which was daily being reinforced in my own house, and instead create a world where "we" flourished. Of course, this was percolating at a level of awareness that only fleetingly came to the surface of my young mind. In my heart, though, I already knew the truth of my feelings and I vowed that I would do everything and anything to somehow create a home for myself within this Jewish milieu.

Chapter Six
Nothing Personal, Just Family

The leather slipper flew fast and accurate, striking me on my left shoulder. My grandfather had thrown it from his perch at the head of the dining room table, thrown it with force and authority straight into the kitchen in an effort to silence my sister and me. We were in our usual chairs, eating in the kitchen while the rest of the household (our grandmother, aunt, uncle, and our two older cousins) sat at the dining room table with my grandfather. My mother was working the nightshift at Woolworth's. In our isolation and boredom it wasn't unusual for Peggy and me to begin talking and laughing, or annoying each other by playing with the food on each other's plate. Inevitably our noise level would rise and, along with it, my grandfather's frustration at children being noisy and unruly. At this point he usually shouted in German, commanding us to be silent. If that proved fruitless, then his slipper followed. If our obstreperousness continued unabated then Uncle Chuck would be sent in as the enforcer. Taking the appropriately stenciled "Board of Education" off the nail on the kitchen window frame, he hefted the wooden paddle menacingly. At this point Peggy and I became deathly quiet, re-gathering ourselves into obedience, though sometimes we could not suppress our laughter even in the face of a paddling. If that happened, our uncle would march us to our room and lay the wood on our asses a few times before returning to the dining room, our wails muffled to the ears of rest of the family as he shut the door on us and his handiwork. Night after night we were socialized into being good, quiet, chaste, Protestant children, corporally remade when necessary, always reminded that under this roof we were most definitely to be seen and not heard.

* * * * *

THE FIRST INDICATION THAT WE WERE DIFFERENT from the rest of the family was our immediate displacement, during dinnertime, to eating in the kitchen while the six other family members ate the evening meal gathered around the dining room table. Dinner was our only communal meal and it became clear that my mother, sister and I would not be allowed to partake in any way that recognized us as members of this family. Breakfast, given everyone's need to get to school or work in the morning, was a hectic launch of individual trajectories into the day. During lunchtime my sister, our two cousins and I – all in elementary school two blocks away – would either take lunchboxes to school or walk home for lunch. On the weekends our separate little family grouplets fended for themselves until the evening meal. It was the dinner hour where our lowly status within this family was first established and nightly reaffirmed. My grandmother was determined to make my mother pay for her transgressions and, because my sister and I were constant reminders of a consummated lower-caste marriage, we would be made to pay as well. This eating arrangement lasted every day for the first seven years we lived under the Saxon Avenue roof, the only breaks coming during the Thanksgiving and Easter holidays when the entire extended family aligned like iron filings around the magnetic demands of my grandmother and pretenses and appearances were of the utmost importance. Even when my mother took the nightshift at Woolworth's on Fordham Road, from 2:00-10:00 p.m., so she could have the mornings to prep us for school and the noon hour to feed us lunch if we chose to come home, my sister and I were never once invited into the dining room to eat with the family. While Peggy and I were at first largely oblivious to the depths of the undercurrents shaping these attitudes and, therefore, our lives, we knew that my mother felt in her gut that returning home to her parents' house was the end of the line – at least for her life. For my sister and me she hoped her decision would give us a new beginning. It turned out to be one more example of the road to hell being paved with the best of intentions.

In addition to the dual dinner arrangement, I had the growing feeling that I had entered a kind of asylum coming to 3987 Saxon Avenue. Even as a five-year-old, try as I might to not think anything was out of the ordinary, the press of bodies in such close proximity to each other made for unwanted intimacies that generated frictions. I was now in a four-bedroom house with eight other people. There was my stern, aging grandfather, who flung German curse words with impunity, and his bloodless, tight-lipped wife, my *hausfrau* grandmother, who rode roughshod by virtue of single, dagger-laden glances. There was also my elegant but sexually repressed, smoldering aunt, the youngest of my mother's siblings, and her husband, my childlike yet angry uncle. Additionally, their children, one older cousin whose huge body size did not match his age and his quirky younger brother, were thrust upon me as role models. Finally, my mother, sister and I were bundled into a single bedroom together. Arriving as we did in the spring, I had months of unstructured time to get to know them all before I would be confronted by the prospect of entering first grade in the upcoming fall. And get to know them I did.

My grandfather, Frederick Christian Scheel, was born in 1867 in Belkow, Germany. He came to America in 1890 at the age of 23. He was an immigrant success story, eventually owning a confectionary (with homemade candy and ice cream) and two apartment buildings in Manhattan (my mother often recounted how her family hardly even felt the press of the Great Depression). He was a businessman, tall and stately in his Teutonic mien; he was a provider, synonymous with being a father. He was as unyielding in his belief that he was a self-made man as he was rigid in his determination that love could only spoil a child. He was 60 when he bought the house at 3987 Saxon Avenue and moved his family to the Bronx in 1927, approximately the same time the First Building of the Amalgamated was moving from blueprint to footprint, and my father was making his way to America from Ireland. By the time we arrived, he was not friendly or likeable, perhaps a product of his resistance to aging and his slowly losing his physical capacities (he was 89 when our family showed up on his doorstep). Additionally he was difficult to talk to, having chosen in his dotage to default to his native German as his preferred form of communication, which only my grandmother understood. He never once spoke up on behalf of me and my family regarding our grandmother's exiling us in the kitchen, adopting instead the attitude of a regal patriarch above the fray, except when noisome children spurred an angry outburst.

At my young age I was shy by temperament and, being a newcomer, I was quite timid. Even when asked direct questions I was not very talkative, attuned as I was to vigilance and making the adjustments necessary to navigate a minefield of new and different social cues under this roof. When my grandfather propelled himself through the house, I was scared by the way his aged body looked and how he navigated his departure from his bedroom toward his favorite chair in the living room – unsteady and shuffling with a cane when we first arrived. Oddly, he was still able to negotiate the long flight of stairs that led out to the front of the house in order to tend to his garden. From there he also had access to the rear of the house where he could enter the basement and putter around his subterranean workbenches. His cane was solid oak, heavy, and intimidating. When he shook it at the television in response to some slight to his favorite wrestler, I imagined seeing bolts of angry lightning flash toward the screen, along with even angrier German words decrying the injustices he perceived occurring in the ring in Madison Square Garden. He steadfastly rooted for Bobo Brazil and his numbing

"Coco-butt," marveled in the high-flying gymnastics of Antonino Rocca, recollected his younger self when strongman Bruno Sammartino went to work, all the while decrying the dirty tactics of the masked Zebra Kid and the fight-stopping pain of Killer Kowalski's "Claw" hold. Initially, I liked to watch him at work in the basement, but from a distance; I was mesmerized when he hand-shoveled coal into the furnace but really uninterested in the tools he handled so deftly. I got bored easily when he had me run back and forth from the front of the house to the rear and bring him his gardening tools; I was frustrated by the menial tasks and wanted to be out playing or with my friends. Listening to his repetitive admonitions about watering the garden only after the sun had moved closer to the horizon so the plants were in shade was information wasted on me. He finally got the message one day, when I was about nine years old and he sent me to fetch a garden implement. Instead of doing his bidding, I hopped the fence in the backyard and sped non-stop to the playground where I stayed until dinner time. I paid the price immediately upon returning home, but I was never at his beck and call again.

My grandmother, Emma Irene Plangemann, was born in New York City in 1885. She and my grandfather married in 1907 on Valentine's Day; he was 40 and she was 22. Nearly nine months to the day of their wedding their first child, Gladys, was born in 1907. Frederick, the first son, was born in 1909; followed by Walter in 1911; my mother, Helen, in 1917; Audrey in 1922 (only to die four years later); Shirley (Sherry) in 1923; and Evelyn in 1928. These were my aunts and uncles who, along with their families, in-gathered at Saxon Avenue during Thanksgiving and Easter. After seven childbirths it is of little surprise that my grandmother, already in her 70th year by the time my mother, sister and I arrived, was tired and impatient. She was stern, the true power behind my grandfather who was but titular head-of-household, and while he received either a wide-berth or deference, she was feared outright. For within her exhaustion she was also vindictive, determined to punish my mother for not only rejecting her family and class, and lowering herself into the blue-collar world of my father and his ilk, but also for spreading her legs for an immigrant Irish-Catholic longshoremen and bringing two of his children into the world. My sister Peggy and I seemed to inspire only disgust in my grandmother. We were uncouth, feral and ill-mannered, desperately in need of re-socialization, a Protestant reformation that she was determined to deliver. Peggy and I were readily scapegoated, always held up and compared unfavorably to our two cousins who apparently could do no wrong. Yet because my mother made it abundantly clear with all her actions and attitudes that I was her favored child, and my sister Peggy was a thoroughly unwanted accident, the wrath of my grandmother's hatred swept into the unprotected vacuum, falling like cudgels upon the vulnerable spirit of my sister. It wasn't long before this emotional brutality began to take its toll.

Chuck Drolet (Uncle Chuck) was eagerly upwardly mobile and he knew that 3987 Saxon Avenue was little more than a necessary way-station for his trajectory into the middle class. He was a veteran of World War II and had served in the Pacific theater in the U.S. Navy. Like many veterans he rarely spoke of his time at war and if he did it was to tell us only the funny stories involving him and his shipmates. Uncle Chuck, like so many in postwar America, was possessed with visions of fleeing farther and farther away from the urban boundaries to the Promised Land suburbs; images of obtaining the Holy Grail of home ownership danced enticingly in his head and allowed him to bide his time – no matter what went on under this roof and under his nose, Uncle Chuck was determined to never rock the boat.

He had grown up poor and countrified in rural Long Island when it was considered out-in-the-sticks compared to Manhattan. How he met my Aunt Evelyn was shrouded in mystery, but there was a noticeable incongruity between his oafishness, her restrained properness, and the upper-class affectations of the Scheel family. Apparently, the family rumor goes, she was a teen mother, having her first son, Brian, when she was 18 and, ten months later, her second son, Ned, when she was 19. How and when Chuck Drolet became their step-father, and whether their biological father died or just took off, was simply never spoken about. It seemed that Uncle Chuck was clearly happy to have a classy beauty like Aunt Evelyn by his side, happy to be out of Long Island, and more than content to wait his turn for secure entry into the American middle class – and what better place to wait than 3987 Saxon Avenue, located as it was at New York's northernmost borderlands right where suburban Westchester County beckoned enticingly.

When we moved in, Uncle Chuck was busily and steadily working his way up the ranks of Western-Electric, first as a cable puller then as a supervisor, moving progressively and methodically from sweaty blue collar to starched white collar. He was a strange combination of child-like silliness, which I gravitated toward readily (his most hysterical laughter occurred as he sat mesmerized watching the antics of Wile E. Coyote in the *Looney Tunes* Road Runner cartoons), while also being plagued with unpredictable and terrifying bouts of red-faced rage when he felt pressured, frustrated, or argued with. He treated my sister and me with general kindness, yet at the same time willingly served as Board of Education henchman when my grandparents deemed us unruly enough to warrant a paddling.

My Aunt Evelyn was the youngest of my mother's siblings. At age 28 when we arrived, she was tall and shapely and fit the definition of

1950s femininity, even as she tried to underplay her physical beauty by donning very conservative skirts and blouses, along with sensible shoes. Aunt Evelyn worked as a secretary in Manhattan, wore stylish cat-eye glasses, and even to my young sensibilities seemed to exude a smoldering sexuality that she had determined somewhere along the way was best to keep tightly under wraps. I once saw her naked, standing in the hallway just outside my bedroom late one night, talking to my grandmother about some blemish on her skin. Even in the dim, shadowy light Aunt Evelyn appeared like an electrifying image. Her naked figure was immediately and forever seared into my young mind as something so transgressive that my eyes had no business gazing upon, yet something so arresting by its very nature as forbidden, I couldn't possibly turn away. It was the birth within me of an inner turmoil between shame and desire that would find regular reinforcement within the repressive Protestant mores that permeated everything in that house. When the light finally clicked off outside my bedroom I could still see, no matter how tightly I shut my eyes, the darkness etched and shimmering, luminescent with Aunt Evelyn's unclothed form.

Aunt Evelyn worked very hard to distance herself from her own physical beauty and strenuously made sure that not a hint of sexuality could ever be associated with her. Perhaps her teen pregnancies and having to live under her mother's roof again with a moderately successful husband had made her contrite, though she certainly did not suffer the steady onslaught of recriminations that my mother labored under. So whether it was as a result of her fall from grace, or an effort at self-purification and penance, she was ever on the alert for sexual innuendos and was constantly on the lookout for transgressions in this arena, seemingly determined that if she had to repress her sexuality then everyone else would have to do so as well. Curiously, she would fail in her Victorian hyper-vigilance when it mattered most.

Aunt Evelyn's children, brothers Brian and Ned, were my older cousins. Only ten months apart they couldn't have been more different. Brian looked like a young man rather than a boy. Even at age 10 (just four years older than me when I came to the Bronx), he was already tall and thick, strong and athletic, with a shock of curly brown hair. Brian was quick to anger and even quicker to use force to resolve anything that complicated his life. Ned was three years older than I. In contrast to Brian, he was thin and gangly, almost frail in appearance, with straight blond hair. He was nervous, sensitive, and quirky, given to intense fits of anguish and alarm simply upon seeing clothing being pinched in dresser drawers. Ned loved complexity and gravitated toward chess, science, and the slide-rule. In a nutshell, Ned was mostly brains and Brian was mostly brawn, and their temperaments seemed to reflect this.

For example, while both brothers were fond of collecting butterflies, Brian clearly enjoyed the hunt and the mothball-filled kill-jar, while Ned enjoyed the beauty of mounting the butterflies with tiny pins that held their wings outstretched in full color. While they loved building things with their motorized Erector Set, Ned loved to figure out the engineering steps involved, while Brian was happy using whatever they built in an action-oriented way. While they regularly busied themselves gluing together plastic models of various World War II armaments, Ned focused on the precision work of adding the delicate decals, while Brian couldn't wait to engage in pretend battle. While they each cherished their collections of baseball cards and Davey Crockett trading cards, Ned appreciated the statistics and the stories, while Brian looked only at the homeruns or the battle scenes at the Alamo. Throughout my formative years, I grew to love them both, though Ned was more introspective and a bit harder to get close to as a result of his sensitivity. Brian, on the other hand, was often friendly and easier to connect with, despite his bouts of rage and anger. When I reached my tenth birthday my relationship with my cousins would veer off into a very dark and unpredictable direction, unimaginable during those early months of acclimating to my new home.

My mother was 39 years old when she brought us to the Bronx, but she looked older. She was crestfallen by my father's submergence into alcohol and violence, which precipitated the entire upheaval that forced us here. She was completely distraught that she had ended up living with her parents again and she constantly sought to steel herself with the mantra that she was doing this for her children. Yet she arrived already beaten, knowing that this was going to be an uphill struggle in a downhill world. In an effort to head-off as much conflict with her parents as possible, my mother's entire focus those first few months was dedicated to incessantly reminding my sister and me that our being able to stay under our grandparents' roof was a privilege and completely contingent on our polite and deferential behavior; in other words, one mishap by us and we would all be out on the street.

When not working nights at Woolworth's five-and-dime on Fordham Road or tending to my sister and me, my mother's days were spent drinking instant coffee and smoking cigarettes. She would often sit for hours at the tiny kitchen table, her legs curled under her, watching her life dissipate like the smoke, repetitively crushing out her dreams with each cigarette butt laid to rest in the ashtray before her. She was dispirited as she struggled those first few months to make sense of all that had happened, struggled to make peace with the end of her marriage. She was reeling at being hurled back to Saxon Avenue by forces she had not predicted and had no control over. She despaired at having to live with her parents once again and, unlike Uncle Chuck, who saw his life stretching outwards and upwards, she knew that she was not going anywhere better. This time the Bronx was forever – and my mother knew it.

My sister Peggy, 15 months my junior, was intensely shy. The fact that she was made to feel decidedly unwelcomed from the moment of her birth imbued her with a tentativeness and hesitancy that caused her to function awkwardly in social situations. This, coupled with the ongoing alienation of eating in the kitchen and my grandmother's undisguised abhorrence, caused her to stay on the periphery. By the time she was eight years old she developed intense rashes in the crooks of her arms and behind her knees, skin disorders that sprung up as a result of the unrelenting stress brought on by the constant berating of my grandmother. Under duress she would scratch them raw, causing them to stand out in bright crimson. This only added to her feelings of ostracization, especially when my cousins, other neighborhood kids and I teased her about it. Paradoxically, this drove her to remain close to 3987 Saxon Avenue for safety, but drove her as well right back into the arms of her tormentor, my grandmother. Peggy always seemed to wait and watch until an explicit invitation to come closer was given. She was cautious, and yet simultaneously desperate to belong, eager to be wanted by anyone who would show some interest. Peggy was like a lonely moth simply desiring to feel warmth from the flame of human connection. In her searching loneliness it did not take very long before she was engulfed by a painful fire that would scar her forever.

This was the cast of characters populating 3987 Saxon Avenue in the spring of 1956. No one in that house reminded me of any of the rowdies of Bradley's Bar. I couldn't imagine anyone here climbing into the vacant lot to play, or feeding pigeons in the shadow of the war memorial statue. It seemed that I had traded the aliveness of Washington Heights for a place filled with dysfunction, decline, and an underlying decay. But these were just intuitions that I quickly brushed aside, for a New York summer was upon the horizon.

MY FIRST SUMMER IN THE BRONX was idyllic. I knew nothing of the neighborhood and very little of the rest of Saxon Avenue. My world consisted happily of inside the house and the environs immediately surrounding: the front stoop, the driveway, and the backyard. The one and only time my mother tried to integrate us into the daytime world of the other mothers and their children was the time she decided to venture out and bring me and Peggy to the playground. She sat on the benches just along the south fence, a safe distance from a gaggle of other mothers, while we romped in the nearby sandbox. According to the story my mother never tired of telling, a few of the other kids ganged up on me and took my plastic pail and shovel away. Without hesitation I fought back, dispatching them with a fury learned on the streets and in the vacant lots of Washington Heights, leaving them in disarray, all crying loudly. Their mothers immediately gathered them up, branding me the instigator, a pariah, and a kid never to be played with again. Within moments my mother was sitting on the bench all alone. She put my sister in her carriage, grabbed me by my hand, and we trooped up the hill back to Saxon Avenue. As we walked she began muttering and cursing, vowing never to return and dismissing all the mothers as arrogant and too haughty to ever be involved with. From that day forward my mother never set foot in the playground again. Years later my mother would recollect this story as both a source of justification for never again attempting to be part of the neighborhood, and to remind me that even as a young child I hated bullying and injustice.

After this incident my whole world that first summer consisted of the house, where the warming weather brought a cornucopia of quinces, cherries, and grapes to blossom in the backyard. My grandmother made sure we collected enough fruit for her jams before she allowed us to ravage the crop. The grapes were available for the taking on the rooftop back porch, accessible only from the top floor and only with permission from Uncle Chuck. The quinces we avoided like the plague; face-puckering-sour in raw form we waited until autumn when, thanks to my grandmother's magic, they were transformed into delicious jam. When it came to the cherries, because there were so many, we had more free-rein. When we had gotten all we could by climbing up the trunk of the cherry tree and shimmying out onto the branches as far as we dared, we then scaled the neighbor's trellis that abutted our garage and climbed to where branches laden with cherries overhung the garage roof. There we would sit, feet dangling over the roof's edge, heads surrounded by halos of leaves, and mouths open beneath bunches of red cherries. We would alternate eating cherries and spitting the pits at each other, using the cherries that the birds had ruined as projectiles to pelt one another. We would laugh so hard we almost fell off the garage. By the end of the day our white t-shirts would be pocked with red stains.

All summer long it seemed like every day merged seamlessly into endless nights sitting on the stoop with my mother, sister, uncle, aunt, and my cousins. The thick, warm, humid air smelled distinctly of summertime, the light not fading until nearly 10 o'clock at night. We kids would compete in front of the assembled adults to see who could jump up the most stairs of the stoop in one bound; my cousin Brian consistently outdid us, taking all five steps in a single leap. On the hottest and most humid nights Uncle Chuck never tired of fantasizing that the huge tree just to the side of our driveway was a gigantic sugar-cone filled with pistachio ice cream. We would look up at the tree and laugh. Other times my uncle would make up stories and regale us with silly characters with sillier names; we would laugh some more and cajole him not to end the story so we could linger when it was announced that it was time to go inside and get ready for bed.

Sometimes we would try to shimmy up the nearby pole, competing to see who could get high enough to touch the sign with the alternate-street parking times on it; even Brian would play along, though he could just stand there and reach up and touch the sign if he wanted to. I experienced my first sensual feelings climbing that pole, my legs wrapped around in such a way as to intensify the sensations in my loins; many times thereafter I would try to recreate those feelings when I was playing outside alone and thought nobody was looking. These summer nights were filled with innocence and discovery, with the carefree and future-less moments of hear-and-now, of getting to know the people who were suddenly my family. Even just watching the ants undulate over the tree bark, or simply playing in the sandy dirt surrounding the parking sign, or sitting with family on the stoop, were sources of pure joy that could mesmerize me for hours.

It seemed like every day I played with either Peggy or my cousins in some combination. Each Saturday, though, I would make sure I was sitting on the front stoop to watch my Uncle Chuck wash his new black Buick LeSabre by hand in the driveway. Over time I remember wondering to myself about the odd incongruency of his regularly repeated remarks criticizing some men for loving their cars more than their wives, spoken in a voice as if he were imparting a life-lesson to me. Yet he spent hours fondly hosing, exactingly washing every crevice, hosing again, waxing and polishing the car until it gleamed in the afternoon sun while his wife, Aunt Evelyn, busied herself inside.

That first summer seemed to last forever. Washington Heights was fading rapidly. I stopped wondering about my father as much. Inside the house it felt mostly peaceful to my sensibilities, especially if my sister and I stayed out of the way and, by virtue of our not being seen or heard, stayed out of trouble. I had accepted the fact that we were eating separately in the kitchen as simply the way it was; I had become adept at denying any longings that I would sit at that dining room table someday as fanciful and not worth desiring. The Bronx was my new home and I was determined to make the best of it. With happy ignorance I made every effort to surrender to this new world, incrementally trying to trust and imagine myself as truly part of this family. All it took was me actively submerging every feeling of unease that regularly bobbed to the surface in that house, effectively pushing them below the waterline of my awareness. It turned out to require fulltime vigilance.

Meanwhile, beyond the confines of 3987 Saxon Avenue, its backyard, its driveway, and its front stoop, a wider world was waiting. My brief forays, under my mother's protection, to the Co-op Market, EM's candy story, or the barber shop for a haircut had given me impressionable but fleeting glimpses into the world surrounding my island-like new home. I knew, from family conversations, that we lived in a Jewish neighborhood but I had no idea what that really meant. Other than periodically hearing snippets of the Yiddish language arising from within the press of people gathered at the deli counter at the rear of the Co-op, or the sudden shift from English to Yiddish when my mother and me passed by, or sensing the strange stillness that permeated the neighborhood streets on Saturdays, the Jewish Sabbath, it was still very much a mystery to me. I already felt a growing sense of alienation since leaving Washington Heights, unshakeable as an unwelcomed but tolerated stranger in my new family. So, as the summer inched slowly toward autumn and the beginning of school, I wondered if it could be any worse out there.

Chapter Seven
An Outsider among Outsiders

I was six years old when she caught me staring at her tattoo. Her unblinking eyes seared me; my head and neck seemed to lose all willfulness and my face was dragged to my chest under a dead-weight feeling of visceral shame. Moments before, I was spinning around on one of the red-topped cushioned stools at the counter in EM's Luncheonette, waiting for my mother to buy her Tareyton cigarettes. I had no idea what had just happened; I wasn't sure what to do. I knew I could not raise my head and meet her eyes, those eyes, again. So I sat there, legs dangling, chin down, and eyes down. Finally, my mother called and without another look I jumped off the stool and raced to her side. As we began walking the three blocks to our house I told my mother what had happened. She listened silently as we walked up the short hill on Sedgwick Avenue past P.S. 95. When we turned onto our street, Saxon Avenue, I asked her why that woman had numbers on her arm. My mother did not reply.

"Why was she looking so mean at me, mom?" I asked. "They were just numbers. Weren't they just a bunch of numbers, mom?"

My mother, as I was to learn about so many of the questions I asked her, never answered.

* * * * *

AS MY FIRST SUMMER WOUND TO A CLOSE, the first day of school began to loom larger and larger as the next step in my journey to further shed the street-urchin sensibilities I had carried from Washington Heights, and begin to integrate the truth that the Bronx was now my home. The administrators at Public School 95 had informed my mother that since my birthday fell at the end of November, and since I would be five years *and* ten months old on the first day of classes, I could, as a new arrival, skip kindergarten and start immediately in first grade. As the opening of school drew nearer I became more terrified. I had only just begun to feel comfortable within the world of my grandparents and the immediate environs surrounding 3987 Saxon Avenue. I was just getting used to navigating the idiosyncrasies of my new family, getting socialized to the Protestant credo. Going to school, despite it being only a two-block walk from my house, meant suddenly being thrown into a social milieu that I intuitively felt I was not yet prepared for. For months I had remained tucked away in a tiny and, therefore, safe and known world, with periodic forays accompanying my mother to the Co-op Market or other businesses clustered in the local shopping area three blocks away. It was only here, in these adult places, where I regularly rubbed up against the images, sounds, smells, and sensibilities that emanated overwhelmingly from the rhythms of a Jewish culture. Now it was time to really be a part of this new world, to begin another level of socialization into an environment populated with not only teachers and other adults, but with all the other neighborhood children, my age and older.

From the moment my mother woke me for my first day of school I cried. While she cajoled me to get dressed, and even while I ate my cereal, I steadily bawled. On the landing at the top of the stairs I resisted leaving the house, tearfully screaming even louder and forcefully pulling on my mother's hand to try to get us back inside the kitchen. My sister stood there wide-eyed; she wanted to go to school and would've been happy for us to change places, as would've I. My cousins were laughing and my grandparents were growing steadily appalled with the transgressive sight and sound of me in a flagrant tantrum. Finally my mother succeeded in getting me down the stairs and out the front door. At the end of our walkway we turned right and began walking down Saxon Avenue toward P.S. 95; it was the march of a condemned child. At the end of our block we made another right turn onto Sedgwick Avenue. We solemnly passed the last and most ornate private house at the south end of our street, framed as it was with two white plantation-style pillars and adorned with two stone lions guarding its entrance. We were in no-man's land now. Then, just to our right and on the other side of Hillman Avenue stood P.S. 95, the main entrance to the school beckoning at the midpoint of the building. I was still crying.

I cried all the way to the front door of the school. As we entered the building I was quieted momentarily by the cavernous lobby and the receding echoes of the other children disappearing like phantoms into classrooms throughout the school. We stood there in the silence, my hand welded to my mother's. Within moments my mother was directed to my classroom by someone who appeared official since she was clearly free and untethered to any particular group of students. We turned right, down a long central corridor with classroom doors along either side. My classroom was at the end of the hallway, on the left-hand side, closest to twin metal exit doors that led to what everyone referred to as the Little Schoolyard, where kindergarteners and first-graders lined up before each school day and where they played during recess. I hesitated at the open doorway and looked in. The face of every single boy and girl in the classroom was turned toward me, staring, as was the teacher's. I began to once again wail my discontent and refused to enter. My mother looked imploringly at the teacher, who walked over to where we stood at the threshold to the classroom. The teacher gently relaxed my hand from the grip I had upon my mother and took it into her own. Slowly, reassuringly in her matter-of-factness, she led me to my seat. Her name was Mrs. Tocker and there couldn't have been a better first-grade teacher for a child as frightened as I was. Something about her caused me to slowly cease my tears. Noticing this, my mother quietly left. I sat in my desk, silently refusing to look anywhere else but at Mrs. Tocker.

The shock of being in school wore off slowly that first day. Mrs. Tocker was kind and attentive and welcoming, to me and to everyone. It seemed that most of the kids knew each other, living as they did in some of the same apartment buildings, or their parents being friends, or having spent time together in kindergarten the previous year (the socializing step that I missed due to my age and sudden arrival in the neighborhood). I was seized by the awkwardness of not knowing a single kid and, as a result, I was determined to remain safe by remaining silent. It was during that first afternoon that I was befriended by a boy named Lenny Baumann. He seemed to want to reassure me that everything was okay, that I wasn't alone. I immediately sensed a kinship with him, a feeling that we were both a little different, both slightly outside the mainstream – I wasn't Jewish and, I found out later, while he was half-Jewish he lived in an apartment on Gouverneur Avenue that wasn't part of the Amalgamated. I was instinctively quiet and he was instinctively gregarious and seemed more certain of himself. Lenny became my guide to life within P. S. 95 and my first friend in the neighborhood.

It was always an unpredictable adventure to go to Lenny's house. He sat in the middle of four other siblings, Bruce the oldest, and Sylvia, next in line; Tim and Charlie were his two younger brothers, respectively. His apartment seemed huge, with windows looking out over Gouverneur Avenue and into the larger of the two recess areas, dubbed the Big Schoolyard. The energy in his house was always frenetic, with Lenny's mother, Roberta, attempting to herd her children in one direction or another. His father was rarely seen, but when I did run into him he was wearing either a button-down shirt or a white, sleeveless t-shirt that showed off a workingman's physique. Lenny's house possessed a distinctively feral feel, reminiscent of Washington Heights, and I was instantly drawn by a sense of comfort and familiarity. It was at Lenny's house that I more than once saw his mother clad in a silky slip as she ran about attempting to get dressed while yelling at the kids to get ready. It was the first time I saw an adult woman in semi-undress (other than the brief accidental vision of my naked aunt), and I was fascinated at the sight and at the apparent freedom within Lenny's family, knowing full well that something like this would never, ever happen in my very proper Protestant household. I liked spending time there and was often invited over by Lenny to hang out at lunch and, as I got a little older, I was allowed to go visit after school as well. Lenny and I stayed close friends until the beginning of fifth grade, when we drifted apart, me toward hanging out with friends who lived on Saxon Avenue, Lenny moving to the beat of his own drum. Lenny seemed to always have the capacity to keep and trust his own counsel. Even at a young age Lenny appeared quite comfortable in his own skin, was never a follower, and was adept at moving between different groups of people, and even between different neighborhoods. This was an attribute that, when we hit our teenage years, would oftentimes turn out to be as helpful as it was problematic.

FIRST GRADE, like so much of elementary school, was structured to provide the basics, those foundational components deemed so necessary to function as citizens in community. We learned patriotism reciting the Pledge of Allegiance every morning, right hands pressed reverently over our hearts. Once a week Mrs. Tocker would roll a huge black, rectangular radio into the classroom and tune in WNYC, the public school channel, where we would listen to the program "Know Your City," and hear about the Empire State Building, the Statue of Liberty, and various museums throughout the metropolitan area. Often, after one of these broadcasts, we would be off on a field trip to the location that had been featured on the radio show.

We learned regimentation, conformity, and control of our restiveness sitting in our perfectly aligned wooden desks, five rows with six desks in each row. Each desk began with a narrow, flat surface with outmoded brass inkwells embedded in it; here we could place our pen, pencil, and ruler. The remainder of the desk slanted slightly downwards to provide a writing platform. Under each platform was a shelf for books and papers. The seat of each desk was attached to the desk behind it and could be raised when we stood or lowered when we sat. The desk and seat were held in place by ornate wrought iron legs screwed into the wooden floors. It was under these desks we would scramble periodically when we were told to "duck and cover" as part of the civil defense air raid drills in case a nuclear bomb was dropped nearby. On top of these desks our arms remained uniformly outstretched, with our hands folded, when not actively engaged in learning. Huge windows towered upwards along one whole side of the classroom, requiring a "window monitor" to wield a long pole with a hook in order to open them in the warmer weather.

Addition, subtraction, and multiplication (known as the "Times Tables"), were routinely recited by the entire class in the sing-song response so typical of prepubescent children. The three alliterative R's – reading, 'riting, and 'rithmetic – figured in specific lesson plans delivered to us throughout the school day. Every one of us practiced scribing the alphabet, images of which ringed the classroom above the blackboard at the front and extended to the wall above the clothes closet off to the side; on yellowing squares of thicker construction paper each letter was depicted in capital form with a lower-case companion alongside, like a parent accompanying a child. We spent what seemed like hours printing block letters and, as we progressed, practicing the unbroken flow of cursive writing. So much of my learning in grade school was motivated by my desire to elicit praise. My need for hearing that I had done something right, in contrast to the disdain I received at home, only increased throughout elementary school and beyond as I sought desperately to believe that I was really okay. Unfortunately, the road that might've led me to feeling okay about myself turned out to be a distinctly unpredictable and bumpy ride.

THREE EPISODES over the course of my first year in P.S. 95 stand out as nodal points of initiation into my new neighborhood. The first was when I drew a Nazi Swastika on the sole of my shoe as I sat bored in class. I had seen this symbol a lot in my house and had drawn it plenty of times, inspired by my cousins' fascination with building plastic models of German World War II weapons. From *Luftwaffe* planes, to *Panzer* tanks, to a huge model of the battleship *Bismarck* – always in gray plastic – my cousins seemed more fascinated by the German army than by the American, though they still built plenty of green-plastic replicas of U.S. weaponry. Yet they seemed more compelled by the imagery and symbolism of Iron Crosses, lightning bolts signifying *Blitzkrieg*, and drawing the fearsome Swastika. At the time I drew it on my shoe I had no idea what it really meant or what it would stir up.

Within an instant of its completion a girl sitting in the row next to me raised her hand and blurted out, "Mrs. Tocker, Mrs. Tocker, Tommy drew a Swastika on his shoe." The entire class gulped a breath in unison and turned toward me. Whatever Mrs. Tocker did next was going to determine whether or not they peacefully released that collective inhale, and how they would treat me thereafter. Without hesitation she called me to the front of the classroom. The rest of the students began breathing again, slowly, with anticipation, their heads turning to follow my sullen march toward her desk. I could feel the tension in the air and a rising, nameless dread oozing throughout my body. As I stood facing the class Mrs. Tocker began by explaining that the Nazi Swastika was a horrible symbol, that it stood for the killing of millions of Jews, Jews just like my classmates. Now the dread I was experiencing was replaced by a distinctive and familiar sense of shame. Tears beaded along my lower eyelids. Mrs. Tocker, in a voice both measured and without anger, continued to make it clear that I was to never draw this symbol again, that it was hurtful to all the students who were my neighbors and friends. I told her and the class that I was sorry and I promised that I would never, ever draw the Swastika. She nodded her head, signaling that the matter was over and asked me to return to my desk. I was quiet for the rest of the school day and found myself alone more often than not, my classmates perhaps responding to some unspoken pariah status that had either been conveyed to the entire group as a result of what I had done, or self-adopted as my way of expressing contrition, or some combination of the two. This was my first lesson in the nightmare that Jewish people throughout Germany, Europe, and Eastern Europe had been thrust into by virtue of simply being Jews. I was rattled, and in that moment in front of the class I made a silent, sacred vow to never allow myself to do anything like that again with respect to my Jewish friends; anti-Semitism, even with my rudimentary understanding, instantly became painful and repugnantly anathema to me.

My next attitudinal shift came as a result of a sledding accident that put me in the hospital for two weeks and separated me from my family and all my new friends and classmates. It was January and the city was blanketed with snow. My cousins each had Flexible-Flyer sleds that they were eager to use. Together the three of us made our way toward the playground. To the east of the playground entrance the asphalt pathway formed a short hill, one steep enough to get some thrillingly fast sleigh runs going. On either side of the path squatted wooden benches, painted green with three evenly spaced concrete stanchions to which the wooden bench slats were bolted. It was a cold day, overcast and sunless, moving toward late afternoon. The track was solid ice after repeatedly being used by the neighborhood kids.

My cousins had each allowed me to lie flat on top of them, double-decker-style, as they maneuvered down the hill between the benches and past other kids, who were off to the sides of the main runway pulling their sleds back uphill for more rides. After a while my cousins tired of having me on their backs and left me to stand idly and watch everyone having fun sledding. As I was looking around I noticed a sled that had been discarded off to the side. It didn't seem to have an owner and it appeared to be intact. I ran over and grabbed the rope that was attached to the wooden steering handles at the front of the frame and began pulling it up to the top of the hill.

What I didn't know was that the sled had been discarded because it could no longer be steered properly. Within an instant of taking off down the hill I was out of control and heading rapidly toward one of the concrete bench supports. I hit the bench head-on at full speed. I was momentarily knocked unconscious and my right hand flopped out onto the icy track where the sleds were whizzing by. Suddenly one of the sleds ran over my hand; I was startled into consciousness by the shock of pain and my own screaming.

One of the kids' fathers who had been watching ran over and lifted me, screaming in pain, into his arms. My cousins rapidly led him up the hill to Saxon Avenue and to our house. Once inside Uncle Chuck carefully removed my glove and there, hanging by a mere thread of muscle and skin, was the top of my right middle finger. I was crying and numb at the same time. Immediately my uncle handed me a napkin and told me to keep it under my hand in case the tip of my finger fell off. He gathered me and my mother and all three of us piled into his Buick, my mother and me in the back seat, him alone in the front driving. My mother told him to drive to the hospital where all my medical records were, the hospital located in our old neighborhood of Washington Heights, Columbia Presbyterian. Throughout the entire five-mile drive I stared at my hand, awaiting the dangling tip of my finger to fall upon the napkin. It somehow stayed attached as my uncle raced like a maniac, speeding from the Bronx to Manhattan. The last thing I remember was being wheeled into an operating room, surrounded by doctors and nurses, and being painfully stuck with needles in the webbing on either side of my traumatized finger. With that I lost consciousness.

When I awoke my right hand was in a cast to immobilize it and lessen the chance that some wrong movement or collision would damage my now reattached fingertip. It took 12 stitches to sew the tip of my middle finger back on. My mother spent the rest of her life praising my surgeon, Dr. Wood, for his surgical wizardry. Still, I was to remain in the hospital under observation for the concussion that caused me to lose consciousness and my hand to fall under the runners of the onrushing sled. I was also being monitored to see whether the reattachment surgery would take.

Over the course of my hospitalization not a single person from my family, other than my mother and, periodically, my sister Peggy, came to visit me. It appeared that now that the immediate emergency that plunged Uncle Chuck into action that afternoon was over, the family could return to its attitude of benign neglect regarding anything having to do with my mother, sister, and me. It was during this time that I began to notice that I was missing my newfound neighborhood friends more than I missed my family members. I began to wonder what was happening back in Mrs. Tocker's classroom and what everyone was doing. This was the moment when a tiny seed of awareness began to sprout; a moment where the definition of what truly constituted family for me began to shape-shift ever so subtly, as I imagined leaving the hospital filled with more excitement to see Lenny and my other friends rather than to return to my own home.

The third initiatory experience during this first year of grade school occurred when I got caught staring at the concentration camp identification numbers tattooed onto the forearm of a woman sitting having her lunch in EM's candy store. Having no real concept of concentration camps or the Holocaust, I was simply struck by the fact that numbers were tattooed on her arm at all, and I stared at them with a mixture of curiosity and perplexity. Once the woman noticed me staring, and let me know that she had noticed me by staring directly back with a fearsome expression, an overwhelming sense of shameful transgression welled up unbidden inside me. I felt small under her gaze and tried to look away; unable to move, I began hoping that I would be relieved from her intractable stare by my mother coming to get me, which wasn't happening fast enough for my liking. Finally my mother called and I desperately grabbed her hand and hurried us out onto the sidewalk.

On the way home, when I asked my mother about the numbers on the woman's arm and received no answer whatsoever, I began to relive how it felt to be caught by the woman and the shame I experienced as she was probing me with her eyes. I somehow began to connect this feeling with how I felt when I stood in front of the classroom and Mrs. Tocker gave me the lesson about the Nazi Swastika. Slowly, as if by some intuitive sense, I began to understand that those numbers tattooed on her arm had to do with her being Jewish and had something to do with Nazis. A life-shaping realization began to take hold of me in that moment of reflection and I knew, at an even deeper level this time, I didn't want to ever again do anything that would cause any hurt to my Jewish friends.

As my mother and I walked along Saxon Avenue together after my encounter in EM's, a distinct feeling that I was truly in a different world, one filled with things and experiences I had no idea about, began to coalesce inside me. Somehow I knew I was being cautioned to tread gently on these streets, to pay attention, to show some respect regarding the complex and unfathomable living memories lurking around every corner of my new Bronx neighborhood. It would take me a few more years to even begin to understand what that woman's defiant stare was all about.

These were the years when I also began to learn about the oppression and subjugation suffered by my father growing up in Ireland. Whenever I began to miss him – which was quite often during my first year in the Bronx – I would sit with my mother and ask her to tell me about his life in Ireland. Piecing together that painful history from my mother's recollections of the fragments of his story that he had shared with her, I began to develop the capacity to build my internal bridges of understanding. I began connecting the wounds and legacies inherited from my father's experiences with discrimination, oppression, and hatred suffered by the Irish, to slowly but increasingly extend empathy toward the indelible scars inflicted onto the hearts and souls of my Jewish friends by the exterminating scythe of the *Shoah*.

Chapter Eight
Daddy, I Hardly Knew You

It was February 1959, a few months after I turned eight. My sister and I were playing in our bedroom, sitting together on the floor with toys strewn about. It was early evening yet dark, with a cold that you could sense lurking just outside the window panes, inspiring a distinctly primal feeling of gratitude for being safe and warm inside. The house was preternaturally quiet, as if the building itself and all of us inside were anticipating something, uncertain as to what it might be. Suddenly, the door of our bedroom opened and there stood my mother, wrapped in a long slate-grey coat, scarf dangling from behind her neck down across the front of her chest. Her hair was disheveled and she appeared as if she had just emerged from a storm, though the chill nighttime air outside was quiet. She looked down at us as we looked up at her.

"You're father's dead," she uttered matter-of-factly.

With that she turned and walked away to another part of the house, making it clear in her departure that we were not to follow. It would take another four years before my mother would speak to me of my father's death.

* * * * *

LIFE IN P.S. 95 went on apace during second grade and the first half of third. Under the stern but fair tutelage of my second grade teacher, Mrs. Bogart, I felt like I was adjusting to being in school, learning each of the subjects presented, making friends, being socialized into the ways of boyhood as practiced in the Bronx, both at school and at home. My life throughout second grade, at the age of seven, was basically structured around sitting in class, enjoying recess, playing after school with my sister Peggy at home, or with friends on the street, homework after supper – repeated the next day and the next until the weekend. Beyond the confines of the classroom I was concerned with attending to life under the Saxon Avenue roof, the unfolding of the seasons, and the shape-shifting vagaries of who at any given moment I was best friends with, and with whom I wasn't. Second grade felt seamless, a smooth sail from the beginning of school in September all the way through the last day in June.

That third summer as a Bronx resident felt beyond the bounds of time, stretching itself like a cat with endless lives toward an unseen and therefore uncontemplated horizon. It was 1958 and I had finally started to feel at home, had fashioned a *modus vivendi* regarding eating in the kitchen separated from the family, and had begun to navigate my not being Jewish in a Jewish neighborhood. Life began to feel easy, secure, and reassuring again. Yet all these sweet feelings were on the verge of suffering tectonic upheaval as my sense of self, and whether I was really safe in this world, was about to be changed utterly and unalterably.

Third grade began as usual, with fresh books and pencils purchased at my mother's Woolworth's; a new shirt and pants from Robert Hall on the Grand Concourse; and a pair of shiny new shoes from Thom McCann on Broadway near 231st Street. This year I was in Mrs. Brown's class. Mrs. Brown seemed incredibly tall, with rows of tight grey curls covering her head like a cap. She had a husky voice which, to my ears, made her seem angrier when she directed the class, told me to do something, or scolded me for not doing something. Nevertheless, all went well as autumn began to reveal itself.

It was once again during the Jewish High Holy Days of Rosh Hashanah and Yom Kippur that I was reminded saliently of my outsider status, of just how different my life was compared to my friends'. Perhaps I hadn't paid enough attention during first and second grade to really notice, or was simply too young to feel it, but this time it struck me just how much our neighborhood and, therefore, important aspects of my own life, were tied to the ebbs and flows of the Jewish calendar. During the High Holy Days none of my Jewish friends attended P.S. 95. This meant that for the entire school day during their time off for religious observance, only about a dozen kids attended school. Assigned to two or three classrooms, sorted by age as best as possible, we spent the day subjected to modified lesson plans designed to have us tread water until all the Jewish kids returned to school.

The one exciting thing for me was that on these strange days I got to be a milk monitor, a job that older students (including my cousin Ned) had during the regular year. Silver metal baskets, each with room for eight cartons of milk, were used to deliver milk to the classrooms. Each morning the metal baskets would be on the floor, lined up beneath one of the grated windows and edged against the wall of the lobby. White cards, similar to cards used in library books, would be in each basket detailing how many cartons of milk went to each particular classroom. During regular days a troop of milk monitors would carry full baskets to each class. During the Jewish holidays, I usually got to carry one or two baskets, each with only three or four milk cartons for distribution, but I felt so important in my official capacity as milk monitor *pro tempore* that I beamed proudly as I went on my deliveries, short-lived as they were.

Not only was the school day in the ghostly confines of P. S. 95 dramatically different, but when I got home from school I found a reality quite unimagined from the reverie I had been having of my friends frolicking throughout the neighborhood while I sat in the classroom. Most of my friends were dressed up, sporting suit and tie and bound by the demands of the Holy Days; many were required to fast, go to temple, be with family, and therefore unable to play. I was terribly lonely whenever a Jewish holiday arrived. On top of this all the local stores were closed as well. It was as if the whole world had tilted on its axis to remind me just how very different my life was, and how much a minority I was in the neighborhood scheme of things. As a result of these dawning revelations I wanted desperately to not feel so separate; I began to ache with desire to be Jewish too.

As THE MONTH OF NOVEMBER wound to a close, Thanksgiving arrived with the usual bustle inside our household. With my birthday on November 28 typically falling close to Thanksgiving Day, any kind of singular celebration of my birth was little more than a passing notion amongst the extended family – barely celebrated except by my mother and sister. My first Bronx Thanksgiving, when I turned six and we had just arrived, was nearly a week after the holiday and therefore never registered as other than a mere afterthought. My seventh birthday actually coincided with Thanksgiving and thereby got completely lost in the holiday preparations. Curiously, this third Thanksgiving fell the day before my birthday. Perhaps, given past experiences of my birthday getting lost in the shuffle, I found myself surprisingly less concerned with my own day and, instead, was determined to observe the family dynamics a bit more astutely.

From the moment I woke up on Thanksgiving morning, I watched as my mother, Aunt Evelyn, and Uncle Chuck, virtually pirouetted hither and thither to prepare the house for the arrival of family members and in preparation for the grand meal. My sister Peggy, I, and my cousins did our best to avoid being underfoot, spending most of the day outside with periodic forays into the house just to imbibe the aromas, or grab a handful of nuts from ubiquitous bowls scattered throughout, only to be shooed out instantly by the adults who simply could not be bothered given the tasks demanded by such a holiday feast. Each breach into the house only ratcheted up our anticipation for the arrival of dinnertime.

Dense, spicy odors emanated from the kitchen, getting stronger as the morning turned toward mid-afternoon. Smells of turkey, sweet-and-sour string beans, mashed potatoes, carrots, jockeyed for position within my olfactory chambers, not to mention the intermingled smells of the mincemeat and pumpkin pies baking in the oven. There was the steady, rhythmic clunk and scrape of pots being stirred or their contents being scooped into serving dishes. My grandmother, wielding the baster like a magical culinary wand, methodically opening and closing the oven door to "check on the bird," unleashed more and more wonderful smells into the already rapturous atmosphere.

The good china and silverware and glasses made music together as they were properly arranged on the dining room table with the formality of creating an altarpiece. The dining room table had sprouted accommodating wings on either side and now completely filled the room. Six matching high-backed wooden chairs sat stiff and erect, three on each side, dedicated by their very sternness to reinforcing proper dining manners; at each end of the table sat near-identical chairs, different only in the fact that these possessed armrests that immediately and regally designated them as reserved for my grandfather and grandmother. Additionally, there were always one or two mismatched chairs taken from the kitchen and designated for whatever kids had reached the magic age whereby an invitation was extended to them to sit at the Great Table with the adults; this was always a welcomed reprieve from continuing another year inhabiting the kids' table, relegated as it was like an outpost in the living room in order that the youngest children in all their holiday excitement would barely be seen and only partially heard.

When I was ten and finally invited to sit in the dining room during the holidays, I studiously tried to mimic the formalities that seemed requisite to moving the serving dishes around the table, echoing the "thanks you's" and the "no thank you's" uttered with barely audible politeness. I was paralyzed by the phalanxes of silverware that stood guard on each side of my plate, holding the undecipherable secrets to what to eat when, what to eat with, and how to eat it. Yet within all my confusion I was ecstatic to be at the table, happy to look around at all the adult faces gathered there. At times like this I could pretend that I was truly wanted here and that tomorrow's return to eating in the kitchen could be postponed indefinitely.

My second-favorite relative (after Uncle Chuck), was Uncle Walter. He always arrived on the Wednesday evening before Thanksgiving, driving his white Chevy Corvair – motor engineered pioneeringly in the rear – up from Washington, D. C., where he lived as a bachelor and worked in the U.S. Patent Office (doing what, I never understood). In preparation for his visit we removed all toys from the sun parlor and my mother made up the army cot for him to sleep. The gathered curtains would be released so that they covered the twin doors of the sunroom, remaining closed throughout his stay to give Uncle Walter a sense of privacy. I was always excited to see him. He was balding, his round face especially thoughtful with his wire-rimmed glasses perched upon the bridge of his nose. I loved the smell of his pipe tobacco when, after the evening meal, he would settle down and light up, the blue-yellow tip of the match being repeatedly and purposefully sucked downwards to enflame the studiously measured and tamped bed of tobacco in the pipe's bowl. Prior to the holiday dinner he would sometimes pace the living room, pipe held aloft in his hand, periodically puffing on it and sending smoke curling upwards, remarking on something he heard about the arts or on the news. At other times he would reach into a bowl of nuts and, grabbing a couple of Brazil nuts he would apply the metal, vise-like nutcracker, saying in a most aloof, scholarly, and erudite tone to no one in particular: "Did you know, these are called nigger toes?" as he tossed the now freed nut-meat into his smiling mouth. Everyone within earshot would snicker in a way that made me uncomfortable but I pushed that feeling down and smiled along with the other family members.

Uncle Walter would always bring my cousins, my sister, and me a gift, always something educational that would improve our minds. This year he brought me a huge pictorial tome about the history of America. The evening before Thanksgiving, I was leafing through it and came upon a painting of a Native American woman swinging bare-chested from a tree branch. As an eight year old I was immediately titillated and walked over to the couch, where my cousin Brian sat, to share my discovery. Within an instant my Aunt Evelyn, ever on high-alert for any temblors of lasciviousness, swooped in and swept the book from my hands, a look of "I caught you" spreading across her face. There I stood, as naked as the picture I was sharing, exposed as the little dirty-minded ruffian whose socialization as a member of this proper family was obviously and woefully incomplete. I was immediately chastised in front of everyone and I raced tearfully to my room covered in shame. As a result, by the time the rest of the extended family arrived the following day for the Thanksgiving feast, I had been sufficiently re-tethered to moral probity and conducted myself throughout Thanksgiving Day with appropriate contriteness.

From about noon to the 2:00 p.m. dinner time, punctuated at unpredictable intervals, the members of the extended Scheel family and their spouses and assorted offspring would arrive, their presence mandated by family tradition and my grandmother's demand that Thanksgiving and Easter be spent together at her house. My widowed aunt, Gladys Speer, her college-aged daughter Patricia, and her son

Butch, always arrived early and left early, since Gladys' steady drinking throughout the day required they extricate her before any embarrassing mishaps and return safely to the suburbs. Aunt Gladys was ever-ready to plant a thick red, liquor- and lipstick-saturated kiss on my cheek the moment she saw me, while her children barely contained their boredom. Aunt Sherrie and her husband, Roger Owen, would arrive from Long Island, their young daughter Kathy and infant son Tommy in tow (by the time I was ten they would add one other child, Susan, but by then the extended family gatherings had ceased). Peggy and I loved playing with Kathy and Tommy since they were the closest to our age. Sometimes our second cousins, Ella Marie and Otto Munk, and their children, Amy and Russell, would attend as well, though theirs was an infrequent cameo appearance at best. Uncle Fred, the eldest of all the male Scheel children, and his wife Kay were there at my first Thanksgiving but none thereafter. Whatever compelled them to attend, that was the first and last time I ever saw them and their three children, Fred, Jr., Billy, and Kathy in the Saxon Avenue house. This was the usual cast of characters that annually populated Thanksgiving at 3987 Saxon Avenue, the configurations around the two tables changing only as new children were born, or kids went off to college, or various family members felt they were too old or too busy to accommodate my grandmother.

This exact family tableau would reassemble itself for the Easter holiday as well; the only noticeable differences were the warmer weather, us kids being deposited at the Kingsbridge Lutheran Church for mass in the morning, a brief hunt for colored Easter eggs afterwards, and the fact that instead of turkey my grandmother served clove-stippled ham. Easter baskets were strategically placed throughout the house, offering all passersby hollow chocolate bunnies, chocolate eggs wrapped in colored tinfoil, variously shaped lollipops and squishy-soft, yellow-marshmallow chicks for the taking. Admonitions warning the kids to "not ruin your dinner" were periodically launched into the air to coincide with our hands approaching one of the candy-laden baskets yet again. We also had to dress more formally than at Thanksgiving, my sister in a dress and Easter bonnet and me in a white shirt and tie. Once again, around both the dining room table and the kids' table, the same family dynamics that occurred at Thanksgiving repeated themselves.

UNLIKE THANKSGIVING AND EASTER, Christmas was a fairly subdued holiday. Except for Uncle Walter's presence there were no other relatives from the extended family crowding around the house. In fact, it was the only other time of the year my family was allowed to eat dinner at the table in the dining room.

About a week before Christmas, Uncle Chuck would come home with a tree roped atop his Buick. He and my cousins would carry it up the stairs and set it up in a corner of the living room, just adjacent to the television. The trunk of the tree rested in a green metal pan. The pan was kept filled with water so that the branches wouldn't turn brown and slough off; the whole base was then covered in fluffy white, cottony stuff to look like snow. Typically the tree extended almost to the ceiling, with just enough room for the white plastic star to be fitted and shine forth. After dinner Uncle Chuck would string the lights and all of us kids would happily – and ever so carefully – alternate between sprinkling strands of silver tinsel on the branches, attaching ornaments, and hanging candy canes. It was a fleeting yet indelible moment of family togetherness.

Christmas morning seemed to activate a wake-up-early signal and all four of us kids would slowly enter the living room, straining not to wake up Uncle Walter asleep in the sun parlor. There we would wait, excitement building at the sight of so many presents wrapped and waiting under the branches of the tree. We would wait as the bath-robed grown-ups began to filter in, coffee in hand, and take their places around the room. Once they were settled we would alternate opening the beautifully wrapped gifts. The presents Peggy and I received were mostly practical: shirts, pants, blouses, dresses and socks . . . tons of socks. Periodically, and depending on the price, my mother would succumb to our pleadings for toys. These amounted to my sister and me repeatedly singing the commercials for our most desired item that appeared on television every Saturday morning. I recall getting toys like a plastic replica of the rifle that Chuck Connors used on the TV show *The Rifleman*; a toy Civil War set, with Blue and Gray troops that included an exploding bunker and wounded soldiers that you could paint red blood onto; and the next book in *The Hardy Boys* series. Peggy received gifts like a *Betsy-Wetsy* doll that cried and wet her diaper; a *Chatty Cathy* doll that spoke whenever you pulled the plastic ring at the back of her neck; a metal dollhouse, complete with a family and plastic furniture for each room; and, as she got older, *Nancy Drew* books. Typically it was a peaceful morning, and so it was on this, my third Christmas in the Bronx. Unbeknownst to me, amidst the happy clamor of shredding wrapping paper and revealing presents, a dark storm was brewing just beyond the shoreline of my awareness.

January, February, and March cluster as the oddest months of the year, especially for children in elementary school. After the past couple of months, tantalizingly salted with Halloween, two major holiday celebrations and nearly a ten-day break from school, there is little to get excited about at the turn of the New Year and therefore time simply drags on. Even with the two days off in honor of the birthdays of Presidents Lincoln and Washington it was a span of time offering little excitement and even less reprieve. The winter was waning, yet spring had not arrived; it was cold and barren, like a *Venus Paradise Paint-By-Numbers Coloring Set* where one is forced to only use the black, brown, and gray pencils for every scene. There was little cheer to be found and when my father died in February, I couldn't find any at all.

In the days and weeks after my mother matter-of-factly informed Peggy and me of my father's death there was simply no conversation at all in our house, nothing uttered about how he died, how anyone felt about his death – or his life – or any talk of a funeral. Instead, my mother went into her own private mourning, the other family members would whisper to each other until Peggy or I came near, and my sister and I were left to make of it what we could as kids, eight and seven year olds respectively. For the rest of the family it appeared that nothing of significance even occurred. Years later when I was 12, in a moment when my mother was fondly recalling my father as the love of her life, I was able to piece together the story of my father's death. Further, unbeknownst to Peggy and me at the time, I was also to discover anguished secrets that his departure revealed which, unsurprisingly, covered me, my mother and sister with another coat of shame and disgust in the eyes of our extended family.

It was after closing time when my father trudged home from his favorite bar that February night. It was cold, the sidewalks of the Inwood Park neighborhood lined with mounds of recently shoveled snow, the concrete icy in places. As he walked unsteadily back to his one-room flophouse on 207th Street and 10th Avenue, jacket collar upturned against the cold, his heart seized up, as if the fist of God was squeezing the life out of it. The shock and pain felled him immediately; he clutched his chest, in too much agony to call out. Yet it was not to be a quick and merciful passing for my father. Like every other step of his life this, too, was going to be without ease or grace. No, instead of dying quickly from his heart attack, my father lay on a frigid street in Manhattan and awaited the *banshee's* call and her arrival. As the coroner explained to my mother when she went to identify his body, my father did not die of heart failure, he actually froze to death over a number of hours. Whether he could not call out for help, or whether no one was on the street at that time of night, or whether passersby only saw another Irish drunk and simply walked on by, is impossible to know.

My father was 59 when he died, and in those accumulated years he had seen his native Ireland convulsed in rebellion and civil war in a bid for nationhood, had immigrated to America, had worked the longshore, and had fathered my sister and me. He had sung me and Peggy to sleep in his native Irish language; he had saved Jimmy Bradley and had become my hero. Finally, he had stood by and allowed us to be taken to the Bronx, causing my love for him to become occluded with confusion, disappointment, and anger. Even those sporadic times before his death, when my mother would take Peggy and me to see him at his one-room walk-up – complete with hotplate, noir-ish flashing neon sign outside the window, and sounds from the Broadway elevated train overhead – I felt the distance between him and me. Even when we all went for a picnic in nearby Inwood Park or for a hamburger in a diner on Dyckman Street, the air was fraught with awkwardness and tentativeness that none of us ever seemed able to overcome.

I don't recall my father ever offering me any father-to-son wisdom. He did take me to a baseball game at Yankee Stadium once, the summer before he died where, in my ache to finally be with him, I watched him more than I watched the game. He also showed me the wonders of the Horn & Hardart's automat in downtown Manhattan, where all kinds of prepared food dishes peered out from behind little glass windows. In his own way he tried to be a father to me, but his world had so narrowed to him and the bottle that there was little left to share and little energy left to imagine anything different. Whenever we were together as a family, he seemed genuinely happy to see me and Peggy, though his tenderness was tinged with a forlorn melancholy, as if by looking at us he could see just how far he had fallen in his life. As the silences inevitably grew during our periodic outings, threatening to reveal the deeper wounds that no one had the wherewithal to honestly set eyes on, my father would resort to singing Irish lullabies. His was a voice so soothing and heartfelt that it would produce tears in anyone close enough to hear. As a result of these songs, sung in his native tongue, I inwardly and secretly grabbed on to my legacy of Irishness as another bulwark with which to defend myself against the denigration I experienced at home in the Bronx. It was a flailing effort to shore up my shaky self-esteem, to bolster my sense of being somebody worthwhile. It was the one gift that my father gave me that I eagerly accepted and endlessly cherished.

THE OTHER PIECE OF INFORMATION that my mother discovered when she went to identify my father's body at the morgue, was that another person was there to identify it as well: his other wife, his still-legal wife, the woman he had married in Ireland and whom he sent for when he first came to America; the woman he had three other children with; the woman he had separated from at some point before meeting my mother. For obvious reasons their existence had been hidden from my mother, yet my father went ahead with their wedding regardless. Now it became horrifyingly clear that my mother's marriage to my father was not legal and, therefore, my sister and I were now officially bastard offspring.

In retrospect it is little wonder that when my mother told my sister and me that our father was dead, she was reeling from multiple shockwaves pummeling her from conflicting directions: the grief over the passing of the only man she ever loved, and the deep anger and betrayal roiling inside over this secret now revealed. It is also little wonder that in the immediate aftermath of my father's passing that nothing was spoken about him inside the confines of 3987 Saxon Avenue. Not only did this revelation about the existence of another family confirm everything that my mother's parents had believed all along about my father, so too was our bastard status the final affirmation for them that we were simply beyond redemption.

My mother's parents neither offered any assistance to see that my father got a proper burial, nor did the rest of her brothers and sisters. My mother couldn't possibly afford the costs to do so, and neither, apparently, could his *other* family. Instead he was considered an unclaimed body and relegated to Hart Island, New York's "Potter's Field," for burial. As a result of this callousness there would be no funeral, there would be no headstone with his name carved upon it, no place for us to visit and remember. Instead a wooden box with a number stenciled on its side awaited my father at the end of his life; he was to be interred with thousands of other nameless paupers, suddenly rendered null and void in the absence of records, as if he never even existed. Good riddance quietly and thoroughly enveloped the entire house after my father died. In my efforts to reconcile my own pain and anger over the loss of my father with the complete erasure of him within my extended family – upon whom my survival now rested unequivocally – all my childlike imaginings of being rescued by my heroic father were dashed. Instead, I too was forced to wrestle with a recurring feeling of good riddance as time and time again I tried to come to terms with who and what my father really was to me.

MY LIFE DURING THE REST OF THIRD GRADE, in the wake of my father's death, was generally nondescript, numb around the edges, and only vaguely remembered; it was mainly a blur, as was the subsequent summer. Come fall and the start of school once again, despite having one of the best teachers in P.S. 95 – Mrs. Stammer – I trudged into fourth grade, approaching my ninth birthday, in a daze. In fourth grade only two things stood out.

Mrs. Stammer had a moment at the end of the day on Fridays when students could come to the front of the room and recite something from memory for the entire class. My first effort was reciting the poem *Hiawatha*, by Henry Wadsworth Longfellow, which, despite my nervousness at never having done anything like this before, went well.

The next time I was in front of the class I sang, *Sink the Bismarck*, by Johnny Horton, which had just been released May 1960. As bad as my singing voice was, I ended up winning a book as a prize for my efforts (and probably for my willingness). This was one of my proudest moments since arriving in the Bronx and the surge of self-esteem that arrived on the waves of my fellow students' applause filled me like a balloon at the Thanksgiving Day parade.

The second thing was our weekly visits to the school library, to research projects, read for book reports or simply for pleasure. It was here that I found *King Arthur and the Knights of the Round Table* and a renewed sense of wonder rushed into the vacuum that had occupied my heart since my father's death. I was astounded and mesmerized by what I took to be a book written just for me, that laid out a code of chivalry and justice that each knight had to follow, that I could learn to follow too. I felt as if the book was telling me how to behave in the world and it touched a tender longing deep within my chest. It reminded me of my father's heroism in Bradley's Bar, rekindling my memory of his knightly ways, swelling my chest with images of exactly how I wanted to be. After my first encounter with the book I decided to hide it in the library so only I would be able to retrieve it when our weekly library period came. As I read about King Arthur, Sir Lancelot, Sir Gawain and all the others, I knew, even as a nine-year-old, that I wanted to be one of the Knights of the Round Table. I wanted to protect everyone that needed protection, like my mother and sister, and my Jewish friends. I hoped that I could find some modicum of virtuousness in those stories that I could use to hide or fix or get rid of the dark stain my grandmother had convinced me soiled my very being. King Arthur was like an antidote, another world I could disappear into where I could be safe, don some shiny armor, remind myself that I was really a noble child misplaced to the wrong family and, for a while, emerge anew.

But other than these moments in front of Mrs. Stammer's classroom, and sitting at the Roundtable with King Arthur in the library, it was mostly uneventful. I sleepwalked through it all, dazed most of the time and driven even more sullen and introspective than ever by the loss of my father. It would take me until sixth grade to write the words "deceased" on any official school form that asked for the name of my father, to admit to myself that he was finally gone forever. As much as I turned inwards for understanding and solace, I wasn't able to find a soothing balm for my heart. Wrapped as I was in my own shroud, I couldn't possibly foresee the pressures building beneath the roof of 3987 Saxon Avenue that would soon be untethered by another death. Nor could I imagine the resulting implosion-then-explosion that would galvanize the entire Scheel clan in a final shaming of me, my sister, and mother that would break and scatter the family constellation forever.

Chapter Nine
Sanctuary in the Streets

The only place I felt free and safe was when I was out of my house. Whether it was in the backyard, or across the street in the First Building courtyard, or down the hill in the playground, I needed to be away from my family drama as much as possible. This desire began as soon as I started going to P. S. 95 and intensified as I moved through elementary school. I wanted to be the first one out of the house in the morning (even going to school had become a relief), and the last one back in at night. My friends were becoming my world and increasingly it was the only world I wanted to inhabit. It was here in the streets where my boyhood in the Bronx began, where my sense of myself started to take shape. It was in the playing of games, in the arguing over who was safe at first base, in winning with humility and losing with determination to return even better, that our ethical selves were forged. It was during fights and making up afterwards, in consoling hurt feelings and ruffled feathers, that our empathetic, compassionate selves were fashioned. It was during the hours in the stairwells, talking about arguments with our parents, shedding tears over frustrations that seemed world-shattering, that our love for each other was birthed and nurtured. Every moment together was like a great sorting of who you wanted to be around and who you didn't – and it changed and changed back again every other day. We were all feeling our way through pre-adolescence, like blind people learning Braille, our tentative yet desirous fingers touching each other awkwardly, seeking safety, affirmation that we were okay, normal in our thoughts and feelings. It was here in the streets that I began to sense that what was going on in my house was not kosher.

* * * * *

I HATED BEING IN MY HOUSE. Everywhere I looked, every person I came in contact with beneath that roof increasingly filled me with a nameless anxiety. I couldn't tell if it was them or me, but I was regularly

91

experiencing a growing discontent in the midst of all these trappings of security and extended family, everything a good life in America was supposed to be about yet, when under this roof, felt increasingly hollow. What I did know, though, was that I was ever on high alert when at home. Even encounters that started out as fun, or relatively benign, soon had me looking to escape. I didn't want to be around my little sister, Peggy, who always wanted to play some game (which usually meant arranging and rearranging the furniture in her metal doll house), or tag along whenever I left to go outside. Being in close proximity to her needy insecurities was like looking into a mirror and that was something I did not want to do for very long; plus, I was not unaffected by the general attitude of neglect that everyone visited upon Peggy and as a result I only sought her out as a last resort to salve my loneliness or boredom. My mom worried relentlessly about money. Tabulating her meager weekly Woolworth's paycheck, ever hopeful that some unexpected expense – usually something to do with the needs of her growing children – wouldn't surface to torpedo the calculations, she prayed she would have enough to get her safely to the next payday.

My grandmother wielded her lacerating denigration like an icy rapier, slashing without remorse whenever my mother, sister, or I happened to be within striking distance.

My grandfather, aging and doddering, slipping more and more from his patriarchal position into his own world of decrease and demise, soon had to forsake his gardening and basement workbenches. He was moving beyond being interested in anything other than his creature comforts: a daily soft-boiled egg in a porcelain egg-cup with dry toast (which my grandmother increasingly had to spoon-feed to him), professional wrestling, and a few other television shows he could placidly enjoy from his chair in the living room. It wasn't long before he stopped donning his work clothes and instead remained in his pajamas, wrapped in a striped bathrobe belted at the waist. And it wasn't long after that he began to smell of old age, infirmity, and urine.

As they got older, my two cousins were mostly in their own worlds, turning to Peggy and me only when they were utterly bored.

My Uncle Chuck, while providing his share of laughter to the household with his periodic outbursts of silliness, was not my parent and didn't want to be, especially since he had two budding teenagers of his own to shepherd.

My Aunt Evelyn, despite her elegant and stately beauty – or perhaps because of it – never seemed able to move beyond the aloof coolness of fine statuary.

Under these circumstances and my growing sensitivity to them, I did everything I could to get out of the house.

IMMEDIATELY AFTER THE 3 O'CLOCK BELL rang at P.S. 95, I would seek out friends from around the immediate environs of Saxon Avenue for a couple of hours of playing together before dinnertime and homework forced me back within the confines of my house. The other thing that drove me out of my home was my grandmother's rule that none of my friends were ever allowed to visit; they couldn't even come upstairs while I got ready to go out and instead had to stand on the front stoop and wait, or linger between the front door and the inside entry door if the weather was bad. It would be well into my teenage years, after my aging grandmother relocated to live with my Uncle Walter, before any of my friends were allowed to actually step into my house to visit and hang out.

During the weekends, though, I made sure I was out in the streets before ten in the morning and home by nightfall with, perhaps, a brief return for lunch – unless I was invited over to a friend's house to eat. While I felt incredibly happy to be invited into the homes of my neighbors, I was equally despairing knowing that I was not allowed to return the favor. My inability to reciprocate caused me all manner of shame and confusion. I felt like I came hat-in-hand like a beggar to receive their generosity.

At the same time, perhaps they sensed my reluctance to go to my own home and invited me out of kindness; perhaps they saw the poverty of my situation and felt my neediness and tried to respond the best they could. Whatever motivated my friends and their parents, I was, even in my silence, grateful beyond measure. It was during those glimpses into my friends' homes that I began to wonder about the possibility that family life could be different, and the pain I was experiencing inside 3987 Saxon Avenue might not be the only way people treated each other. If there was anything going on other than the perfection I perceived within my friends' homes and amongst their families, I was oblivious and perhaps willfully so; I desperately needed the ideal that I was imagining.

These visits were also my chance to learn more about what being Jewish meant. I keenly noticed whenever someone kissed their fingers and transferred that kiss to the *mezuzah* attached to the threshold of their apartment door, my mind spinning at the fantastic idea that a secret parchment lived within with a verse from the Torah indelibly inscribed upon it. In these visitations I glimpsed menorahs on bookcase shelves, I saw photographs of grandparents and great-grandparents who had emigrated from Europe; I was mesmerized as I gaped at pictures of men and boys, some wearing *yarmulkes* and prayer shawls, staring back at the camera with serious, deep-set eyes that demanded I not turn away and instead return their look. All of it fascinated me with the allure of difference, a difference I increasingly wanted to overcome and be part of.

Throughout most of elementary school I played with kids who lived on or near Saxon Avenue. I met two of my earliest friends, Levi Mencher and Abe Vogel, in my first grade class and they became my closest companions throughout most of grade school. Levi lived in the Sixth Building and possessed a stolid demeanor. He was already athletic, even at this young age, and he wore the aura of a quiet, natural leader, commanding respect by virtue of his self-possession. My first experience with overt and angry anti-Semitism happened when I was with Levi. He and I and a few other kids were exploring along the railroad tracks that ran past Van Cortlandt Lake. As we walked northwards toward the suburb of Yonkers we came to a fenced warehouse area that prohibited us from going any further on the tracks. As we clambered up a set of metal stairs to a footbridge that spanned the tracks we were confronted by a group of kids who blocked our way. There was menace in the way they stood and looked at us. I was in the lead and, when I got close, the first kid asked me if I was Jewish; I said no and he let me pass by. I turned and waited. Next was Levi. He was asked the same question and he unhesitatingly and proudly answered yes. Instantly you could feel the air thicken and grow icy. The kid who had been asking the questions yelled, "Get them! Get the Jews!" Immediate chaos ensued as we pushed and dodged our way across the bridge and down the steps on the other side and raced as fast as we could back toward the Bronx. We made it back unharmed, our eventual laughter aiding in relieving the fear and tension that had gripped us all. But something was shaken inside me. How could someone want to harm my friends just because they were Jewish? What kind of world did I just experience? Why was Levi so brave? My head was spinning and my heart was breaking; once again I was angered by prejudice and distraught by the surrealness of sudden violence and irrational injustice. While it made no sense to me at the time, inside I was inspired by both Levi's courage and my growing conviction that I had to find a similar courage to take a stand against acts like this one.

Abe lived in the First Building and was easygoing, joyful, and simply fun to be around. When Abe's family decided to move to New Jersey in 1962, just as we were all finishing sixth grade and about to move onto junior high school, I was once more confronted with loss – both of a dear friend and with the now-fading safe familiarity of P.S. 95. Not knowing how to convey my sadness to Abe, or express it even to myself, I stuffed the difficult emotions down inside by seeking out my other friends even more. Yet no matter how many people I surrounded myself with, I acutely felt all my friendships slipping from my hands in a wave of transition that was about to take us all out of the neighborhood and into a new school.

Dennis Blumstein and Ezra Baum, my other close friends on Saxon Avenue, though one grade behind Levi, Abe, and me, were also part of our pack. They both lived in the Sixth Building. Dennis was quiet, affable, and given to tearful bursts of frustration when things didn't go smoothly. Ezra had a stubborn intensity that, especially during these early years, caused most of us to defer to his wishes rather than rile him up by expressing our own desires. Curiously, whenever he said he did not want to do something we typically followed suit, even if we were previously excited about our original plan. Dennis and I forged a friendship around his toys and we would spend hours playing with my favorite of all: the tiny, plastic figures of his "Ski Patrol" set. On the steps to the entrance to his apartment after a snowfall, or on the rocks across from St. Patrick's Home for the Aged, we would imagine all manner of predicaments for the ski patrollers to get involved in. I loved being invited to Dennis's house for lunch and I spent as much time there as I was allowed. His mom, Nancy, and his older sister, Hazel, were always so welcoming. Most importantly, I felt a deep kinship with Dennis since, like me, his father was also dead. Without us ever directly speaking about this shared fact, I simply knew that *he knew* exactly what I was going through and that made all the difference.

WITHIN THE EVER-CHANGING ORBIT of kids fluidly coming and going that marks so much of the ever-reconstituting friendships of adolescence, the endless recycling of best-friend status, we all nevertheless spent endless hours playing together. "Army" was one of our favorite games, where we would chase each other, pretend fist-fight and, with sticks as pistols and rifles, shoot the bad guys. The area we called The Woods, or The Bushes, directly across Van Cortlandt Park South from Saxon Avenue, became our battlegrounds and the battles raged for hours. All through elementary school and into junior high our budding masculine imaginations were fired by military-inspired television shows that alternated between comedy and drama, like *McHale's Navy, Hogan's Heroes, The Wackiest Ship in the Army* and the more serious *Twelve O'Clock High, The Rat Patrol,* and *Combat.* Through the mid-1950s and into the mid-1960s it was the war-movie genre that caught our attention most profoundly, as the culture at large painted a portrait of American soldiers as larger-than-life figures. Shows like the *Million Dollar Movie* piped first-run war movies into our living rooms. As we got older, our adventures to the local movie theaters, witnessing the heroism, sacrifice, and ultimate triumph of the American soldier buoyed our youthful idealism and our spirits, while shaping our views of World War II as the noblest effort ever undertaken by America. It was patently obvious in every film about World War II that the Germans were methodically evil, the Japanese were maniacally evil, and the Americans were innocently noble. Films like: *To Hell and Back* (the Audie Murphy Story), *A Walk in the Sun*, *The Bridge Over the River Kwai*, *Stalag 17*, *From Here to Eternity*, *Sink the Bismarck*, *The Guns of Navarone*, *The Longest Day*, *The Dirty Dozen* and, of course, *The Great Escape* kept us all proud to be Americans. Even if we sometimes thought that the German armaments and uniforms looked cooler, we knew who the good guys were and who the bad guys were, and as we played throughout our neighborhood we never deviated very far from this script. Enacting many a heroic demise as we charged a German machine-gun nest, or raised our stick rifles to shoot at a diving Japanese *kamikaze*, we fell in agonizing slow motion trying to create the best death scenes possible.

But even more ubiquitous in inculcating the attributes of masculinity were the Westerns. As we were growing up playing "Cowboys and Indians," dozens and dozens of Hollywood films poured forth onto the American landscape celebrating the civilizing conquest of the horizonless West via the propagation of the Code of the West, which included everything from killing off "redskins" in the name of progress, to protecting women and children. Perhaps more than the films themselves it was the particular image of the Cowboy that was seared into our tender psyches. Moving beyond the often stilted classic cowboys like Gene Autry, Gabby Hayes, Roy Rogers and Hopalong Cassidy, a new breed of stalwart tumbleweed hero was offered us: John Wayne, Randolph Scott, Joel McCrea, Kirk Douglas, Robert Ryan, Gary Cooper, Glenn Ford, Jimmy Stewart, all stood ramrod straight on the silver screen for us to measure up against. These were typically loners, men of few words and decisive action, often eschewing women and children as things to be protected rather than human beings worth relating to (neither the sunny purity of Dale Evans, nor the dead-aim, rough-around-the-edges style of Gail Davis' *Annie Oakley* could withstand the engulfing testosterone).

New television shows offered a slightly more varied hero to us, ranging from the flamboyant to the existential, from the comedic to the loner, and from the gregarious to the strong silent type; amidst it all the Cowboy Code never faded. Our nightly television was saturated with Westerns: *Wanted Dead or Alive* with Steve McQueen; *Wagon Train*, led by Ward Bond; *The Rebel*, with Nick Adams; *Rawhide*, with Clint Eastwood; James Garner as *Maverick*; Clayton Moore playing *The Lone Ranger* and Jay Silverheels as Tonto; *Gunsmoke*, starring James Arness; Fess Parker as the legendary *Davy Crockett*; *Cheyenne*, with Clint Walker; *Bonanza*, with the Cartwright family and, of course, *Rin*

Tin Tin. There was also *Zorro,* starring Guy Williams as the scion of a wealthy Spanish landowner in California, and *The Cisco Kid,* with Duncan Reynaldo as "Cisco" and Leo Carrillo as "Pancho" (the first time we ever saw Mexican cowboys). From every angle the Western manly ethic of heroism, chivalry toward the "little ladies," and good triumphing over evil, was pumped intravenously into our tender hearts and minds by hours of television watching as we strove to embody these role models being offered up to us.

Between the movies and the television shows that overtly and subliminally inculcated us as budding men, our lives remained swathed in postwar excitement and innocence. It felt like my young boyhood days were a never-ending fairytale. When we weren't puzzling over math homework, memorizing names and dates for a current events quiz, or writing book reports, we were immersed in a timeless, imaginative playland, made available to us in every corner of the neighborhood. We played "Red-light, Green-light" in the Sixth Building and King of the Hill on the hillocks abutting the Major Deegan Expressway, near Dickinson. At P. S. 95 we all played punch-ball, kick-ball, dodge-ball, and "corners" whenever we were at recess in the Big Schoolyard.

As we moved into the fifth and sixth grades we took these games over to the playground, using the wading pool for dodgeball and the area where the basketball courts were for punch-ball. Kickball, while always inducing laughter, was eventually considered a kids' game after fourth grade. Punchball, on the other hand, was an incredibly fun game, requiring at least five people to play. Played exactly like baseball, each batter had to punch a small rubber ball in order to get a hit. After designating certain spots as our bases, we would spend hours pretending we were the New York Yankees, most of us knowing the starting line-ups by heart: batting first, Bobby Richardson, then Tony Kubeck, then Clete Boyer, then our heroes, Mickey Mantle and Roger Maris, and on and on. If you could punch the ball over the three-tiered fence that enclosed the basketball courts it was an automatic home run. When we got a bit stronger we modified the rule so that over the fence was an automatic out and only hitting the top tier of the fence was a home run.

In the winter my cousins and I would build snow forts in front of our driveway on Saxon Avenue, challenging other kids to snowball fights. They would assemble on the other side of the street, behind parked cars, and we'd battle each other from opposing barricades all day long, reluctant to return home even when we were wet and freezing and turning blue. As we got older the snowball fights erupted spontaneously whenever two groups of kids encountered each other anywhere in the neighborhood. It was nonstop activity and we reveled in our freewheeling imaginations.

In the summertime, my mother tried to make our weekends a bit more fun. Once or twice during school vacation she would gather me and my sister and make the three-bus trek to Orchard Beach, the only public beach in the Bronx. There we would camp as close to the water's edge as possible so my mother could keep an eye on us while we made sand castles and padded in the waves. Using public transportation exhausted all of us, and by day's end we would drag ourselves home and fall happily into bed. But the most amazing place she ever took us was to Freedomland amusement park. Divided into six American-history-themed areas, encircled by an 1800's-style train, a day at Freedomland was a dream come true for my sister and I. But it was way too expensive for my mother, with one visit setting her back significantly, so our visits there were few and far between. So, mostly, I, my cousins, and the kids who did not attend either sleep-away camp or day camp, would spend our days in the schoolyard or in the playground. One of our favorite transgressions, one that got us gleefully excited, was picking the crab apples that grew atop the rocks across from St. Patrick's Home, in preparation to ambush the kids in Circle Pines Day Camp as they unsuspectingly ambled by on one of their neighborhood outings.

As they passed unawares, we would emerge from The Bushes to pelt them with these hard, green projectiles. A chase would always ensue, with the campers and their counselors easily scattering us into retreat for fear of our getting caught and getting in trouble. One time, as we were being chased, I did get captured by a counselor named Moishe. He was high-school age, handsome, athletic, and quick to smile. As he held my arm firmly and marched me toward the Canteen, with a posse of campers dancing and yelling alongside, I could tell he wasn't really angry. On the contrary, he seemed concerned about me, as if he was sad or disappointed or confused as to why I had been throwing crab apples at him and the other kids. Rather than berate me, or escort me across the street to my home and to my mother's inevitable wrath, he invited me to sit with the rest of the campers outside the Canteen. He even offered me an ice cream bar as he distributed the afternoon treats to the other boys and girls.

Then, as everyone settled down, he took out his guitar and began playing Hebrew songs. Before long everyone was joining in. I was in awe of Moishe. Those moments sitting there, feeling like I finally belonged somewhere, listening to the voices singing in a language I did not understand, brought back fleeting memories of my father singing to me in Irish. Somewhere in my young heart I felt the stirrings of deep appreciation for Moishe's fairness and generosity, as well as gratitude for the other kids, many of them my neighborhood friends, for following his lead and welcoming me into the group despite my throwing crab apples at them only moments before. Even the songs, whose words I could not decipher, elicited wonderful feelings inside my body. When camp ended that day and I walked across the street and into my house, I knew that I had been touched by something that I could not put into words.

MY COUSINS OFTEN ALLOWED ME to tag along with them. The group they prowled the streets with included kids closer to their age: Larry Neuman (before he moved away); Bobby Chaikin (a fanatic Giants baseball fan, despiser of our favored Yankees, and inveterate comic book and baseball card collector); Jerry Penzig (whose younger sister Hadar often befriended my sister Peggy); and Aidan Cleary (the troubled neighborhood juvenile delinquent). With this core group and, from time to time assorted others, we would split into opposing teams and spend hours chasing each other in "Ring-o-leevio," or chalk the sidewalks playing "Follow the Arrow." Either of these games would take nearly all day to play and the entire neighborhood was our canvas.

Most often, though, since nearly everyone was fanatically in love with baseball and the New York Yankees, we would all eventually convene in the Big Schoolyard and play "pitching-in" stickball. All along the wall of P. S. 95, alternating between the metal-grated windows, rectangular boxes with X's running from corner to corner were painted on the bricks. This was the strike zone above an imaginary home plate. At a specific distance from the wall (50 heel-to-toe paces), a chalk line was drawn and this was designated the pitching mound. In the old days the bat was a broom handle and the owner used either black electrician's tape or Mystic tape in their favorite color, wrapped in a barber-pole spiral, to provide extra grip on the handle and make the bat look cool. When I was a kid we used a manufactured stickball bat with black tape already wound around the handle. The ball was pink rubber, usually the favored *Spalding* (in our vernacular a "Spaldeen") or, if in a pinch, the lesser quality *Pensee Pinky*. Both the bat and ball could be purchased at EM's. Any pitch that hit either inside the box or on the painted borders was a strike. Of course, just like in the Big Leagues, there was always debate as to whether any given pitch was a strike or not. If the batter hit the ball and it struck the second floor of the building across the street it was a double; the third floor was a triple; a homerun was either the top floor or onto the roof.

This was my least favorite game of all. First, I was a terrible pitcher and my cousins would systematically crush the ball over the fence or, in the case of Brian, regularly onto the rooftop; this meant that I was chasing Spaldeens all day long. Second, I was even a worse batter; terrified by the incoming pitch I would swing wildly, eyes half-closed, or turn away and "step into the bucket," so fearful was I of being hit by the ball.

When I got older I had better luck with another version of stickball that we called "long-stick," or "bases." For this game we used the entire length of the schoolyard, with home plate on the south side and the field stretching north, with designated bases. It was played just like baseball. In this game we usually had teams of seven, three at each base and four in various points in the outfield. There was no pitcher; instead we played fungo, where the batter tossed the Spaldeen up and then swung the bat hoping to connect and send the ball past the fielders for a hit. If the batter hit it over the three-tiered fence at the distant end of the schoolyard it was an automatic home run. I usually played in the outfield and had my share of one-handed catches right against the chain-link since everyone wanted to launch a homerun. I remember the first time I hit it over the fence. I felt like I had come of age athletically, passing another neighborhood milestone; for a moment I was a young god.

It was always a mixed blessing for me to be included with my cousins and this group of older kids. While I loved being with my cousins, being the youngest and smallest meant that I was inevitably the subject of Aidan's sadistic attentions. Aidan was a troubled kid. Perhaps it was his way of compensating for being a non-Jewish minority, or not living in the Amalgamated apartments, or trying to compete with his clearly college-bound older brother. Perhaps there were problems at home that forced Aidan to vent on kids smaller and weaker than him. Whatever sword drove him, inevitably, at some point during the day, he would tease me, then push me, then hit me; all the while I begged for my older cousin, Brian, to help me. Each time Brian halfheartedly told him to stop, or ignored my pleas altogether, Aidan would become more emboldened. Before long, as he realized that Brian was not going to intervene, Aidan would finally dispatch me into a puddle of tears with either an onslaught of verbal denigration or a punch in the stomach, and I would run home crying.

Aidan and I would continue to have minor run-ins as I grew into a teenager. Whenever he and his group of cronies encountered any of us in the neighborhood, he would have us line up and stand rigidly at attention. Then he would act like a drill sergeant. As he inspected his troops he would often grab long sumac stems, strip the leaves off, and whip us on the backs of our legs, demanding that we stand even more rigidly at attention. If we complained a sharp jab in the solar plexus would drop one of us to our knees while he and his friends departed laughing. But once I entered junior high school and shot up over six-feet tall, he and I kept a respectful distance from each other and avoided any serious altercations, reserving our confrontations to the basketball courts.

The other main friendship I developed in elementary school when I reached fifth grade, was with Solomon "Solly" Goldhirsch, a kid who like me lived in one of the private houses on Saxon Avenue. Because of this I felt slightly less different around him than I felt around my Amalgamated-dwelling friends, even though he was also Jewish. As close as we got during fifth and sixth grades, it was difficult for me to completely trust that Solly had concerns for anyone but himself. Solly was bigger and stronger than most of us all throughout elementary school and he reveled in demonstrating this fact whenever he could. He delighted in challenging anyone of us foolish enough to take the bait to trade punches to the arm with him; back and forth the punches went, getting stronger with each exchange. I lost every time, succumbing to the power of his jabs and eventually turning away to hide the tears in my eyes. He redundantly tried to pull off the trick to see who could punch the softest, pointing to his shoulder and requesting that his opponent go first. After the unsuspecting kid tapped Solly's shoulder ever so gently, Solly would haul off and pound his adversary's shoulder has hard as he could, laughingly exclaiming "I lost!" Consistently, the fear of being called "chicken" compelled me to engage in these regular pummelings even though I knew the outcome.

Yet Solly was also a charmer, handsome and articulate beyond his years. I envied these qualities in him and, at the same time, hated myself for being so envious. Solly and I developed quite a love-hate relationship over the course of our last two years in grade school, periodically doing homework together at his house, walking to school together nearly every morning, and then eventually annoying each other to the point of falling out and not talking to each other for a few days. In fifth grade we got into the most serious trouble of our entire elementary school years.

We both shared in the delight of our mutual crushes on two of the girls in our class, Shoshana Morgenstern and Rivka Fisher. We thought they were incredibly beautiful and while we daydreamed and mooned over both of them, Solly was more attracted to Shoshana and I was more attracted to Rivka. We would stare at them and then shyly turn away when they noticed us. With our clumsy and ill-formed understanding of what happens physically between boys and girls, coupled with our hormonal frustrations and feverishly agitated stirrings, we got to the point where one day Solly and I penned what our young imaginations thought of as a sexually graphic letter to Shoshana. It contained many references to "boners" and "breasts." In the lobby of her apartment building, on the rise where Cannon Place and Orloff Avenue met, overlooking Snake Hill, we debated whether to put the letter in her mailbox or not. When Solly got cold feet I grabbed it out of his hands and stuffed it through the slot anyway. We ran away laughing while a sickening feeling of worry welled up in our stomachs at the same time.

The very next day we were marshalled to the principal's office, where Shoshana's father, Hyman Morgenstern, one of the top board members of the entire Amalgamated stood shaking with silent anger. We were terrified, literally petrified as we stood there. The fact that we both signed the letter made it quite easy for them to round us up. We were royally chewed out by our principal, Miss Flynn, and by Mr. Morgenstern. We were told, in no uncertain terms, to never do anything like this again and to keep away from Shoshana completely. We were both severely relieved as we left Miss Flynn and the seething Mr. Morgenstern behind. For the rest of fifth and sixth grade our crushes on Shoshana and Rivka only got more intense, but we succeeded in keeping silent and only dreaming about them from afar. It was one of the last times Solly and I did anything together again. By the time we both graduated to junior high school our relationship had developed into open antagonism.

ONCE MY FRIENDS AND I MADE IT INTO FIFTH GRADE, the Big Schoolyard gave way more and more to the playground, especially on the weekends and during the summer months. The playground was the real heart of our neighborhood, no matter what your age. It was enclosed on three sides by a three-tiered chain-link fence, while along the fourth side – the front, facing Van Cortlandt Park South – the fence was a single-tier high. This was where the entrance was situated. The gate, which in our early years was kept closed and padlocked at night, eventually was removed altogether as more and more kids were able to climb over it before the park department employees arrived to unlock it.

The hub of the playground was a brick parkhouse. About 15 feet from the parkhouse door was a flag pole rising skyward from a circular granite base. The bottom third of the pole was painted black; the uppermost two-thirds was white. A lock-box, about five feet up from the base, held a cleat that secured the rope that the park employee used to hoist the American flag each morning and lower it each evening. Inside the main part of the parkhouse was a desk for the staff person to sit, a first aid cabinet, and lockers that held a variety of sports equipment and assorted games that could be checked out for use if you gave some collateral (often this would be a house key, a jacket or, for adults, a wallet). This room took up the front half of the parkhouse and was typically disheveled as kids came back and forth all day long to checkout different equipment and board games.

The rear half of the parkhouse was divided between a men's bathroom on the left and a women's bathroom on the right. Near the door to the men's bathroom was a water fountain that was quickly mobbed whenever a basketball game ended. The single step leading into the women's bathroom was frequently used to play "off the point."

102

This game involved the "batter" throwing a pink Spaldeen toward the edge of the single step in an effort to launch it past the opposing team's fielders. Most often the ball hit the step obliquely making for an easy pop-up or grounder; but when it did hit off the point, the ball would rocket over everyone's head for extra-bases or, if the fielder had to navigate the dreaded see-saws, a homerun. Again, the Yankees' starting line-up was reverently invoked.

On one side of the playground, toward the east, it was the little kids' paradise. A sandbox, ringed by a waist-high, black metal fence with one narrow entrance and a stone step for easier access, sat within the semicircular embrace of a series of park benches. These benches were situated to provide perches for the regular brood of mothers tending their toddlers. Nearby, painted on the ground in yellow, were the outlines for potsie (also called hopscotch and played mostly by girls tossing house keys into the appropriately numbered box and hopping on one leg to pick them up and return to the start). Nearby, also framed in yellow paint, a Skully board beckoned.

Skully consisted of 13 boxes, sequentially numbered. There were four boxes at the corners, plus four-paired boxes making up each of the sides (for a total of twelve), and box numbered 13 that sat directly in the middle. Using bottle caps propelled by a flick of the forefinger (or sometimes the middle finger), the idea was to move your bottle cap sequentially from box one to box thirteen and thereby win the game. One obstacle was that box thirteen was ringed by a moat of smaller, unnumbered boxes; if your bottle cap landed in one of these you had to start over again from the beginning. But the greater obstacle was when your opponent's bottle cap landed next to yours; he now had the ability to "blast" your bottle cap right off the Skully area, making your return to the playing field that much more difficult. Of course this led to all manner of imaginative responses and the fashioning of bottle caps for different situations, similar to a set of golf clubs. For example, some Skully players melted wax crayons into their bottle caps; not only did they look colorful and sharp but the bottle cap blasted opponents further due to its added weight. Once, Bobby Chaikin, in an act of inventive genius, actually melted a lead fishing sinker into a bottle cap and swapped it out for one of his lighter caps when an opponent was about to blast him; needless to say, it was a dramatic blasting-in-reverse that took place, leading to cries of "foul" from opponents, with a "there's-no-rule-against-it" shrug and smirk from Bobby in response. It was amazing to see the creativity that Skully competition inspired.

In the southeast corner of the playground where the younger kids played, a complete set of swings stood, each with a safety bar across the front to keep toddlers firmly in their three-sided bucket seat as their caregivers pushed them higher and higher while they squealed in delight. Next to the swings was a small metal slide, barely six feet tall at its highest point. Mothers would guide their children carefully up the metal stairs and get them seated at the top. Then, just as their child began to slide down the chute, they would race to the front of the slide to catch their laughing child right at the bottom. Four seesaws, each one made of wood painted green, sat like expectant catapults seeking the balance of two willing bodies.

A huge, fenced-in wading pool took up most of the northeast corner of the playground. With a forceful stream of water gushing out to fill the pool to about ankle-deep, and four sprinkler heads emitting a continuous cascade of showers, this was the perfect spot to cool off from the remorseless sweltering sun and the thick mugginess New York summers are infamous for.

Closer to the parkhouse, between the wading pool and the fence that marked the eastern edge of the basketball courts, was playground equipment designed for older and bigger kids. Nearest the wading pool fence stood two very tall slides. Between these slides, and the fence enclosing the basketball courts, were six adult swings with metal, bench-like seats; they were attached by chains fastened on either side of the seat to an overhead metal pole twelve feet above. A small, chest-high chain-link fence allowed for only one entrance to this area, protecting people from walking into the moving swings. Nearby stood a set of metal monkey bars shaped like a tiered castle with one single turret-like cube at the top waiting to be scaled.

The next section, fully one-quarter of the entire playground, held the basketball courts, which could be utilized for playing four half-court games or two full-court games. In the final part of the playground, in its westernmost edge, the area was divided up between a tennis court to the south and a concrete handball wall divided into four courts to the north. The playground was the recreation spot for the whole neighborhood, the hub of so many activities, providing something for every age group to enjoy.

JUST OUTSIDE THE PLAYGROUND FENCE was a grass-less, dusty area, populated by a few medium-tall trees, their roots periodically emerging from the dirt to interrupt the relatively even ground. This spot served as the staging area for two of the neighborhood's most communal events – chestnut fights and penny pitching.

In the fall kids would trek down past the lake and over to Van Cortlandt Mansion, the stately historic home of the original landowner, Jacobus Van Cortlandt, now owned and preserved by the city. Most of us had rarely been inside this historic landmark, except for the single, mandatory "Know Your City" fieldtrip in elementary school. But we did not gather here to go inside and study history; what we wanted was outside, high up in the trees that dotted the grounds. What we wanted were chestnuts.

Access to this treasure was barred by an eight-foot, wrought-iron fence with spear-tip points that enclosed the biggest trees and marked the area as definitely off limits. Since I was the smallest, my cousins would boost me up to the top of the fence where I could grab one of the close branches, swing my legs up and over, and shimmy toward the main trunk. Once there I would begin looking for the limbs with the most chestnuts. I would gather as many chestnuts as I could, dropping them down to my cousins who were rapidly dumping them into brown-paper shopping bags. Typically we had about fifteen minutes of undisturbed harvesting before some mansion employee would spot us and sound the alarm, launching two or three uniformed guardians. "Hey! Get the hell out of there or we'll call the cops," they shouted as they ran, red-faced with their sudden call to exertion. In a flash I was down the tree, dropping to the other side of the fence, and off we ran with our contraband chestnuts.

Other days we would try our luck in the Fieldston area of the Riverdale section of the Bronx. It was a much richer neighborhood, home to a wealthier class of people, including foreign diplomats assigned to the United Nations in Manhattan. The streets of Fieldston appeared easy pickings, lined as they were with unprotected chestnut trees. The dilemma was that Fieldston had its own private security patrols and our vagabond dress screamed that we didn't really belong. In the face of this high-gain/high-risk situation, we usually walked through as fast as we could and scoured the ground for our prized chestnuts, ever on high alert. Needless to say, our pickings were slim.

Once home we would break the green, spikey outer covering to reveal a shiny brown chestnut with a much lighter brown collar ringing the top. Brian would select the ones he thought were best for fighting, utilizing some kind of accumulated expertise that Ned and I did not possess. Brian would take what he considered the prime chestnuts for himself, then Ned would pore over the remaining ones, and I would be given whatever was left. The next step was to drill a hole through the middle of the chestnut. This was done by using a nut-picking tool and gouging slowly from one end to the other. When this was complete, various methods of hardening were undertaken, ranging from soaking them in vinegar to putting them in the freezer. When they were ready, the next step was to push a string through the hole and tie a knot at the bottom to hold the chestnut on the string. We used a thicker, stronger white twine that Uncle Chuck gave us from one of his toolboxes. We gathered our chestnut weapons and headed to the playground to engage our foes in "Conkers," as it was formally called.

How Conkers worked was that two people would challenge each other, deciding who would go first. Standing face to face, the person who went second simply held the string with the chestnut dangling about eight to ten inches below his hand. The other person gripped the string of his chestnut and, using it like a medieval flail, wound up and walloped the opponent's chestnut in the hopes of smashing it to smithereens. It was rare that a first-blow would end a match so each person would alternate taking turns at trying to demolish the other's chestnut. These battles took place all over the area in front of the playground, with shrieks of delight from the crowd and howls of triumph from the victor whenever a chestnut exploded. The crowd reveled in the shock and surprise of chestnut shell and meat flying everywhere. As the day wore on, amidst the debris of chestnut shards and pieces of now limp twine strewn on the ground, the legends of super-strong, unbeatable chestnuts grew. Challengers would inquire "how old is that chestnut?" meaning, how many fights had it won. In a complicated ranking system the winning chestnut gained a year for every victory and took the years of the defeated chestnut as well. So not only was it about straightforward victories, it was also about beating battle-tested competitors. My cousin Brian regularly had chestnuts that made it to well over ten years old, with half the crowd rooting for his chestnut to live to fight again, the other half rooting for its shattering demise. Eventually the brief, seasonal eruption of chestnut fights would wane with the approach of winter.

In the spring, kids would also descend on this very same area for a week or so to engage in penny pitching. This annual event had people dusting off their accumulated comic book collections and bundling them down to the playground with the aim of commercial gain. Like stalls in a North African bazaar, comic-laden entrepreneurs would stake out a plot of dirt and lay a few rows of single comics on the ground, perhaps three-comics-by-three-comics, across and down. They would then take a stick, or use the toe of their sneaker, and draw a line at a distance they deemed appropriate in front of their comics. People would have to stand at the line and pitch pennies at the comic they desired. If the penny landed on the comic it was yours; if it missed or slid off, the penny was theirs. All manner of comic books were on display: The Dell stable of *Superman*, *Batman*, *Wonder Woman*, *Green Lantern*, *The Flash*, *Justice League* and *Aquaman*; the entire Marvel line-up, including *Thor*, *Silver Surfer*, *Captain Marvel*, *Hulk* and my two favorites, *Daredevil* and *Spiderman*. There were also plenty of *Caspar the Friendly Ghost*, *Little Lulu*, *Ritchie Rich*, *Archie* and *Classics Illustrated* thrown in as well.

Like barkers at a carnival each seller would entice penny pitchers to their offerings: "Over here! Batman fights Superman!" "Daredevil killed in this comic!" "Superman and Lois Lane Get Married," and on and on. Similar to a carnival as well, there were plenty sleights-of-hand to navigate. On windy days sellers would place medium-sized rocks on the comics to keep them from blowing away. Of course, when a penny hit a rock and bounced off into the dirt, cries of "do over" would rise up, with the seller replying "no way"; the argument was usually resolved in favor of who could verbally outlast the other or who was bigger.

Other sellers would sprinkle imperceptible amounts of sand on the covers of the comics, making them even slicker than usual; they would rack up profits galore as the coins slid off until the scheme was discovered and all hell broke loose. Occasionally, someone would stuff the pages of a *Caspar the Friendly Ghost* comic inside the cover of a highly sought after comic. Crowds would vie for this particular edition, the pennies raining nonstop until finally someone was successful. Just as the new owner of the comic was discovering the bait-and-switch, the previous owner, pockets jingling with pennies, was laughing and racing home.

Another tactic was to have the penny pitcher pretend to toss a coin super high to get all heads looking up, while a confederate standing nearby the comics dropped a coin on the one they wanted. This ruse rarely went undetected and always resulted in hilarious claims and counterclaims about what really happened.

As the days wore on and the supply of good comics found their way to new owners, weary sellers eager to get rid of their remaining comics would build a pile of perhaps ten to thirty comics. Here, they advertised loudly, a single, properly placed coin could claim all of these at once. The pitching lines was moved further back and no longer were pennies accepted; depending on the size of the stack it was now nickels, dimes, or even quarters one had to pitch. Even here you had to employ *caveat emptor* savvy as a stack presenting a compelling *Fantastic Four* on top could actually be sitting on a dozen *Little Lulu* comics. This annual ritual was our foray into bartering and bamboozling and bickering in a great festival of primitive commercial exchange over the course of several days of surprise and merriment. It was here, as well as when engaging in sports, that we learned about handling different personalities and temperaments, about understanding our own individual limits in a variety of social situations and interactions. It was but another training arena in which our developing young lives flourished.

OVERSEEING THE ENTIRE LANDSCAPE, inside and outside the playground, was an on-duty park employee. We called them "Parkies". Chief among the Parkie's responsibilities was to open the gate in the morning and raise the flag, then lower the flag and lock the gate in the evening. In our grade-school years, since we were already in school by the time the playground was opened, it was on Saturday and Sunday mornings when we would eagerly await the Parkie's arrival to open the gate, and the same every morning throughout the summer months. When we reached our teenage years we would simply scale the gates and begin playing without adult supervision – eventually leading to the gates being removed altogether, providing us with round-the-clock access. The Parkie, sometimes aided by a younger college student working for the summer, would also hand out sports equipment and games, like chess and checkers; provide first-aid when necessary; and maintain the area by sweeping, raking leaves, and spearing trash.

Our longest reigning Parkie was Joe. He was clearly a lifer in the New York City Parks and Recreation Department. He was short, rounded by middle-age, and sported a greying, walrus-style moustache. All year long he was there to open and close the front gates, to sweep up around the benches or shovel snow, and to raise and lower the flag on the flagpole that towered just outside the parkhouse doors. He was friendly and caring, much like a grandfather in his interactions. While Joe did not venture much outside the fenced confines of the playground, periodically he would lock up the parkhouse and take his green burlap bag and his trash-spear to tidy up the grounds, meandering around the benches along the asphalt path that ran along the front edge of the playground, east through The Bushes and west to Gale Place. On other days, especially in the fall, he would spend his time raking leaves and burning them in a 55-gallon metal drum, sending that unforgettable smell of autumn wafting across the neighborhood. If for some reason a pile of leaves was left unburnt we would have a field day jumping into it over and over again, laughing and scattering the leaves in every direction. Day after day, year after year, Joe would show up like clockwork.

One year, there was a Parkie who caused such uproar that he was sent packing before the summer was over. He was young, with slicked-back dark hair, never without his shades on; he was muscular and enjoyed showing off bare-chested on his weight bench right outside the parkhouse. He wore out his welcome fast when he tried to spy on one of the older girls in the bathroom. As soon as she told her friends the entire parkhouse was surrounded by dozens of the older neighborhood guys ready to beat the crap out of him. He locked himself in the parkhouse while people yelled for him to come out and pounded ferociously on the door. I was in junior high school and this was the first time I saw anything like this in our neighborhood. I was both scared and proud at how people were protecting each other and I knew there was a lesson to be learned here. Eventually, Joe the Parkie was able to call the cops. They arrived to calm things down and escort him safely out of the area. He was never seen in the neighborhood again.

One of the last Parkies I remember was Harvey. He was Jewish and he loved baseball, especially Los Angeles Dodgers pitcher Sandy Koufax, one of the few Jews in professional baseball at the time. Harvey loved to sit on the benches near the parkhouse and talk sports with anyone who was interested. Rather than be overly responsible to Parkie duties, he let Joe take care of the daily checklist. Instead, he would spend his days waxing about who were the best and worst teams in baseball and sharing his wisdom as to why and what he'd do to improve them.

BEYOND THE PLAYGROUND FENCE TO THE NORTH, across verdant, rolling hills, an 18-hole, city-run golf course stretched as far as the eye could see. By the time we were in junior high school this was our paradise, our escape valve, another type of playground paved only with grass, and rocks, and trees. It was here where we could be in a world that felt natural and so very far away from anyone and anything that we sought refuge from. What we considered our part of the golf course consisted of four holes, the 15th, 16th, 17th, and the 18th. From almost any part of our neighborhood, access points into the golf course punctuated the surrounding fences.

On The Plateau, near the east side of Ghost Town, enough dirt was dug away that you could crawl under the fence and into the rough behind the 16th tee. Another hole had been cut behind the handball wall. This hole led onto the 16th fairway and was actively maintained by some of the older guys as a way to retrieve handballs or Spaldeens that inadvertently went over the fence. Another hole presented itself just halfway up the asphalt path west of the playground entrance towards Gale Place; this led, with a little bushwhacking, right over a hill to the 16th green. Behind the Big Rock at Gale Place a hole led into the rough behind the 17th tee. Finally, at the furthest southwest corner of the fence, just above Daisy Field and the road to Van Cortlandt Lake, a hole led into a tangle of bushes, brambles, and trees far from any of the greens or tee-boxes.

As children our first golf course adventures involved sledding down the Big Hill in wintertime. This was a part of the final fairway, the spot where the gradually sloping hill that left the 18th tee-box dropped suddenly and steeply into a valley where the 18th green sat in the distance. After every serious snowfall the Big Hill was populated with what seemed like the entire neighborhood; kids, parents, sometimes even grandparents, all sledding or watching the sledding. It was a long, fast ride downhill and a long slow walk back up, but we did it all day long, happily.

As we got older we still sledded, now without parents along. We tried all manner of ways to sleigh down the Big Hill. There were always people atop one another, sledding in double- or triple-decker formations. Some daredevils would stand on their sleds, both hands gripping the ropes attached to the wooden cross-piece handles used for steering, and try to make it all the way down without falling off. Sometimes we would make airplanes out of our sleds by placing a sled crosswise atop the bottom sled; this way you could have one main driver steering with his feet, two others sitting out on the wings, and sometimes one person kneeling on the back with their arms around the wing-men. With particularly longer sleds we tried to add two more sled-wings, stacking and balancing six or seven riders in a Keystone Cops' effort to make it all the way down the hill without tumbling off. Rarely did any of these approaches succeed but they were hilarious to watch. Kids without sleds brought huge, flattened cardboard boxes to use as downhill transport, which always led to a great piling on of bodies as the cardboard got underway. It seemed to never fail that each winter a car hood would magically show up at the Big Hill inviting only the brave or the foolish to risk the uncontrollable whirling and spinning descent this mode of sleighing offered.

One night, when I was in high school and under the combined influence of beer and hard liquor, a few of us decided to see if we could find something to slide down the Big Hill on. It was after midnight and the day's sledding had long ceased. Kevin Hurley, Natty Lefkowitz, and I found a refrigerator door left on the sidewalk for the Porters to pick up. Inspired by the sudden possibilities, we proceeded to muscle it through the hole in the fence behind the handball courts and dragged it to the precipice of the Big Hill. We excitedly piled onto the door, poised for our descent. What we didn't know was that at the very bottom of the hill, extending outwards over one hundred feet, the snow that had been flattened smooth during the day had frozen solid with the coming of night and the plummeting of the temperature. With Kevin in the front, me in the middle, and Natty in the rear, we pushed off, our drunken shouts turning into screams of abject terror as we hit the flats and rocketed across the field of ice faster than any one of us had ever experienced. Not only was the door unstoppable but we were going much too fast to jump off. We held onto each other for dear life as we raced toward the chain-link fence just to the left of the 18th Green. Oddly, it appeared for an instant that we were slowing down, but it was just the optical illusion that the fence looked like it was now racing toward us. Finally we smashed into the fence with a complete and sudden stop that knocked the breath out of us, immediately silencing our cries and sending us toppling like dominoes: Natty into me, both of us into Kevin, and Kevin into the fence face-first with all of our combined weight and force behind him. Sensing that something bad had happened by the moans coming from Kevin, we gathered ourselves as best we could and stumbled back out of the Golf Course. We went into one of the laundry rooms in the Seventh Building to check on Kevin and blood was pouring from above his right eye where the fence had gouged out a significant chunk of flesh. As tipsy as we were we all knew that this needed stiches and we proceeded, wobbly, to the Montefiore Hospital Emergency Room on Gun Hill Road with another golf course story to add to our list.

By high school the golf course was a place to take a walk with friends, sit and talk about life, rest a bit after basketball games, make out with girls, drink alcohol or smoke pot. When it was really hot and humid we'd strip off our shirts and run under the sprinklers that were saturating the nearby 16th Green. We always had to be on guard for rocketing golf balls from errant tee shots, and also alert for the golf course Parkies swooping down in their green flat-bed trucks to chase us out of the area. But during our teenage years, despite our regular skirmishes with the Parkies, we boldly claimed this part of Van Cortlandt golf course as our idyllic pastureland, our safe domain to freely roam about as we chose, day and night. It was the perfect proving ground for our coming-of-age adventures, safe from the prying eyes of the neighborhood adults.

Chapter Ten
House of Cards

We all clustered just outside the doorway to my grandparents' bedroom, the silence alive with dread and expectation of more. My grandfather lay in his bed, his breathing becoming increasingly shallow; my grandmother at his side, looking at her weak and helpless husband while the doctor rummaged around in his tattered brown leather bag for his stethoscope. The contrast between my grandfather's now inert form and the forceful man who not that long ago shook his cane and hurled German epithets whenever frustration crossed his path, yelling loudly enough to make his domain go quiet, could not have been more stark. The patriarch was down and as a result the air throughout the house was stilled, filled with uncertainty, and we each dared not breathe it in too deeply. Dr. Herman rarely made house calls anymore, especially on a cold January afternoon, but given his and my grandfather's long relationship he could hardly say no to my grandmother's worried voice on the phone. Now he moved the stethoscope slowly, with all the dexterity his decades as a practitioner had given him, using it to follow the life of my grandfather as it receded further and further away from his hearing. Within what seemed like mere moments, Dr. Herman turned to my grandmother and told her that her husband was dead. My grandmother's body issued a barely perceptible shudder as she turned toward the rest of us crowded in the hallway. Aunt Evelyn moved to embrace her. I stood there looking at my grandfather's face, the only part of him not covered by the bedding. He was dead. Just like my father.

* * * * *

IT WAS SEPTEMBER 1960 and there was a new faculty member at P.S. 95 when I began fifth grade. His name was Vincent Abata and he was my teacher. Mr. Abata was joining Mr. Black and Mr. Christiansen as the only male teachers in the entire school. Male elementary school teachers were a rarity in this female-dominated profession. For me, as I neared

113

my tenth birthday, he was a godsend. In the wake of my father's death a year-and-a-half prior, I needed an adult male in my life that I could imprint on. At home, my grandfather was simply too old and I had long ago distanced myself from him by refusing to be at his beck and call. Uncle Chuck was busy being distracted by dreams of suburbia and the demands of his own family; plus, I had already figured out that he was too cowardly to go against the family current by befriending me in my time of grief after my father's death, so he was not my idea of a role model. I found the other two male teachers daunting: Mr. Black was given to red-faced outbursts of anger and felt unpredictable; Mr. Christiansen was enveloped by a three-foot wall of cologne that served as an odiferous barrier. But Mr. Abata was different and I felt it immediately. Somehow I could see some of myself mirrored in his way of being and I responded by always wanting to be around him, always wanting to please him.

He was strong and wide, built like a wrestler or a football lineman. He appeared to wear the same rumpled and creased dark blue suit every day, always with a white shirt and matching blue tie misaligned at the collar. It was difficult to tell whether the suit was poorly fitted or whether Mr. Abata just felt confined and at odds with the dress code of his teaching profession. He was ruggedly handsome, his olive Italian complexion darkened by a 5 o'clock shadow that lengthened across his chin and jawline by 10:30 every morning. He had been an Army paratrooper in World War II, stationed at Ft. Benning, Georgia, braving the arduous survival training in the Okeefenokee Swamp. He brought down-to-earth, rough-and-tumble sensibilities to the classroom that all the students just loved, especially the boys, especially me. He designated one row of desks as his disciplinary section, dubbing it the "8-Ball Row" and those consigned there as his "8-Ball Squad." No girls ever landed in the 8-Ball Squad; on the contrary, various boys filtered in and out each day, based on the type of infractions. Before long, my best friend and Saxon Avenue neighbor, Solly Goldhirsch, and I took up permanent residence in the 8-Ball Row and we loved it. I could not get enough of Mr. Abata's attention. Whether it was volunteering to take the chalkboard erasers to be vibrated clean by the electric machine in the Eraser Room in the lobby of P.S. 95, or doing something just to get sent to sit in the 8-Ball Row, I did everything and anything to get his attention. He was like a mentor, especially when he kept the 8-Ball'ers after class at the end of the official school day.

During those moments he would sit on the front of his desk, feet irreverently placed atop the two closest student desks, while we sat randomly at the desks in front of him. Mr. Abata would loosen his tie and light up a cigarette and begin telling stories. We would ask him questions and he would answer, while we sat there with upturned faces, enrapt by his honesty and what I experienced as a felt-sense of wisdom being passed from this man straight to me. He would tell us stories about being in the Army and, in his own way, try to imbue us with the attributes that would enable us to become honorable young men. Even though it was getting into trouble that resulted in us being "8-ballers," it seemed that Mr. Abata found us to be his more interesting pupils, more open to taking risks, more adventuresome and, therefore, potentially more absorbing of his after-school teachings about life.

In addition to being enamored with Mr. Abata himself, I developed my first crush on a girl in Mr. Abata's class – two girls, actually. Each day from my back-of-the-classroom perch in the 8-Ball Row, I would be magnetized by both Shoshana Morgenstern and Rivka Fisher, often sending alternating moon-eyes toward each of them. I was mesmerized by them and terribly nervous whenever I was near them, doubly so because they were friends and nearly always together. In my emotional disarray I either stood awkwardly, mouth agape, or teased them in an effort to find equilibrium and restore my internal ballast. Rivka was clearly of Sephardic Jewish ancestry, exotic, with dark hair and dark skin, while Shoshana was Ashkenazi, with lighter hair and pure, blemish-free skin, her beauty possessing a more classic American look. Both were distractingly gorgeous to my eyes. This was the first time that I had felt sustained sensual stirrings associated with girls. Perhaps some of Mr. Abata's manliness was being transmitted straight to my hormones. Even when Solly and I made the terrible mistake of sending Shoshana a letter filled with dirty words, getting ourselves chewed out by her father and the school principal, my sense of wellbeing remained undamaged due to Mr. Abata. Even when he rolled his eyes at our stupidity, he refused to shame us. Between gazing at Shoshana and Rivka, daydreaming during lessons, and getting in trouble as a charter member of the 8-Ball Squad, my days in Mr. Abata's fifth-grade class were heavenly.

Those first few months of fifth grade were an incredible antidote for my state of confusion and grief over my father's death a year-and-a-half earlier. My heart grew lighter and I fairly danced through autumn, kicking my feet through the piles of yellow and red leaves that carpeted our neighborhood streets, or diving into the really huge piles of leaves raked together around the playground area for eventual burning by the Parkies. The crisp air was even more invigorating than usual in this my favorite of all the seasons. I was energized and happy, soon to turn ten and so alive to my young life. I thought I was free and clear of all my sadness and nothing could possibly happen to change this feeling of sheer exhilarating flight.

THE DEATH OF MY GRANDFATHER, on January 24, 1961, sent shockwaves throughout the household. The patriarch was gone, released from the family constellation and in the disarray that followed no one knew exactly who they were, what spot they now held, or quite how to act. The first thing I noticed was that my family continued to eat in the kitchen. The second thing I noticed was that Uncle Chuck moved to the head of the dining room table. The next thing that became noticeable was how much quieter and subdued my grandmother became in the aftermath of her husband's death. As a result, almost like an unconscious adaptation to her new bearing, the entire household ratcheted down a notch. Without my grandfather at her side, for *raison d'etre* as well as his unspoken backing of her as matriarch, it began to feel like the center could no longer hold. I became increasingly watchful, unsure and unsteady in this apparent vacuum left by my grandfather's departure; I felt like I was waiting for another shoe to drop from somewhere and made myself scarce by being around the house as little as possible. This was the second death of a family member in my young life in barely two years. I couldn't tell if I was sad, or numb, or just trying to imitate how everyone else was feeling so as not to stand out in any way and avoid calling attention to myself. Besides, none of the adults really cared about what I was feeling, so most of the time I just put it all out of my mind and immersed myself in my own daily world.

My mother was mostly out of the house, working at Woolworth's from 2:00 to 10:00 at night, Monday through Saturday. Peggy, my cousins, and I were getting older and, when not in school, were playing outside more and more, simply to escape the pall that filled the house after our grandfather died. My aunt and uncle were beginning to plan their escape to suburbia. There was an implicit feeling of uncertainty and change in the air and everyone was feeling the restlessness that accompanies such transitional times.

My cousin Brian was feeling a particularly hormonal restiveness. Already into his teenage years at 14 and looking more like a man than a boy, his sexual energy was percolating on overdrive, his curiosity and desire ablaze, determined to find expression and relief. I have no idea if Brian had been abused by someone in his childhood, or if his sexual advances toward my sister and me were simply a combination of time, place, and opportunity, along with an air of *de facto* permission. What was true, and what had been made clear ever since my family arrived in the house and we were consigned to eating in the kitchen, was that we were something less than family, people who one didn't really need to care much about. Early on my grandmother had made it clear that we brought our misfortunes upon ourselves and, therefore, got whatever we deserved. There was no clearer definition of who constituted potential

116

prey under that roof than Peggy and me. In Brian's mind, as he surveyed his domain for sexual experimentation and manipulation, it must've looked relatively safe and completely wide open, and we must've looked like easy pickings.

The first time my cousin Brian took me upstairs to his family's living area and into their tiny, pink and white bathroom, I was so excited. We were about to have a "boner party," as Brian called them, a time where he and I would be alone, touching each other's penises. I was ten and he was 14. It must've been a weekend, most likely a Saturday, my mother working at Woolworth's, everyone else out somewhere, my grandmother alone downstairs, reveling in the quiet, thinking Brian and I were upstairs playing – if she thought of us at all.

This was not the first sexual contact I experienced with my cousin, but this was the first time he and I were alone together, and the first time it was in daylight rather than darkness. Previously, both my cousins and my sister and I had gathered in the garage at the back of the house. With the door closed, the only available light shone through the six glass panes running horizontal across the door, just under the uppermost edge. Within this darkened, shadowy confine it felt mildly damp, the concrete floor cool to the touch, the smell of car exhaust, oil, and rubber tires permeated the air. Peggy, my cousin Ned, and I all sat side by side against the wall while Brian put his hand down my sister's shorts. He had me open my fly and pull my penis out so he could touch it also. His penis was out and he began slowly stroking it, cajoling his brother to participate. But Ned, who could hardly stand to see clothing pinched in a dresser drawer much less hurt another human being, would have none of it; he refused and just sat there rigid, unmoving, unspeaking. Whether Brian had finally satisfied himself or had gotten nervous regarding his brother's absolute resistance, Brian opened the garage door and we all emerged into the sunlight. To his credit, Ned never again participated in his brother's sexual gamesmanship.

Brian, on the other hand, seemed insatiable. Thanks to the previous four years of watching me and my family being consigned to eating in the kitchen, of us being deemed pariahs because of my mother's carnal descent with my Irish-Catholic, working-class father, and us being treated with a combination of pitying tolerance, neglect, and shaming recriminations, Brian knew exactly where it was safe to go to experiment sexually.

Brian seemed to alternate in his choice of sexual guinea pig between groping Peggy, who was eight, and seducing me with his boner parties. He also became careful not to have both me and my sister together with him anymore, perhaps fearing one or both of us would blurt out the truth, or simply because it was easier to manipulate us individually. We were both so starved for love that any form of interest, of being sought after, desired, accepted, was like food to Peggy and me – and our hearts were ravenous. Because it would've seemed odd for him and Peggy to be alone upstairs, the backyard garage and the basement was his favorite site for fondling my sister. How many times he took her there, and what he did to her or had her do to him, is unknown. This abuse, though, on top of all the other maltreatment my sister received throughout her young life, would leave Peggy forever deformed.

That first boner party, Brian had me unzip my pants and pull them down to my ankles. Then he had me pull my underpants down. He did the same. I was excited and nervous; I knew we were doing something that could get us in trouble, but I was with my cousin Brian who I looked up to and loved. I was with him and I felt special; this was our private, secret time together, just ours. My penis was skinny and flaccid, barely stirring as Brian cupped my testicles with his hand. I could feel warmth enveloping my entire scrotum; it felt good and sent a rush of blood into my penis, stiffening it slightly. When I looked at Brian's penis my breath caught in my throat – his erection was huge, thick and cylindrical, hard like a piece of wood. We began by rubbing our penises together, tip to tip. It felt good and I was excited. He then asked me to wrap my hand around his penis and when I did I could barely close my fingers. His penis was hot and pulsing, red at the tip with blue-grey veins worming their way up and down the penis shaft. He asked me to move my hand up and down his penis. Within minutes the tip was glistening with a droplet of clear, shiny liquid.

Meanwhile, Brian was doing the same thing to my penis, stroking it into a state of erection that seemed miniscule compared to his. I was breathing rapidly, partly due to the forbidden nature of what we were doing, partly due to the increasingly good feelings I was experiencing as Brian's hand moved faster and faster. With my hand on his penis I imitated the movements that he was performing on me. He was also getting more excited, telling me not to stop. As I continued masturbating him he reached over and grabbed a wad of toilet paper in his free hand. Suddenly his body jerked. He clamped the toilet paper down upon the head of his penis and ejaculated forcefully and spasmodically into it. I kept moving my hand up and down until he grabbed it and pulled it off of his penis. His breathing was beginning to slow. He also stopped stroking my penis. I do not remember ejaculating that first time, but I was still happy; I knew there would be more boner parties with Brian in the future – and there were.

Our mutual masturbations always took place in that pink and white bathroom and they always happened when most of the other family members were either out of the house or busy in such a way that whatever the kids were doing became distant afterthoughts. Due to the fact that Saturdays, when everyone was gone or otherwise preoccupied, were difficult to come by, these boner parties were episodic over the course of the year, something left to spontaneity, which only seemed to add other dimensions of anticipation and titillation. The rest of my year in fifth grade after my grandfather's death was tedious and superficial, submerged as I had become in the sexual machinations of my cousin. With each weekend my mind turned toward wondering if this would be a weekend when Brian and I would have another boner party and I would feel good and feel special for a while. Perhaps it was the intermittent nature of our dalliances that stimulated a new level of sexual frustration within Brian, or perhaps he had grown bored with my sister, or had tried something with her that he now wanted to try with me; whatever it was, during the next boner party it was clear that Brian wanted something more than just masturbation.

The next time we found ourselves alone in the house (except for my grandmother), Brian and I raced upstairs and into the bathroom. He shut the door and locked it. This time he did not ask me to pull down my pants and underwear. Instead, he closed the toilet lid and had me sit on it, facing him. When I was sitting, Brian unbuckled his belt and unzipped his pants. In one move he pushed his pants and underwear to the floor, his huge erection springing outward toward my face, which was now at the exact same level. I stared, mesmerized; never before had I looked this close at his penis. I watched as he wrapped his own hand around the shaft and aimed it right at my lips. I was breathing unevenly, feeling the sexual energy stirring in my own penis and feeling a distinct sense of foreboding that something very different was going to happen. "Kiss it," Brian whispered. "Just kiss it," he urged.

I froze and looked up at him. His face was looking down at me, an anticipatory expression silently imploring me to kiss his penis. The tip of his penis was so close that I could feel the heat rising off of it; the huge, mushroom-shaped helmet of his penis head was etched indelibly into my mind. I wanted to please the cousin I loved so much, but somewhere inside my ten-year-old brain and heart I knew that this was too much, this was too far for me to go. He continued to stroke his penis slowly, moving it slightly closer to my mouth. "Kiss it," he repeated. I pursed my lips tighter, mustering the courage and determination to turn down my cousin's demand. "Put it in your mouth," he said as he now wrapped my hand around his penis. I was frozen in fear and refusal and disgust. After a few more frustrating moments he pulled up his pants and we left the bathroom in silence. I was confused, feeling like I simply couldn't go through with it but at the same time fearing that I had jeopardized our boner parties forever and, worst of all, I had also let Brian down.

It turned out that I was wrong about the first part. Twice more Brian brought me upstairs into the bathroom and twice more he tried to convince me to kiss and suck his penis. Both times I refused. Then everything came apart.

IT SEEMED THAT MY SISTER PEGGY had learned well from Brian's gropings and God knows what else. She had figured out that if she let other third-grade neighborhood boys put their hands down her pants or did the same to them she was very popular, and being wanted was all Peggy ever desired. But eight- and nine-year-olds could hardly keep such an occurrence secret for very long, especially since the number of boys being attracted to my sister was increasing. One of the boys' mothers finally discovered what Peggy was doing and immediately told my mother what was going on.

The subsequent family gathering in the dining room was oppressive with the air of silent condemnation. My sister and I stood silently, marinating in our slowly rising shame, while my grandmother basted my mother with equal amounts of outrage and holier-than-thou condescension. My mother was brought to task for her complete inability in both controlling my sister and me and for her failure to raise us with any morals whatsoever, all of it explained by my mother's transgressive shacking-up with my lowlife Irish father. Peggy was wordlessly denigrated with despised looks of outright disgust, coupled with tsk-tsking attitudes of "what can you really expect, anyway?"

Then the adults turned on me, my mother screaming, "Why didn't you protect your sister!?" I felt encircled by them, all glaring down at me with stern looks, wagging fingers, and words of blame. I glanced toward my cousin Brian, who just turned away and kept silent; my cousin Ned did the same. Somehow the weight of all the family shame was falling only on Peggy and me. Inside I was reeling, wanting to say that it wasn't my fault but knowing at an even deeper level that if I told the truth I would never be believed and would probably get in even more trouble. I might even get my family kicked out onto the street. After all, I knew full well by then the reasons why we were the ones that ate separately in the kitchen, knew why we were the ones nobody really wanted: we served as constant reminders of the consequences of lower-class, Irish-Catholic, feral blood seeping in to contaminate the Scheel family lineage. In an insidious Catch-22 fashion, everything we did or did not do was constantly seized upon to prove and reinforce my grandmother's original assessment. I felt trapped between defending myself and implicating my cousin, and swallowing it all in hopes of weathering this latest nightmare. But inside I could not hold it together.

In that bullying family trial, under their intense shaming, two paradoxical things exploded within my very being as I desperately tried to maintain my equilibrium. The first explosion was really an implosion: the anchoring of my belief that I was indeed irreparably bad at the core. After nearly five years under my grandmother's roof of being told every day that I was damaged goods, I was now certain that this was the truth and that it would only be a matter of time before I would do something else to cause the people in my life to find out just how fundamentally rotten I truly was. As a result, from that moment of realization on, I began to construct my life knowing full well that no matter how good I behaved, I was truly an imposter, forever living on borrowed time before I would be discovered, shamed, and inevitably rejected. As part of this I made a sacred vow that I would do anything not to let people see the true badness which I now knew was the real me.

My second response to being singled out and wrongfully blamed for what happened to my sister, while witnessing Brian get away with it all and Ned chicken out from telling the truth, was to make another sacred vow: I swore to myself that I would not tolerate unfairness and injustice in any form. If I couldn't defend myself and Peggy, then I would defend others and, perhaps, in this way I could counterbalance the ugliness that lived inside of me, ever threatening to be exposed. These two forces, erupting in my soul at the tender age of ten, one fearing the revelation of the darkness lurking within, one yearning for nobility of action as a temporary mask behind which I could hide, created the psychological and emotional dynamics that would – for good and ill – shape my actions and color my relationships for the rest of my life.

LIFE AT 3987 SAXON AVENUE was never the same after that. Everyone was more estranged than ever before. Tension lingered, threatening to burst forth into angry conflagration at any moment. I felt distanced from Brian and didn't like that at all; I wanted things to go back to the way they were before. Once, after a few weeks of walking on eggshells of shame, I noticed that he and I were again alone in the house with my grandmother resting in her room. This time I approached him and tentatively asked if we could go upstairs together for a "boner party." Brian looked at me with horror, clearly appalled that I would ever bring this up again. He whispered angrily, "No!" and stormed upstairs alone. I was so hurt and confused. My heart felt broken; I loved my cousin and I had enjoyed many of the sexual feelings that I experienced, yet I knew that what we had done was wrong. This must be my shameful bad side coming out, I thought, though later I also wondered fearfully what I might have agreed to if Brian had said yes. I was in such turmoil and despair, with no one to talk to. As a result I decided to weather my internal storms the best I could – and that meant stuffing everything down deep into my inner darkness and tightening the lid on as securely as my young, frightened mind could conceive.

The next shockwave came less than a year later. It was summer 1962. Sixth grade was over and I was done with P.S. 95. It had gone by in a slow blur. Nothing felt stable. If I felt anything at all it was numbness. After my father's death, my grandfather's death, and the nightmare of being blamed for what happened to Peggy, I stumbled through my last year in elementary school in a state of dissociation, my own pain and confusion remaining unspoken and therefore unknown.

What I did know was that in a couple of months I would be on my way to John Peter Tetard Junior High School 143 in the coming fall, and that I would be turning twelve shortly after my arrival there. But now it was summer and I clung desperately to the hope that everything would return to some state of normalcy in the tranquilizing heat and long days. I wanted to forget all that had happened. I wanted to go back in time and be an innocent little boy again. I wanted to stop summer in its tracks but, try as I might, life asserted itself.

It was at this moment that my Uncle Chuck had decided to finally make his move out of the Bronx. Within weeks he packed up his family and relocated north to a two-bedroom apartment in Bronxville, just over the Westchester County border, his first imagined stepping-stone to eventual home ownership and undoubtedly a welcomed relief to the growing oppressiveness beleaguering 3987 Saxon Avenue. I was devastated. Even after all the misery and pain brought on by the sexual abuse and the false accusations, I still loved my cousins and my uncle; plus, once again, change and upheaval was undoing whatever stability I had achieved since moving to the Bronx and weathering the deaths of my father and grandfather. Now my mother and sister and I would be all alone in the house with my grandmother growing daily more embittered and vindictive. I knew full well that nothing good could come of that arrangement.

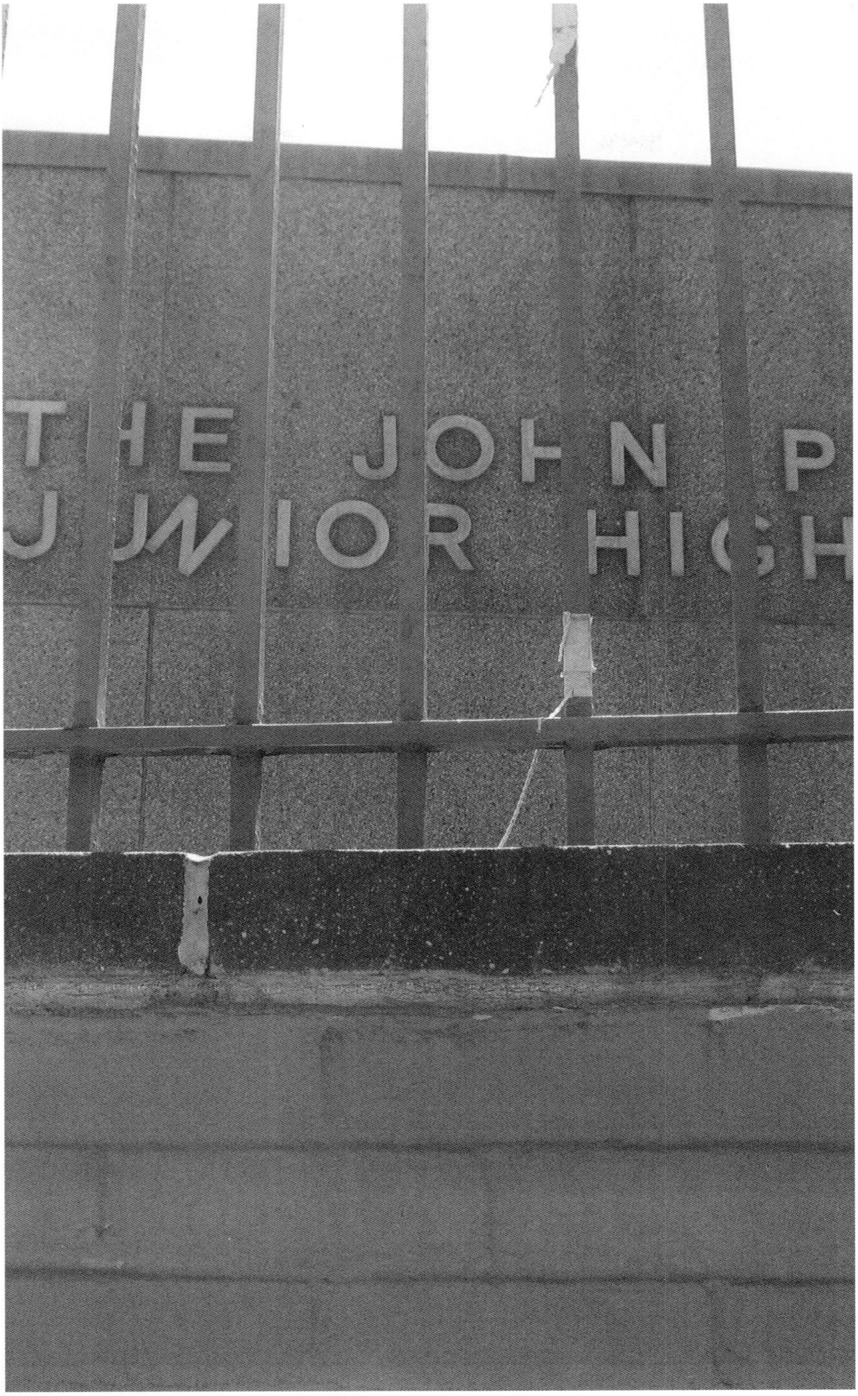
THE JOHN P
JUNIOR HIGH

Chapter Eleven
Adrift

*A*pproaching *my twelfth birthday was vertiginous, as if I was high upon an unstable and dangerous mountain peak. Whatever I looked on from this height, in whatever direction, all I saw was either the painful, frightening wreckage in the valleys of the past, or a pathless terrain disappearing into an unclear future. I was dizzy and nauseous in the face of it all.*

To my rear it seemed like nothing but hurtful change characterized my first six years of living in this neighborhood: leaving my father and moving to the Bronx, to a house void of love; arriving in a strange neighborhood where unfamiliarity was around every corner; the unacknowledged death of my father; the death of my grandfather imploding the family constellation; the sexual predation of my cousin and the blame and shame my sister and I were doused with as a result; and, finally, the paradoxically disheartening disappearance of the Drolet family into suburbia.

When I looked forward everything in that direction promised even more change and upheaval and, therefore, looked equally confusing and terrifying: me and my family alone in the house with my angry and mournful grandmother; the end of elementary school and the threshold of junior high school – with its industrial efficiency and racial diversity beckoning like a potential daily gauntlet; the embodied confusion of my budding interest and attraction to girls; and on top of it all, the cultural expectations about becoming a man, which seemed to offer only one rigid, uniform template of masculinity within which to surrender my soul – a surrender I had been working instinctively to refuse.

* * * * *

ALMOST BEFORE UNCLE CHUCK'S rented moving van had left the driveway, turning right onto Van Cortlandt Park South on its way to the Major Deegan Expressway to take them to Bronxville, my mother, sister, and I immediately filled the vacuum of the Drolet's departure by relocating upstairs to their now-vacant living quarters on the third floor. It was necessary for two reasons: first, I was old enough to require my own bedroom and second, we desperately needed physical space between us and my dispirited grandmother. I moved into the bedroom that my cousins had previously shared, while my mother and Peggy moved into what had been Uncle Chuck's and Aunt Evelyn's bedroom. My sister and mother had access to their own rooftop (the front porch); I had access to the rooftop at the rear of the house (appropriately designated the back porch). In summer, despite the scorching heat of the half-melted tarpaper, I also had access to the grape trellis and its mouth-puckering bounty. It was my private domain and at night, when I was alone, it felt like freedom. We all shared the little pink and white bathroom, which mixed the still-lingering feminine smells of my Aunt Evelyn's toilette with the predatory dalliances that my cousin Brian had arranged for him and me. It would take some time for all of those energies and associations to dissipate.

Thus our upstairs refuge was settled uneasily into. Regular contact with my grandmother was abbreviated as much as possible now that we all weren't living crammed together on the same floor of the house. With my mother working nights, my sister and I still ate dinner in the kitchen, while my grandmother made her own meals and dined solitary at the huge table in the dining room. An invisible yet visceral threshold separated the two rooms that proved impossible for anyone to cross, the tenacious power of habit coupled with my grandmother's determination that our family would always be banished to the kitchen, made living in this near-empty house more surreal than ever. Yet, during the daylight hours, when Peggy and I went off to school, my mother continued to have her morning coffee and cigarettes at the kitchen table, often ending up sitting with my grandmother in stony silence, little conversation passing between them. This must've been a fate even my mother could not have imagined when she pondered all the scenarios in her decision to move us back to the Bronx. Now, thrust together by virtue of their aloneness, they formed an odd couple, bound by mutual mistrust and seething animosity that mothers and daughters can so often be ensnared by. Sadly, this was the model of relationship being handed down from my mother to my sister, a distinct reflection that both daughters were unwanted by the women who had brought them into this world.

As a result of this in-house schizophrenia, my comings and goings weren't subjected to quite as much scrutiny by my grandmother and that seemed to lessen her capacity for complaining to my mother about me. Peggy, on the other hand, being the youngest and now a shame-laden figure for her past transgressions, had less freedom to stray from the immediate area in and around 3987 Saxon Avenue. Therefore she continued to be the brunt of my grandmother's ire, tormenting her, it seemed, simply on general principles, while my mother's growing lethargy about her own life and her habit of parental neglect left Peggy completely unprotected. Needless to say, in this environment of regular, daily proximity my sister and grandmother grew to hate each other with intensity. They could hardly pass by each other without an instant conflagration being sparked, by despised looks, by words slipped harshly under their breath. Hardly a day went by without my grandmother complaining to my mother about Peggy's spitefulness, or laziness, or disrespectful manner; all of which would reduce my sister to curse-filled, tearful raging, professing her innocence until she would finally storm upstairs or out of the house, slamming one door or another in complete frustration.

I was in seventh grade now, entering John Peter Tetard Junior High School 143. Tetard was located at 120 W. 231st Street, just shy of a mile from our neighborhood. We all knew that it was less than a mile away because, in New York City at the time, students could receive free bus passes to use on the city transit system if they traveled a mile or more to school. The furthest edge of our neighborhood, Dickinson Avenue, was literally a few blocks under the mile marker. Thus we were denied free transportation and it periodically chafed. A few enterprising individuals began forging bus passes on the appropriately hued construction paper to match that month's bus-pass color, oftentimes with great success. After all, if you got caught you only lost a fake bus pass and were tossed off, which meant having to wait for the next bus and pay the fare, or simply walk to school . . . less than a mile away. Our other acts of rebellion were to hand our bus passes out the back window to one of our friends who would take the very next bus, or push open the back door to let our classmates sneak on. This sometimes caused the irate bus driver to push his way to the rear of the packed bus to try to stem the inflow. Our travels to school were always exciting.

In decent weather, my friends and I would walk to school together. Each morning we would meet at the east entrance to Pigeon Park, or in front of EM's candy store, and begin our reluctant trek to school. All along the way we would hassle each other, show off for the girls, and meet other classmates in a slow accretion of bodies trudging along Sedgwick Avenue, past Ft. Independence, in pilgrimage to another day in junior high school. Coming home was similar, though less subdued and more joyful, as we made our way back to the safety and familiarity of our neighborhood.

TETARD WAS THREE STORIES HIGH and shaped like a T. The hallways were covered with light tan-brown linoleum and had a white stripe running down the middle of each corridor. This was our "lane divider," and during class changes everyone had to keep to the right of the stripe and move in an orderly fashion to their next classroom. During this time of controlled chaos in the hallways, faculty members were strategically placed on each floor. This was designed to keep students moving, to prevent them from cutting across the stripe, to keep the noise down, and to defuse any altercations. For most of us, cloistered and protected by familiarity in our various neighborhoods, this was our first real interactions with this many kids of different races, class backgrounds, and ethnicities, all piled into one building for seven hours a day. While my friends and I met most mornings and walked to school together, once inside the doors of Junior High School 143, it felt like survival of the fittest. It was a scary environment for a new, seventh grader like me, coming from a primarily monochromatic neighborhood. Tetard was filled with blacks, Puerto Ricans, Irish, Jewish, and a smattering of Asians and other students from various mixed backgrounds. Perhaps the hallway logistics, complete with floor stripe, was the administration's attempt to mitigate conflict and tension, their reminder to us that we were all in this together, always moving in the same direction. Despite the best intentions by the powers-that-be overseeing Tetard, within the comings and goings of the general population, on the frontlines of student-to-student interactions, it was a complete zoo.

Within my first month in seventh grade, as I settled into the daily rhythms of homeroom, I was fascinated by two of my black classmates, Henderson Heinz and Donald Washington. Henderson was stoically cool, quiet and intense; Donald was the joker, the goofball. They were both obsessed with the female *derrière* and spent every class change in the halls in single-minded determination attempting to cop a feel of as many girls' asses as possible without getting caught. Walking behind Henderson and Donald was an experience in intense, fearful titillation as they each zoomed in on a likely target, walked as close behind one of the girls as they could and, in rhythm with the girl's stride, slid their palms right against one or the other buttock, keeping it there for a full step or two. It was amazing to watch and even more amazing to see how rarely they seemed to get caught – except for Donald, who could hardly keep his excitement at bay and was regularly getting chewed out by a very agitated girl right in the middle of the hallway. Needless to say, Henderson's cool demeanor prevailed in the competition when he and Donald tallied their daily "feels" at the end of each school day as I sat with them shaking my head in disbelief.

At another extreme, was Leslie Mendon, the biggest and toughest girl in the entire school, standing nearly six-feet tall, curve-less, and built like a refrigerator with glasses. She was incredibly strong and willing to mix it up with any guy in the school if she felt disrespected. When she barreled through the halls, all the students parted to allow her past. Leslie spent every lunch hour in the cafeteria surrounded by a huge

128

crowd of students, as guy after guy tried to best her in arm wrestling – which never, ever happened.

Meanwhile, sitting right behind me in homeroom, was Jessup Kingman, a super-smart, bespectacled student who brought an orange to school every day. When the teacher was distracted Joseph would open a rectangular wooden case, within which lay a shiny stainless steel syringe purloined from his father, a doctor. Nestled inside the metal housing of the syringe, a glass cylinder contained a clear liquid that sloshed from side to side as he positioned the syringe near to the peel. The liquid was alcohol and it was Joseph's daily project to inject the orange, allow it to ferment throughout the morning, and then drink the juice – usually after lunch – and get a buzz. Perhaps this was his way of coping with the boredom, the chaos, or with the fact that the end of the school day meant going back home.

Then there was the day when two students came to school wearing suits, ties, hats, and sunglasses, with attaché cases handcuffed to their wrists, all planned in honor of the new James Bond movie, *From Russia with Love.*

And the day Turner, an older black student who had been "left back" and was repeating ninth grade, flashed a revolver in the cafeteria. Watching him remove the gun from his jacket was like watching him handling a deadly snake, repulsive and mesmerizing precisely because it was so dangerous. I had never seen a gun before that day and the surreal nature of that moment in the JHS 143 lunchroom evaporated ever so slowly when Turner finally pocketed the pistol, glanced nervously around, and disappeared into the crowd of students going about their midday business.

It was like a daily immersion into an asylum; and these were just some of the students in a population of hundreds.

Tellingly, there were only two teachers that made any impression or impact on me my entire first year in Tetard, both for very different reasons. Perhaps moving from having a single teacher the entire day in elementary school, to having at least five or six teachers each day in junior high, was simply too much for me to take in; so teachers really had to stand out for some particular, memorable reason other than the simple fact that they droned on interchangeably in front of the classroom. In any case, without these two to provide regular spikes in the flat-line that characterized my engagement with my first year of junior high school, I might've simply faded into the oblivious shuffling mass or joined Jessup Kingman in sucking alcohol-laced oranges in order to numb out.

MY HOMEROOM TEACHER WAS MISS MANCINI, a dark-haired, voluptuous woman who also taught my first-year Spanish class. I cringed every time I had to stand up in class and regurgitate a sentence, or when I was called on to answer a question in Spanish. Though I tried mightily, I had no aptitude at all for language acquisition and I imagined she cringed even more than I did since she was forced to listen to me butchering the language she loved. That I even passed her first-year Spanish class is a wonder. My attention toward Miss Mancini, though, was directed elsewhere; far away from anything to do with Spanish *per se*. Miss Mancini exuded palpable sensuality, from her curvaceous physicality to her dark unruly hair, and from her dark-framed eyeglasses to the exotic nature of her voice speaking Spanish as she tried so hard to have the language stick in our brains. I was enamored by her breasts, which were large and pressed outward against her blouse in such a way that the fabric bowed open between the buttons, giving me periodic glimpses of her bra and sending me into daydreams the likes of which only inexperienced adolescent boys are capable – void of any context yet somehow completely titillating in the mystery of it all.

Every single day I prayed to see just a little bit more. I watched her every movement, every turn and twist, hoping. I longed for those moments when she would come to the aid of a student sitting at a desk in the row next to where I was sitting, and she would bend over and a brief hint of cleavage would imprint itself on my fevered brain. Sadly, these moments were always short-lived; it seemed to never fail that she called on me to say something to the class in Spanish at the very moment I was lost in my world of fantasizing. Perhaps she knew what I was doing, or she tracked the angle of my stare, or saw the dreaminess of my glazed-over expression; whatever it was, Miss Mancini had an uncanny knack for dragging me away from her breasts and bringing me forcefully back into her classroom. Nevertheless, she provided a wonderful distraction in the midst of the mayhem erupting throughout my initiatory year as a seventh grader.

In stark contrast to Miss Mancini was my math teacher, Mr. Bailey. Mr. Bailey was an Irish hellion. Wearing a rumpled suit, a thin tie and white shirt with the first button always undone, he was an elemental force with little patience for rule-breakers. He wore his thinning hair plastered back, while behind his glasses his eyes missed little and tolerated less. In moments of clarifying school protocol and procedures to unruly students his eyes would widen and bulge, his voice would bellow, and his rage would turn his face deep crimson. He was like the Tasmanian Devil cartoon character, only worse. In math class he just shook his head over my utter failure to show any aptitude for math at any level. Sometimes I think it was sheer pity on Mr. Bailey's part that allowed me to barely pass his classes and stumble onward through junior high school math.

He was relatively calm in the classroom but once kids started pouring into the halls *en masse*, moving from one class to another, all bets were off with Mr. Bailey – at that moment he became like a bird of prey, waiting to swoop down on any scofflaw stupid enough to transgress the rules of the hallways. Once, when I had stopped in the hallway to take a forbidden drink at the water fountain, he came up behind me and kicked me in the ass so hard I nearly smashed my head into the wall above the fountain. He then spun me around, pushed his reddening face only inches from mine, and told me to get the hell to class. Yet, despite his maniacal unpredictability, I loved him and sought him out every chance I could, reveling equally in his tempestuous outbursts as well as in those more calm, conversational moments when, probably unbeknownst to him, I imagined I was receiving some masculine mentoring and insight. I rejoiced in just being around him. Mr. Bailey became my "Mr. Abata" for my junior high years, another father figure I felt, somewhere inside, that I desperately needed in order to survive this new world.

My first year at Tetard I spent dancing awkwardly between navigating the unknown, the unfamiliar, and clinging to my neighborhood friends whenever the chaos became too much to bear. What this meant on a day-to-day basis, in addition to banding together to walk to and from school, was longing for the noontime solace and sanctuary of the cafeteria, where I could once again see the faces of the kids I had grown up with and relax my guard, albeit briefly.

Eating in the lunchroom was exactly like any other large institution depicted on television or in the movies, exactly like being in the army or in prison: rows of tables aligned in a single direction, chairs along each side, low ceilings with light fixtures glaring, grated windows that looked into a shadowy culvert since the cafeteria was slightly below ground. Smells of cooked food, discarded food, and decaying food clung to the tepid and immobile air. Moving through the serving line was like a reflex, requiring less animation than a zombie. The staff on the other side of the metal-and-glass display counter was as robotized as the students they were serving food to on this seemingly endless assembly line of hungry mouths. The menu was the same for each day of the week – with a special surprise thrown in now and then. This meant gorging on as much food as possible when it was something edible – my favorite was spaghetti and meat sauce – or opting for the comfort of milk and dessert when it was something unrecognizable.

Sometimes it was just better to bring lunch in a brown paper bag, with my name written on it in crayon by my mother's own hand. When enough of us brought lunch from home, this unleashed the hilarious haggling of a food-trading frenzy. My standard (and favorite) lunch from home was Skippy crunchy-style peanut-butter and Welch's grape jelly on

Wonder Bread, an apple or an orange, and three or four Oreo cookies. When I got this there was no trading that could interest me.

Like the movie prison scenes, each lunchroom table was commandeered by a particular group of people: some clustered by race, some gender segregated, some with boys and girls mingling, yet even the most mixed of tables belonged to a particular clique and was not welcoming of strangers. At the end of one table, closest to a window, our neighborhood rag-tag group of white, mostly Jewish kids, gathered each day to commiserate about grades, imagine about girls, and warn each other about tough guys to watch out for (while nearby the girls we knew from our neighborhood carried out their version of the very same conversations). It was like a brief oasis of stability and familiarity in a desert of shifting social sands, a much-needed respite to the high-alert energy required to survive in Tetard.

MEANWHILE, ON THE SURFACE, life in the neighborhood went on apace for me, despite the interruptions of having to be in seventh grade and having to devote more time each evening to doing more homework than ever before. On the periphery, though, especially via the nightly news broadcasts, the wider world appeared to be edging ever closer, challenging our ability to remain naïve and safe in our childhood. More military advisors were being sent to support the unpopular government in South Vietnam. Nuclear testing was continuing, as were the growing protests against it. Black students in the South were being refused admission into schools and colleges, with race riots breaking out and local elected officials barring the doors. Tensions between our government and Cuba were ratcheting up after the thwarted Bay of Pigs invasion, supported by American policy and aid, and the Cuban Missile Crisis was mere months away. At age 12 it was still easy, most of the time, to brush these events to the side and return to our self-involved lives. But more and more, troubling things were beginning to find purchase in our minds and hearts. Every day it felt like something was being added to the global pressure cooker and it was becoming harder and harder to ignore it all.

At a more intimately personal level, just breaching the surface of our social awareness, other things were beginning to stir for me and my friends. While it still felt like we were all part of the same neighborhood, it appeared that we were now under a hormone-driven centrifugal force that was re-shaping who we were, separating us beyond our control and largely without our conscious consent, pushing us to determine who we really wanted to hang out with and who we didn't. Suddenly it seemed that one major result of leaving the intimate confines of P.S. 95 was a compulsion to fashion a completely new reconfiguration of friendships. We all knew, divined, or intuited at some level, that this movement toward creating subgroups had to be one based on a very serious re-determination of who we perceived it was cool to hang out with. Yes, "cool" was now a part of our adolescent radar, which meant developing our sensibilities to *be* cool, recognizing when something or someone *was* cool and, most importantly, be especially aware and cautious when something or someone *was not* cool.

While friendships were mostly fluid throughout elementary school, because everyone under 12 was so uniformly and decidedly uncool, it now became important for us to coalesce into different configurations, seeking those with more like-minded interests and those possessing complementary temperaments. For most of us, this process did not generally incorporate the non-neighborhood kids we met at JHS 143. During the school day there was plenty of intermingling with other kids, and while at-school friendships did develop, our neighborhood was nearly a mile away from Tetard. More vitally, though, our neighborhood possessed a communal quality that magnetized us powerfully toward each other as an organismic whole, making these social reconfigurations very much intra-tribal. As seventh grade came to a close, the kids close to my age – within a year on either side – began to separate out from under the common umbrella of "neighborhood kids" and congeal into various subgroups. Even though sports continued to serve as a mutual meeting ground for most age-groups in the neighborhood, these sub-grouplets represented new alignments taking shape as a matter of an inexorable adolescent urge. Because of the powerful pull of our community it became a coming-of-age reorganization *within* our neighborhood, rather than a fracturing out beyond the bounds of our enclave. Despite the growing impulse to differentiate and fashion new identities, it was hardly a willful, conscious reordering. More akin to a Braille-like exploration, people seemed to sort themselves and start hanging out together, as if drawn irresistibly by a vague sense of kinship – you just seemed to know who you wanted to be around.

But even more crucially for people like me, who were so brutally alienated within the family drama, this movement was about forging a new family, in contrast – and often in direct opposition – to my family of origin. This, I believed, would now be the group into which I could pour my love, speak my truths, express my hopes and fears, and never be rejected. I wanted this for myself and for all my friends. In this new tribe I hoped that finally we could be who we really were, accepted by and accepting of each other, facing this world together. This was what my 12-year-old heart was imagining as that first year of junior high school ended and another summer emerged.

Chapter Twelve
Coming of Age

*W*hen Jacob Schenck called me and told me to come over to his apartment, I could sense the excitement in his voice. As soon as I arrived he took me into his room and explained that it was time we formed a gang. It was summertime 1964; we were both 13 and percolating with vibrant coming-of-age adolescent male energy. About to enter ninth grade, I had rocketed to over six-feet tall, making me bigger than most of my friends; yet like a Great Dane puppy I came clumsily into my newfound physicality and athleticism. Jacob, though shorter, was muscular, with a backlog of pent-up anger coiled behind his polite, manicured boy-next-door presentation that caused him to radiate a "don't-mess-with-me" intensity when necessary. He figured we could be co-leaders of the gang. We began laughing and imagining out loud how we would dress, and what a cool thing it would be to form a gang together. We decided that Gale Place was going to be our turf. We weren't about to wait our turn for the older kids to vacate The Rail so we could move up; we were restless to step out and stake our own claim. That The Rail was only two blocks away at the other end of the retaining wall didn't matter to us; what mattered was that this was going to be our world and we were set on shaping it in our own image.

Suddenly he grabbed an Archie *comic from his bed and quickly thumbed it open. There, on the lower left-hand corner of the page, was a picture of Archie looking teenage-tough and wearing a black leather jacket with a gang name arcing along his upper back across his shoulders. "This should be our name," Jacob said tapping his finger repeatedly on the picture. "We'll call ourselves 'The Panthers'."*

* * * * *

WEATHERING MY FIRST TWO YEARS OF JUNIOR HIGH SCHOOL caused me to feel worldlier. After all, in grades seven and eight I had spent seven hours a day, five days a week, and ten long months in a seething cauldron of hormone-driven anxiety and insecurity that we all were trying to sort out, most often – due to our limited and flailing self-awareness – at the expense of each other. Each day was filled with unscheduled collisions that rocked our tender psyches just at the moment when we thought we'd figured out the previous day's entanglements. Distinctly different and otherworldly than our womb-like elementary school nestled in the bosom of our own neighborhood enclave, Tetard JHS 143 presented us with hundreds of kids who were not white or Jewish. Now we were mingling every day with blacks, Puerto Ricans, Asians, and other white kids who each came to school with their own attitudes and perspectives on the world and how to navigate it; attitudes and perspectives that did not always jibe with ours – or ours with theirs. Beneath our freshly scrubbed budding adolescence, behind our button-down shirts and ties, within our slacks and nice dress shoes, awe and stark terror were barely held in check. Whether it was instantly falling in love with someone you regularly passed in the hallway during class change, steering clear of the designated tough guys, looking and acting cool in front of your friends, or dreading the next exam – or worse, the report cards – life in Tetard was a daily minefield of potential and actual social disasters. Further, the age differences between incoming seventh graders (I was barely 12 at the beginning of junior high school) and the soon-to-be-departing ninth graders (some even 15 or 16 years old by the time they graduated off to high school after being left back), created vast chasms of relative immaturity, physically and emotionally. Most of the time during my first year I felt like a shoplifter among felons; I kept my head down and tried to find friendly faces, mostly keeping as close to my neighborhood friends as any given day would allow.

THEN, AT THE BEGINNING OF EIGHTH GRADE, during the autumn of 1963 with my 13th birthday approaching, something unimaginably out of character happened. I got up enough courage to ask Pat Baker, a complete stranger from a completely different neighborhood, to go to a movie with me. We had been making eyes at each other in the hallways of Tetard since the very first day of the school year. I felt magnetized to her, an electric current zipping through me with such voltage that I was completely smitten beyond my control. Each time we passed each other our looks got longer and more direct, as if our eyes were daring each other to take a chance and break the silence. Pat was beautiful, Irish like me, with blond hair and what I saw as an implicit "bad-girl" curl to her smile. Since she was not from the neighborhood, and definitely not Jewish, I figured I had a real chance at romance this time. When I finally asked her to go out with me, we decided a movie would be best.

I met her in front of the RKO Marble Hill, on Broadway near 231st Street, closer to her neighborhood. Once inside we made a beeline for the balcony, a move that signaled to me that I was going to have a great time. Neither one of us watched the movie and instead spent nearly the entire time kissing awkwardly. I was in heaven, marinating in the smells of her make-up and hair spray. As we cuddled and became more and more playful with each other, I knew the door that would allow me to finally feel a girl up was about to swing open here in the darkened balcony. But even after I had assumed the requisite position of having my arm casually slung around her shoulders, my right hand dangling just inches away from her breast, I was still too shy, or too gentlemanly, to make my move. I was paralyzed by my own ethics. I just sat there frozen, not even kissing her any longer. Suddenly, toward the end of the movie, a bunch of her friends piled into the row of seats right behind us. Somehow they'd gotten wind that Pat was up in the balcony with a stranger. They began catcalling, smacking their lips, and promising Pat that they were going to tell her boyfriend that she was cheating on him. Finally the movie was over and Pat and I walked outside together. Her friends were grouped nearby, snickering and pointing. Pat and I smiled at each other awkwardly; then she turned and walked away, her friends quickly surrounding her. I headed in the opposite direction for a long walk back home. As confused and awkward as the whole date was at times, my whole body was zinging, alive with the memories of her pressing against me, of kissing her, and all the feelings that had been activated and were still recycling through my flesh. I felt so good that even her friends' threats to tell her boyfriend about me did not register. I was so excited to see her again that for the first time in my life I was actually looking forward to the weekend being over and going back to school.

Throughout that following Monday, I saw Pat only once and she quickly avoided my gaze. It seemed unreal that this chasm had suddenly appeared between us when mere days ago we were making out in the balcony of the movie theater. That afternoon though, as school let out, Pat's boyfriend, John, became all too real. He confronted me right outside the doors that emptied onto West 231st Street, right next to the dead-end barriers that stood above the concrete stairs that led down to Kingsbridge Terrace. John was already in high school at De Witt Clinton. He possessed the perilous, reptilian eyes of a skilled juvenile delinquent embedded in a huge head fixed upon the body of what looked to me like a football player. With the collar of his pea-coat turned up against the autumn air, barely concealing his 5 o'clock shadow, he emanated menace. As the other students gathered around, ready to enjoy a potential dust-up, John simply said, "She's my girlfriend.

Understand?" I nodded and stammered, "Yes." "You will never see her again. Understand?" I nodded. With that John walked off down the stone steps and disappeared into the Irish neighborhood just below Tetard. I breathed out my anxiousness, began the trek home and, stumbling over my words, explained what had just happened to my friends. It was our sole conversation all the way back to the neighborhood. In the conflicted world of adolescent boys I was momentarily a hero; my friends were equally amazed that I had actually gone out on a date *and* had nearly gotten beat up over it. In a strange way it felt good to be the center of attention for my transgression. Back home in my room, though, I returned to my despair, resigning myself to never having a girlfriend.

LIKE AN EVER-LENGTHENING SHADOW, events beyond our day-to-day concerns continued to periodically shroud the sun that not long ago had beamed steadily down upon our innocence. That past June I had watched the grisly footage on the television news of a Buddhist monk setting himself on fire in protest of the U.S.-supported government in Vietnam. I was stunned, confused, and troubled by what could've caused a person to do something like that. Throughout the late summer and into the fall the news was abuzz with Martin Luther King Jr.'s "I Have a Dream" speech, delivered to hundreds of thousands of people on the Mall in Washington, D.C., as well as the increasing tensions across the South as more and more black people stood up for their civil rights. Then, within weeks of his speech, just as my friends and I were adapting to the start of eighth grade at Tetard, four young black girls were murdered by a bomb set in a church in Birmingham, Alabama. What was going on, my mind screamed silently. Meanwhile, baseball fans across the country – even those who hated the Los Angeles Dodgers – were lauding pitcher Sandy Koufax throwing a record-setting fifteen strikeouts in a single World Series game. The world was making less and less sense, and making me more and more anxious.

But the event that indelibly stained my entire year as an eighth grader at Tetard was the assassination of President John F. Kennedy on November 22, 1963, just six days prior to my thirteenth birthday. The one indelible image that freezes my memory is our teacher, Mrs. Kafka, being called outside the classroom and then returning with tears streaming down her face. We waited expectantly, tears forming in our own eyes because we were scared, we'd never seen anything like this and we knew it must be very bad. She quieted us down and, between her sobs and ours, told us that President Kennedy had been shot in Dallas, Texas, and as a result school was being let out early so we could all go home to our families. So many emotions pummeled me in that grave moment: shock that the President had been shot, and near-equal shock at seeing one of my teachers openly crying; momentary delight that I was getting out of school early followed by pulsations of guilt for thinking such a thing; and cascading fear, confusion, and more tears as to what was really happening in our country and what it had to do with me. As we moved through the corridors in an eerie silence I could not fail to notice that every single adult we passed was weeping. Stunned, my friends and I trudged aimlessly home, trying in our own way to make sense of it all.

When I arrived home my grandmother, mother, and sister were in the living room watching the CBS News with Walter Cronkite on the television. As disorienting as the news coverage was, especially since the television was strangely on in our house in the afternoon, it quickly became even more surreal. After it was announced that the President had died, felled by the bullets of a lone assassin, there was one thing I clearly felt – the world in that instant grew more somber and much darker, like a light switch had been flipped off. Whereas three years ago I had joined my cousins in nighttime marauding, tearing down Kennedy election posters around the neighborhood (my whole family was voting for Nixon), I had, like so many Americans, grown to revel in the youthful optimism of progress and possibility that every one of the President's speeches seemed to convey. Even as a soon-to-be teenager I could feel the energy that had been percolating in the country since his election. A spirit of optimism had swept the land, taking me and nearly everyone I knew in its embrace. In the immediate aftermath of the assassination, as the reality of this heinous event began to set in, I felt at some visceral level that a chunk of meaning had been violently cut out of my life. I hurt in places I had never felt hurt before, and I could not articulate why.

Yet despite all the angst that surrounded this tragedy, coloring the winter holidays and launching the New Year onto unsteady seas, before long it was summer again. I had once more muddled through and, even though I was in summer school for failing Spanish, I felt I had indeed survived eighth grade both academically and, more importantly, personally. But something was missing. Perhaps it was my generalized teen-age angst, coupled with the lingering, destitute emptiness trailing the President's assassination. Perhaps it was some of our older, college-aged friends talking about the Free Speech Movement that had galvanized the University of California at Berkeley campus the previous school year, calling into question the role of education in this country and the dangers of corporate control and influence. Perhaps it was the face of poverty, now more revealed than ever in America's inner cities and undermining all our Social Studies classes that tried to convince us America didn't have these issues. And even though I was years away from being eligible for the Army's ever-looming Selective Service draft, many of our older neighborhood friends had already begun worrying. The escalating war in Vietnam, and images of fire hoses and police dogs being set upon black people marching for civil rights in the Deep South, were beamed incessantly into my living room on the nightly news. As a result, I was feeling a growing need to be part of something, to be wanted, to be needed, and at the same time discover a place of safety that I could never manage to find in my own house. The only move that made sense to me, the only direction I could trust turning toward, was once again in the direction of my friends.

Every day it became more palpable; I could feel it in the tension between how I felt at home and how I felt in the streets. It was time for me to coalesce with like-minded souls, time to move beyond the simplicity of grade-school friendships where the only draw was the easy, often habitual, familiarity of either being in the same class at P.S. 95, or living in proximity of each other, or having parents who were friends. I felt like a reordering of my social cosmos was being compelled by an unspoken hunger as I began to intuitively and imaginatively craft a coterie of male friends that somewhere in my heart, I prayed, would become just like the Knights of King Arthur's Roundtable.

Perhaps it was this mythic story, or all the westerns and war movies I was nurtured on, but in my adolescent fantasy I wanted to surround myself with friends who would protect each other, who would love each other and, if necessary, who would die for each other. This was radically different than my confused and burgeoning attractions to the girls in our neighborhood. It wasn't about sexuality or the urge to bond with a single individual; this forging of friendships with other young men, even in this nascent stage, felt like it was a bonding that, once sealed, would last a lifetime. With wave upon wave of coming-of-age libidinal energies building, surging, and crashing everywhere inside me, pounding incessantly against the shores of my skin inside and out, I needed a place for all of these forces to go. I wanted to share it among people who would be able to recognize it and, most crucially, among people who would be able to reciprocate. I wanted to pour myself into the hearts of male friends who could receive my offerings of love and camaraderie. What I discovered in fairly short order, as if they were searching for the exact same thing, was a lifeline of brothers that would tether me safely through years of self-discovery and years of darkness. Joined by a mutuality forged in trial and tribulation, buoyed by our shared coming-of-age revelations, made whole through revealing our hopes and dreams and joys, we nurtured each other with care and compassion – as best we understood these sentiments – testing our limits against the world around us while testing each other's limits as well.

ODDLY ENOUGH IT WAS A MOVIE that galvanized us into action to form a gang – *West Side Story*. By the time most of the boys I hung around with were in junior high school we had seen *West Side Story* what felt like dozens of times. We were transfixed by the opening aerial view, gliding over *our* city. The jazzy combat during the "Prologue" as Baby John is chased by the Sharks got our blood racing, as we imagined being in that position or coming to the rescue of one of our own. We memorized the lyrics to "The Jets' Song," "Tonight," "Quintet," "Officer Krupke," and especially "America," sung and danced by the Sharks and their girlfriends during the rooftop scene. We could easily recall pieces of dialogue: "Womb to tomb; birth to earth," exchanged like a sacred vow by Riff and Tony; and, "I wanna bust! Bust cool," as Ice tries to calm Action and all the Jets after the rumble. We liked the toughness of the two gangs, particularly the Jets' Riff, Action, and Ice, and the Sharks' Bernardo and Indio. If we were expected to like the Jets any better because they were white like us, it didn't wash – while the Jets were in many ways just like us, the Sharks dressed cooler than anything we'd ever seen, mesmerizing us in their tight-fitting, colorful shirts. We wanted to be *both* gangs at once.

We even imitated the street-dance ballet. Together, in a line, we'd snap our fingers and move through the dance moves we memorized, pirouetting in the middle of the street or in one of the basements. Then, in unison at the appropriate moment, we'd stop and pull our K-55 knives from our back pockets and, with a flick of our wrists, snap the knives open as if they were switchblades. We all knew every self-respecting gang member had to carry a blade, but switchblades, cool as they were, were also illegal. When we found a store near Fordham Road and Southern Boulevard that sold the Mercator K-55 knife, and it was legal, we became instant customers. The fact that it was emblazoned with a leaping cat logo, outlined in gold which we immediately determined was the outline of a Panther, we were hooked. We'd race to our hangout at Gale Place with our purchases and, with a can of 3-in-1 oil, work the blades until with a minimal amount of wrist-action we could snap them open into their locked position.

Even the book, *West Side Story*, influenced us. As we read, citing chapter and verse to each other, we learned things like needing to walk in the middle of the street to prevent being stomped by someone emerging suddenly out of an apartment entrance. Thereafter, our pilgrimages from Gale Place to the playground always took place in the middle of the street. We took seriously the mandate that gangs always had to have a hidden cache of weapons stashed somewhere in case of a rumble. As a result Jacob and I created an arsenal just over the fence surrounding the reservoir, at the east entrance to Pigeon Park, hidden in a cluster of weeds and sumac bushes. There we had collected chains, scraps of wood and lengths of pipe that we found, even a broken piece of metal fence the shape and length of a spear. We were preparing for our mythic rumble but every one of us, beneath the bravado, hoped it would never come.

Yet try as we might to be bad-ass, we were also different from the generations of really tough guys before us. We actually liked the whole Romeo and Juliet drama depicted in *West Side Story* and we re-cast it into our world which, by virtue of growing up in the Bronx, provided our fevered minds with images galore. There was gang folklore everywhere, with the names of the Fordham Baldies, the Ducky Boys, and the Golden Guineas emblazoned into the fear centers of our young brains. Individual toughs like the Watts brothers (Tommy, Mikey and Alfie), the Lurie brothers (Billy, Bobby, and Michael), and Roy Drillich became names one would evoke in hushed tones and as cautionary tales as to what could happen if one crossed into the wrong neighborhood. Legend had it that Billy Lurie and Roy Drillich beat up ten cops at Orchard Beach one night before being subdued and carted off to jail. These were serious Bronx bad-asses. Yet our vision of being in a gang was desperately romantic, imagining ourselves fighting other gangs but praying we'd never have to. But being Panthers was deeply serious to us and therefore central to what we imagined as a vital ingredient for our budding, complex masculinity.

OUR NEXT STEP WAS TO HAVE A UNIFORM that identified us as the Panthers. Most of us had graduated from the childish blue jeans, cuffs rolled up, to black jeans with no cuffs. Around our waists we wore black leather Garrison belts, the square chrome-metal buckle pushed away from the front to sit coolly on the left side near our hip. Most of us wore black loafers or brown suede Desert Boots with white socks, especially when we went to school or were going to a party on the weekend. During the daylight hours when we weren't in school we usually wore white Chuck Taylor Converse sneakers, because during the day we played basketball every chance we could; plus, as we all understood, sneakers were needed to climb over fences and walls in case we needed to get away from the cops or rival gangs. But the *couture d' resistance* was our discovery of dungaree jackets.

There was simply nothing like standing in front of the mirror before going out into the neighborhood or to a party. A perfected pompadour labored stylishly in place with a plastic pocket comb, a long-sleeve white shirt open at the neck with cuffs rolled halfway up our forearms, and a muscle-shirt beneath it providing a flash of color just below our throats. Slipping into the dungaree jacket was like putting on invincible armor. After assessing that everything in your reflection was perfect, the final flair was taking the edges of the jacket collar and snapping it out and up so it covered the back of your neck. There was no cooler image imaginable. With all this in place you were ready – and you knew it. Every teenaged boy knew it. But what distinguished us from every other teenager in the world, or so we felt, was the Panther-head patch that we wore on the right shoulder of our jackets.

We had found these patches at Hi-Jinx's Sporting Goods on Jerome Avenue. Hi-Jinx was owned by one of our neighbors, Mr. Isaacson, and everyone went there to get school jackets, athletic equipment, and sneakers. When we came upon the Panther patches we bought them all. We then excitedly brought them home where we watched with anticipation our mothers sewing them onto our jackets. The irony of this domestic act being responsible for the completion of our rebellious gang image was completely lost upon us as we donned our uniform and raced to Gale Place to gather, finally, as Panthers.

We claimed the Gale Place dead-end as ours. It was here we would assemble, slowly trickling from our houses and apartments to create a critical mass of aimless energy seeking something to focus on. Most often we just hung out, sitting on the railings of the retaining wall during the daylight hours, waiting for Uncle John's ice cream truck to make a stop, going to the playground to play basketball, or making forays to EM's candy store.

As we surged hormonally into our teens, EM's went from simply being the favorite neighborhood candy store of our youth, where we bought the Sunday newspaper and cigarettes for our parents and candy for ourselves, to being a cool place to hang out. Co-owned by Milton and Morris (hence the name EM's), the store seemed to be stocked with a little bit of everything. Just to the left as you entered the store sat the cash register. Either Milton or Morris always stood guardian there, making sure that everything was paid for before anyone exited. To the right of the main door were spinner racks for comic books, which Milton and Morris never tired of reminding us had to be bought before we read them. Through the middle of the store an aisle ran from the front door to the back of the building, where a janitorial closet and a tiny employees-only bathroom were stuffed. At the beginning of the aisle, just to the right, a metal rack stuffed with small blue bags of Wise potato chips – with the trademark winking owl – beckoned. Nearby, on a wooden shelf, sat a circular plastic container filled with pretzel rods selling at two cents apiece. Right next to these, a tall rectangular box stood, filled with large soft pretzels, salted and braided, and stacked one on top of the other and held in place by a wooden dowel.

Also on the right side of the aisle, four tables with Formica tops and four chairs took up the area almost to the back wall. This was a favorite hangout for the older kids, especially in the winter. Just beyond these tables was a phone booth where all manner of shenanigans took place; from jury-rigging the phone to make free calls, to shoplifting, to couples closing themselves in to make out in the tight and titillating space. Needless to say, Milton and Morris made regular reconnaissance patrols to this part of the store. In fact, Milton and Morris ran a very tight ship, with the express purpose of keeping us teenagers from discouraging their other customers. They instituted a 15-minute rule, whereby you had to finish your drink in 15 minutes or you had to buy another one or leave the premises. In wintertime, the ability to nurse a cup of hot chocolate beyond the 15-minute rule became an art form.

The heart of EM's was the soda fountain, complete with Formica counter and seven or eight revolving stools topped with red plastic. Once through the door we would make a beeline to the counter, pile onto the stools, and begin ordering drinks: plain coke, cherry coke, vanilla coke, thick chocolate malteds, lemon-lime rickeys in tall, narrow glasses, and the perennial favorite, egg creams (with chocolate syrup, milk, and seltzer water – but definitely no eggs). Bottled soda (Coke, Hires Root Beer, Fanta Orange, and 7-Up) was also available for the walk back to the schoolyard or the playground. A menu consisting of hamburgers, grilled and cold sandwiches was also available.

It was a cool, somewhat prestigious job to be the soda jerk at EM's. You had to be personable and you had to be quick. Drinks had to be made and sandwiches constructed. All the dirty glasses had to be run through the vertical scrub brushes in the three sinks: one with soapy dirty water, the next with less soapy dirty water, and the third with clean water. It was demanding and you were on stage for the whole neighborhood to see. The first neighborhood kid I remember having that job was Al Weiss. Al was big and jovial. He moved with methodical purpose. He smiled constantly, was unflappable and always welcoming. Next was Jerry Penzig. Jerry was bespectacled, wiry, and moved with quick and darting motions. He was friendly, while at the same time often prone to letting the stress of a crowded counter and our inevitable teasing get to him. The last soda jerk I saw working at EM's was a black man in his late 20s or early 30s. His name was Gerard and I liked him immediately, especially his tell-it-like-it-is honesty.

Gerard and I would have long talks about the civil rights movement in America which, as he got to trust me, were always quite candid. Because he was older, he was hired to provide some consistency at the position since neighborhood kids were always leaving for school or better jobs. Gerard was proud, highly image conscious and determined to project a professional, uptown persona. To this end he was always nattily dressed with an expensive jacket or coat, scarf in the winter, and a cool hat. He also carried an attaché case, which we later discovered was empty except for his lunch. I often imagined him riding the bus, looking like he was on his way to an office job, only to arrive at EM's, ditch it all and don an apron. In the racially troubled atmosphere permeating America, Gerard was quite brave in accepting a job in an all-white neighborhood. This was underscored when one night, right before closing, Aidan and a few of his cronies started calling Gerard a nigger and challenging him to come out front and fight. A few of us were watching, fearing for Gerard and seething at this turn of events, but none of us was brave enough to go up against Aidan. Eventually, Milton and Morris escorted Gerard from the store and drove him home. Nothing like this ever happened again and most people accepted Gerard as a sweet guy behind EM's soda fountain.

Now, in addition to Gale Place and the playground, EM's had become an important part of our neighborhood circuit. Yet these venues were out in the public eye and we soon realized that we needed a spot where we could be shielded from prying adult judgment and recriminating stares.

IT BEGAN WITH AN OLD MATTRESS propped up against a phalanx of metal trash cans on the sidewalk awaiting the garbage collectors. Someone had the idea that we should take the mattress back to Gale Place and use it as a trampoline. We instantly hoisted it and began carrying it to our turf, having no real idea what we were going to do with it. Once back at Gale Place we dropped it on the ground and stood there staring at it. Someone flopped on it; another guy jumped on him, then another and another, a wrestling free-for-all quickly ensuing. When it was over the mattress just lay there. "I have an idea," someone yelled excitedly. "Let's bring it into the golf course." A few of us ducked through a hole in the chain-link behind the Big Rock, while the others lifted the mattress toward the top of the fence. The guys inside the golf course climbed the fence and grabbed the mattress, lifting it up and over and dropping it into the foliage. The remaining guys entered the golf course and with one mind we pulled the mattress straight to a clearing right below a huge tree. "This is it," someone said. "This is where we can come to get away from the crap out there. Let's call it The Cove."

145

Every time we saw any old discarded furniture we brought it to The Cove. Eventually we had two mattresses, an overstuffed chair and a couple of kitchen chairs, an old, tattered rectangular rug, and a small end table. What we really had, though, was our privacy. It was a version of the vacant lot in Washington Heights where I used to play as a child. The Cove, like the lot, was hidden enough to make it our world, only this time I was a teenager, which meant I wanted and needed a very different world – a place to make out with girls, talk heart-to-heart with my friends, and step out of the bustle of the neighborhood. We all needed that it seemed. Most of the time The Cove was populated by us guys, hanging out on the chairs and mattresses, musing about our lives. Often we would end up sitting in the tree carving our initials with our knives (sometimes adding girlfriends' initials, if we were lucky). Amazingly, if someone did take a girl into The Cove to make out, it was like a group radar signal was set off and everyone knew to make themselves scarce and give the couple privacy. The Cove became the perfect hidden complement to our Gale Place perch and we used it to the fullest extent possible.

NOW I HAD THE PANTHERS. I was finding my new family and in that discovery I was beginning to find myself. Jacob and I were acknowledged as co-leaders, though this was hardly a top-down arrangement and rested mostly on the fact that we had come up with the original idea. It was a rather loose affiliation of people who regularly gathered at Gale Place, drawn to each other by virtue of age and by the fact that there wasn't a rigid social hierarchy to navigate. A handful of us, though, truly took the Panther ethos to heart, wearing our jackets everywhere and feeling our identities and our self-esteem solidify by being part of a gang.

JACOB SCHENCK was my first close friend after leaving grade school. He lived right across the street from me in the First Building. He cut a dashing figure, with close-cropped, wiry hair, a gleaming smile that made him highly attractive to most of the girls he encountered, and inquisitive eyes. Jacob was the kind of guy who could take over the dance floor just as easily as he could an argument. When pushed he was quick to anger, his face reddening and fists clenching as he fought to keep it all managed. He was determined to project a manly image.

One summer, he had his mother drive me and Kevin Hurley up to Camp Wel-Met on visitor's day. Wel-Met was a sleepaway camp where Jacob spent a good portion of the summer. He wanted us to come and show everyone just how tough his friends from the Bronx were and, by extension, how tough he was. Kevin and I donned black jeans, white log-sleeved shirts opened in the front to reveal colorful muscle shirts, and our trademark Garrison belt buckle pushed to our left hips. We certainly looked like the toughest kids at Wel-Met that weekend, and the most out of place in the blazing sun with everyone else wearing shorts, t-shirts, and sandals. Our only saving grace was that Jacob, Kevin and I were undefeated in every half-court basketball game we played.

Jacob was adamantly anti-drug and when that whole scene began to unfold he made himself more and more absent at The Rail, especially after graduating high school. One day the rumor spread that he had up and joined the United States Marine Corps. We were shocked, partly because it seemed so unexpected and partly because our growing antiwar sentiments made this kind of voluntary choice anathema to our sensibilities. One day I saw him was at the playground. He told me he did not make it through the Marines' training. He was vague about the reasons why so we left it at that.

Jacob was a restless spirit, always seeking adventure, always prodding us to explore beyond the confines of the neighborhood. Under his urgings we would take the Broadway train to South Ferry and ride the ferry for a nickel; or take the commuter train north to explore Poughkeepsie; or venture into other gangs' territory and walk across the condemned High Bridge span that connected Manhattan and the Bronx. Perhaps it was our mutual restlessness that drew us to each other. From him I learned the power of self-confidence.

PHIL PASTERNAK lived beyond the confines of our immediate neighborhood, in an apartment on Gates Place, closer to Jerome Avenue. Unlike most of my other friends who had their eyes set on college, he was determined to attend Samuel Gompers vocational high school and learn a trade. We bonded instantly over the fact that we passionately hated our home life and did everything in our power to get out of our houses and into the streets. Throughout junior high and high school, no matter what the weather, when everyone else was doing homework after dinner, Phil and I would be prowling the neighborhood looking for any open window or unlocked door, wandering the streets or sitting in one of the apartment building stairwells or basements, commiserating and philosophizing. We would spend long hours discussing Tolkien's *Lord of the Rings* trilogy, immersing ourselves into the fantasy world of Hobbits, Elves, Orcs and Wizards. Our other favorite books to talk about were Ian Fleming's James Bond series which, coupled with the movies, gave us an endless supply of fantasies of besting the exotic villains and falling into bed with the bikini-clad women. We largely disregarded school and felt above it all, reveling in our scofflaw attitudes and feeling like we were really being rebellious teen-age delinquents. He was the first one to get me to drink hard liquor after he snuck two bottles of booze out of his father's supply. Not long after we smoked pot, we both jumped headlong into the deep end of drug scene, our motto: "Try anything once."

Phil was short and didn't like it. He attempted to compensate with braggadocio and belligerence, more often than not getting us into trouble instead of actually intimidating anyone. He fancied himself a ladies man and he never tired of regaling us about how many times he had gotten laid, despite our chorus of laugher and synchronized eye-rolling. For a few years we were utterly inseparable and from Phil I learned the complex nature of loyalty.

KEVIN HURLEY lived in a private house on Orloff Avenue, close to the Irish neighborhood near Bailey Avenue. He was originally recruited to play on our neighborhood football team and we immediately hit it off; soon he became a regular part of the Panthers. Our friendship was more than simply the fact that, like me, he was Irish; it felt like we had both found our missing brother. In fact, we became so close that we even started dressing alike, especially donning our Army jackets and our Australian bush hats (popularized by the television show, *The Rat Patrol*). I was so unconditionally welcomed in his house by his mother,, that I began to feel I was part of the family. His father, Brendan, was a New York City detective with about a half-dozen other hustles, both legit and partially legit; he was a colorful character who was as charming as he was determined to physically whip his son Kevin into manhood. Kevin was smart and his parents had high expectations of him, enrolling him in the prestigious Cardinal Hayes High School. Kevin had two younger sisters, Angela and Kathleen, respectively. It seemed they were forever in their Catholic school regalia, either coming from or going to school, whenever I saw them.

Kevin and I got our first real jobs together at the Bronx Zoo animal rides. When we went to apply for working papers, because we were under sixteen, we also got our Social Security numbers with one digit separating them. The Bronx Zoo was the perfect job for us. Sent to the interview by my mother, who was friends with the boss, Frank Bean, we got the job immediately. For two summers, and every weekend during school, we took kids on one of three animal rides: donkey cart for the littlest ones; camel rides, where we got six passengers near seasick due to their swaying gait; and the ponies. Everyone who worked there hated the donkey cart; it was simply too boring. Loading kids on and off the ship of the desert was tedious, and trying not to get bitten, spit on, or kicked while leading the camels around was unpredictable in its outcome. It was the ponies that we all lusted after. Not only did we get to run around (which kept us in shape for basketball), but everyday dozens and dozens of girls gathered along the fence on one side of the oval and flirted with us. We must've appeared studly as we sweated in our denim shirts, the words "Bronx Zoo" and a horseshoe embroidered in red thread on the back. More than a few dates resulted as we circled the track and flirted back, asking names and getting phone numbers. Kevin and I were constantly pinching ourselves, remarking to each other how incredible it was that we were actually getting paid to do this. The other unexpected benefit of our job was that unbeknownst to our already desensitized noses, the animal smells permeated our clothes so thoroughly that we were guaranteed seats on even the most crowded of buses during the end-of-day commute.

Together, shoulder to shoulder through high school and beyond, we followed the predictable trajectory from drinking to drugs, until one day Kevin was gone – our first friend to be drafted and shipped off to Vietnam.

Kevin was the epitome of the stand-up guy. From him I learned that friendship demands a serious level of commitment and a dedication to nurture and protect each other through thick and thin.

ARI KRAVITZ arrived in our neighborhood in 1966, at the beginning of our high school years. He was a serious weightlifter, a black-belt in Karate, and incredibly strong. One day when we were playing touch football in the playground, Ari caught a pass and started running across the asphalt. Somehow, in trying to elude being touched he ran full speed into one of the basketball poles, bounced off onto the ground, and bounced up again, announcing loudly: "I'm okay!" One of the exercises his *sensei* had developed at the *dojo* was to blindfold Ari and surround him with a circle of students. Then the lights would be turned off and the students would attack Ari *en masse*. When the lights went back on only Ari was standing. For entertainment he would do twenty push-ups with me, at over 150 pounds, lying on his back. Fortunately for us he was more like Ferdinand the Bull rather than a bad-ass gang member. His home life also drove him into the streets and as a result of hanging out with each other our mutual respect grew. Ari was always down for anything and everything, whether that was playing sports, having an adventure or, in later years, taking drugs. He put a level of intensity in his *joie d' vivre* that was infectious. From Ari I discovered that life was meant to be lived to the fullest.

It was rare to find any of the five of us without our Panther regalia.

Other friends that I drew close to in the Panther years were Barry Roth, Adam Sokol, Aron Rose, Peter Mandel, Harry Lefkowitz, Gregg Kai, and Michael Katz. While for the most part eschewing the whole Panther bravado and dungaree-jacket look, these friends hung out regularly at Gale Place and, more importantly, understood the meaning of having each other's backs – something I loved and cherished about them all.

BARRY ROTH and I grew our friendship as a result of basketball. He was a tenacious player, driving to the basket through the toughest defense. We played a lot together, including one year each on the junior varsity and varsity teams sponsored by the Mosholu-Montefiore Community Center. When the drug scene seduced us, we both went down some very dark and dangerous paths together, but we never lost our true bearings when it came to the value of our friendship. Barry radiated intensity. He could talk, could bargain, could sell, and could wheedle his way out of trouble with the best of them. From Barry I learned the meaning of *chutzpah*.

ADAM SOKOL and I first bonded over my protecting him from a few of our neighborhood bullies. He was less athletic, and more given to pursuing music and academics, so it was hardly surprising when he passed the entrance exam to Music and Art High School. At the same time he was smart and highly opinionated. For a person looking for someone to pick on, this was the perfect combination of automatic agitation and easy pickings. One year, I spent nearly an entire summer intervening on Adam's behalf when anyone started to pick on him. When I succumbed to drugs he returned the favor by relentlessly arguing and pleading with me not to throw my life away.

Somehow, Adam was magical when it came to getting into events for free or finding his way backstage, or even onto the stage. Whether it was a Mets' game, a classical music concert at Tanglewood, or a local band playing at one of the community centers, Adam would find his way into the mix. I found Adam to be compelling, appearing and disappearing at will, always returning with something to share that he knew was going to be "intense," and "far out." Whenever we talked I found him pondering the social and political issues of the day and constantly worrying about how the world could be made better. He never seemed to lose sight of what was most important in any given situation. From him I experienced the power of being a humane and caring person.

PETER MANDEL and I also came together through sports, especially softball (where he was a star as our fast-pitching ace) and basketball (where his baseline jump shot won many a game). In our later teens our conversations would turn toward the state of the world, especially Civil Rights and the Vietnam War. Peter was smart and worldly-wise, able to look beyond our singular lives and wonder about the plight of people everywhere. He turned me on to the music of Bob Dylan, where every song was like a shot of expanded social consciousness. His apartment was the first place I saw paintings of African-Americans; I would stand there mesmerized, in that moment becoming suddenly aware of their humanity and, by extension, my own. Peter's house exuded social awareness and a striving for fairness and equality that most neighborhood apartments I entered simply did not. We both became enamored with Fidel Castro and Che Guevara, so much so for Peter that he was part of the first Venceremos Brigade harvesting sugarcane in Cuba. We spent an entire summer dropping acid and pondering and debating the pros and cons of revolution in America. From him I learned about social justice and the need for political activism.

Aron Rose was another friendship forged on the basketball courts, where his attacking style and deft passing ability made him a highly sought after teammate and a highly respected opponent. We both shared a growing disenchantment with the Vietnam War and racial discrimination in the South. We would have long talks about books we were reading, like Jerry Rubin's *Do It* and Abbie Hoffman's *Steal this Book;* both authors were part of the Yippies and both, therefore, appealed to Aron's sense of humor and sense of the absurd. Aron was especially adept at articulating his views, researching the facts, and bringing humor and insight into debating his position. He epitomized *mensch-ness*, exhibiting a solid, salt-of-the-earth embrace of people in their complex humanity. He was so motivated by justice and standing up for the underdog that he even backed down one of Bailey Avenue's most psychotic Irish toughs, Brady Gavin, when Brady was about to beat up an old man for no reason other than being pissed off about life. Aron consistently walked his talk with grace and forthrightness. From him I learned the power of the spoken word backed up by logic, patience, rationality, and compassion.

Despite knowing Harry Lefkowitz since grade school, he and I became much closer as friends battling each other on the neighborhood basketball courts. By the time we were in eighth grade we had sprouted from relatively short guys into budding teens, both over six-feet tall. As two of the taller players we often were on opposite teams guarding each other. What Harry lacked in athleticism he made up in tenacity. There was a level of mutual admiration and respect that developed between us that extended beyond our basketball playing and into our friendship.

Harry was a decided pacifist and throughout high school, as the Vietnam War raged and civil rights heated up, we would debate the question of peacefully changing society versus violent revolution. As the drug scene worsened, he and I would be the first of our group to try to make a break for it and leave the Bronx forever. Harry wore all of his emotions on his sleeve and met life by leading with his heart. He had a huge smile and possessed a playful spirit and was always laughing. From him I learned the power of love.

GREGG KAI was our only Asian friend and he was of Japanese descent. The minute puberty hit, Gregg seemed to epitomize "cool." Whether it was the way he half-rolled the cuffs of his dungaree jacket up his forearms, or smoked cigarettes, or played basketball with grace and flair years beyond our still maturing athleticism, we all held him with a sense of quiet awe. He could muster a steely look when necessary and project an aura of "don't mess with me." Yet the overwhelming feeling he exuded was joy. Gregg was the first to wear desert boots and tight jeans, the first to French kiss and feel up a girl, the first to smoke cigarettes, the first to smoke pot, and the first to have a real love relationship that involved actual sex, and he did it all without a trace of arrogance. He was also one of the first to sniff glue, perfecting the art of using a black magic marker to hide the glue spots on his black jeans. Before high school was over, though, Gregg would be plunged into a very dark labyrinth. While he and I never became the closest of friends, it just felt good to be around him, as if his cool might rub off onto me. From him I learned what image looked like and what classy felt like.

MICHAEL KATZ was lean and lanky and excited about life. He was smart and funny, handsome, erudite, athletic and debonair. All the girls liked him. All the boys liked him, too. Close in height, he and I bonded first on the basketball courts, where he possessed an uncanny hook shot. Over our teen years we would often find ourselves sitting in one or another of the hallways commiserating about the challenges at school, at home, the ups and downs of the drug scene, and especially our love lives. We were always honest with each other, and from that honesty a deep and abiding love began to grow. During our heartfelt conversations, Michael demonstrated over and over again a capacity for sweeping philosophizing that seemed to provide a comforting context to whatever angst I was going through. I always felt a resurgence of my spirit after talking things out with him and I came to rely on his perspective and counsel. Despite being a teenager, he was an astute listener and a natural therapist. I always felt better after we talked. Unpredictably, he would play a crucial role in helping to save my life when things seemed the darkest. From him I learned the meaning of *savoir faire*.

It was these eleven brothers-in-arms who helped shape me as a young man. As if they were called directly from the pages of the book I hid so carefully in the school library when I was in fourth grade, these friends, without their knowing, became my Roundtable Knights. Whether it was challenging me to be better, or supporting me in my darkest moments, one or more of them were always there.

Another tier of friends, who kept their focus primarily on school and other interests safer than the Panthers, included Sam Prinz, Paul Riese, Jon Wolff, Michael Landau, Asher and Marvin Shapiro, and Ira Feigenbaum, all of whom congregated regularly at Gale Place and considered themselves Panthers by association, however tenuous that connection might appear at times. A handful of other guys – including Jake Carter from the Sixth Building, George Ippolito, Paul Steinmetz, and Gene Bronfman, all from the Cannon Place neighborhood on the far side of Pigeon Park – constellated a more informal orbit of friends of the Panthers; they split their time between the Panthers' domain at Gale Place and hanging out at the playground or closer to their own homes.

Whether formally Panthers or not, these were the friends that shaped my day-to-day reality. With them around I felt like I could handle anything.

As Panthers, we moved in packs. Whether it was going to Frank's Pizza on Jerome Avenue, or to the nearby David Marcus movie theater, or to Schweller's or Epstein's deli for a corned beef on rye, we felt like we owned that stretch between Gun Hill Road and Mosholu Parkway, that it was an extension of our neighborhood. But when it came to meandering up and down Fordham Road and the Grand Concourse, going to the Loew's Paradise movie theater or Jahn's Ice Cream Parlor, trying our hand at shoplifting in the aisles of Alexander's department store, perusing the 45's in myriad record shops, it was a different story. Even with five or six of us Panthers banding together and strutting our stuff, we kept our eyes ever peeled for the infamous Fordham Baldies gang who were known to hang out between the Army and Marines recruiting stations situated on the Fordham Road overpass. Even when we moved out of our Gale Place turf to the playground, or to EM's candy store, we sauntered through the streets of the neighborhood, ignoring the catcalls from some of the older guys, while reveling in the disapproving stares from the adults and the wide-eyed awe in the faces of the younger kids. Like all true gangs, we forged our identity in opposition to another group, who we began to harass and challenge every time we saw them. These were kids from our own neighborhood who we had grown up with. As fate would have it this group was led by my former friend and elementary school nemesis, Solly Goldhirsch.

The collision course between Solly and I had been set in motion by years of accumulated petty hurts, jealousy, and competitive tension. It felt like part of our destiny was to duke it out at some point. So, when we hit our teenage years and he banded with Mark Kirsch, Robbie Hochberg, Ira Lehrer and Steve Feld, and I co-founded the Panthers, the stage was set for us to become the neighborhood version of the Jets and the Sharks. And just like *West Side Story*, everywhere we encountered them, in the schoolyard, the playground, or just walking down Gouverneur Avenue, we would get in their faces and call them out, threatening to kick their asses, telling them to get the hell off the streets. They would argue back as best they could. Particular antagonisms developed between Kevin Hurley and Mark Kirsch, and between Phil Pasternak and Robbie Hochberg. These guys would literally get nose to nose and curse each other out in no uncertain terms. Sometimes our guys would shove one of them, daring them to fight, but with ten or twelve Panthers surrounding them that impulse remained in check. Despite the open hostility, no one was ever quite ready to escalate to the next level of actually throwing a punch. Eventually these altercations would run out of steam and we would warn Solly and the others that this was our neighborhood and to keep out of our way. We'd head back to our Gale Place hangout, or to the Cove, recounting our bravado in the face of Solly and his cronies.

Then one sunny, carefree day it all came to a head. About a half dozen of us Panthers found Solly cutting through the walkway just north of P.S. 95 that connected Hillman Avenue and Gouverneur Avenue. He was alone. What followed were instinctual reflexes. The moment he saw us he froze and began scoping out his getaway options; the moment we saw him someone yelled, "Let's get him!" Upon hearing that, Solly instantly turned and fled back toward Hillman Avenue in a bid to make it safely to his house on Saxon. We took off in pursuit, an angry pack driven by an inflamed group-mind determined to catch Solly and pummel him. To our disappointment he made it home and we came to a breathless halt in front of his house. We gathered ourselves and began yelling for him to come out and face us. Solly tentatively opened his front door and motioned for me to come over, alone.

At first he tried to talk me out of beating him up, recalling all the times when we were friends, when we did homework together, when we had crushes on Shoshana and Rivka. I would have none of it, especially with my Panther brothers restless behind me. I told him to come outside and face us, disregarding his efforts to talk his way out of this standoff. Finally he said he would come out on one condition: that he and I fight one-on-one in the golf course and that no one else jump in. I immediately agreed.

Solly and I began walking down Saxon Avenue toward the playground, the rest of the Panthers right behind us. They were giddy at the prospect of Solly and I fighting it out. It seemed that word had spread that Solly and I were about to have a showdown because by the time we cut through the Sixth Building and headed down Van Cortlandt Park South, a throng of neighborhood kids were following us, their voices energetic and clamoring in anticipation of a fight, and more continued to join in behind us as we made our way toward the playground entrance. Solly and I were both over six-feet, athletic, and strong enough for most neighborhood kids our age or younger to not want to mess with us. Solly was handsome, articulate, and smarmy when trying to manipulate people or situations to his advantage; I was an acknowledged leader of the Panthers, feared by some but respected by most because while I tried to be tough I was inherently fair in my interactions. As we entered the playground all activity ceased as kids stopped what they were doing and swarmed to join the crowd already following us. We made our way into the handball courts and toward the hole in the golf course fence. We ascended the small hill and stood face to face, like gunslingers about to duel under a sunny, autumn sky. I looked to my left, toward the playground, and was stunned to see what looked like hundreds of people watching Solly and I.

At that moment it suddenly dawned on me that I was about to have a fist fight with Solly Goldhirsch and the whole neighborhood was gathered as witnesses. I became nervous. How was I supposed to start this fight? Should I just let loose and throw the first punch? What if I lost? What if I won? Did I really want to go through with this? Could I even back out if I wanted to? Solly spoke to me in a pleading voice. Once more he recalled our friendly past in an effort to wheedle and charm his way off this hill. Again, I would have none of it, telling him to start fighting, to throw a punch. Back and forth we went, the crowd below silently tensing, waiting for the epic battle to begin. Finally, Solly spoke. "Listen, Tommy," he began. "I will not fight you; I will not throw a punch even if you hit me. I am not going to fight." I felt immediately relieved. Just like that it was over, the neighborhood drama between Solly Goldhirsch and Tommy Donovan dissipating into the hill where we continued to stand, facing each other.

I turned toward the assembled crowd, spreading my arms with my palms outward, and shrugged. "He refuses to fight," I yelled, loud enough for those behind the fence in the handball courts to hear. A small but audible groan arose from some of the more bloodthirsty in the crowd, including some of the Panthers who wanted this resolved for good. But I was glad to not be fighting. "It's over," I yelled, and

155

began walking down the hill into the already retreating crowd, leaving Solly alone.

From that moment on whenever we saw Solly and his group of friends in the neighborhood, we simply looked at them with superior disdain and walked on by. Gone were the altercations, the name-calling, and the desire to mix it up and fight. Gone also was whatever remnants of friendship that might have been salvaged between Solly and I. It felt strange whenever Solly and I crossed paths without our friends along. In those brief, estranged moments I would look at him and wonder what exactly had happened to drive us so far apart. I could never find an explanation, nor did I linger very long in my wondering, preferring instead to chalk it up to the mysteries of coming of age in the Bronx.

THE CLOSEST THE PANTHERS EVER CAME TO AN ACTUAL RUMBLE was one day when a bunch of us were hanging around the Big Schoolyard. Someone got into an argument with Lenny Baumann. By then Lenny had nothing to do with the Panthers, having chosen instead a sort of free agency that allowed him to move through various neighborhoods exuding a sense of self-interested neutrality and therefore safe passage. The argument ended with a group of us gathered around Lenny, yelling and cursing and telling him to get lost or else we'd kick his ass. He walked off to the sounds of our derision and laughter. A few hours later he returned with a group of guys he had recruited from Jerome Avenue, chief among them Bobby Wexler of the Jerome Avenue Jokers, who we all knew was pretty tough. Also amidst the crowd was a huge, wider-than-tall black guy who held an enormous rock in this hand. It wasn't the rock that was intimidating, though, it was the fact that the size of his hand made the large rock he was holding look like a Spaldeen. Lenny was smiling and his reinforcements made it clear that they had not agreed to come all this way without busting some heads. As the tension mounted, our guys, through some inter-psychic survival mechanism, all suddenly bolted in opposite directions toward the two schoolyard gates and out onto Gouverneur Avenue, scattering in myriad directions into the neighborhood we knew so intimately. Momentarily surprised, Lenny and his cohort quickly followed in hot pursuit. But we were fast and we had a lead, and we knew where we were going. Jacob and I ran into the stairway of the Twelfth Building, racing up the nine floors as fast as we could go. We stopped, almost at the top, terrified and breathing heavily and listening intently to see if we were still being hunted. Jacob and I, so scared shitless that we finally had to burst out laughing to relieve the tension, eventually made it home. We found out the next day that so did the rest of the Panthers. We were all shaken and spent the next few weeks avoiding Lenny and laying low, mostly out of sight at Gale Place.

While most of the time we would gather happily in our own Gale Place cocoon, demonstrating to each other and the girls gathered around us how tough we were, periodically we would have run-ins with kids from the neighborhoods bordering ours. To the west, Bailey Avenue was a shorthand reference for the nearby working-class Irish neighborhood. Because a long flight of concrete steps connected Gale Place with Bailey Avenue, Alfie Watts, Mikey Riordan, Brady Gavin, and a few others from the that neighborhood – uniformly donned in blue windbreakers and white chinos – would regularly saunter through our world, freezing us in terror by virtue of their dissociated stares and by the fact that we knew they were all crazy. Alfie and his sidekick, Brady, were small and edgy, like landmines begging to be stepped on so they could explode with psychotic fury at whoever made the misstep. Mikey Riordan had fists the size of sledgehammer heads. A few of our guys would nod ingratiatingly to them in an attempt to say "Hey, we're cool like you too." They never nodded back. Instead they moved silently past us like a pack of sharks. We tried to avoid them at all costs and subsequently never had any fights with them.

A rival gang, The Jokers, lived on the eastern edge of our neighborhood, around the Jerome Avenue area. They rarely came into our neighborhood but we frequented Jerome Avenue regularly, especially going to Frank's Pizza on weekend nights and during the summer. Most of the time when we crossed paths with the Jokers we would, in a shower of bravado, curse and call each other names: "Fuck you!" "Yeah, you prick? Your mother! Fuck your mother!" After this last epithet it was either time to either fight or run. Mostly we ran.

One afternoon, though, as a bunch of us were walking up Gun Hill Road toward Jerome Avenue, a band of Jokers confronted us. It looked like a melee was about to break out when I pointed to their biggest guy and said, "Me and you." He agreed and we squared off. I immediately adopted the only fighting stance I was familiar with, the one that Ice used when fighting Bernardo in the rumble scene in *West Side Story* – crouched and compact with both of my fists extended outwards at about chest height. As my opponent moved in, instead of punching, I launched a vicious kick to his thigh causing him to jump back. He circled and moved in again. This time my kick caught him in the stomach and he doubled over and fell to the sidewalk. I was on him in an instant, punching him. He waved me off, surrendering. It was over in seconds. The Jokers ran off, vowing to get reinforcements. We ran back toward our neighborhood, the entire way my friends looking at me with a new level of respect and admiration. I was a bit shaky but I felt really good. I felt I had stood up for my friends. Eventually we turned the animosity between us and the Jokers into more constructive energies, taking out our aggressions by challenging each other to play tackle football.

My own reputation as a tough kid reached another dimension in junior high school, when I was in ninth grade and 14 years old. The Panthers had been in existence for nearly a year. We were mostly a force unto ourselves, gathering in our own territory at the dead-end at Gale Place, or in The Cove, especially on the weekends and evenings if homework didn't shackle us inside. When we would walk through the neighborhood, either to the playground or to EM's, especially in our Panther-emblem dungaree jackets, we *knew* we were something, and we tried hard to talk, act and saunter like we were. Some of the parents and elders in the neighborhood looked at us in a tsk-tsking sort of way, thinking we were either being silly and wasting our time or misguided troublemakers destined for no good. We usually just stared back at them in disdain, knowing full well that they were just too old to understand.

One spring day during our post-lunch break in the Tetard schoolyard, we were playing our usual keep-away game using a ball of rolled-up tin foil, garnered from the preferred wrapping that our mothers used to preserve the freshness of our sandwiches. We'd designate someone as "it" and we would then toss the tin-foil ball over their heads to each other as they tried to grab it. Whoever threw the ball, or dropped it, and allowed the person in the middle to get it, was the next "it," forced to run frantically around to the sounds of our laughter. This time someone threw it way over the head of their intended recipient and it bounced and rolled right into the clutches of Mackey Hagan, an arrogant, pugnacious bully feared by many in Tetard. Hagan was part of the Bailey Avenue crowd and was always surrounded by three or four other Irish toughs. When asked to give the tin-foil ball back he sneeringly refused. When asked again he not only refused, he pushed one of our friends to the ground in response. This was too much for me.

I walked over and stood in front of him, feeling determined to right this wrong here and now. I held out my hand and asked him for the tin foil. Around me, almost imperceptibly and on cue, the noise in the schoolyard suddenly ratcheted down a notch; even Mr. Hecht, a science teacher and our faculty monitor for the recess, turned to observe. I repeated my request and when he refused I pushed him and said "Give it to me." Now the schoolyard was deathly quiet as the tension eerily made its way throughout the entire crowd. Hagan again refused and this time dropped the tin foil on the ground, taking up a fighting stance, smiling all the while. His minions smiled in unison and stepped back to give us room. I balled my fists, raised my arms like a classic boxer, and waited. He suddenly swung his right hand in an arcing motion toward my head. I crouched slightly, blocking his punch with my left arm, like I had seen in dozens of Westerns, and countered with a right hand of my own. My fist smashed perfectly into the side of his jaw and he went down like a deflated balloon; I was on top of him faster than he or his friends could react. I rained punch after punch upon his head and face as he squirmed to cover up, releasing all of my anger at the injustice of his bullying and feeling the righteousness of sticking up for my friends. No one moved, not even Mr. Hecht. Suddenly it was over, Hagan signaling he was through, his friends paralyzed in shock and me motionless above his sprawled-out form. His friends picked him up, hissing that they would get me for this, and the schoolyard slowly returned to life. I walked over to my friends who surrounded me with shouts of victory and with pats on the back. Mr. Hecht came over and whispered, "Good job."

At the end of the day, as we were leaving the building, Hagan appeared and said he wanted to fight me again. I said okay. He said we should do it away from the school and I agreed. So, accompanied by a group of my friends, I followed Hagan and his entourage down the stone steps that led to Kingsbridge Terrace right below the school. He led us into an apartment building and we all followed him and his guys to the rooftop where he had what he thought would be my certain comeuppance. As I emerged onto the roof I was confronted by Hagan's ace-in-the-hole, a guy who was older, bigger, and clearly brought in to avenge Hagan and to pummel me. It turned out that this was John, the same guy who had warned me not to ever date his girlfriend back in eighth grade. As we both recognized each other, I knew I was in for a serious beating since John was already a senior in Clinton High School and way tougher than I was. As John nodded a smirking hello in recognition of me and our earlier meeting under similar tense circumstances, I braced myself for what was to come. After a few minutes of considering the whole situation, perhaps detecting irony where the rest of us junior-high-schoolers couldn't, John turned to Hagan and slowly, derisively, said, "Fight your own fucking battles" and disappeared. Hagan looked even more deflated than when I clocked him. Even his friends sagged a bit in the wake of their hero's departure. Hagan and I looked at each other and it was clear that he was not going to fight me again, not here and not ever. My friends and I turned and left. I breathed a deep sigh of relief at how whimsical fate had saved my ass that afternoon.

IT JUST WASN'T IN MY NATURE to conjure or adopt any kind of serious tough-guy persona, but in the 1950s and 1960s, guys were supposed to be tough – especially in the Bronx. Tough was cool. Tough was not being a girl, a sissy, a faggot, or a pussy. If you were tough you stood your ground; if you weren't you got pushed around. If you were tough most people gave you a wide berth; but sometimes if you were tough people came looking for you. Maybe the news spread through the Bailey Avenue network that I had kicked Mackey Hagan's ass, disturbing something tribal in the Irish psyche, but one day not long after I had an unexpected visitor.

It was hot and humid. I was leaning against the chain-link fence that enclosed one side of the basketball courts. My shirt was off and I was sweating from the full-court basketball game my team had just lost. I had next game and was waiting so the team I had assembled could return and take on the winners. Suddenly I saw Mikey Watts approaching. He had peeled off from a group of guys who were making their way toward a hole in the fence and heading into the golf course. Under one arm he carried a plain brown grocery bag crumpled down tightly over the contents. He stopped in front of me and looked me directly in the eyes. Mikey Watts was about a half-a-head shorter than me and at first glance did not seem a threatening presence, but everyone knew he was Alfie Watts' older and tougher brother, one of the mad Irish guys from Bailey Avenue. He stood silently in front of me, our faces almost touching. Slowly, he reached into his pocket and withdrew a metal can opener and placed the sharp, pointed end against the spot at the bridge of my nose, right between my eyes. "I've been hearing about you, Tommy," he said. "I know that we are going to fight one of these days." I could feel the point of the can opener pressing insistently between my eyebrows. "But it ain't happening today. Today I am going into the golf course to drink these beers," he said, his eyes indicating the package cradled under his arm. "See you around." With that, Mikey Watts turned and walked away. As I was beginning to learn in my adolescent stumbles, sometimes in the Bronx this is just the way it is.

GRADUATING TETARD JUNIOR HIGH SCHOOL 143 and heading off to serve three years in De Witt Clinton High School held its own terrors. This was brought home to me one day close to the end of my time at Tetard. Dennis Blumstein and I were walking home from school through Pigeon Park. Another guy, older and bigger than us and clearly coming from the direction of Clinton, was walking through the park toward us. As we came together he stopped and asked me if I was going to Clinton next year. I said that I was and he immediately hauled off and punched me in the stomach. As I doubled over and fell to the ground, tears welling in my eyes and mouth sucking for air, I heard him say, "Well, I guess I'll see you there" before he continued on his way.

Clinton High School squatted with institutional foreboding two blocks from my house, across Sedgwick Avenue, right near the reservoir. It was three stories high with a central tower rising to create a fourth story above the front entrance, topped with copper roofing which gave it a pale green hue at certain times of day. Emerging southwards out of the main building that held classrooms and the auditorium, was another, squat three-story structure that housed two full gymnasiums on the top two floors (one with a raised indoor track suspended from the ceiling that required 17 laps in order to cover a mile, the other for Clinton's basketball home games). The bottom floor contained the swimming pool and a few smaller, specialized workout rooms. Clinton was the Bronx's designated all-male high school (Walton, located just southeast along Reservoir Avenue, was the all-girls high school). Over 6,500 boys spent some portion of their weekdays inside the halls of "De Witt C," as the school's fight song began. Everyone was subjected to a staggered class schedule that could begin as early as 7:15 in the morning. No matter what time you had to be in school you were guaranteed to be mere flotsam and jetsam in a turbulent sea of maleness – a seething *male*-strom, if you will. During class change thousands of boys filled the halls of the school, percolating with a barely controlled desire to bust down the walls and escape or, barring that, find someone or something to vent frustrations on. As a soon-to-be newly arriving 10th grader, I wasn't about to call any unnecessary attention to myself by wearing my Panther jacket into this unruly madhouse. High school would soon demand new and creative ways of navigating my coming of age.

Chapter Thirteen
Music to My Ears

*P*erhaps *it was my grandparents' advanced ages. Or the strict German Protestantism of my grandfather, where the sounds of singing, or hands clapping, or images of proximal bodies gyrating in rhythm to the music were deemed sinful and therefore* verboten. *Perhaps the experiences of demanding lives, pressed dysfunctionally under one roof, had just wrung all the joy out of the adults living at 3987 Saxon Avenue. Whatever it was, the sound of music was rarely heard in the house throughout my entire elementary school years. Not even Christmas music was played. There was one sanctified exception:* The Lawrence Welk Show *every Saturday night. This was at the top of the list of my grandfather's three favorite television shows – including* The Ed Sullivan Show *and professional wrestling – and his only consistently must-see show. Every Saturday night the entire family gathered in the living room to partake in Welk's traditionalism (for us kids it was either suffering through this or go to bed, something to which we never voluntarily acquiesced).*

Once seated and silenced we weathered the old-fashioned tunes, the waltzes, the polkas, the accordion solos, and the bubble machine attempting to make real the show's tag-line: "champagne music." The one saving grace for me as I got a bit older, that enabled me to not run screaming from the living room, was my developing crush on the show's renowned female singing quartet. By the time fifth grade arrived, along with burgeoning hormones, school dances, and the growing suspicion that girls were more than just playmates with longer hair, I actively marshaled my reserves to bear another Saturday night with Lawrence Welk just to get a glimpse of the dreamy Lennon Sisters. After a steady starvation diet of this old folks' music, I was completely unprepared – and completely turned inside-out – by the door-smashing arrival of rock-and-roll into my world.

* * * * *

JUST BEFORE MY COUSIN BRIAN entered the Navy at the age of seventeen, with a signed consent from his father, he visited me bearing gifts. Brian was in the process of paring down his material life in preparation for his departure into the arms of Uncle Sam. Given the escalating ground war in Vietnam, the Navy was seen as a softer, safer place to be by many; images of visiting exotic ports-of-call rather than slogging through the muddy jungles of Southeast Asia were much more appealing. One of the items Brian bequeathed to me was his short-wave radio. I was mesmerized. It was black, squat and heavy, and at night from behind its glass window where the bandwidths were read, an amber glow beckoned like a primitive campfire. Sometimes I would lie on my bed, long after everyone was asleep, and listen to languages I had no knowledge of: Russian, Spanish, English with a British accent, Voice of America and Radio Free Europe broadcasts, and wonder about the wide world so far away out there. The radio became a portal for me to look beyond home and imagine myself a part of something bigger. Along with this imagining came the idea that someday I would escape into that world in a bid to shed all my perceived shackles.

Yet even more vitally, the short-wave radio provided something else that was so profound to my thirteen-year-old soul. It connected me directly to the music that was shaping the psyche of my friends and me. I no longer had to hear music on one of my friends' transistor radios, or look longingly at the collection of 45's spinning on the record player at a party.

The first song I heard blasting over the airwaves and filling my bedroom was on WABC's "Cousin' Brucie" show. On that June evening in 1964, "Going to the Chapel of Love," by the Dixie Cups, the number one song for most of the month, rattled me. Compared to the other Top 40 songs, this was a light, trite song about getting married, something that was so far out of my imagination as to be a completely alien idea. Still, I memorized it immediately and sang it out loud whenever it was played which, given its number-one status, was about every hour. Regardless of the song's content it provided me a key to another realm, a place where my parched and desiccated spirit could drink freely from streams of music that percolated from aquifers so radically different than the ones fed by Lawrence Welk. What better moment for Brian's largesse than mere months after The Beatles' appearance on the Ed Sullivan Show, February 9.

On that jaw-dropping night, even the usual stolid and conservative energy that normally permeated our living room whenever the television was on was no match for The Beatles. We all sat there stunned. My mother and grandmother, slowing shaking their heads in a silent

164

disapproval of what they were beholding; my sister, simply happy to be there at all, bobbing her head to the music. Me? I was completely blown away, like Moses being handed the Ten Commandments by a transcendent entity. For the first time since they moved away, I was glad that my Uncle Chuck and my cousins Brian and Ned weren't there. All I could imagine was all of them jeering about how the Beatles' long hair proved they must be faggots. I don't think I could've restrained myself in the face of such disrespect.

Each song that night shot through my veins with a jolt. First, I watched as "All My Loving" wrapped its words around the hearts of every girl in the audience and I wordlessly joined them in their screaming. Next, the lover's serenade, "Till There Was You," made romance suddenly palatable to my budding, confused teenage self. The final song in the first set was "She Loves You," and that brought down the house. Even with a commercial break and the rest of Ed Sullivan's guests, I barely recovered by the time the second set commenced. When "I Saw Her Standing There," burst forth, I had to control myself from leaping to my feet and dancing up the walls and across the ceiling of my living room. When The Beatles signed off with "I Want to Hold Your Hand," I was smitten beyond belief.

As I looked around at the faces of my family members, I knew in that moment that I wasn't really a part of them. I felt like my world had just been shattered open while their world had slammed shut as a result of their shock and rejection of what we had all just witnessed. Beyond explanation and beyond my conscious awareness it felt like a path, vibrating with colorful paisley, had suddenly diverged from the drab and sepia road being offered by my family's values: go to college, get a good job, get married, raise a family, retire and then die. I suppose if they had seemed happy or engaged with their lives I might have felt different. But they had always looked so sad and angry and despondent; even now, after witnessing something that I beheld as miraculous, they were unmoved. I was inspired and determined to choose a more life-affirming path, even if I had to blaze it myself.

Suddenly The Beatles were everywhere. As a result of the Ed Sullivan Show they trampled Bobby Vinton's "There I've Said It Again" right out of the number-one spot and claimed the top position with three different songs over the next three months. Before 1964 was over another three Beatles songs would sit atop the charts. More importantly they were embedding themselves in our hearts and minds. Girls wept tears of joy at the mere mention of their names, John, Paul, George and Ringo; boys altered their hairstyles in imitation; people everywhere were singing and dancing to their songs; romance, and a softer, gentler innocence were once again in the air mere months after JFK's assassination.

What I saw in The Beatles was a bridge to a new style of masculinity. With their tenderness, their silliness, their devil-may-care *joie de vivre*, their lyrics of love and heartbreak willingly and openly confessed, I felt a new image being offered of what it meant to be a man. Theirs was a sharp departure from the schizophrenic oscillations between cold aloofness and jealous possessiveness that had passed for decades as the way for men to relate to women and to the world. Previously, my only choices were suppressing all my emotions but anger, forcibly quelling and hiding my own tears, looking at girls as objects and only a means to one particular end, and, under no circumstances, was I ever to admit to feeling pain. Somehow, to my eyes, The Beatles made all this seem ridiculous.

ONCE I WAS TUNED INTO THE RADIO and learning more and more about the songs and bands, it wasn't long before I convinced my mother to buy me a record player that could be carried to dance parties – or socials, as we called them. It was a little square box that allowed for the playing of either a single album or, with a plastic insert, could be adjusted to playing a single 45 rpm record. There was also a tower-shaped adapter that accommodated about ten 45's, allowing them to drop automatically when one song was finished so you did not have to manually change the records each time and could keep dancing. I also had a small file box with a latching top and a handle in which to store, behind alphabetically arranged index cards, my small but growing collection of 45's. At less than a dollar each, and with two songs by a favorite artist on the A and B sides, this was musical bliss that even with my meagre allowance I could not afford to miss. So, whenever we got our weekly allotment, my friends and I hopped a bus and flocked to Cousins, or to Sam Goody's, or to the Spinning Disc.

I was so entranced by my newfound discovery of music that I ended up joining the mail-order Columbia Record Club, where I was initially seduced by the "3 Albums for Twenty-Five Cents" offer. What I didn't understand was not simply the fact that I had to purchase an album each month (at a price I certainly could not readily afford), but also that they pre-selected that month's offering so that I either had to refuse it and choose one to my liking, or be automatically sent their selection. By the end of the year-long commitment and after receiving a few unwanted "Sound Effects" albums along with severe chastisement from my mother for costing her this monthly outlay for my music (over and above my allowance), I was happily done with the Columbia Record Club. But this music was part of me now and Lawrence Welk's bubble machine lay in a heap, my memory banks scrubbed of accordion music for good.

Not being anywhere near musically inclined (I was convinced early on by peoples' response to my singing that I had a tin ear and a horrible voice), my appreciation for the songs that populated the radio waves became less about their musicality. I became more deeply attached to the poetry of the lyrics. I was compelled, oftentimes to tears, by how the words touched or evoked feelings I was having that I could not articulate, either to my friends or to myself. In this way the music clarified and crystallized my hopes and dreams and fears, and held them up to me like a mirror where I could gather my thoughts and see who I really was in that moment.

My taste in music was completely mood driven and context based. When I was with my friends and a Four Seasons song came on, like "Sherry," or "Big Girls Don't Cry," we all desperately tried to match Frankie Valli's falsetto, so much so that we quickly devolved into a cacophonous caterwauling that had others grimacing and covering their ears. Whenever the distinctive Motown sound wafted across the airwaves it was time to sing *and* dance (as best I could) to the likes of The Supremes, The Four Tops, The Temptations, Little Stevie Wonder, The Impressions, Anthony and the Imperials, Martha and the Vandellas, Marvin Gaye, Gladys Knight and the Pips, Smokey Robinson and the Miracles, and more. Every song exhorted us that the time was right for dancing in the streets. This was the indelible sound of Black urban America and it infiltrated our white neighborhood and galvanized us with music and lyrics that went beyond skin color.

At the other end of the spectrum, the Beach Boys sent our imaginations California dreaming and had us all trying to visualize a world filled with beach sand, surfing, drag races, and bikinis. So inspired were we by this West Coast fantasy, that Jacob Schenck and I, co-founders of our gang The Panthers, would race to his apartment after school each day and tune into *Never Too Young*, our own age-group soap opera set in Malibu, California.

At another point along the musical spectrum, the bad-boy Rolling Stones jacked up our energy and "Satisfaction" became an anthem of sorts signaling our growing discontent with the endless materialism that we felt was being fed us. "Paint It Black" was raw and offered me a contemplative moment whenever I was disconsolate in my growing pains. As I became more worldly wise, Creedence Clearwater Revival offered an anti-establishment political edge in "Who'll Stop the Rain" and "Fortunate Son," while providing us with an over-the-top dance groove in the 11-minute break in "I Heard it Through the Grapevine."

The mellifluous voices of Simon & Garfunkel transported me to an entirely different and more depthful level of introspection. The first time I heard them sing "Richard Corey," it was like I was pulled through an existential wringer and deposited on the other side with a completely different perspective on the human condition. Paul Simon's lyrics sent out shards of poetic insight that lacerated whatever pretenses blocked me from being real with myself. Whenever I heard "I am a Rock," or "Sounds of Silence," new and insightful avenues of thought and feeling were revealed. Theirs was a musical profundity that always stopped me in my tracks.

When drugs began to reshape the doors of perception, the music took me to new dimensions. Vivid summer days dropping acid, sprawled on the floor of Kevin's house listening to The Young Rascals sing "Groovin'," tumbled me gently into dreamy states of carefree, psychedelic bliss. On the other hand, listening to The Yardbirds' "Over Under Sideways Down" and "Heart Full of Soul," in the dark and shadowy confines of Steven Pascal's apartment after ingesting LSD, was way beyond trippy. When Grace Slick and the Jefferson Airplane seduced with "White Rabbit," we nodded knowingly to each other that indeed we were experiencing the pills making us larger and smaller. Iron Butterfly's "In-A-Gadda-Da-Vida" sent paroxysms of tribal energies straight through us. Jimi Hendrix's surreal guitar playing mesmerized us, as did his voice on "The Wind Cries Mary," "Foxy Lady," and especially "Are You Experienced?" Janis Joplin, with her signature bottle of Southern Comfort, offered us new definitions of soulful with her rendition of "Summertime," "Piece of my Heart," and "Down on Me."

GOING TO CONCERTS quickly became important and a sure-fire way to demonstrate that you were really into music and really cool, but for me they were simply too expensive. Despite my lack of money, though, I did save up enough to make it to see Traffic, Blue Cheer, and Iron Butterfly all on the same bill at the Fillmore East on 11th Street in the East Village. In those few hours, pressed flesh to flesh with worshipful kids just like me, I felt lifted right out of my mundane life. Thanks to one of my friends buying me a ticket, I also had the good fortune of witnessing The Chambers Brothers in an amazing concert at The Electric Circus on St. Mark's Place. What was memorable about this concert was, first, that during the opening set the Chambers Brothers were backed up by the otherworldly voices of a gospel choir, something I had never heard before. Second, I got to stand next to Willie Chambers at the urinal during the break. In the last set they ripped into a beautifully endless version of "Time" that sent me beyond the confines of Earth and into my own orbit.

But perhaps the most profound, the most cerebral, the most kindred to my growing spirit of rebelling against a society rife with hypocrisy and injustice, was Bob Dylan. He called out the deadening nature of

American life and the absurdity of playing the "be-successful/get-ahead" game. More importantly, simultaneous with my growing awareness of the war in Vietnam and the Civil Right movement, Dylan seemed to come up with song after song that tilted me off my complacency or deepened my desire to make the world a better place. Whether it was "Masters of War," "Blowin' in the Wind," "The Lonesome Death of Hattie Carroll," "The Chimes of Freedom," or "A Hard Rain's a-Gonna Fall," Dylan was an unrelenting social *tummler*, a tweaker of our collective conscience, and I loved it . . . and him. I took his songs as sacred vows, solidifying my developing commitment and idealism to do something to make the world more just, fairer, and a more peaceful place for all of us to live.

Yet, ultimately, it seemed my friends and I always returned to The Beatles. When Michael Abrams was the first one to buy *Sgt. Pepper's Lonely Hearts Club Band*, we gathered at his house as if by telepathy, filling his dimly lit bedroom like a cabal that had just received a secret message from our mystical leaders. We played the album over and over again until the wee hours of the morning. When Adam Sokol appeared one day with the first copy of the two-disc *White Album* (obtained with the help of his father's connections even before the record went on sale), we crowded conspiratorially into his bedroom like we had contraband. We stood or knelt reverently in front of his record player like devotees awaiting anointment to transcendence.

From the moment they appeared on The Ed Sullivan Show singing "I Want to Hold Your Hand," to the arrival of *Abbey Road*, to the sad day on April 10, 1970 when The Beatles broke up, it felt like they walked along with us every step of the way. It seemed that they were influencing us on subliminal levels, growing as we grew, experimenting as we experimented, and suffering joy and heartbreak just as we did.

Chapter Fourteen
The Sheer Poetry of Basketball

When I finally realized that I was good at basketball my entire inner world shifted off its axis. At home I felt less than unwanted; I felt unseen, as if it didn't really matter if I was there or not. Perhaps that's why I got into trouble so often – it was my way of saying, "Hey, I'm over here, look at me." But on the basketball courts everybody noticed, everybody watched. I was an athletic force, lean, tall, with arms like windmills blocking shots, snatching rebounds, and tipping missed shots back in for the score. Since I mostly played center and forward, I began perfecting my hook shot which I could take from either the low-post pivot or moving across the middle just beneath the free-throw line. When, under my Cousin Ned's tutelage, I finally developed an outside jump shot, I no longer had to rely on the one dimension of always being under the boards; now people had to defend me all over the court. I was not particularly graceful, but I possessed a blue-collar ethic and gave everything I had in every game. As one of the older guys once remarked about my presence on the courts, he just "liked to watch me work." I felt as if I'd found the secret poetry of the game in the dueling dance movements with opponents, in the newfound freedom and artistry that every new game offered, and in discovering my own unique self-expression. Perhaps, most importantly, I was sought after to be on everyone's team, and even after losing a game I never sat out waiting for "next."

* * * * *

IT WAS BASKETBALL THAT SAVED MY YOUNG SOUL. Between the relentless self-esteem pummeling that permeated the environment within my grandparents' house, and my utter dislike of the entrapment called "going to school," the playground basketball courts felt like the another place where I gained respect and admiration. It was an uphill struggle that took years to stake a claim as a basketball player in our neighborhood, for we had some excellent talent: Harvey Bender, who at that time held

171

the scoring record at Bronx Science High School; Bobby Carney, who played for Manhattan College; Stevie Greenberg, who honed his skills at an Midwest college; and Steve Young, who was among the original, funniest trash-talkers with skills to back it up.

Throughout most of elementary school I was quite short, usually standing third in line when the teachers organized us by height. During those years my athleticism was expressed and strengthened by running everywhere and fearlessly climbing anything. I filled the daylight hours playing dodgeball, punchball, and a variety of hunt-and-find games like Hide & Seek, Sardines, Follow the Arrow, Ringolevio, Cowboys and Indians, and Army, all of which involved endless chasing and being chased. When I did play basketball at the after school Night Center in P.S. 95, I was ungainly, flailing about, heaving the ball in a one-hand pushing motion. If I tried to dribble the ball it was immediately taken from me by an opposing defender.

Then, between sixth grade and eighth grade, I grew from a diminutive five-foot-one to a towering six-foot-two. While this growth spurt held promise, I remained clumsy, uncoordinated, and continued praying that my highly inaccurate one-handed push shot would eventually go in the basket. The only apparent benefit of my sudden gain in height was that I was taller than most of my friends and by virtue of that fact obtained the lion's share of rebounds in most of our games and, in turn, I made lots of shots from close under the basket. My surge in height also aided in my growing shot-blocking prowess. While I was hardly a force to be reckoned with, especially when playing with the older guys, I was growing to love basketball and could sense with each flash of competency that I might be able to fill the deep hole of inadequacy I always felt gnawing inside.

My first experience with organized basketball was in a league in neighboring Fieldston, organized and directed by Hap Richards. When we were in 6th grade, Levi Mencher, Dennis Blumstein, Gregg Kai, and I and a few others formed a team and had our first taste of refereed games complete with time clocks and free throws. Donned in our yellow t-shirts emblazoned with green numbers on the back, we had flashes of brilliance, especially with the skills brought to the floor by Levi and Gregg, both of whom could dribble like little Harlem Globetrotters as well as shoot accurately. Even though we failed to win a single game and finished last in the league, we could've gotten an award for "most tenacious" since we always showed up and battled to the end, causing fans and opponents alike to cheer us on. As a result of this first league experience the taste of full-court competition was impressed into my body and mind.

IN THE FALL OF 1964, just as I entered ninth grade at Tetard, Barry Roth and I went to try out for the junior varsity basketball team at the Mosholu-Montefiore Community Center. When we both made the team we were elated, especially since we didn't know any of our other teammates; being together, though, we could offer support to each other in this new environment. More importantly, now we were going to play ball under the tutelage of a real coach.

Coach Ron was quiet and steady, extremely personable, more like an older brother than a frustrated adult trying to relive his glory days by coaching kids to fit his image. As a result, we all immediately wanted to do well for Coach Ron. The other thing we enjoyed was the fact that Coach Ron always brought his wife to every game. She was droolingly beautiful to us – percolating hormone factories that we were – and we wanted to show off and do well in her eyes also.

After a few practices Barry was made the off-guard because of his outside shooting skills and his ability to penetrate the middle for slashing drives and, if guarded, dishing off a pass to an open shooter. I, of course, was placed at center. This was a whole new experience for both of us. We had uniforms *and* we had warm-ups, with black pants and a satiny blue pullover with black piping. Our gym was the entire basement of the community center and it had glass backboards, a linoleum-type floor, and a scoreboard and sound system; it was like entering a professional arena. And our coaches demanded we act like professionals too: for our home games we had to wear ties and slacks, while for our away games we had to add a sport coat to our already dapper wardrobe. Once again my athletic pursuits cost my mother money she did not really have, yet somehow she always came through.

Our team played all over New York and even travelled to Connecticut for tournaments, which always meant driving the coaches crazy and sleepless with our antics when we stayed overnight at a local motel. Our biggest nemesis and the usual league champion was the team from Bensonhurst, Brooklyn. They were big and scrappy and had no qualms about trying to knock us out of the game with their physicality, in ways both legitimate and below the belt. With each succeeding game I felt my raw skills becoming honed finer and finer. Under the patient guidance of Coach Ron, I developed from a player who would often foul out to a player who learned to appreciate the movements and patterns of both the players I was guarding and the entire flow of the game. By the time that first season ended, I had added a more complete offensive repertoire to my game, though my outside shot remained suspect. Furthermore, thanks to Coach Ron, I had also added the art of boxing-out to my already strong under-the-boards skill-set, which made my life as a center a whole lot easier. My first season on the junior varsity we finished second behind Bensonhurst, and Barry and I returned to the playground a bit stronger and a bit more skilled. As the season wound to a close we were both being recruited to play on the varsity team for the community center the following season, and that meant playing for Coach Julie.

Coach Julie was an Italian wild-man, with a shock of black hair that touched the bridge of his dark-rimmed glasses. When we practiced we warmed up to the Four Tops singing "My Girl" over the gym's speaker system, one of Coach Julie's favorite songs and one he thought brought an up-tempo energy to our practices. He was the epitome of up-tempo: quick to laugh, loved talking and telling stories, and he loved playing and coaching basketball. He was a bowling-ball type of basketball player who reveled in driving the lanes and knocking defenders down like pins at the end of the alley. His gregariousness was infectious and his angry frustration at bad playing and dumb fouls absolutely paralyzing. We would often stand motionless on the court in utter silence while we waited for his rant to subside. Unlike Coach Ron, who was like our older brother, Coach Julie felt he was one of us and we loved him differently because of that.

As expected, the varsity team demanded another level of skill and physicality than junior varsity. The players were a little older, more skillful, and stronger. Our shooting forward, Joey Figaro lived on the baseline, either shooting from outside when open or slashing to the basket like a razor when he found himself guarded on the outside; Mitch Knorr was our point guard who could readily take and make the open shot or find the open man with uncanny court-sense; Warren Abelman was our 6'4" starting center who, despite being bespectacled and having no meat on his bones, could easily control the jump balls and score down low. Barry became second-string on the varsity while I usually started at power forward, with brief stints at center if Warren got in foul trouble. While I had definitely improved, I still lacked confidence in my shooting and focused instead on rebounding, defense, and starting the fast break off an opponent's missed shot. As varsity players we were grittier and more determined to win than we were as junior varsity players and that had everything to do with the Tasmanian-Devil style and demeanor of Coach Julie.

Game after game we poured our hearts into each competition and every single time left our bodies wrung out by the effort. We sweated with each other and for each other, fighting not to let our teammates down. We had each other's backs and we were seriously in love – with our coach, with each other, and, most potently, with the game itself. At the end of it all we finished in third place and then, just like that, it was over. Each of us was suddenly called elsewhere, to school, to jobs, to other responsibilities. We drifted apart like a disappearing mist, receding back into our respective neighborhoods and lives, rarely seeing or speaking to each other again. For Barry and me that meant going back to the basketball courts of the neighborhood where plenty of hoop action awaited.

THERE WERE FIVE PLACES around our neighborhood where you could play basketball: two indoor gyms and three outdoor courts. For a while De Witt Clinton High School had open gym in the evenings. Its biggest draw was that players could use the same court where the Clinton team played their home games, complete with shiny, springy wooden floors and beautiful glass backboards, the exploits of Willie Worsley, Nate Archibald, and Mike Switzer lingering and inspiring. Even when relegated to half-court games by the size of the evening's turnout, if you happened to be on one of these courts you felt like a pro in Madison Square Garden. Periodically, Gregg Kai, Aron Rose, or Lenny Baumann and I would venture over to Clinton to play. We got a chance to play with black and Puerto Rican guys, which was a rare and welcomed opportunity for us dedicated street-ballers living in a white neighborhood. We always held our own but for some reason, despite Clinton being only blocks away, it never became our favorite place to play basketball. Whether it was the size of the crowds that made for long waits if you lost a game, or the erratic scheduling of when the gym was open, we always gravitated back to the comfort within the confines of our neighborhood.

In the fall and winter we would regularly convene in the third-floor gym at the after-school Night Center in P.S. 95. This venue drew players from our neighborhood and from adjoining neighborhoods as well. The competition was fierce and the only drawback was that it was typically too crowded to play full-court, so 3-on-3 was the game of choice. The basket nearest the gym doors was reserved for the older guys – more than a few of them with college playing experience – and this court saw the most serious action. The opposite court at the far end of the gym was where my age group mostly played. Every so often I would get picked to be on one of the older guy's teams and there I would test my skills against guys stronger and better than me. It was a rough-and-tumble coming-of-age process for me, with guys like Bobby Carney using his quick cross-over dribble to fake me out of my jockstrap and glide past me to score easily. Even my rebounding prowess was put to the test, as I placed my raw athleticism against the skillful boxing-out techniques of Stevie Greenberg or Bill Campion. At game's end I had gotten few rebounds and instead suffered a night of frustration and bruising elbows that battered my ribs as I jockeyed for positon. In every game, and from every opponent, I watched, and studied, and learned another new thing about the art of basketball.

175

There was also a couple of basketball courts wedged into Pigeon Park. One nice feature at this location was that the backboards were attached directly to the fences and, therefore, the absence of a solid steel pole holding them up meant unleashed artistic abandon in juking and spinning when driving in for lay-ups. But even this luxury could not turn this into a place where we were eager to play hoops. Perhaps it was the chain-link nets that dangled menacingly from the rims, ready to snag an errant finger, or the flat, unreliable backboards, or the Friday nights of drinking and broken beer bottles strewn on the courts that would have to be navigated come Saturday morning. Whatever it was, these courts held no appeal and for the most part they remained unused by us.

There was also one lone basketball court that sat ghost-like in the southwest corner of the Big Schoolyard at P.S. 95. This was the province of the kids who chose to hang around this part of the neighborhood rather than at the playground, or chose to have no truck with the Panthers at Gale Place. These were the kids who were studious and identifiably college-bound: Levi Mencher, Dennis Blumstein, Steve Feld, David Gass, Stuie Sitz (and his younger sister Dana), Michael Krakowski, and Malka Blumenthal (one of the few girls who could hold their own in most sports). Because this was their preferred venue, when it came to playing here they owned these courts. They knew every bounce on the pebbled concrete and every sweet spot on both the backboards. Whenever I played there the pavement had no spring, the baskets looked taller than 10 feet, and the thin rusting metal hoops jutted out into the air in a way that offered no real target. It all made for a disorienting perspective and a typically poor game. With my court sense radically discombobulated in this strange, black-hole basketball environment, I unequivocally hated playing on the Big Schoolyard court and avoided it religiously.

As a result of the erratic quality and conditions of the other basketball venues, the heart and soul of neighborhood basketball, therefore, resided in the playground. This became my home. This was the place where I first felt loved and admired from so many in the neighborhood; this is where I first felt sought after, wanted in a way that never manifested in my home life. When my team won, we stayed on the court; when my team lost I was instantly picked to return to the court without having to wait for what could be a number of games, depending on the size of the crowd. I could literally play all day, from ten in the morning until suppertime in the summer and on the weekends.

And I wanted to play all day. I wanted to be seen, to bask in the oohs and aahs when I blocked a shot and sent it flying onto the benches; when I flew upwards into the rarified atmosphere at hoop-level and tipped in an errant shot high above everyone else; when after a rebound I launched a full-court pass for a successful fast break. It was sheer poetry and every move, every scrape of our sneakers, every foul and subsequent argument, and every play – defensively and offensively – sang both within and to my soul. And I danced to that music to the point of ecstasy.

MY RELATIONSHIP WITH BASKETBALL changed dramatically over the summer of 1965. I was 14 years old and I had one year of playing junior varsity for the Mosholu-Montefiore Community Center under my belt. I had also just graduated Tetard Junior High School and was about to enter De Witt Clinton High School that fall. Three years prior, my cousins Brian and Ned and their parents had moved to the suburb of Bronxville in Westchester County, just north of the Bronx. I had only seen them periodically over the years and I missed them all terribly; their absence had removed a buffer between the bitter anger my grandmother seethed with and her favorite targets: my family. With my cousin Brian now in the Navy, there was more room in their apartment which allowed me to visit and spend the night more frequently. This particular summer I made the most of it. Nearly every Saturday I took the earliest bus I could find to Bronxville, spent the night and returned home late afternoon on Sunday. Once I arrived on Saturday, my cousin Ned would call his friend, Mike Dalman, and the three of us would hop into Mike's sports car and patrol the playgrounds of Bronxville looking for three-on-three basketball competitions. We found plenty and we won most of them.

We comprised a threesome with quite complimentary basketball skills. Ned was six-foot-two, wiry, and had an outside jump shot that almost never missed. Mike was quite a bit shorter, but stocky, and he drove the lanes for lay-ups with the aggression of a pulling football lineman, yet with more skill than his bulky appearance would initially portend. I crashed the boards for tip-ins and snatched rebounds like a crazy man. Brandishing all my six-feet-two-inches fearlessly, I could often "sky" high enough to get most of my hand above the rim and as a result this lofty aerie became my domain. If Mike missed a lay-up, I was there to follow it up; if I grabbed a rebound and had no put-back, I fired it outside to Ned and *swish* ... automatic two points! On defense Mike would strip his man almost on the first dribble, Ned would snatch errant passes with uncanny reflexes, and I would block shots like I was Bill Russell. All day we would play, stopping only for some sodas and candy and soft pretzels. When we were done and heading back home, we would revel in our conquests, recalling particular plays that stood out, making each other feel good.

On Sunday mornings before I went back home, in a tiny fenced-in basketball court in the playground below my cousin's apartment, Ned would teach me how to dribble while protecting the ball. More importantly for my skill as a taller player, he taught me how to shoot a jump shot. Over and over again he would pass me the ball and I would dribble once and leap as high as I could, arcing the ball toward the basket. He corrected my form relentlessly, pointing out how I needed to release the ball at the apex of my jump so as to not get the shot blocked. By noon other kids would begin showing up and I would practice my newfound skills in more three-on-three competitions. I ate up Ned's coaching for the entire summer and I got better. By the beginning of high school that fall I was ready to play some serious basketball, both on the Moshulu-Montefiore Community Center varsity team and, more importantly, especially in our neighborhood playground.

WHENEVER THE WEATHER WAS GOOD, be it after school, on the weekends, and especially over the summer months, basketball ruled the playground. Before noon, three-on-three half-court games dominated play. These games had an intensity all their own. Especially when guys like Barry Roth and Aron Rose teamed together and put on a clinic on the grace and beauty of the pick-and-roll; their third teammate became superfluous in the wake of their passing and scoring skills.

Later, as afternoon arrived, and as more and more people began showing up at the playground, the full-court games began in earnest. Oftentimes these contests would pit the guys 20 and older – Freddie Davis, Tom Chartier, Ed Yaker, Paul Birnbaum, Harold Shallin, Eddie Gerwin, Danny Meisner, and the like – versus guys under 20 – me, John Carter, Harry Lefkowitz, Peter Mandel, Gregg Kai, Michael Katz, Kevin Hurley, Barry and Aron. We would battle each other relentlessly, us upstarts seeking to topple the self-proclaimed kings of the courts. These games were always filled with intensity and, as the day wore on, with arguments erupting more frequently as the older guys began compensating for mounting fatigue and age-related slowing of their reaction time with increased intentional fouling. All day long, day in and day out, the full-court dramas would rage, with people lining up at the parkhouse water fountain between games, or grabbing an ice cream from one of the competing vendors regularly stationed in front of The Rail – Uncle John's, Bungalow Bar, Good Humor, or Carvel soft-serve. By mid-afternoon the migration toward EM's would begin. We grabbed sodas, soft pretzels, or candy bars to fuel up before returning to the playground.

But it was during spring break and over the summer when older guys who had played high school or college ball returned to the neighborhood to play. A feeling of rising anticipation would begin weeks in advance. This was when the competition amped up to an incredible intensity. This was an opportunity for glory, for imprinting your basketball prowess on all who were playing and watching by creating an unforgettable play. It was a moment where anyone could become part of the ongoing memory of neighborhood basketball and, perhaps, even an immortal legend.

Stevie Greenberg was always a solid basketball player. Standing six-foot-three, he was strong and quick with an accurate shot. He was always a force in every game he played. The summer he returned from his first year playing college ball it was as if a bionic makeover had taken place. Now he was even stronger, more aggressive, and defensively tenacious. His boxing-out technique was punishing and frustrating. As a big man, given to my style of play under the boards, he became my greatest teacher. I was determined to use everything he taught me on the court against him – and even some of my own creative moves of my own.

During one game, as we battled each other head-to-head under a blazing summer sun, I got a chance to even the score which was decidedly in his favor. On this play I was leading a fast break with my teammate Dennis Blumstein on my right side. Stevie was the sole defender as Dennis and I made our way toward him. Just as I stepped over the free-throw line I launched myself skyward, straight toward the rim, for an attempted lay-in. Stevie closed to meet me, rising up as I elevated, his hand attempting to block my shot. At the apex of my leap, my body still going toward the rim, I realized that he was going to block my lay-up. At that moment I noticed Dennis standing by himself, in perfect position for an easy basket. In one motion I switched the ball from my right hand to my left hand in mid-air and brought my left hand down and around my back, deftly passing the ball to Dennis for the score. The people on the sidelines went crazy and the rest of our teammates looked stunned. When Stevie and I landed, we both looked at each other, my eyes and smile saying "Gotcha!" and his eyes and smile replying, "Next time." These were the kinds of mini-competitions that were always taking place inside the larger game.

Going up against Bobby Carney, who played for Manhattan College, there always seemed to be a one-sided dimension to guarding him – the side where he came out on top. He wasn't tall, perhaps 5' 10", yet he possessed what at first appeared to be a slow, methodical approach but upon closer inspection turned out to be quite mercurial and uncanny. Somehow the bounce of his dribble never went higher than his knees, making stripping the ball from him nearly impossible. Both his hands were equally adept at ball control and he could maneuver through defenders with ease for a graceful lay-up. He rarely out-jumped anyone but by virtue of superior positioning, came away with more than his share of rebounds. His outside shot, from 12-15 feet, was quick and accurate and, with what appeared to be three-dimensional court vision, he could pass in ways that made all his teammates look like scoring machines. Few of us wanted to guard him and all of us wanted to be on his team.

Harvey Bender, who at six-foot-one held the scoring record at Bronx Science High School, was another dominating force in the playground. He had deceptively fast hands, both dribbling and on defense. Dribbling past him was nearly impossible because he pick-pocketed the ball from whoever he was defending almost willfully. He was not much of a jumper but possessed the quickest release in the playground when shooting. Even when I was in his face and leaping to block his shot, it was gone and through the hoop before I even launched. He was the only player who used the metal poles that held up the baskets to his advantage. Like a ballet dancer he would tip-toe along the out-of-bounds line just behind the pole, using the solid metal to screen defenders, slip the ball from hand to hand, and then flip it off the backboard for the score. Whenever I defended Harvey there was at least one moment of full-on embarrassment as he had his way with me. It was always a learning opportunity.

Steve Young lived near the bottom of Snake Hill and did not hang out in the neighborhood except to play basketball. Just shy of six-foot-three he was built solid, as if he was meant to play both shooting guard and mix it up on the inside as well. Steve was one of the original trash talkers but rather than be demeaning he was funny. He'd keep a running tab of the game, especially of his own made baskets: "Steve say shoot, ball say in!" he would announce, laughing. Add this to his defensive prowess and he was good enough in both categories to keep talking virtually non-stop. He could dribble effectively and had a lot of moves to shed defenders and get open shots. Sometimes he would narrate, in third person, his own moves on his way to the basket: "Now he spins. He hesitates and fakes. He's open. Too late for the defender! Swish!" He was always a tenacious match-up for me but even when he beat me I reveled in the sheer joy he brought to the game.

I always got pumped up when any of these players showed up in the playground. I especially looked forward to the spring break when, not only did the weather free us from the indoors and allowed us to return to our favorite basketball courts, but it was the first time since the winter holidays when all the best players appeared *en masse* to duke it out. I refused to miss these games, come hell or high water. In fact, one spring I badly sprained my right ankle after landing on a warped spot in the wooden floor of the P. S. 95 gym. This was barely a week before the coveted games of spring break were going to commence. In desperate determination I went to a surplus store and bought a pair of black Army boots that went up nearly to mid-calf. Clamping down on

180

the laces as tightly as I could, I created a type of splint for my wounded ankle and proceeded to play in every game I could, holding my own despite my injury.

As MY BASKETBALL SKILLS IMPROVED so did my reputation on the court. I was often chosen first when teams were being decided and rarely had to sit out long if my team lost. One afternoon as I was shooting around by myself, I was challenged to a one-on-one game by Bobby Diamond. Bobby was four years older and a solid ball player. He was my height, six-foot-two, but he was a wide-body, thick in the shoulders and midsection and with hips that were hard to get around when he rebounded or when he backed toward the basket for a short turnaround-jumper. Given his bulk, he moved quicker than one would imagine and he had a consistently accurate outside shot. He had been bringing his friend, the actor Elliot Gould to the neighborhood for a taste of playground basketball, but on this occasion he was by himself and he zeroed in on me. Perhaps he'd been noticing my growing competence on the courts and had gotten a hard-on about beating me. Whatever the original motivation, we all knew Bobby was a talker and a gambler, and this match-up was definitely going to involve talking trash and betting cash.

Bobby began working the benches near the basketball courts, challenging anyone and everyone to bet on the outcome of a match-up pitting him against me. I could see that it wasn't easy for people to bet on me since I was still young and honing my skills, but there was also the factor of shutting Bobby up. Finally, Freddie Davis, one of the older, well-respected guys held up a fistful of dollars and said, "I'll take Tommy." This unleashed a frenzy of betting, people lining up to put money on their favorite. Finally, someone was designated to hold all the money and Bobby and I began to shoot around and loosen up. I looked over at the crowd standing around Freddie, who had first bet on me to win, and tried to convey my nervousness and hopefully lower their expectations in case I lost. After all, not only was I playing Bobby one-on-one, but now I had the responsibility of not losing peoples' money on top of that. I was flooded with anxiety but it was quickly eased by a smile and a reassuring glance from Freddie, and words of encouragement coming my way from the ever growing crowd of onlookers.

One-on-one basketball is a game of stamina, intense defense, and lucky bounces. The first player to get 11 points (by ones) was the winner, as long as there was at least a two-point margin of victory; if not, the game went on until someone won by two. If you made a basket it was "loser's out," where your opponent got the ball and was on offense. If you missed a shot, and your opponent rebounded, he had to take the ball back out behind the free-throw line to reset his offense.

Bobby magnanimously allowed me to take the ball out and be on offense first. While the betting was taking place word must have spread as the crowd began to grow and all eyes were focused on the single basketball court closest to the parkhouse. My first move was to try and blow past him for a lay-up but he quickly blocked my way and I missed badly. His ball now. I sagged on defense, thinking that he might use his wide-body and try barreling his way closer to the basket. But with the little space I gave him he quickly released a jump shot for a score. My mistake. 1-0, his favor. My ball. This time I dribbled left. He blocked my way and I spun and dashed across the free throw line; leaping suddenly skyward I arced a hook shot right into the basket. 1-1; my nerves settled.

We battled back and forth, Bobby alternating between backing me down the lane and then turning for his patented jumper, and taking advantage of any lapses in my defense to connect with sweet outside shots that rainbowed in. For my part I relied on my quickness to gather up the rebounds of my missed shots, sometimes maneuvering around him to tip the ball back in for easy scores. I still didn't have complete confidence in my jump shot so I tried a little of his game – backing him down the lane and then executing a hook shot way above his outstretched arm, caroming the ball off the backboard for scores. Every shot made by either of us set off cheers from the crowd. The summer heat was draining us as we dug in, the score see-sawing with no one able to pull away.

Finally it was 11-10, Bobby's favor, and he had the ball after I missed a shot. One more basket by him and the game was over and all the money bet on me would be lost. I could feel the crowd sensing a Bobby Diamond victory. He began his move to finish the game. He dribbled to his right on the outside and I closed to defend. We bumped hips and his bulk backed me off enough for him to square up and shoot. The ball arced upwards, like it had for so many of his other points. I turned to watch while moving toward the basket. It clanged against the front of the rim, bounced upward, spinning toward the hoop but hit the backboard instead and rolled off. A miss. I raced to retrieve the rebound and scurried behind the free-throw line. With Bobby confident that his previous shot was the game winner he allowed himself to get out of position and I raced in for an uncontested lay-up. 11-11, tie game.

Bobby's next shot missed again and I rebounded quickly. He closed to defend me and I moved gracefully across the middle and lofted my running hook shot for a score. 12-11, my favor. The screams from the crowd, especially those who'd bet on me, ricocheted off the buildings across the street and reverberated over the playground. I was pumped up; marshalling all the energy reserves I could gather. Bobby took the ball out and began dribbling, first one way then the opposite way, trying to find an opening in my defense for his outside jump shot. He didn't have much room but he turned and shot anyway. The ball was way off but it ricocheted off the rim with such force that it sailed over my head and back into Bobby's waiting hands. Now there was plenty of space between us and time for him to square up and shoot at his leisure. This was his favorite shot. No way, I thought as I raced toward him. Just as he launched his shot I leaped as high as I could, my right arm extended as if I was trying to touch the clouds. My hand met the ball on its way up and I swatted it behind Bobby. The force of my leap propelled me past Bobby and I scooped up the ball just before it went out of bounds at the half-court line. The crowd was screaming and cheering.

Now I began to dribble, trying to outwit Bobby on my way toward the basket. I moved right, he moved right; I moved left, he moved left, each time cutting me off from getting any closer to the basket. Finally at the top of the key I dribbled right and he went to swipe at the ball. I instantly crossed the ball over to my left hand and he missed, his weight carrying him far enough away from me that I was now free to take an uncontested jump shot. I relaxed, dribbled once, and jumped. It felt like I just kept on rising. With Cousin Ned's voice in my ear I waited until I reached the apex of my elevation and, with the five fingers of my right hand perfectly in place, I calmly released the ball. It floated toward the basket, rotating with precision and accuracy. As it fell through the hoop I felt like I was still up in the air and might never return to earth. 13-11. Victory.

Immediately I was swarmed by people from the benches and the sidelines. I was stunned and elated. In the midst of the crowd Bobby and I hugged and smiled at each other. "Great game," he exclaimed. "You too, Bobby," I replied, and then we lost each other amidst the throng. Freddie made his way over to me and handed me $10, my part of the spoils that day. I thanked him and melted into the embrace of the crowd. It meant everything to me to beat Bobby Diamond, one of the older guys, who was a damn good basketball player and a tough competitor. It felt especially good since money was riding on the game and I came through in the clinch for those who had bet on me. But it meant even more to me to be so lauded, so recognized, so loved in that moment.

I didn't quite have the insight or the capacity to realize it then, but every time I stepped onto the playground basketball courts, I was seeking love. After each blocked shot or above-the-rim escapade, I looked deep into the eyes of my teammates, my friends, hoping that I would find reflections of myself that told me I was okay, that I was good enough, that I was accepted. That's what I wanted to see and that's what I always saw whenever I looked. Always.

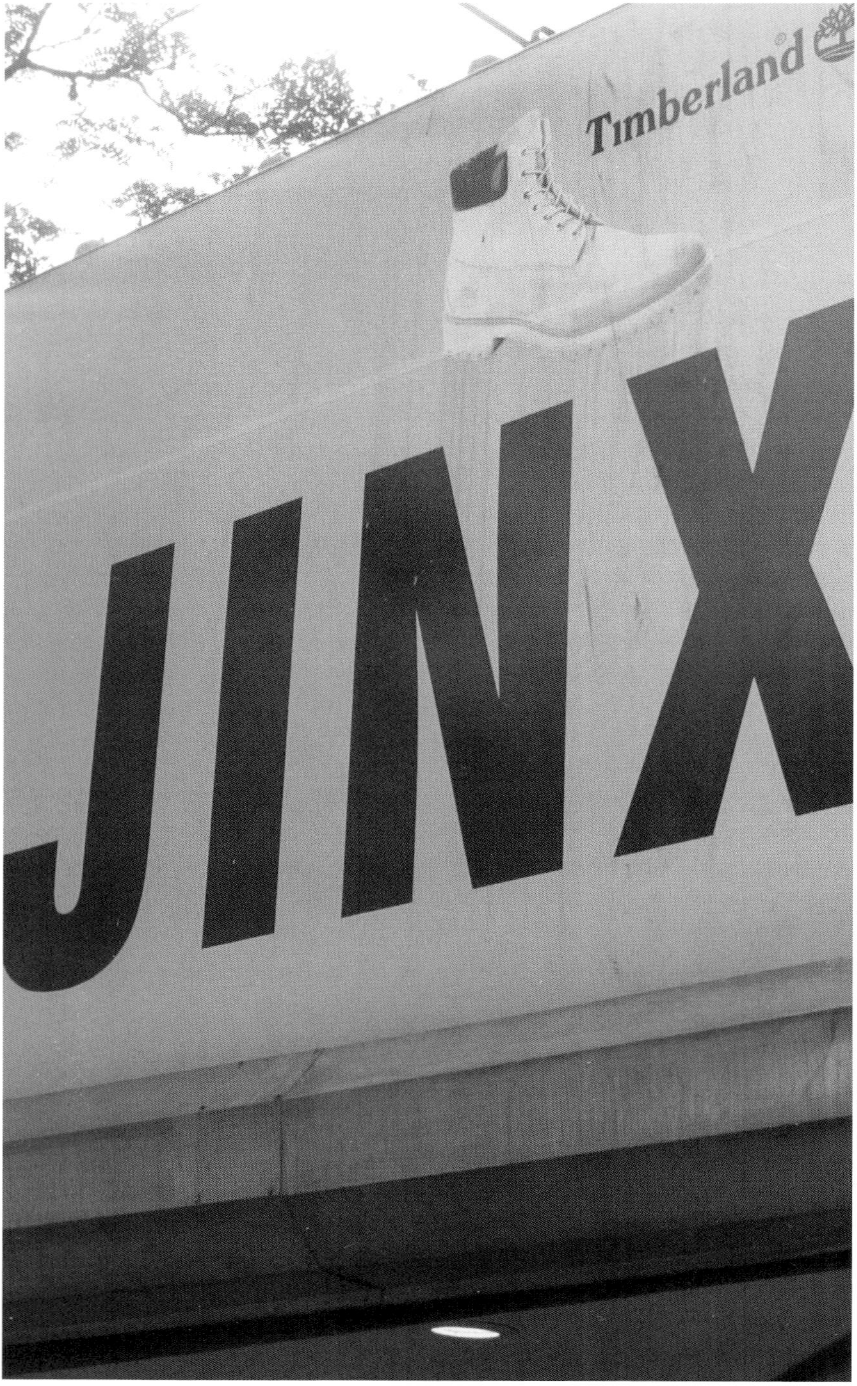
Timberland®
JINX

Chapter Fifteen
Football: Another Kind of Respect

We've been talking to Coach Prezioso about you," Eddie Gerwin explained. Joe Fried stood alongside of him, nodding. "You need to go see him about getting on the team," added Joe. Eddie and Joe had been the coaches for our neighborhood football team and they had watched me develop into a sure-handed receiver. To them it made sense that I should be playing for the same high school team they had played on – De Witt Clinton. It was October 1966 and I was in my junior year at Clinton. Their football season was nearly half over, but the following day I was standing in Coach Prez's office telling him that Eddie and Joe had sent me. He clearly remembered their conversation and without hesitation or even a "welcome aboard," he directed one of the team managers to get me outfitted and assign me a locker. Down in the bowels of the gym building was the football team's lair. I was fitted with cleats and pads, given two jerseys, one red and one white, and assigned a locker. I held up the white jersey, marveling at my good luck to even be on this team. A crimson number 88 shone back at me. It was time to step up into a very different world than neighborhood football.

* * * * *

EVEN WHILE WE WERE FASHIONING our image as Panthers, we were still boys and we loved to play sports. Simultaneous with our efforts to embody coolness as members of a gang, sports – especially football and basketball – had always been venues within which to create a reputation, to gain self-esteem. While many of my friends played little league baseball in grade school or, when they got a little bit older, tried their hands at ice hockey at Kelton's skating rink on Broadway, the equipment for these sports proved too expensive for my mother. Besides, I learned early on by playing stickball with my cousins that I did not like having a ball thrown at me, so that immediately soured me on taking up America's favorite pastime. Further, my one and only time on roller skates sent me crashing painfully into a tree. Given the resulting shoulder dislocation from using skates with four wheels, I could hardly fathom the idea of navigating a sport that required you to speed around on ice with a single blade.

When we were in junior high school two-hand-touch football was played in the playground basketball courts. This was where I first tasted some measure of athletic accolades. Most of the time we had four or five players on each side – a quarterback, one person in the backfield, and two or three linemen. Everyone was an eligible receiver. On defense one player would toss the ball to the quarterback and begin counting: "One Mississippi, Two Mississippi," until they got to Three Mississippi when, at that point, they could rush the quarterback and try to touch him with two hands to affect a "tackle." Each team had four downs to try to score. If on the fourth down the team was too far away from the end-zone they punted the ball, usually by throwing it since our kicking was horrendous. We played in the fall and, every once in a while after a significant snowfall, we'd turn touch into tackle, reveling in the frosty air and the soft landings the snow provided as we pretended to be our favorite N. Y. Giants players.

It was here also that my height came into play. I could catch passes that were over everybody's head and I could defend other receivers due to the length of my arms. On kick returns I could block effectively and even make a little yardage if I was carrying the ball, using my speed and gyrating ability to avoid being touched. It was in these games where I began to become proficient as a receiver. One-handed catches, two-handed catches, passes that were thrown too low or too high, all became opportunities for yardage or scores if I was anywhere near the ball. As we continued playing all of us seemed to improve apace; at the very least we had all gotten bigger and stronger. Halfway through high school, we decided to organize a football team and start playing tackle.

It broke my mother's heart and her pocketbook when I asked her if I could play on the neighborhood tackle football team. At first she adamantly refused, explaining that she did not want me to get hurt. I begged and pleaded, telling her that I didn't want to be the only kid in the neighborhood not on the team. Finally she relented, with these words: "I guess it's okay. After all, I don't want you to become a Mary." Now that my manhood was certified it was time to trek to Hi-Jinx's Sporting Goods on Jerome Avenue – the one-stop shopping destination for all things related to sports. My mother could only afford the essentials (helmet, shoulder pads, a jersey, and a jockstrap and cup), but not football pants with thigh pads, or a pair of cleats. Instead, I resigned myself to playing in my black jeans and my sneakers. Mr. Isaacson, the owner, was really kind in reassuring my mother that I would be safe in

186

the equipment he was suggesting. I remember when he had me don my helmet to check it for fit; he grabbed the face mask and had me move my head up and down and side-to-side, pronouncing it A-Okay. By the time we left with my equipment I was jazzed to be a real football player. My mother was quiet all the way home.

DESPITE THE FACT THAT A SMALL GROUP of us had gone out and purchased identical jerseys – blue, with red and white circling the shoulder where the outer edge of the pads reached – we would always be a ragtag team as we recruited bigger and better players from nearby neighborhoods, each with their own different jerseys. When we were in formation on the field we looked like a patchwork quilt or a team drawn from *The Little Rascals*. At first, we played just like we looked. Games were organized without adult intervention or supervision; we simply had a conversation at school, laid down a challenge, and picked a time and place. Our first game was against our rival gang, The Jokers, from the Jerome Avenue area. For this skirmish we designated Pine Island, across from Clinton's main entrance and approximately midway between our two neighborhoods, as our field of choice.

Pine Island was a tiny sliver of grass and dirt, long enough to play football on but narrow enough to prevent running any serious outside sweeps. There was a slight rise full of pine trees along the Mosholu Parkway side that narrowed the playing area slightly at about midfield, but not enough to pose serious logistical problems. With traffic whizzing by on both sides it was a perfect urban football venue. Fifteen of us met at The Rail on a warm September Saturday morning, carrying our gear, eager and ready to play our first tackle game ever. As we trooped up Van Cortlandt Park South our adrenaline was pumping. When our two teams gathered we immediately set about marking the field, using gym bags as the end zone markers and piles of jackets and sweatshirts to designate the sidelines. We would play 10-minute quarters. We then flipped a coin to decide who would receive the kickoff. We won and both teams slid instinctively into position on their respective sides of the field.

What I discovered on the first play of the game was that I did not like tackling and getting hit. It was one thing during our disorganized practices, when the hits were benign. Here, on the field against another team dead set on driving you into the dirt, it was a whole other reality. It was obvious we were out of our league when, on their opening kickoff, The Jokers started pounding their palms on their thigh pads in unison, creating a rising crescendo as their kicker approached the ball. It was their attempt to intimidate us. They succeeded. But I was determined to be on this team and that meant joining the melee wholeheartedly. Most

187

of us played both offense and defense, but our rudimentary knowledge of the game kept us scurrying around the field like Keystone Cops to get in position for each play. Gregg Kai led our team at quarterback and played in the defensive backfield. Phil Pasternak claimed the position of center and played on the defensive line. Jacob Schenck was one of our running backs and a linebacker, and I played end on offense and in the defensive backfield. Paul Siskin played both ways at tackle and Adam Sokol played defensive safety. It was a harsh reality for all of us as our opponents pummeled us throughout the day.

At quarterback, Gregg had difficulty seeing over the onrushing defensive line; our offensive line could not block well and our runners suffered as a result. We had no set plays, which meant that Gregg had to dream up each play right in the huddle: "Fake run to Jacob. Tommy, you go long." But even when I got open, I was all thumbs, dropping ball after ball in an unusual display of "hearing footsteps" every time the play was designed to go to me. The only saving grace was when Bobby Wexler, the star running back and tough-guy for The Jokers' team, swept around the left end of his offensive line and broke into the open field. It was the final play of the game and insult was about to be added to injury with yet another touchdown. We all turned dejectedly to watch him run toward our end zone. Suddenly, out of nowhere, Adam appeared. Adam was our least physical, least athletic player, more suited to playing music and debating than to tackling an oncoming fullback. Adam stood his ground though, stretching out both arms like a scarecrow. We could feel the arrogance exuding from Wexler as he made his decision to run over and through Adam rather than try to elude him. In the anticipatory silence of both mesmerized teams the impact was explosive. We all thought Adam was dead. But out of the tangle of bodies colliding, Wexler began running over Adam's prone body. Just as he was about to proceed into the end-zone, the toe of Wexler's cleat got caught in Adam's face-mask and down he went, sending up a cloud of dirt. Touchdown denied. We couldn't believe it. Our team instantly swarmed Adam, hoisting him to his feet and dancing around him in celebration; our least likely candidate for the game's hero began laughing and acting like he'd known all along that he would make the play. Momentarily, it felt like we had won the game.

As we shook hands with The Jokers and made our way to the sideline to take off our equipment, Eddie Gerwin and Joe Fried made their way over to where we were changing. They had both played football at De Witt Clinton High School and they continued to play touch football in the Big Schoolyard every Sunday between Labor Day and the first snowfall. They were both good football players, and I had played against Eddie in some full-court basketball games. They explained that they had been watching us play football in the playground over the past few weeks and had tagged along to watch our first tackle game. We listened quietly. As a result of what they had observed they wanted to volunteer as our coaches, to mold us into a more competitive team. We were elated and we all quickly agreed. We immediately scheduled our next practice for Daisy Field, at the bottom of Snake Hill near the entrance to Van Cortlandt Lake and the on-ramp to the Major Deegan Highway.

Word spread quickly that Eddie and Joe were coaching us and that we were looking for more players. We quickly recruited Kevin Hurley, Paul Steinmetz, Jake Carter, and Steve Horowitz to come to the next practice. All these new additions were bigger and stronger than much of our current squad. As practice progressed it became clear that we had some reshuffling to do in a variety of positions to strengthen our team. Kevin could play tight-end and linebacker. Paul was tall and could throw the ball with accuracy and was the natural replacement at quarterback since Gregg had trouble seeing over the opposing linemen; he would move to defensive backfield. Carter was a sure-handed wide receiver and a rangy defensive end, and Steve Horowitz was huge and cat-quick in close quarters and could anchor our line on both offense and defense. Eddie and Joe began the grueling task of taking raw athleticism and enthusiasm, and molding it into something approaching football know-how. They showed us how to block in a way that leveled the opposing player; taught us many of Clinton's running and passing plays. They taught us how to not use our hands on offense by grabbing handfuls of our own jerseys when blocking; taught our linemen how to pull and lead a running play. At the end of the first practice we were exhausted, but as we looked around at each other, breathing heavily and sweating, we knew we were on our way to becoming a team.

A few more after-school practices and we scheduled our next game – a rematch against The Jokers. We played on the scruffy field behind the Clinton gym building. It was an area that was used for outdoor gym classes and it was necklaced by a quarter-mile cinder running track. The entire area sat sunken in a field below street level. This time we were ready to play and on the ensuing kickoff, when The Jokers pounded their thighs, creating that intimidating rumble, we just smiled. It was a titanic battle and with our new players manning their positions it became clear to The Jokers that we had shored up most of our previous weaknesses. Paul could easily throw over the rushing defensive linemen, and Kevin, Carter, and I provided reliable targets for his passes. Our defense was much better stopping their running plays. On one play, Steve Horowitz, playing defensive tackle, recovered a fumble and started running downfield. We knew how strong he was but until that moment

189

we had no idea just how flat-out fast he was as well. His combination of size, speed, and strength sent would-be tacklers flying. Both teams watched in awe as Steve barreled into the end zone for a touchdown.

Toward the end of the game, just after The Jokers scored but were still many points behind us, they kicked off to our team. I was playing on the far right side of the field, preparing to lead the blocking if the play went my way. But the kick sailed all the way over to the left side of the field and as I turned to watch, knowing I was out of the action, Bobby Wexler ran full force into my back, crumpling me to the ground. As I was writhing in pain I saw him look back and smile. I was more shocked than seriously hurt. It was beyond me at that moment to understand the mentality of the cheap shot, imagining as I did that sports were supposed to be fair and sportsmanship imbued players with some notion of nobility. As I slowly walked to the sidelines at the end of our first victory, I knew I would not stoop to that kind of act and I also knew that I would have to be a lot more vigilant because, as I just painfully learned, in the realm of competitive sports some people would do anything to inflict harm on their opponents in order to win.

Our third game was arranged by Lenny Baumann, our de facto and self-appointed emissary to various Bronx neighborhoods. Lenny had gone over to the Marble Hill projects near 225th Street and Broadway, boasting about our football team and suddenly we were squaring off with an all-black team that we really knew very little about. We had heard about the reputations of only two of their players: Kenny Wylie, their quarterback, and Clint Jones, their fullback. Wylie was tall and superbly athletic. He was known to us as one of the smartest and toughest guys in the projects. Jones had played for Clinton and was a powerful runner, with thighs that moved like steel pistons as he shed tacklers and devoured yardage every time he carried the ball. The game was set to be played on a small patch of turf on the Van Cortlandt Park parade grounds, a vast expanse of flatland that spread west from the Van Cortlandt Mansion all the way to Broadway, and was used on the weekends for softball, soccer, horseback riding, and family outings.

We met them on a Saturday morning and while we tried to be nonchalant and go through our warm-up drills, we couldn't help but throw regular, astonished looks at them. Just watching these guys warming up made us feel like we were witnessing a pro team. It was immediately clear that they practiced regularly as they moved through their drills with fluidity and coordination. Unlike our eclectic, colorfully clashing football jerseys, pants, and helmets, every one of their team members was outfitted with matching royal purple jerseys with gold trim around the shoulders, gold pants, and gold helmets like the Fighting Irish of Notre Dame. We immediately took to calling them "The Purples."

It was a long morning for our team. We did our best and succeeded in holding our own for half the game. After witnessing his powerhouse performance during our last game against The Jokers, we had moved Steve Horowitz to fullback and he pummeled his way into the end-zone a few times. Nevertheless, we were clearly outmatched. Kenny Wylie shredded our secondary and Clint Jones had a field day churning out yardage through the middle of our line. The few scores we did manage were obliterated under what felt like an avalanche of touchdowns by The Purples. It was a long walk back to the neighborhood, with the triumphant sounds of our victorious opponents echoing behind us.

AT OUR NEXT PRACTICE Eddie and Joe patiently explained what we did right and what went wrong, rejecting the screaming-coach stereotype. Then they drilled us in overcoming our weak spots; over and over again we worked on new offensive plays and on defensive formations. We were almost as exhausted after practice as we had been at the end of the game with The Purples. As a result we could feel our teamwork begin to gel and our team spirit begin to rise again. After another practice we were ready for another game against The Jokers.

Somehow for this game we got access to the brand new field that Clinton High School was building as the site of its first real home stadium for the football team, finally rejecting the rundown area behind the gym for the relic it had become. There were freshly painted stands rising upwards along one side of the field. A brick locker room for the home team and visitors stood locked behind one of the end zones. There were real goal posts and a sea of fresh green grass beckoned. All it lacked on the day of our game were the chalk lines marking out the field, which we once again solved with gym bags and jackets placed along the sidelines and designating the end zones. It was scheduled to be fully ready for Clinton's Thanksgiving Day home game against traditional rival Monroe High School. On this Sunday morning, though, it was all ours and we reveled in the fact that we were playing on a real football field.

We had recruited a couple of new players. Dave Stolarz was added as a halfback; though not big or particularly strong, he was scrappy and elusive. Bob Glesser joined us as a lineman on both offense and defense. Glesser was a few years older than us, tall and thick and not easily moved. He was also the only one of us playing that day stoned on marijuana. As if to underscore the Trickster nature of his participation, he wore his shoulder pads outside his gray-green hooded sweatshirt, along with an old-fashion helmet with a single face-guard bar, clearly too small for his head, his hair and beard sprouting in all directions. Glesser was ready to have a blast bouncing off other bodies as a kind of peaceful, stoned and spaced-out football warrior. He was a formidable comic sight, easily ignored as not much of a player, which The Jokers did to their misfortune as he ended up wreaking havoc on their offensive backfield throughout the game. Glesser's presence and our recent practices made us all feel loose and ready.

As we warmed up we horsed around, taking action photos that I demanded the guys pose for since my mother had just bought me a new Kodak Brownie Instamatic camera. A few of us even dropped our pants and mooned Clinton High School, just across the way, for the deadening institution it felt like to us. As the game began it became clear that our team was just too fired up after our recent loss and The Jokers felt the brunt of it all. It wasn't much of a game as our offense seemed to stay on the field the entire day. When it was over we were elated and eager for a rematch with The Purples.

IT MUST HAVE BEEN ARRANGED by some adults in the Projects, or someone connected to the Park Department, but somehow our rematch with The Purples got scheduled to be played in Van Cortlandt Stadium. The venue was huge to us, like playing in a professional football stadium. Along the west side of Broadway sat the concrete stands, decorated with wrought-iron railings and circular concrete posts at each stairway. It was ornate, with round, turret-like stanchions at the back corners supporting the stands' steep skyward angle. It was more suited for watching track-and-field events, and schools from all over the city came there to compete. The football field ran north and south. Ragged patches of grass covered most of the field except in the middle, where field events and football games had worn the grass away until it was pebbles and dirt. Circling the entire field was a quarter-mile track.

Our teams arrived simultaneously, this time with a bevy of fans from our respective neighborhoods. As The Purples began to warm up, flashy and smooth as we remembered them, the stands began to fill up. We gathered around Eddie and Joe. Whatever they told us we believed every word. This time we were ready and we knew it and felt it. Our warm-up was quiet and determined; this was serious business to us as we went through some passing and running drills. Throughout our rag-tag season I had gotten better about getting tackled and mixing it up in the fray. Unlike the really good football players I never really enjoyed it, but I was definitely not as gun-shy anymore and today I was more ready than I'd ever been. The signal to start the game roused me from my musings.

The game was our version of smash-mouth football. The Purples ran Clint Jones all day long and, while his legs still moved like pistons, this time our defenders were not about to be pushed aside or run over. Our tacklers dropped below his furious knees and wrapped up his ankles

192

instead; or we gang-tackled him, piling on four or five players to bring him to ground. When Kenny Wylie tried to pass, our onrushing lineman continually disrupted the plays and forced him to scramble. If he did get a pass off our defensive backs either broke up the plays or limited his receivers to short gains. When we were on offense, Steve Horowitz, our freight train of a fullback, did yeoman's work in completely bowling over their defensive line; aided by our now confident linemen, he was simply unstoppable. I caught a few passes for decent yardage and on defense, as a cornerback, I had busted up a number of plays when Wylie tried to pass to the player I was defending. We refused to budge this time; The Purples' intimidating flash faded like the afternoon sun in the face of the grit and grime of our determination.

Late in the third quarter, I was still playing cornerback. As the ball was snapped it was like I had been inside their huddle; I just knew the play was coming my way. I watched as their split end started to race down the sideline. I back-pedaled just to keep him in front of me, but I sensed this was not going to be a long, downfield throw. Three steps in front of me he turned suddenly and sprinted straight across the middle of the field between our linebackers and our defensive backs. Just before he pivoted, I moved to close the gap, riding him just off his right shoulder. Wylie had thrown the ball just before his receiver made his cut. It was an excellent, on-target pass, but I was there. As the ball sped over the outstretched arms of our linemen I pushed myself to another gear and cut right in front and intercepted the ball. As I looked up all I could see was an open lane straight to the end zone. I tucked the ball and took off, completely oblivious to anyone around me. It was like slow motion as I scampered in for the score. As I ran to the sidelines, my teammates began cheering and patting me on my shoulder pads and helmet. Later they would tell me that I had eluded numerous defenders, but I was so in the zone that it felt like I was running on the field all by myself. It was on the basis of my performance in this game, my steady improvement as a player, and the fact that in the playground I could catch anything thrown to me, that Eddie and Joe set up a meeting between me and Coach Joe Prezioso.

As a result of my joining the Clinton team, the game against The Purples was my last game of neighborhood tackle football. It turned out this was also to be the last game for our team. As autumn began to fade and the chill of winter began being felt just over the horizon, people began turning their attention to school, homework, and other pursuits. Our one and only tackle football season was over just like that, but we continued to revel in the camaraderie that was built by our coaches, immersed for a while longer in the wonderful feelings that Eddie's and Joe's belief in us had coaxed to the surface.

DE WITT CLINTON FOOTBALL HAD A STORIED TRADITION among New York City high schools. As an all-boys' school with thousands of students to choose from, it was never difficult to build quality teams in nearly every sport, from basketball to bowling. On the walls of the gym building, on each of the three floors, were pictures of the sports teams that Clinton had fielded over the years, especially in football. Historically, three things seemed inextricably linked, even synonymous, when one looked back over the decades of New York City high school football: Clinton, Coach Doc Weidman, and regular contention for City Champs.

When I arrived on the team the glory days for football were clearly starting to fade. Doc Weidman had retired, replaced by his former assistant, Joe Prezioso. Basketball, fresh off a championship season with Nate "Tiny" Archibald and Mike Switzer, was definitely the king. With the football season just half over, the team was already sporting a losing record. As an unproven, late arrival, I was made third-string end, playing both offense and defense. What this meant was mostly duty on special teams or, if the score was lopsided one way or the other, I might see some playing time toward the end of the game. But I was loving being on the team.

After one week of daily after-school practices I went up to Hi-Jinx on Jerome Avenue to order my team jacket. Rather than the classic letterman's jacket, I chose the loden coat (or benchwarmer coat as they were affectionately known) that came down to my knees, sported a hood, had snaps for buttons, and made me look bigger and broader than I was. The coat was black and heavy wool. Over my heart was a white football-shaped patch, with "Tommy" embroidered across it in red thread. On my right shoulder was sewn my number, 88. Wearing this jacket around school and on the streets gave me a sense of belonging to something bigger than myself, similar to what my Panther jacket had done but now on a much larger stage. In Clinton's hallways during class change, people moved out of my way, instinctively knowing that if you messed with one football player you messed with the whole team. In what felt faster than a New York minute, I had moved out of the shadows of anonymity within a sea of 6,500 boys and into the light of being a Clinton footballer. Significantly, the power went far beyond the halls of Clinton.

One night, some friends and I were on our way to a party at an apartment on the other side of the reservoir, near Tetard Junior High School. We were in front of the building trying to find the right doorbell to ring when a group of guys, not recognizing us as familiar faces from their neighborhood, started to hassle us. It looked like it might erupt into a fight until I stepped from the darkness in my Clinton team jacket. They all turned in my direction, their eyes suddenly wide. I must've looked huge to them. One of them stuttered, "You play for Clinton?" "That's right," I responded in my deepest, most baritone voice, stepping closer to the one who spoke. They silently checked with each other, assessing the now changed situation. "Let's go," another guy mumbled and they skulked off into the night.

JOINING THE CLINTON FOOTBALL TEAM demanded that I make some changes in my habits, especially when it came to getting high. I was committed to being healthy and to not jeopardizing my chances to play next year when I would be a senior. I decided to significantly modify my beer drinking on the weekends, cut out smoking pot entirely, and devote myself to being a football player. The team practiced every day after school, with a much lighter workout on Fridays before our Saturday games. Since Clinton's new football field would not be ready until Thanksgiving, we continued the tradition of practicing on Harris Field, located on the south side of Bronx Science High School. It was a mixture of dirt, pebbles, broken glass from beer bottles, and tufts of grass randomly spotting the surface. The team's favorite part of each after-school practice was jogging from Clinton to Harris Field as a warm-up. With our cleats scraping along the concrete sidewalk like rolling thunder, we would barrel through what we perceived as the less-than-athletically-minded, egg-head students of Bronx Science who were just getting out of school. Amidst their shrieks, we would delight in scattering them off the pavement. We felt big and strong and intimidating and it hyped us up for the grueling practices that waited.

At the daily practices I felt a bit over my head with regard to my strength and skill level, particularly in relation to the starters, and especially with regard to my football killer instinct – or significant lack thereof. Practices meant lots of blocking and lots of tackling, over and over again. One of Coach Prez's favorite drills was to surround a single player with a dozen or so teammates. Then the coach would call the name of one of the players in the outside ring and that player would run full force toward the encircled player who had to block the onrushing guy. The intensity of this drill came from the fact that a player could be called to rush from any direction so the guy in the middle had to be ever-ready, moving his feet constantly and pivoting in expectation of the next onrushing body. Needless to say, I hated this drill with a passion.

One day, after all the warm-ups and drills, I was practicing pass routes with the third-string quarterback while being defended by one of the cornerbacks. I ran a stop-and-go route and my defender bit on my fake just enough for me to get a step on him and race downfield. He was still close but a step behind me when the quarterback launched the ball. It sailed in a perfect arc and my defender and I both leapt skyward. My height and my ability to sell the fake gave me the edge as the ball sailed over his fingers and into my hands. As I cradled the ball to my chest, he tackled me. We both came to a sliding halt at the feet of Coach Prez and Coach Wasserman. "Nice catch, Donovan," was all Coach Prez said as he proceeded toward the starting team. I felt like I was definitely on the team now.

It was shortly after that catch that Coach Prez called me into his office and explained that he had high hopes for me next year, and that he was already talking to the head coach of St. Lawrence University in Upstate New York about a partial scholarship for me. It all depended on how I finished out the year and how hard I worked over the next summer to stay in shape. I was blown away. I thanked him profusely and as I left his office my mind was vibrating with images of going to college and playing football. Given my family's hand-to-mouth existence, and my unshakeable belief that I was really too academically stupid, I had erased college right out of my imagination. But now the prospect suddenly seemed possible.

The rest of the season went smoothly for me even though we continued to lose game after game. I continued to play solidly on special teams without making either outstanding plays or costly mistakes. In one of our last away games, I got put into the line-up as a defensive end late in the game. We were winning and all we had to do was to hold on. Our opponents were driving down the field when I came into the game. I was playing left end and I was determined to show Coach Prez what I could do. On the first play from scrimmage their quarterback dropped back to pass and I raced in untouched and blocked the ball just as he released it. The next play they ran the ball away from my side of the line for little gain. On the third play their quarterback dropped back again, looking for an open receiver. Once more I had a clear line to the passer and I tackled him for a loss. At that point they punted and we eventually ran out the clock for a victory. I was elated when Coach Prez said, "Nice game," as he walked by.

Our final game of the season was on Thanksgiving Day against Monroe High School, located in the Soundview section of the Bronx. We were playing our first game on our brand new home field. It was a brisk autumn day with a clear, sun-filled sky offering little warmth. The stands were filled. That pre-game moment would be the only beautiful spot the entire day as Monroe pummeled us soundly. With their defensive line anchored by six-foot-six Wilbur Young at tackle, we simply could not run to that side of the field nor could we find time to set up for a pass play without him tackling our runner, disrupting the timing of the throw, or sacking our quarterback outright. It was a very long day as the coaching staff sent lineman after lineman to try to fill the breach created by Wilbur Young. At the close of the game I had to face him for four downs. Each time we snapped the ball, I would plow my shoulders into Wilbur Young's midsection as hard as I could. I had negligible effect on him as he would smash his forearm down upon my head and shoulders. Upon impact I would be flattened to the ground, my mouth stuffed with the fresh sown grass, and he would run over me into our backfield. I had never felt so helpless and ineffectual on a football field before. For a brief moment I wondered if college football was really the place for me, but in the next moment I swore that I would work my ass off over the summer and come back bigger and stronger. If I could land a football scholarship to college my entire world would change. Dare I allow myself that dream?

Chapter Sixteen
"And My Soul's been Psycedelicized"

Everything about him was shamanic. The beads he wore, the pouch at his hip, his walking stick, his unruly beard. His pace was slow and his voice was methodical, as if he chewed his words into place before uttering them. Wild, curly brown hair edging below his ears gave him a just-woke-up kind of look, which his hooded eyelids only enhanced. Months ago he had offered to initiate me into the drug culture and I refused. Now, as one of the last of my friends to turn on and smoke pot, I thought I was ready.

* * * * *

THE DRUG SCENE SEEMED TO SPREAD SLOWLY throughout the neighborhood, finger-like wisps of marijuana smoke reaching up and tapping each of us on the shoulder, one after another. It was like the mysterious rabbit-hole in *Alice in Wonderland*, beckoning us to come hither and discover reality anew. When we reached our early teens, it was just a handful of guys a few years older than us – T-man, Ignatz, Big Ed, Morty, Bean, Aidan, Fish, Schnur and a few others – who were the first to begin smoking pot and hashish. We'd see them stoned at The Rail and think they were crazy. When Marvin grew the fingernails of his thumb and index fingers extra-long to serve as a way to hold and smoke a joint down to the tiniest roach without getting burned, we marveled. When Ignatz, in his zealousness for cannabis, actually shaved all the hair off the front of his torso except for a thin, hairy strip that ran from his belly to his chest, and another wooly band that ran across his nipples to form the shape of a "T" (slang for marijuana), we were convinced they really were insane. But their weirdness was surreal in a way that we could not always look away from. In our efforts to deny our growing curiosity we held fast to what our parents said: pot leads to harder drugs, so stay away. These guys were the bad influences we were warned about, the people we were told to avoid. But they were also part of the neighborhood. Whenever they saw us they would tease us by sinisterly asking if we wanted to come into the golf course and get high with them; we nervously and laughingly declined. Instead we turned to our typical choices of beer and booze to brace us into Friday and Saturday nights.

Once we were good and drunk and stumbling around The Rail they'd tease us even more, condescendingly dubbing us the "Alkies," while we referred to them as "Heads." Somewhere in between the drinkers and the potheads, the vast majority of our friends were paying attention to school and their futures, for a time successfully avoiding either polarity. But there were others of us who wanted and needed to belong, and to our way of thinking that meant getting stoned, one way or another.

By the time we were in our mid-teens and in high school, nearly every Friday and Saturday night some combination of, me, Kevin, Carter, Paul Steinmetz, Jerry Penzig, and Dave Stolarz would either trek to one of the Jerome Avenue delis, or to the liquor store at the foot of the Cannon Place stairs, and buy our booze. Someone always had a phony I.D. Once when we didn't have any fake identification they had me put on two coats to look bigger and, along with my height, supposedly older. The proprietor looked me up and down, knowing full well that I was still in high school and underage. I just knew that because of my lame disguise I was going to get busted and tossed out on my ass. For some reason, though, he let it slide and I walked out of the store with eight quarts of Schaeffer beer and bags of munchies to the cheers of my friends. Even those times when we did get carded and refused service, there was always another liquor store or deli within walking distance.

In the summertime especially, we would find some hidden spot to drink our beer (two quarts each), and munch our pretzels and potato chips. If we had purchased our contraband from one of the delis on Jerome Avenue we would walk down Gun Hill Road and duck into a wooded area along the eastern fenced border of the golf course. At other times we would descend into Ghost Town. There we would sit on a fallen tree and crack open our bottles of beer. At some point an inevitable chorus of Bob Dylan's "Rainy Day Woman #12 & 35" would erupt, the cacophony of all of us screeching "everybody must get stoned" barely muffled by the surrounding trees and the earthen embankment of The Plateau. Once, on our way into Ghost Town, a police car drove right onto The Plateau and called us over. They were looking for potheads, they explained, and when we opened our plain brown bags and revealed only our beer they were clearly disappointed. In their frustration they ordered us to open all the bottles and empty them on the ground. They told us to get lost and if they ever saw us there again we would get arrested for drinking in public. Undeterred, we were back in Ghost Town the very next weekend, imbibing and singing and laughing.

If we happened to buy our booze at one of the stores near Bailey Avenue we would make our way into the golf course through one of the holes in the fence nearer to Gale Place. We would find a spot hidden by the tall grass, or meander over to our Cove, and drink and talk for hours. During the winter we would hope for a night when someone's parents were going to be out, which was quite often, and descend upon their apartment. There we would drink and sprawl out around the living room, singing to our favorite records. Otherwise, we shivered on one of the more secluded benches or huddled behind the handball courts as we chugged. Despite the fact that the majority of us typically ended up sloppy drunk, this weekend ritual provided us with a wonderful camaraderie. As the alcohol went down our spirits went up. We talked about our fantasy exploits with girls, argued about the best players and teams and, in one of the only forms of love available to adolescent boys, mercilessly teased each other.

THE FIRST TIME I GOT DRUNK was with Phil Pasternak on the New Year's Eve that ushered 1965 into existence. I had just barely turned fourteen and was halfway through my last year at Tetard Junior High School; Phil was a sophomore at Samuel Gompers Technical High School, studying heating and air conditioning. Phil had called and told me he had a surprise. When he rang my doorbell I raced out of the house, telling my mother I would be home by midnight; it was New Year's Eve after all. Phil had somehow procured a bottle of Old Mr. Boston pre-mixed screwdriver and he flashed me the bottle of liquor from under his coat and we immediately ran across Saxon Avenue. We entered the door to the Canteen, which had long since stopped being locked. Once inside we found the door to the room where the *alte kaker* men played cards and smoked cigars oddly unlocked as well. We entered slowly, as if stepping into a sacred chamber previously off limits. We sat at one of the tables and began sipping the screwdriver mix, both of us grimacing with each swallow, and each swallow getting smaller and smaller as we struggled not to gag. By the time half the bottle was gone we were giggly. We explored the room, finding one deck of cards still out but everything else locked up. In the winter silence, we felt like we were the only ones alive on that New Year's Eve. Before long our taste for drinking became completely subdued. We sat staring at the orange liquid in the half-empty bottle, neither one of us possessing the desire to drink, our taste buds curling up in disgust at the mere thought of another sip. Instead we talked until midnight, philosophizing like only young men can.

We shared our angst about life at home, Phil telling me once again how physically brutal his father was and the intense arguments he would have with his stepmother. I told him about the downright meanness of my grandmother. We both hated being in our homes and fled every chance we could. We forged a deep friendship during these years by escaping every night after dinner to hang out together while the rest of our friends were busy doing homework and living in what we believed were normal families. Our conversations that night were free-ranging, from our delight in reading Tolkien's *Lord of the Rings* trilogy to how far we'd gotten in Ian Fleming's James Bond books; and from how much we hated school, to imagining what it would be like to kiss a girl, or feel a girl up. Phil loved bragging about how he'd already done all sorts of things with girls, but through our mutual laughter we both knew that his exploits were all talk. A few minutes into January 1, we each took one more swig, grimacing as we toasted 1965, and then meandered reluctantly back to our homes.

By the completion of my first year in Clinton and the arrival of summer 1966, the once enthralling notion of being in a gang, of identifying ourselves as Panthers, was seriously fading. Somehow all that now felt childish and drinking felt more adult, another step in our coming-of-age. Instead of hanging out at Gale Place in our Panther jackets, our drinking ritual had begun to shape nearly every Friday and Saturday night. Beer was our typical drink of choice since it went down easier. Our periodic experiences with hard liquor always seemed to lead to throwing up or to belligerent interactions. Yet the scuffles that seemed to naturally attend alcohol consumption – I had a few dust-ups with Kevin and Carter – were quickly forgiven long before the next weekend arrived. After we drank our fill we eventually made it back to The Rail or to some party, all of us loud, boisterous, and obnoxious.

As drunkenness became the desired state, it seemed that we were consuming more and more alcohol, swigging whatever was available, as if we were all in some kind of competition to see who could get the most fucked up. Gone was the idea of just talking together and getting a buzz to enhance our weekend endeavors. At this level of inebriation, it became harder and harder for me to sneak into my house and up to my room without waking my mother. While she suspected that I was drinking my weekends away, her fear that I would turn into my father and her stiff-backed refusal to entertain such a possibility, kept her in vivid denial . . . until one night.

I was stumbling-drunk as I made my way through the front door and up the stairs toward the kitchen. Thinking everyone was asleep, I was shocked to see my mother at the kitchen table when I opened the door from the landing and entered. The scowl on her face said she was clearly waiting up for me. "Are you drunk?" she demanded. "No way," I slurred in response. I began to take slow, exaggerated steps across the kitchen toward the stairway that would lift me to the safety of my bedroom upstairs. It was the walk that my mother had seen my father take a thousand times, the telltale, uncoordinated movements of a drunk. "You son of a bitch," she shrieked. "You are fucking drunk!" Again I steadied myself, refused to answer, and resumed my ambulation in an effort to escape. As I began to squeeze past the refrigerator the whole room spun radically. Instantly losing my balance, I grabbed on to the refrigerator, nearly upending the bulky appliance and sending it crashing to the floor. As I steadied myself, the figure of my grandmother appeared in the doorway to the dining room, her robe clenched tightly in her bloodless hands, staring in disgust. "You are just like your father," my mother howled, tears streaming down her face. Silently, with my head and eyes downcast, I disappeared up to my bedroom, leaving my mother and grandmother staring after me.

The next morning, nursing a screaming hangover, I swore to my mother that I would never drink again. I made every promise I could think of, agreed to her every request, in a desperate effort to repair my mother's mechanism of denial in order to get back in her good graces. After a few hours of agonizing and mutual lamentation over the dangerous road I was on, we were mother and son, peaceable again. My grandmother, on the other hand, had seen enough. She explained to my mother that she was too old for all the mayhem and noise that my sister and I endlessly plagued her with. As for my behavior the night before, she was convinced beyond doubt that I was indeed the incarnation of my Irish drunkard father and she would have no part of it. She had already called her bachelor son, Walter, and set in motion a plan to leave 3987 Saxon Avenue for good and move to Washington, D. C., to live out her days with him. Within weeks Uncle Walter whisked her out of the Bronx and into his home. Once more another relative was leaving without a word of goodbye. I would never see or speak to my grandmother again. But this time I was glad.

It was the repetitious tedium of the weekends, at least as much as being worn down by the puking and the hangovers, which eventually sapped my resolve to never try drugs. As I looked around the neighborhood, we were becoming outnumbered by the potheads. Increasingly, as more and more of us "alkies" transformed into "heads," it seemed that it was just a matter of time before I crossed the line into the land of the Lotus Eaters.

Among my closest friends I was one of the last holdouts to smoke pot. Finally, in the summer of 1966, halfway through my fifteenth year, I made my decision. I had grown tired of so many of my friends going off to get high and me staying back out of fear. Frankly, it was a gnawing loneliness as much as my curiosity that compelled me to take the step I never thought I would take. One thing I was certain about, though, I was not going to do this capriciously; I was very scared and I was determined to find a trusted expert to turn me on. I felt like I needed a ritual of initiation in order to make what I knew was going to be a huge leap into another world.

Despite our age difference, Bob Glesser and I had always been friendly whenever we ran into each other around The Rail or in the playground. He'd watch some of the basketball games and we'd chat a bit about my athleticism and superior playing skills. We all knew he was a pothead yet he never teased me or any of my friends about our weekend drinking; he simply knew what he liked and went about his business. Bob had matter-of-factly offered to get me high once or twice before and I had refused. Now, as I approached this momentous decision, standing on the precipice of what appeared in my beleaguered conscience as a choice between remaining in heaven or toppling into hell, I scanned the neighborhood each day for someone to guide me across this threshold. Bob Glesser appeared to be the only person that made sense to me.

It was late June, school was out and the heat and humidity of the New York summer was in full, sun-drenched display. On the appointed day, Glesser and I met in the playground. As we took what felt like a long, slow walk I could feel every eye in the neighborhood on me. I had told only a few of my friends, who had already started smoking pot, about my plan to get high for the first time with Glesser. Yet to anyone even half aware of the drug scene in the neighborhood, there was no conceivable reason other than getting high that would have Bob Glesser and I disappearing into the golf course together and moving out of sight beyond the grassy hill behind the Sixteenth Green. I knew what I was doing and now it seemed like everyone else knew it too.

We walked in silence until Bob felt we had found the appropriate spot. We sat in the tall grass, under the open sky yet mainly hidden from golfers and Parkies and everyone else. He pulled a pack of Zig-Zag white rolling papers from his shirt pocket. He laid these out on the ground. Then he reached his thumb and forefinger into a grey plastic film canister with a black plastic cover that he had taken from another pocket. He took a pinch of marijuana and spread it on the rolling papers. Within seconds, with barely a twist of his fingers and a slither of his tongue on the gluey edges of the paper, we had, sitting before us, two nearly symmetrical joints. Bob had me pick one up and place it between my lips. As he lit it with his lighter he told me to puff gently and inhale, keeping the smoke in my lungs for as long as I could. As I withdrew the joint from my mouth and held it in my hand, I finally exhaled a huge cloud of smoke. Bob nodded his head, remarking, "Good lungs." Exuding a supremely serene and sagacious countenance, he lit up the second joint and began smoking it. We sat there and smoked the joints slowly, with care and a sense of purpose, ritually savoring the growing feeling of peace and well-being, smiling at each other between tokes.

Few words were uttered, except when Bob asked me how I was doing. I could feel my eyes and body relaxing, getting heavier. I could feel the heat of the sun warming me inside and out. "I felt good," I told him, "really good." When we were finished, Bob suggested we simply sit there and enjoy the fine summer day, and we did, for what seemed like hours. As the heaviness in my body morphed into a generalized mellowness we began to make our way back. I walked as if in a dream, stepping gently in respect to the grass; I never felt so light and in my body at the same time. It was such a good feeling. Re-entry back into the playground caused me to shift suddenly into a sharp-edged feeling of self-consciousness, because I was sure that everybody else knew what had transpired just over the hill in the golf course. With a sudden protective intuition Bob placed his arm around my shoulder in the most reassuring manner, calming me instantly, returning me to my blissful state.

When we arrived at The Rail a few of my friends were waiting in expectant anticipation. They immediately gathered around, patting me on the back, welcoming me into the pothead tribe. As Bob turned and left, quietly disappearing into the neighborhood, I told my friends what an incredible experience I had. For me the Sixties had officially begun. Marijuana had opened my mind and my heart. I had turned on and was definitely tuning in. Dropping out, though, was still a ways off on the horizon.

DURING THE SUMMER OF 1966 it seemed like pot was everywhere. While some of us continued to drink our quarts of beer, the alkies were definitely on the wane and weekend nights imbibing in the park definitely took a backseat to smoking a joint or filling the bowl of a corncob pipe with marijuana. The rituals of rolling joints (which I never mastered), and the process of rigging up a pipe with either perforated tin-foil or a hand-cut fine-meshed metal screen pressed down into the bowl (easily found in the plumbing section of any hardware store), fully occupied us and became art forms for some. Amidst the ubiquitously abundant supply of pot, periodically someone would come along with a deep, earthy greenish-brown ball of hashish to smoke – hash being the concentrated and more potent resins of the pot plant. Beneath the cloud of smoke that enveloped our neighborhood, there was a joyful headiness in the air. A mere five dollars, shared amongst a few friends, would buy a small manila envelope (a nickel bag as we called it) bursting at the seams with pot, enough for a group of people to smoke together. While *caveat emptor* was a wise approach, particularly checking whether the bag was filled with smokeable leaves and not chock full of stems, seeds and twigs, the mood in the neighborhood was gracious and a share-and-share-alike atmosphere prevailed. Part of what cultivated and sustained this generous energy was the fact that smoking pot was a communal exercise that brought people together. Another aspect of this was that pot simply made everyone feel good and mellow and kind toward each other. Perhaps, though, a greater contributor to this was that pot was emblematic of the developing spirit of the Sixties – a spirit of tolerance, acceptance, and love toward all living things. It wasn't long before manifestations of this loving, sharing mood were evident everywhere.

For the first time The Rail itself became the gathering place of multiple generations. We were all magnetized by what felt like a great co-conspiracy to undermine and move beyond the dreary 9-5 lifestyle, beyond the greed and get-ahead-at-all-costs mentality, and beyond war and racism and sexism. The guys and girls who were older, and who previously shunned our group simply because of age differences, were now willing to hang out together and get high; guys we once feared as tough guys to be avoided, were now mellow and human in our eyes – and we in theirs. In any gathering where pot was being smoked, one only had to look around to see men and women from different generations sharing with one another, both the pot and a growing perspective on what constituted a new way of being in the world together. A great leveling was taking place and the whole neighborhood – at least among those of us under the age of 30 – was aswirl in the alchemy of what we felt was a visionary change sweeping the entire country and us along with it.

Between the summers of 1966 and 1968, it was definitely a transitional time for us, very much betwixt and between, a contradictory time characterized by a liminality where the old was fading out but the new was only just getting established. We smoked pot and hash but we still played basketball and football. We still went to our classes in high school, but sometimes we went there stoned. Kevin and I were in our final summer of working at the Bronx Zoo, but every night we would be back in the neighborhood and either drink beer or smoke weed.

One of the biggest transitions was the opening into the world of drugs more generally and what awaited us there. While we had scoffed at the authorities' dire warnings that pot would inevitably lead to the use of heavier and heavier drugs, nonetheless our very decision to smoke marijuana did in fact present us with a pharmaceutical cornucopia of uppers and downers, psilocybin, and LSD, all there for whatever level of experimentation we wanted to risk. It seemed like the *zeitgeist* invited risk and experimentation and, for a while, many of us were all in, boldly making our credo, "Try anything once."

As THE SUMMER OF 1966 faded into autumn, I had quickly gone from being one of the last of my friends to smoke pot to one of the earliest to try

LSD. It seemed like every few weeks someone arrived at The Rail with hits of LSD to sell, marketing their wares with brand names like Orange Sunshine, Micro-dot (drops of acid on paper or sugar cubes), Barrels (due to their cylindrical shape), or Blue Cheer. Each time they showed up I was there, ready and eager to experience an acid trip. Try as I might, I never once was catapulted into the realms of psychedelica. In fact, it wasn't until the seventh time I tried LSD that I finally tripped out. I, Gregg Kai, and an assorted cast of seekers desiring entrance into the mystical Promised Land met at The Rail on a sunny, but chilly, autumn afternoon. The guy who was selling the hits claimed that this acid was pure, direct from the Audsley Laboratories. Whatever it was, we were promised that is was going to be really intense. What we discovered over the course of the next 12 hours was that this acid was so intense, in fact, that one of us would not make it back from this trip ever again.

We all purchased a hit apiece and walked to the water fountain on the side of the parkhouse. We each took turns placing the LSD into our mouths and then lowering our heads so our lips could catch the arcing stream of water. After we all had swallowed the dose we looked into each other's faces with anticipation, wondering when we'd start getting off, when the fun would begin. As we walked back to The Rail to await some signs that this was the real deal, somehow I could sense in my gut that I was definitely not in Kansas anymore and that this seventh time would be the realest deal ever. I didn't have to wait long for the butterflies to begin beating their wings rhythmically against the walls of my solar plexus. It felt like all manner of chemical reactions and responses were unfolding within my body. I looked at my friends, imagining that they were going through the same thing, only to see each of their faces moving and distorting into constantly changing expressions, all of them shadowy, grotesque and disconcerting. The build-up was like the moment when the first roller-coaster car slowly and inexorably makes its way to the peak of the very first drop-off. I knew I was beyond going back and all I could do was hold on tight and exclaim, "Oh shit!"

Someone suggested that we go into the golf course and get away from all the intensifying comings and goings at The Rail and we all agreed. Once away from the eyes of the neighborhood we relaxed as best we could. We began to slowly walk around on the soft grass. We picked up leaves and looked at them, watching their secret patterns reveal themselves to us. Some of us lay down on the grass and watched the clouds, fascinated by their relentlessly shifting shapes, as well as by what we perceived as the direct energy from the heart of the universe that was giving them – and everything else including us – form and substance. When we turned our gaze upon our own hands it was like we had x-ray vision as we peered beneath the skin, beyond the muscles, and watched our blood and our very cells move and flow together, communicating with each other. For the next few hours we all felt a distinct oneness with each other, with our bodies, and with the world around us. We had crossed over and the entire golf course had morphed into a distinctly mystical realm, separated from everything outside in the neighborhood. Within this imagined verdant, undulating bubble we explored and experienced and expanded. We were in a place that we could barely imagine, much less navigate; for a while it was unbelievably magical. Then it all went dark.

Where this trip had taken us thus far was powerful enough, so when the LSD ratcheted up into another level of intensity we were all abruptly and forcefully hurled beyond whatever limits we possessed at that point. First, it was the waning afternoon light and the rising cold that assaulted us. We could feel the chill piercing through our clothes while the lengthening shadows began to turn our golf course wonderland into a writhing and sinister environment. Quickly we headed back through the fence and back to the familiar sanctuary of The Rail. Once there we still could not relax as all of us turned suddenly quiet and introspective, trying to contain and manage the edginess as it continued to build on the inside. As if there was some psychic communication we all began to separate and silently turn toward our homes, perhaps knowing that safety lay there rather than out here in the streets, familiar as they normally were.

As I began to trudge up Van Cortlandt Park South toward Saxon Avenue, I was overcome by the urge to go up on the roof of the Seventh Building. I scooted under the archway, walked into Section D and made a beeline up all the flights of stairs to the rooftop. Once there I began walking from edge to edge, peering out over the golf course and then turning to the other side of the roof to look down into the courtyard. I walked all the way across the roof until I was looking down on the walkway leading into Section A, at the far south end of the building. As I stared down I saw the figure of Dickey Ganberg making his way toward Gouverneur Avenue. I suddenly yelled out his name. He looked around, perplexed. "Up here," I shouted. He stopped and looked up. In a flash his face, grotesque and misshapen, flew up from his body and stopped nose-to-nose with my face. I was stunned and horrified at the hallucination that was assaulting me. I closed my eyes tightly and pushed myself away from the roof's edge; when I opened them the face and Dickey were gone. I shakily walked down the stairs and emerged out of Section A, desperate to get safely home.

Once home I still could not relax. I sat on the edge of the cot in the sun porch, with the two doors pulled shut. My heart was racing. As I tried to calm down the heavy wool turtle-neck sweater I was wearing began to feel like it was alive and choking me. I quickly pulled it off. I decided to get undressed and get under the blankets to see if I could just breathe and relax. As I lay there I began to feel congested and sick. I became more and more convinced that something bad was happening to me and my health was deteriorating. An image of how my mother used to take care of me when I was younger flashed into my mind, and I got up and went to the bathroom and opened the medicine cabinet. There I saw the bluish canister of Vick's Vapor Rub and thinking of it as a soothing and reassuring balm, I began smearing it onto my chest. By the time I got back into my bed I felt like the ointment was branding a hole into my chest, everywhere I spread it was aflame with searing heat. I felt like I was about to lose control.

I decided to lay still, breathe slowly, and look up at the ceiling. Afternoon had turned into evening and soon my mother would be home from work. I forcefully reminded myself that I was on LSD and that all of what was transpiring was only magnified by the drug and not real. I don't remember seeing my sister, or my mother, arrive home. My mind was stumbling and tumbling over itself, with ideas and endless streams of images none of which I could latch on to. With thoughts percolating so rapidly that they just took over, I was forced to simply go along for the ride. Rigidly I stared wild-eyed at the ceiling of the room for hour upon hour, not daring to leave for fear of running into my mother or sister. Somewhere in the quiet of the night I finally went to sleep.

When I awoke the next day I was beyond fatigue, both mentally and physically. I wasn't sure I ever wanted to drop acid again. I wondered what it had been like for the rest of my friends. It would be a couple of days before I would find out that everyone was okay, except Gregg Kai. He had completely flipped out during the LSD trip and, as a result, was definitely not the same person we all knew mere days ago. As tragic and as scary as the sudden transformation of our friend was, from a gregarious, animated person into a subdued shadow of his former self who could hardly look anyone in the eye, the casualty of Gregg ultimately did nothing to deter us from our drug adventures.

DURING THE SUMMERS OF 1968-1969 the scene at The Rail resembled a bizarre conglomeration of young people reveling in new-found freedoms trying to discover who they really were and to live from that place. Every night during those two summers, literally hundreds of people converged on The Rail. Cars were doubled-parked on Gouverneur Avenue; on Van Cortlandt Park South the cars stretched almost to Gale Place two blocks away and, in the other direction, halfway up the street to Hillman Avenue. It was a festival, oftentimes with Uncle John's ice cream truck right in the middle of the milling crowds until daylight began to ebb. People would arrive from neighborhoods all over the Bronx to buy or sell bags of pot, balls of hashish, uppers and downers, mushrooms, and LSD, anything to alter the mind and launch us into a different sensibility – even if for a fleeting moment. Those whose aims were purely commercial arrived and left quickly. Others stayed long after the sun went down, drifting to a secluded spot in the shadows of the playground or into the golf course to get high, returning later to partake in the communal energies, mingling as a welcomed member of the larger tribe. Joy and happiness permeated nearly everywhere and through everyone.

Late at night, under cover of darkness, dozens of us would enter the golf course and make our way toward the 17th Green. There we would fan out, like the scientists in the movie *The Thing* when they walked the circumference of the alien's flying saucer, to the edges of the green. Then we would sit, thigh-to-thigh, in one great circle. Multiple pre-rolled joints, and pipes filled with marijuana, would be passed from hand to hand, each person drawing deeply on the mellowing weed and instantly being filled with sensual feelings of love and peace, for each other and for the whole world. The orange flag on its pole in the center of the green fluttered in the cooling breeze, while we lay back and communed with the stars dotting the sky directly above us. It was a magical time, filled with hundreds of magical encounters in people's apartments, in the playground, on the streets, and in the golf course. We reveled in what we perceived as a dawning of a new way of being. The Rail was our magnetic north and we felt secure in this knowledge.

THERE WAS ONLY ONE NIGHT when things almost got out of hand. It was the night that Lowell Amos pulled a gun on Bobby Lurie right in front of The Rail.

Amos was a short, petty drug dealer and would-be drug smuggler with purported connections in hashish-laden Afghanistan. It was hard to tell if any of the stories were real or simply Amos's own public relations efforts to inflate his tough-guy credentials. It would be just like him to resort to using a gun to threaten someone, especially someone bigger and tougher than him.

Bobby was the middle brother in the Lurie clan, wedged between older brother Billy and younger brother Michael. The Lurie name was not to be trifled with and people all over the Bronx knew it. Bobby was six-foot-three and built like an Adonis. He was beautiful in every way, from his curly hair to his olive skin, from his sculpted musculature to his sparkling eyes and captivating smile. He was as tough as they come, but a reluctant warrior, pressed as he was between the machismo of his older brother's crowd and the more reasonable, tolerant ways of his younger brother's generation. Bobby was a sensualist, a sensitive, loving soul trapped in a tough guy's body and fading paradigm. He was loved and respected by all of us. I could tell that he hated being in such inner turmoil, and I was sure that he wrestled with many a demon as a result. In this way I felt some kinship. On this night, though, it appeared like he wasn't going to be allowed a choice.

It seemed that Amos had shorted Bobby in their drug exchange and Bobby wanted things to be made right. Amos became cocky, espousing a street version of *caveat emptor* and trying to dismiss Bobby as having to live with a little less because he had made the deal and what's done is done. Bobby continued to make his case, making it clear to Amos that this would be resolved here and now. Their voices grew louder and reason was quickly pushed aside by threats. At that point Amos pulled out his gun and stuck it in Bobby's face. The people closest to the altercation drew quickly back, sucked in a collective breath and held it. Time froze and the energy around both of them crackled.

Suddenly, like a coiled rattlesnake, Bobby struck Amos's right wrist with his left hand knocking the gun to the pavement, disarming him. Before Amos could even turn to look for the gun, in a single, continuous serpentine motion, Bobby's left hand reversed course and he back-handed Amos across the jaw with such force that it lifted him momentarily off the ground, flinging him into the gutter. The crowd expelled its collective breath. At that point Bobby just walked away as the stunned onlookers shook their heads and went back to their business. An even more stunned and embarrassed Amos retrieved his gun, got into his green Austin Healy 3000, and sped off. It felt like good had triumphed over evil. Before long though, for the rest of us, it was another night at The Rail.

This altercation revealed some of the underlying tensions that inevitably accompany the world of drug deals. The pressures to make money by cutting corners, by selling inferior product, or by ripping people off outright were always just beneath the surface calm as we tried to live by a different code and peacefully share with each other. It would take a while for these dark tentacles to push their way forcefully against the loving energy we were all trying to cultivate at The Rail. It would take something more powerful than the communal neighborhood spirit, more powerful than, and antagonistic to, the spirit of the Sixties that we were happily awash in.

The destabilizing fissures would arrive sooner than we could have possibly predicted from our present vantage point. They would widen with incredible speed, unleashing monsters and darkness that we naively believed we were immune from. Huddled together at The Rail we were in for one hell of a ride.

Chapter Seventeen
Desire Awakened, Desire Fulfilled

The first time I saw her she was standing outside of EM's candy store, back against the brick wall, bundled against the cold. She was new in the neighborhood. I had no idea who she was, where she came from, or what her name was but I was instantly attracted to her. She was five-foot-six, had light-brown hair, bordering on blond, with big eyes and a beautiful face. Even wearing a winter coat I could see that she was buxom and curvaceous, looking more womanly than girlish. Despite her being new to my eyes, I would learn later that she had already been befriended by Lenny Baumann, his sister Sylvia, and Ari Kravitz, but I never saw her at The Rail, or the playground, or anywhere else in the neighborhood. After that initial sighting, though, it seemed that I started running into her more regularly in or around EM's. Yet even though I continued to feel drawn toward her, I never mustered the courage to talk to her; I simply walked by and gazed dreamily at her.

One spring day in 1967, Kevin, Carter, and I were at one of the tables in EM's, replenishing our energy with sodas and some large soft pretzels after an afternoon of full-court basketball. The walk to EM's was our regular post-game pilgrimage, made multiple times a day, whenever we were playing sports in the schoolyard or playground. This time the blond girl was sitting at the counter toward the rear of the store, eating a hamburger. The three of us suddenly started talking about who we thought were the most beautiful girls in the neighborhood. Without a bit of self-consciousness or inhibition I proclaimed, with enough vocal force for her to hear me: "See that girl sitting there? Now that's beauty!" Her head turned ever so slightly and I caught a hint of a smile, which I took to be directed solely at me.

A few weeks after my outburst, I was standing outside EM's and she came up to me and, without a word, handed me an envelope with a card inside. Before I could open it she was gone, walking across Sedgwick Avenue and into the apartment building where she lived. The card was an invitation to her 15ᵗʰ birthday party. We still hadn't spoken a word but I found out from her signature that her name was Shira.

* * * * *

I WAS PAINFULLY AWKWARD and incredibly shy around girls. Throughout junior high and high school, I was also plagued with outbursts of facial acne that periodically erupted on my nose, or chin, or cheek with such prominence that I regularly refused to go to school until it subsided. Further, being *goyim* in a Jewish neighborhood effectively predetermined that just going steady with a girl, much less making out, would constantly elude me despite my best efforts; few parents or grandparents would give their blessing to such a transgressive idea. Plus, the whole mystery of girls was further complicated by stories that some of the older guys would tell us, stories that both confused and frightened us in our pre-adolescent curiosity. Aidan was fond of reminding us that sex was dangerous because, during the act, girls could become scared and tighten up their vaginas so hard that boys' penises could get stuck. This was a fate, he told us ominously, that required either being doused with a bucket of cold water, like dogs in the street, or being rushed to the emergency room to be separated. Other guys tried to convince us that the vaginas of Asian women ran horizontally, like their eyes. And every single older guy warned us about the excruciating pain of blue-balls, the condition brought on by being too long sexually frustrated. We were taught that this could only be relieved by begging your girlfriend to agree to have sex, or at least for them to bring a blow-job or hand-job to completion.

By the time we were in high school though, we found our role models, the three coolest guys in the neighborhood: Harvey Bender, Ross Taub, and Marty Semedorff. These guys were the epitome of suave, from wearing pea-coats to the way they combed their hair; from their desert boots to the way they walked the neighborhood streets; from their unflappable demeanor to their unbelievable ease around girls. They didn't tell us strange stories about women, or brag about their conquests. They just suavely glided through the neighborhood and through our imaginations. We watched them, keen on finding their secrets and, failing that, hoping that their mere proximity would confer some masculine blessings upon us. Whenever they were around we became attentive, like puppies eager to learn from the big dogs. Learn what we weren't sure specifically, but we knew we wanted what they possessed. Even if we could not define it we recognized it in our bones.

Needless to say the push-pull between being curious about sex and being terrified about it filled our heads with all manner of conflicting images, creating many strange beliefs and making for many awkward moments. But over the years, whenever I could burst out of my self-

214

protective shyness, or risk stepping beyond my pariah status as a non-Jew in the quest for romance, I periodically tried in my clumsy way to alter what I imagined was going to be my fate of unrequited love as long as I lived in the neighborhood.

Early on in P.S. 95, I developed my first crush-from-afar on one of my fourth-grade classmates, Linda Blum, whose red hair and freckles I found completely intriguing. We'd glance at each other throughout the day and smile and giggle. Once when we were paired in one of the dance classes, I was riven with both excitement and trepidation since, on the one hand, I was in heaven holding her close, but on the other hand, I was also terrified of making a wrong move and ruining everything by crushing her toes. But my hormones really began flowing in fifth grade, where I spent the entire year completely crushed out on Shoshana Morgenstern and Rivka Fisher. Even after the risqué letter episode with Shoshana, I could not stop thinking about them or stealing surreptitious lovelorn glances at them during class. I tried my best to feign aloofness as so I wouldn't draw anyone's ire by appearing too interested.

The years between sixth grade and toward the end of ninth grade in junior high school were utterly barren, except for my near fatal mistake of asking Pat Baker to a movie without her boyfriend's knowledge. I could not figure out how to be other than painfully shy whenever I was around girls and as a result I suffered. Except when it came to Connie Steiner.

Connie lived in the Seventh Building, in a second-floor apartment. One of her bedroom windows looked right out on The Rail, though she never really hung out there; she just showed up when she wanted to. Nor did she hang out at Gale Place with the Panthers, though she was friends with all of us. She was simply never a follower and instead exuded a sense of grounded maturity beyond the capability of most teenagers. For many of us, our first brush with having to navigate the ebbs and flows of our hormonal tides started with our friendship with Connie. Somehow, the air around Connie was mixed with a strange combination of maternal energy and innocent budding sexuality. She had a way of dancing between being sisterly and seductive, especially when she let loose with her feline smile. Like curious moths a number of us boys would gather almost nightly in her bedroom to talk and laugh, and share our lives. With her parents in the living room she would hold court and hold us transfixed. There was an enticing energy in that room, of abiding and trusting friendship and the electric charge of gender polarities. It was like we all had a safe place in which to practice having our adolescent feelings. Connie had the shape of a woman, a Cheshire smile, and piercing sensual eyes. She also had the heart of a true friend and the ability to listen and advise us – and perhaps even the greater ability to surround herself with teenage boys while holding clear boundaries between us, boundaries that were always respected.

She was an old soul, mature beyond her age and beyond all of us. Each night we talked until her parents came in and told us it was time for us to go. Reluctantly we would depart, half of us filing out the front door and down the single flight of stairs into the night. The other half would climb out onto her fire escape and drop to the soft ground below. Once outside, we would all look up at Connie's window for a final goodnight. There we would linger until that warm light faded to black and then we would drift in our separate orbits toward home, private thoughts and dreams filling our heads after another night in Connie's room. While all of this was wonderful, I still could not figure out how to translate anything I was feeling or learning into the ability to talk to any of the other neighborhood girls, much less ask them on a date.

In contrast, my closest friend, Jacob Schenck, was ultra-suave and seemed to have girlfriends from summer camp at his beck and call all year long; he even briefly dated someone who lived in Queens. When Gregg Kai and Connie started dating, one of the first couples to emerge from our group of friends, they seemed like they'd been destined to be together forever. They seemed so in love, so close and committed, that all manner of speculation began to arise as to whether or not they actually had sex. They were my and many others' role models when it came to imagining the commitment of going steady.

Phil Pasternak definitely talked like he had plenty of experiences with females, explaining in graphic detail what it felt like to unhook a girl's bra and slip his hand under it and onto her breast, or describing the wetness and smell that lingered after fingering a girl. At the same time we had never seen Phil with anyone, except a raggedy *Playboy* centerfold he would periodically produce to titillate us, so he was immediately dismissed as nothing but a big talker.

I was certain that Kevin Hurley, being so handsome with piercing blue eyes, had little problem dating the Irish-Catholic girls that populated Visitation School and hung out around Bailey Avenue. If he did, though, he kept it to himself. I envied my friends' exploits, those that were true and those that were not. But for me, having a girlfriend remained an elusive fantasy in a season of unrelenting drought.

By the time the Panthers inhabited Gale Place, a number of girls had chosen to hang out with us. I thought all the girls who clustered around were wonderfully attractive and mesmerizing; just being in their presence flooded me with excitement.

Susan Meyer, short and bouncy, was dating Marvin Shapiro. Sherrie Bieber, a dark-haired beauty, lived in the Gale Place apartments and was both smart and funny. Esther David was exceptionally beautiful in a curvaceous, voluptuous way, but since she lived up Sedgwick Avenue past the library she was an infrequent yet arresting visitor to Gale Place. Diane Fishman lived near Jerome Avenue, as did Rona Abrams. Rona was gangly and goofy and all the boys considered her a pal. Diane was exotically pretty, with dark hair and a radiant smile. Both Rona and Diane were best friends with Susan, who lived on Hillman Avenue; they always seemed to travel together. When Connie Steiner met Laurie Herschel and Cynthia Belman at Tetard, and brought them into the neighborhood fold, the possibilities of dating and going steady increased exponentially. Laurie lived in the Marble Hill Projects on 225th Street and Broadway, and Cynthia lived very close to our junior high school. Laurie was radiantly beautiful, with blond hair and bright, clear skin; it wasn't long before debonair Peter Mandel asked her to go steady and she agreed. Cynthia looked like a model, hair perfect and her figure slim, topped off with an amazing personality, but because she lived halfway around the reservoir we did not see her as often as we would've liked. Red-haired, freckle-faced Fern Haber was going steady with Jacob. All of these girls, whether they were dating someone or not, stimulated our masculine pheromones from time to time, mostly in the realm of fantasy and guy-to-guy banter. And then there were times when things just magically happened.

One autumn afternoon at Gale Place, I found myself sitting next to Esther David on the metal railings that served as bannisters on either side of the Big Steps that led down to Bailey Avenue. Esther had positioned herself close to me and leaned back, pressing herself gently into my chest. I was shocked when she allowed me to put my arms around her waist and didn't push me away. I was in ninth grade and close to being overwhelmed, the sudden waves welling up inside my body caused sweat to bead everywhere on my skin. Our bodies were close, my thigh touching the outer curve of her hip. With my arms wrapped around her waist, I could feel her stomach lifting my forearms as she breathed, the lower part of her bra-cradled breasts enticingly touching my wrists with every inhale. She was beautiful and warm and smelled so fresh and wonderful. I was drawn into a fairytale for that brief moment. We sat together for what seemed like a heavenly eternity, no one else around, simply enjoying each other's heat with the innocence and curiosity of puppies. Then it was over. She stood, smiled silently, and headed back home to her apartment on Sedgwick Avenue. We never spoke about our encounter, each of us satisfied with our mutual exploration.

FINALLY IN SPRING 1965, I GOT UP THE NERVE to risk engaging in the ritual of actually laying my heart on the line by asking Diane Fishman to go steady. Diane had long dark hair, stood erect, shoulders back, like a dancer or model. Her posture accentuated and lifted her beautiful breasts, riveting my attention whenever she appeared. Despite her own struggles with teenage acne, her eyes, her smile, and her lovely personality carried the day. She was captivating and slightly mysterious, especially since she was not around us every day. I had become totally crushed out on her and I had been working hard to get up the courage to ask Diane to be my girlfriend. I had confided in my closest friends, Phil and Jacob, and they had encouraged my plan by reassuring me that they knew she felt the same – they claimed they had both seen it in the way she acted around me.

One afternoon, as we all hung out at Gale Place, I walked over to Diane and took her aside. As we stood together in the street, next to a parked car, I asked her if she would go steady with me. She got quiet. She looked me straight in the eyes and said no, explaining that she was not ready to do that with anyone. I was devastated. I couldn't believe that she said no. As I reeled in shock she called to Susan and Rona and they began walking away toward the playground. I stood there crestfallen. Looking over at my friends anxiously awaiting my confirmation, my own disheartened energy seemed to emanate out from me and permeate all of Gale Place. Immediately picking up on my devastation, Jacob and Phil rushed over and asked what had happened. I told them. Instantly they got angry and began defending me, saying over and over that she made the wrong decision. I shook my head and muttered one of the stock phrases of teenage heartbreak: "Well, at least she let me down gently."

A week later, as all the Panthers were sitting on the retaining wall at Gale Place, Diane arrived with her new boyfriend in tow, Steve Zingel. Steve, who also lived in the Jerome Avenue neighborhood and close to Diane, tried briefly to ingratiate himself into our group. He ceased immediately, backing away and seeking Diane's hand the minute he felt the stiff wall of unwelcome. In the thick awkwardness that permeated the atmosphere, he and Diane began to walk back toward the playground, repelled by the entire group's iciness. I was stunned. As tears welled up in my eyes, Phil came over and said protectively, "Do you want us to kick his ass, Tommy? Just give us the word and we'll do it." I shook my head and silently headed home. I was flattened. I didn't know if she had turned me down because I wasn't Jewish, or because she liked this other guy better, or what. One thing was clear: she lied about not wanting to go steady with anyone at all; what was even clearer was that she did not want to go steady with me. I was more confused than ever about what it would take for me to have a girlfriend.

MY LOVE-LIFE DROUGHT resumed for another year until the summer of 1966, when I was 15 and had just completed my freshman year at Clinton High School. Out of the blue, I found myself making out in the golf course with Rebecca Schwartz. It was completely spontaneous; a bunch of us had been sitting there talking and suddenly it was Rebecca and I alone. Rebecca took the lead in every way. She was at least a couple of years older, soon on her way to college. Someone had brought her around the neighborhood that summer. She was tall and smart and seemed to possess a sophistication that I hadn't encountered before. I was intimidated and unsure what to do. At her initiative we embraced and began rolling around in the grass, on the hill just behind the handball courts. I was under her control and tutelage and I surrendered willingly. She laid half on top of me, willfully orchestrating her every move and mine. She was very animal-like, driven by an energy that was simply raw and instinctual. She kissed me forcefully. She unbuttoned the white blouse she wore and slipped my hand inside. I touched her breasts; this was my first time and they were so soft and warm and amazing that I nearly fainted in ecstasy. My head swirled and my mind flew away. She rubbed my crotch on the outside of my jeans until I had an erection; this was the first time a girl had ever touched me there. I was arching my back with lust and desire. She continued rubbing until I convulsed in an orgasm. Then she smiled, stood up and began buttoning her blouse as I crumpled back into the grass, breathing heavily. It was as if she was leaving in triumph, another male carcass dispatched as only a woman who knows herself and her desires can. As I lay there recovering she walked down the hill and, without a single look behind, stepped through the hole in the fence, back into the playground, and disappeared. I saw her once more that summer, in a crowd of people at The Rail. We didn't speak; I was too unsure to even approach her. We just looked at each other for a while. After that I never saw her again in the neighborhood; her bodily imprint fading into a summer memory that sustained my own fantasy life for a little while longer.

After my episode with Rebecca, I continued to remain uncertain about girls but now, because of the explicitness of our encounter, I was percolating lust on top of my confusion. By now, most of my closest friends had already found girlfriends and had sex, and I had experienced neither. My summer was spent working with Kevin at the Bronx Zoo, playing basketball, smoking pot, drinking quarts of beer on Friday and Saturday nights and, quite often, puking somewhere afterwards. The idea of having a girlfriend moved decidedly to the periphery of my thoughts but, frustratingly, it did not disappear altogether, only faded to fantasizing every night before I went to sleep. It was nearly nine months later when Shira Langer entered my life.

SHE HAD MOVED TO THE NEIGHBORHOOD from Valentine Avenue, just off Fordham Road and the Grand Concourse. In many ways her life paralleled mine. I often felt out of place not being Jewish; Shira had fled to our neighborhood to find a safe haven from the alienating prejudice she found living in an area populated by mostly Irish-Catholics who entertained themselves by calling her "kike" and "Christ-killer." Like me, one of her parents was deceased and she had been forced into a reconfigured family structure. When her mother passed away her father felt he could not handle the burden of raising a daughter on his own and had given her over to the custody of her mother's two spinster sisters, Mabel and Fruma Gold.

Mabel was extremely timid, easily browbeaten by her older sister, Fruma. Mabel had never been with a man in her life but she knew that the world was often a painful place and more than anything she was devoted to making sure Shira was protected from any harm. Fruma, on the other hand, had been jilted in love. She had given herself, in all innocence, to a cad who took the gift of her love and shattered her heart, leaving her bitter and angry at the things she knew men could and would do if given the chance. Mabel and Fruma were like a two-headed Cerberus in their determination to protect Shira's maidenhead and ensure that she married a nice Jewish man. They thought they were protecting her from the hell of a prematurely lost virginity, while the only thing I knew was that they were guarding the entryway to what I perceived to be heaven. They were like America's Distant Early Warning system, fiercely on the lookout for male invaders and their incoming missiles. It caught them completely by surprise when right under their radar the gates of Shira's heart swung open and an invitation was extended to me, a *goyisher* Irish boy no less, by Shira herself.

When I arrived at her apartment for her 15th birthday party, the music was blaring and the living room was filled with friends from her old neighborhood and from Walton High School, where she was a sophomore. Similar to Clinton, Walton was a single-sex high school, with thousands of girls packed together. As she invited me in, I shyly handed Shira a small gift and a birthday card in which I had written, as poetically as I could muster, how beautiful I thought she was. She read the card immediately and for the rest of the night we became evermore attached. We danced periodically, which was an excruciatingly painful display of my utter incapacity to affect any sense of the rhythm or grace that I showed on the basketball courts. Even the slow dance caused me to sweat, since I had never held a girl I really liked for that long or that close, feeling every curve of her body undulating full-on against mine. I was sure everyone in the room knew I had an erection, or at least was making fun of me turning in a patternless, shuffling circle unrecognizable as dancing. One thing I was certain about in my heart of hearts was that they were definitely all wondering why their beautiful friend Shira had chosen such a loser.

Whenever we weren't dancing together I planted myself in an overstuffed chair, too shy to engage with anyone of these strangers who all seemed to know each other. Toward the end of the evening Shira stopped dancing and sat for a long time on my lap. I was in heaven, even under the steady hail of daggers being launched from across the room from the eyes of her ever-watchful aunts. By the next day, we were an item; I was finally dating.

WHEN I WALKED DOWN THE STREETS OF THE NEIGHBORHOOD WITH SHIRA I felt like a Cape Canaveral rocket ready to launch. I could barely contain myself at the good fortune that was spreading out before me. I had staked a reputation as a leader of the Panthers. In that role I was respected as tough when necessary and always fair. I had also just completed my first season as a member of the varsity football team at De Witt Clinton, wearing number 88 and playing offensive and defensive end. As a result of my commitment and steady improvement, Coach Prezioso had hinted at working on a partial scholarship to St. Lawrence University in upstate New York if I played well in my senior year. My basketball prowess caused me to be constantly sought out to be on a team the minute I entered the playground, no matter what time of day, whereas latecomers had to wait two or three games because of the crowds. It seemed I never left the court and it felt great. My self-esteem was at an all-time high and now I had my first girlfriend – and she was beautiful, and she was Jewish, and she was falling in love with me as fast as I was falling in love with her. I was proud to be seen with her, and I knew she felt the same. She was the final piece in the puzzle of my life. Looking into her eyes, I felt like I had finally found sanctuary; her look back into mine told me it was mutual.

As school ended that June, the summer heat and humidity gradually made itself felt, both externally and internally. Shira and I were full-throttle into our courtship dance. I had finally gotten the nerve to ask her out on our first real date. Since my job at the Bronx Zoo had ended the previous summer, I was virtually penniless. I borrowed five dollars from my mother for my date with Shira and we decided take the bus to the Loew's Paradise Theater to see a movie. The Paradise, as we called it, was a classic, ornate, old-style movie house with a spacious lobby and a broad, red-carpeted staircase that curved sweepingly up to the balcony area. The walls in the theater were made to look like an old European skyline with silhouettes of rooftops framed against a blue-black sky that arched over our heads. When the houselights went out tiny lights twinkled like stars across the ceiling, giving the impression that this was an outdoor theater and a glorious firmament held us gently. The whole scene was beautifully romantic and for both of us an extraordinary first date.

I wanted to bestow everything I could upon Shira, take her to movies, buy her lunch and ice cream, take her to the zoo, and more. But my mother's pocketbook was too thin to continue asking her for date money. Even the meager allowance she struggled each week to offer my sister and me was hardly going to be enough. I was sixteen and I had a girlfriend, and that required a steady income. Fortunately, it was a time when everyone was hiring and even if you lost one job you could walk down the street to the next establishment and get another, just for the asking. Within days I was hired as a stock clerk and grocery bagger at the neighborhood Co-op Market which, in addition to paying well, was just across the street from Shira's apartment.

THE CO-OP WAS THE ANCHOR for the tiny shopping area at the intersections of Sedgwick Avenue, Gouverneur Avenue, and Van Cortlandt Avenue West. Everyone shopped here, with periodic forays to Jerome Avenue, Fordham Road, or 231st Street and Broadway to buy specialty items or clothing. The Co-op was our social hub, where neighbors would regularly cross paths, catch up on gossip, and *kvetch* about food prices and the quality of the fruits and vegetables. Before getting a job there, my connection to the Co-op was quite limited.

Whenever my mother got her Woolworth's paycheck, we would grab our rolling metal shopping basket and off we'd go to the Co-op on our weekly expedition. We would stock up on all the necessary things for her to make dinners and lunches for my sister and me. Before checking out, my mother always made a beeline to say hello to Nathan Greenspan, who worked in the deli at the back of the store. He was gregarious and sincere in his interactions with my mother and everyone else, thus becoming one of the few people my mother felt comfortable talking to, and someone she felt would not look down on her or talk behind her back. After our groceries were rung up, bagged and in the cart, I would serve my real purpose: pulling the

222

heavily laden basket up the hill and then down Saxon Avenue to our house. The real test came when I had to use my strength to haul the basket up the stairs to the kitchen.

My other connection to the workings of the Co-op, tenuous as it was, was the rare invitation by Donnie Zorn to lend a hand on the huge, turquoise-colored delivery truck that he contracted to the Co-op. Donnie was bold and brash, and drove with reckless abandon as he tried to make the deliveries in a timely manner. He had a full complement of helpers – most often Aidan and his friends, Fish, Schnur, Sidney, and others – who worked mostly for tips and the novelty of being part of Zorn's crew. Sometimes a few of the older girls were on board, which was an added treat. The few times I was allowed on board, I either just hung out or held on for dear life. Every so often I helped by grabbing one of the bags of groceries that wasn't enough to fill one of the cardboard delivery boxes, and trailed after one of the older guys as he hoisted the heavy box on his shoulder and headed into an apartment building. But once I was actually working there, privy to all the people and their idiosyncratic interactions, the Co-op took on a larger-than-life reality.

There was Murray the manager, who, when he wasn't running around the store like a madman, sat watchfully in the open-air office perched next to and slightly above the express lane register. From here he could gaze out upon everyone entering or exiting the store. Shortly after hiring me, Murray was replaced, for unspecified reasons, by a debonair new manager recruited from one of the Manhattan Co-ops, named Tony LoBianco. One of his first acts as the new manager was to fire Donnie Zorn and create an in-house delivery service, complete with a green panel truck emblazoned with the words "Co-op," along with the Twin Pines logo. He and I would quickly form a love-hate relationship.

And then there was Faye. She was the store's resident *yenta* and she was greatly loved because of it. She was the longest working cashier in the Co-op. All gossip seemed to begin and end with Faye, making hers the checkout line that people would willingly wait for. She was short, dark red hair, and possessed the gift of gab. She trained me in working the cash register and kept a watchful eye on me when I was making change – a task that I had to do quickly in my head which, given my horrible math skills, took me some time to master. But under her tutelage, I was soon ready to handle the rapidity of the 10-items-or-less express lane. In many ways, Faye *was* the heart of the Co-op.

The market was also the only place in the neighborhood, with the exception of the Co-op building maintenance department, where black people worked. Bernice started out as a cashier and quickly moved into a bookkeeper's position. Alfonzo was always dapper and nattily attired, like a version of Sammy Davis, Jr.; he worked the floor and *schmoozed* the customers with an abundance of charm – so much so that it was rumored that when he went out on deliveries he always returned late due to various trysts along the route. Eli was a bear of a man, given to monosyllabic responses if he spoke at all; he never stopped working, helping out mostly in the produce department and wherever else he was needed. Finally there was Clarence, a stately figure, lean and erect, composed with a no-nonsense demeanor. He and I forged a *modus vivendi* of mutual respect when he saw how hard I worked sorting out the roach-infested chaos of the bottle-return area deep in the bowels of the Co-op. While I worked on one end of the basement, he worked on the other, stamping prices on groceries before sending the cases onto the conveyor belt to be off-loaded upstairs and shelved. As we both tended to our tasks, he would burst out into song, his Johnny Mathis-like voice filling the air with the most incredible sounds. Whenever I knew he was working downstairs, I would instantly volunteer to tend to the piled up bottles just so I could bask in his music.

I worked at the Co-op after school and on weekends. I stocked shelves, worked the register, helped on the delivery truck when it was backed up, and swept the floors before closing. During the Jewish holidays, especially Passover, Tony the manager and I would set up a section of shelves to display the boxes of *matzah*, bottles of borscht, gefilte fish, and *schmaltz*, plus cans of macaroons. When delivery trucks double-parked, Tony would have the deli department whip up a couple of sandwiches and I would deliver them to the policemen sitting in the patrol car to avoid getting a ticket. Tony was something to behold; he worked all the angles, and bending the rules or *schmoozing* his way around them, was an art form for him. I loved working there and I loved the people I worked with. I even liked most of the customers. I arrived every day, grateful beyond measure.

I ASKED SHIRA TO GO STEADY with me as soon as I had the job. To sanctify this step I went with my sister, Peggy, to a jewelry shop on Fordham Road to pick out an ankle bracelet. I found one made of white gold, fashioned into two adjoining hearts with a tiny diamond chip in the center of each heart and held by a delicate chain and clasp. I instantly put it on lay-away and Peggy and I walked home incredibly happy. For what seemed like an eternity, with each Co-op paycheck I dutifully brought another installment to the jewelry store until I finally paid it off. When I presented it to Shira, I watched her emanate so much joy as she strapped it onto her ankle; I stood there beaming with love and pride at this next step of committing to our relationship.

Going steady meant we were exclusive, off limits to others. Daily it meant always holding hands when walking anywhere, with our special way of entwining our index fingers together. It meant perfecting our kisses, moving from lips to tongues. It meant stealing away to the golf course to make out every chance we could, braving the envious howls of those in the playground watching us duck through the hole in the fence and disappear beyond the grassy hills in back of the 17th tee, or into the Cove near Gale Place where an overstuffed chair and a couple of mattresses beckoned. In these intimate moments, fraught with barely contained urgency, I was following what I understood to be the manly code of gently and insistently pushing the boundaries in order to feel Shira's breast *under* her shirt and possibly unhook her bra to hold her warm flesh in my hands. Once these milestones were reached and accepted by her, the next step seemed to be to try to get my hand down her pants, or get her to put her hand down mine. When these monumental moments were achieved, our making out became full explorations of pleasing ourselves while pleasing each other.

While we were both enjoying everything we discovered about each other, Shira struggled with her own desires, their vital urgency held in check by demur protocols of resistance, beset with fears of being called a slut, fears of being used and then dumped, or worse, fears of getting pregnant. Yet we both knew that we had been brought together by fate and our attitudes and behaviors toward each other were never other than respectful; even in the throes of passion, as we both surged toward the edge of ecstatic surrender, we consistently pulled back when it became clear that taking the step of full sexual consummation was beyond either of our capacities. We both wondered when we would make love with each other – "going all the way," as it was termed – since, as a result of our deepening relationship, it now felt all but inevitable.

One evening, Shira and I were upstairs on the top floor of my house, in my bedroom; my mother and sister were downstairs in the living room watching television. We were making out on my bed. As the passion spread, I hooked my fingers under the waistband of Shira's stretch pants and began to slowly tug them downwards. She grabbed my hand and held it in place, stopping her pants from going any lower. I tugged; she resisted. We kept kissing. Finally she let go of my hand and I knew instantly that she was saying yes, make love to me. I stopped kissing her and looked into her eyes for reassurance and affirmation. Love and trust radiated between us as we looked deeply into each other's' hearts. I moved to my knees and placed my hands on her hips, gripping the pants firmly. I started to pull and Shira arched her back to help make it easier. In one movement I slid her underwear and pants down below her knees. My eyes widened and my breathing stopped. As I gazed down upon her nakedness I knew instantly I was in the presence of a sacred, mysterious energy, way beyond my comprehension. I was trembling, with excitement and fear, just staring at her shining skin and the curves that beckoned me to touch and explore.

I gently lowered my head and placed my cheek upon the tangled fur covering her womanhood, felt its softness, and breathed in her heat. I could hear her breathing quicken and feel her bare stomach rise and fall against my face. I lay like that for what seemed like endless minutes. It was the only position closest to prayer that I could think of and I wanted nothing more than to show reverence, gratitude, respect, and love for what Shira was offering me. I rose up enough to unbuckle my belt and pushed my pants and underwear below my knees as well. I was beyond excitement; I was terrified and shaking, a thousand half-formed thoughts and ideas colliding in my head. I finally lay on top of her, and Shira and I made gentle love with each other. The beauty of that first moment confirmed for each of us that we would be together forever.

As I walked her home Shira began to cry, realizing that she had given up her virginity and now had to go home to her aunts. I struggled with all my heart to reassure her that I loved her and nothing would break our relationship. By the time we reached the front door of her apartment building, after talking and crying together, we both felt good about making love and we were certain as well that this act had sealed our lives as one.

FOR THE NEXT TWO AND A HALF YEARS we reveled in our time together, taking each other on a journey of discovery that led us deeply into each other's hearts and bodies. In the summertime, when her aunts were at work, I would take my lunch break from the Co-op at her house where she would make us hamburgers or tuna fish sandwiches, always garnished with kosher dill pickles. Then we would make love and I would race back across the street to work, always breathless and always few minutes late.

During my senior year in high school, I would periodically convince her to feign sickness. On those days I would cut school, wait in front of EM's until her aunts boarded the bus for work, and make a beeline to her apartment door. There Shira would greet me sleepily and press her body against mine in a hug that flooded me with the warmth that

226

had been building as she lay under her covers. We would go back into her bed and make love throughout the day, listening to *The Doors* sing "Light My Fire" and reveling in the luscious sounds of *The Bee Gees'* "To Love Somebody."

After we ate lunch we would listen to Gene Pitney singing "Town without Pity." His voice and lyrics brought tears to our eyes as we remembered all the difficulty we experienced in our respective neighborhoods to feel accepted. We knew that to finally get to this point and find each other was our miracle. Against the backdrop of the song and our cascading memories, we spoke tenderly together, reinforcing with every word and gesture just how life-saving our love had been for each of us, and how the cruelty of the world would never, ever change that.

Shira's aunts, though, were determined to thwart our growing love for each other every chance they could. At first they simply used their power over Shira's freedom, restricting her comings and goings as best they could. Shira loved her aunts deeply and tried to abide by their strictures. It was very difficult for her to lie to them but her desire to be with me often overruled her aunts' ability to shackle her, especially when they had to work and especially during the summer when Shira and I were out of school.

For the first year of our relationship Shira's aunts did their best to keep us apart, hoping that the whole thing would blow over and Shira would come to her senses and find a nice Jewish boy. Instead, Shira and I, much to the dismay and consternation of Aunt Fruma especially, were busy deepening our love. Aunt Mabel, on the other hand, left to her own devices would've happily celebrated Shira's happiness, but she always acquiesced to Fruma's dictates. Whether they knew it or not, or even dared consider it, Shira and I were in the throes of a fiercely heated, innocence-shattering exploration of our sexuality, a mutually driven quest that only pressed us deeper into each other's arms. Every moment together we cemented ourselves into the other's heart with a mortar mixed with the sincerest love, an achingly tender lust, and a long hoped-for sanctuary finally arrived. Under the power of our exploding desires all of her aunts' machinations proved not only fruitless, but only added more impetus to our determination to be together no matter what. Their frustrations grew more intense each day.

The proverbial shit hit the proverbial fan during the Jewish High Holy Days in the fall of 1968. We'd been together for over a year and Shira's aunts had seen and heard enough; they were through alternating reason with threats. Terrorizing Shira with the fear of pregnancy, coupled with Fruma's own personal stories of how horrible men could be, just wasn't working. Under the cover of taking a five-day vacation they staged an intervention and whisked Shira away to the Catskills for a type of intensive therapy that only two maiden aunts could conjure. Against the backdrop of the High Holy Days, they were dedicated to exorcising everything about me, an interloping *goy*, from Shira's heart and mind. Meanwhile, unbeknownst to them, Shira had given me the keys to their apartment, providing me with a welcomed respite from my own house. The entire time I was there I reveled in the smells of Shira's bed; smells that I imagined were left over from our last lovemaking. I pretended that this was my own apartment, imagining myself as an adult coming home from work at the Co-op and having dinner, or coming back from playing basketball or football and jumping into the shower. The only thing missing in all my reverie was Shira herself.

The next time I saw Shira I knew immediately that nothing had changed between us. In fact her honest, tearful professing of the love she felt for me had actually softened her aunts' hearts somewhat, especially the more sensitive and inexperienced Aunt Mabel. Yet even Fruma, ever staunchly the foe of all things male, relented enough to allow the gates barring our love to budge ever so slightly. It seemed the intervention had worked in reverse.

Throughout our entire relationship our only real tangle was over my continued use of drugs. Shira felt that if I was stoned on pot or any other drug, then I was not really with her, that I was choosing the drugs over her. My drug use was relatively benign when we first got together, confined mostly to smoking pot. I also stepped away from drugs entirely when I was training for my senior year on the Clinton football team, but over time she eventually demanded that I quit smoking weed and that I not be high at all whenever we were together. I agreed – up to a point. Given that she was highly monitored by her guardian aunts, Shira lived an extremely curtailed, almost cloistered existence. During the school year she needed to be home for dinner and focused on homework. On the weekends throughout the year she had to regularly check in with her aunts and not stay at The Rail for too many consecutive hours. Permission was required for her to go out on a date with me or even to visit a friend's house. It was only in the summer, when school was out and her aunts were at work during the week, that we were able to be together all day long. It was during the times when Shira was bound in her protected tower – and there were many of these – that I surreptitiously continued my drug use with my friends every chance I could.

Nevertheless, when Shira and I were together we always made the most of our time, whether it was sitting at The Rail, walking in the golf course picking flowers, going to a movie, planning our futures, or making love. We clung to each other with an intensity that most others marveled at. Yet while in our heart of hearts we continued to imagine our love would go on forever, perhaps we sensed in the growing turbulence of the times some underground tremors spreading spidery cracks into the foundation of our vision of everlasting love. Over the course of our next twelve months together, these temblors would be felt by each of us acutely.

Chapter Eighteen
High School Redux

After suffering under the distinctively puritanical regime of my grandparents' house for over ten years, I thought I had endured just about all the shameful experiences a young man could possibly have. But one of the biggest was yet to come, inflicted, no less, by my own hands. Entering my senior year of high school I felt so together, cocky, on top of the world. I was all set on flying the coop and, come that final June, kissing Clinton goodbye forever. Imagining a possible football scholarship, I allowed myself to believe that I would not be left behind when my friends went off to college; it was suddenly within the realm of possibility that I could make something out of my life. Yet by the end of the school year my life, along with what seemed like the whole world, was in shambles.

* * * * *

As my last year at De Witt Clinton High School stretched out before me, I felt as if I was in complete control of my fate. Summer was coming to a close and my 17th birthday was just three months away. Shira and I continued to be head-over-heels in love and, as the song by *The Turtles* went, we were simply "So happy together." My job at the Co-op Market kept me busy, both in the store itself and running across the street to eat lunch and make love with Shira. It also provided me with a weekly paycheck with which to take Shira on dates and have a little spending cash as well. And, I was playing football for Clinton. Across the board my cache had risen. In the eyes of many in the neighborhood I was living a charmed life, a life that might possibly keep me out of trouble and lead to college where, as a result, I would finally amount to something. Despite the fact that the only dark cloud on the horizon after I graduated was that I'd have to register for the draft, I felt exactly the same way too. Besides, I had more pressing things to focus on.

School would be commencing right after Labor Day. I was looking forward to playing on the football team again. I hoped that I would

231

continue to impress Coach Prez into getting me the scholarship to St. Lawrence University in Upstate New York he had hinted about at the end of last season. Whenever I had time within my full-time job at the Co-op, I trained hard in the blazing summer heat on the cinder track in the rear of Clinton's gym building, sprinting and doing grass drills the coaches had designed and given us a handout to follow. Endless repetitions of sit-ups and push-ups tortured my body until my muscles no longer ached. I was honing my entire physique in ways that simply playing basketball was unable to do. It was the first time in my life where I felt supremely healthy. When I awoke each morning I fairly flew out of bed, ready for anything. Smoking pot and drinking beer on the weekends seemed to have little negative effect, the sheer resiliency of my youthfulness appearing as a potent antidote to any possible detriment. Besides, it wasn't like I was getting stoned every day; I was more committed to playing football than I had been to anything in the past. Of course, I also continued my love affair with basketball every chance I got, reveling in the days when I was not working and I could play full-court hoops from ten in the morning until six o'clock at night, especially now that I was getting in tip-top shape. As the summer wore on and I got football-ready, I began to eagerly look forward to the resumption of Sunday morning football against the older guys in the Big Schoolyard. I was hoping to use the first couple of games like a tune-up, to strut my stuff a bit before the Clinton football season began in earnest.

Touch football in the Big Schoolyard was an autumn ritual that lasted from Labor Day until Thanksgiving (or the first serious snowfall, whichever came first). After our neighborhood tackle football team dissipated, a number of us eventually began migrating over to the Sunday morning games, which previously had been the sole province of guys older than us. These were guys in their late 20s and early 30s, some who had been through the Army, others who had played college football – Freddie, Yaker, Murray, Tom Chartier, Steve Pear, our former coaches, Joe and Eddie, and a host of others. More and more we infiltrated their previously sacrosanct domain, to mixed reviews. We were welcomed by some of the guys who appreciated our athletic abilities, but others wanted to do everything to knock us on our asses every single play, to show us that they were still young enough to prevail and we'd better remember that this was their schoolyard. As a result, when enough players our age began showing up and our numbers reached critical mass and we could field a team of our own, it was immediately decided that from now on the games would be older guys vs. younger guys. They had a point to prove and they were determined to do so at our expense.

They were all bigger, stronger, and more football savvy than we were, and it showed. The first couple of seasons playing against the older guys we were demolished every Sunday. On defense they blasted through our offensive line like it wasn't there, half-dozen hands easily "tackling" our quarterback, Paul Steinmetz. They had a field day disrupting pass plays and shutting down all our attempts at running the ball. On offense, their quarterback Eddie Gerwin had all the time in the world to sit back, survey the field, and find an open receiver. When he handed the ball off to Freddie for a sweep around the end, there were blockers galore as he barreled over the concrete and into the end zone.

Finally, after a particularly humiliating defeat, someone convinced Harvey Bender to come play quarterback for us. Harvey stood over six-feet tall and was deceptively athletic. He was already a neighborhood basketball legend for his sterling career at Bronx Science High School and for his playground prowess. He was strong and could pass nearly the entire length of the schoolyard. With him at the helm our fortunes during Sunday morning football made a complete 180-degree turn. We started winning, and winning, and winning. With every win our confidence soared and the mystique of invulnerability that previously surrounded the older guys evaporated with every touchdown pass. Harvey and I made a particularly potent duo since I could easily get open and rarely missed a catch if the ball was anywhere near me. Needless to say, our walks to EM's candy store after the games were boisterous and cocky, while the older guys gnashed their teeth and plotted how to beat us come next Sunday. Now, as the leaves once again began their seasonal turning, and my body had re-shaped itself over the summer, I couldn't wait to get back to the Big Schoolyard for some Sunday morning football.

THE FIRST JOLT TO THE SPELL I was living under was an all-encompassing trauma that toppled the entire line of dominoes that I had planned to follow from the neighborhood right into college. Ironically, and tragically, playing *touch* football put an end to my playing *tackle* football. Right before Clinton's football season started, I decided to show up for the first Sunday morning football game in the Big Schoolyard. I was in great shape and itching to mix it up. Once again it was the younger guys against the older guys and once again we were having our way with them. Late in the game I went out for a pass on a sideline pattern. The ball was thrown to me just as I made my cut. The ball was high and slightly behind me. As I leapt to catch it my upper body rotated one way while my defender's two-handed touch on my thighs rotated my lower body in the opposite direction. I felt and heard the crunching inside my lower spine. I knew before I landed that I was really hurt. Intense spasm gripped me as I stepped off the field and sat down against the brick wall of P.S. 95. The pain was so great that I could not get comfortable. When I stood I felt like I was listing to one side, twisted and unable to straighten out. I asked Shira to help me get home. As I slung my arm across her shoulders for support, we jerkily hobbled out of the schoolyard and up Sedgwick Avenue toward my house. As I disappeared around the corner I could hear the sounds of the game fading behind me.

For the rest of that Sunday I lay on the floor of my bedroom, with Shira, my mother, and my sister Peggy tending to me as best they could. On Monday, my mother took me on a short bus ride to see Dr. Liebman, a general practitioner and our family doctor since Dr. Herman had retired. He explained to us that I had slipped a disc in my lower back and it was pressing on my spinal nerve. He further explained that he was not a fan of surgery, especially for someone my age, but thought that a regimen of traction would be the best route to follow. Before I knew it, my mother and I were in a taxi speeding northwards to be admitted to Cross County Hospital, housed in the Cross County Shopping Mall, located in Westchester just across the northern border of the Bronx. I was to stay there a full week, trussed up with a wide belt around my hips with weights attached to the belt. The weights dangled off the foot of the bed while I lay there waiting for the traction to pull open the vertebrae so the disc could slip back into its rightful place and relieve the pressure it was exerting on my spinal nerve. I was not allowed to get out of bed during the entire week. The mattress could be raised whenever I ate or watched television, but most of the time I was lying flat. Since the bathroom was off-limits, I had to try to pee into a plastic hand-held urinal and direct my bowel movements into a cold, steel bed pan while lying down. But even my small efforts to arch my back in order to position myself on the bed pan, or to bear down to aid elimination, caused excruciating pain.

Adding insult to injury, between the unpalatable hospital food, the pain pills and muscle relaxers, and the fact that I rebelled against the frustrating impossibility of trying to defecate while supine, I became constipated within a few days of my arrival. Every two days I got sponge baths from the nurses, which were titillating and embarrassing all at the same time. My mother would visit every evening after work, bringing my sister along as well. Shira would arrive most days after school and spend a couple of hours with me, her face alternating between loving encouragement and brows furrowed with deep concern.

On a couple of occasions a troop of my friends arrived to cheer my spirits, awkward in the environment of the hospital as well as from witnessing me in pain and utterly vulnerable. Ezra Baum brought me two books, *A Confederate General at Big Sur*, by Richard Brautigan, and *The Origins of Totalitarianism*, by Hannah Arendt. While I wasn't much of a reader at the time, except for comic books, I devoured these books in what was to be a foreshadowing of things to come regarding my developing relationship with reading and its connection with my

234

gaining a deeper understanding of the wider world. In the middle of the week I was sent to radiology for a myelogram, a process where they injected dye into my spine and maneuvered me into various positions on a movable table while taking x-rays to see what the dye revealed about my discs. The injection was painful and left my back throbbing and my head aching for hours after the procedure.

By week's end I was feeling decidedly better, with a lot less pain. When they finally unharnessed me and allowed me to get up from the bed and use the bathroom, I was so dizzy and nauseous that by the time I made it to the toilet, with the nurse's help, all I could do was kneel down like I had so many times before and throw up into the porcelain bowl. For the rest of that day they had me sitting up and taking only brief walks around the room to try to restore my equilibrium. During my final day in the hospital, when Dr. Liebman explained to my mother and me that I could leave and go home, he left me with an ominous warning: While I would likely be able to return to most of my normal activities, if I wanted my back to stay healthy, I would never be able to play tackle football again.

THIS TURN OF EVENTS WOULD BE MORE DEVASTATING than I could've possibly imagined at the time of his pronouncement. Initially, I had gotten on the team as kind of a lark, vouched for to Coach Prez by Eddie and Joe. I joined the team more to not let them down than out of any strong desire to play football for Clinton High School. But flashes of my ability had shown through, both on the field and during practices. What I considered simply my natural ability, talent that certainly earned accolades around the neighborhood, was now being noticed by the head coach of my high school football team, noticed enough for him to think I might be eligible for some kind of scholarship to a small college. As a result it was the first time I ever really considered going to college, since when it came to academics I was convinced that I was too stupid to ever make a go of it at that level. Besides, given my mother's dire income at Woolworth's and our reliance on Social Security support checks to keep us in food throughout the month, I had always considered college way beyond my means. But the idea of a football scholarship made me reconsider my possibilities, made me risk dreaming of something beyond a dead-end, blue-collar future.

When I returned to school and went to Coach Prezioso's office with all of the doctor's paperwork, and explained that I wasn't able to play for the team any longer, he was business-like, aloof and very matter-of-fact in the way he received my news. It felt like now that I was damaged goods and no use to the team, he had a lot more important things to tend to. He barely looked up from his seat as he took the doctor's notes from my hand and set them down on a sea of disorganized piles of paper atop his desk. In this cold, suddenly uncaring atmosphere my eyes began to well up with tears. Somehow I expected more, needed more, and in that difficult moment I needed Coach Prez to be a father or a friend of some kind. But that's simply not football, at least not how Coach Prez played it; once you're out, you're out. Why bother with someone who could not play when he had fifty other guys in good health and ready to play. It made practical sense: football is a machine and the calculus is weighted toward those who had not been ground up in its gears. In the estranged silence that permeated the air, I finally turned and left without another word. As I emerged onto the main floor, class change was in progress and wave upon wave of bodies, swelling into a great masculine sea, buffeted me about as I tried to find an exit. When I finally pushed one of the metal doors open I felt I could breathe again, a surge of free-flowing energy swirled around and through me. "Fuck Coach Prez and fuck this place," I muttered aloud to myself, stifling my tears. Without football I knew that my senior year was going to be radically different; without football I felt unconstrained by any commitments or structure. It was an untethered feeling that both thrilled and terrified me.

IT DIDN'T TAKE LONG before the vacuum was filled by cutting school to hang out with friends and smoke pot, or get high in some fashion. Since my mother had switched back to day shift after my grandmother had moved out, she now went to work early each morning. I was able to skip homeroom whenever I felt like it and, without her knowing, fall happily back to sleep as soon as she left. Since Peggy also left with my mother, because she had to take a bus to Walton High School, she presented no obstacle to my newfound creative scheduling and my lackluster attitude. With both of them away for the bulk of the day, my house became "get high central," safely indoors and imperceptible to omnipresent neighborhood eyes. This was especially useful during the winter months when it was too cold to sit in the golf course and get stoned. Further, because I got out of school long before my mother returned home from work, I was also able to intercept the mail whenever a notice of my absence arrived in its telltale postcard format. I would then forge her name on the card and return it to the school office, allowing me to keep my mother and the school in happy ignorance. I decided that I'd only go to the classes I actually enjoyed or ones where a test was scheduled. As far as I knew I was getting passing grades in my individual classes. But because I missed so many homeroom periods where the attendance for the entire day was taken, as far as the main office was concerned I showed up in their records as more absent from school than present – and this proved my ultimate undoing.

With my new plan in place, the beginning of the year went along apace. I was still riding the fumes of being on the football team as I strode the halls of Clinton with shimmers of my remaining confidence still intact but fading rapidly with each passing day. Senior year in high school is typically of much lighter concern, especially the latter half of the year. With the SAT exams basically done, and the GPA as good as it is likely going to get for college recruiters, the energy is one of living on the cusp, of being essentially done with high school but still going through the motions. While most of my friends were talking animatedly about attending college, I figured that without the football scholarship I had no chance. My SAT's, especially in math, were decidedly mediocre. Plus, as difficult as high school continued to be even just attending classes that I liked, I quickly returned to the notion that college was really not for me anyway.

Then one night I got into a conversation with Peter Mandel about the school he was planning to attend next fall – Goddard College in Vermont. He explained how the program was an alternative approach to education and might be very accepting of someone like me from a poorer, more working-class background, even to the degree of obtaining grants and scholarships. He thought I would fit nicely at Goddard and spent half the night singing the praises of the school and how cool it would be to go there together, and the other half cheer-leading me to at least apply. He also suggested Old Westbury College, a part of the State University of New York that had just opened its doors in Oyster Bay, Long Island, as another alternative program I might look into. When I went home that night I actually rekindled the thought that it might be possible for me to find a college to attend. The next day I wrote to both schools for an application.

It seemed that I wrote for hours filling out the Goddard application, plus writing a number of essays and a personal statement describing who I was and what I wanted to do in college. I was nervous when I dropped it in the mailbox in front of the Co-op Market. The application to Old Westbury was a bit more standard and therefore quicker to fill out. Once more the mailbox greeted me stoically as I added another plea for my future. As I waited for the replies, I tried to stay detached, aloof, and I forced my expectations lower and lower as the days passed without hearing from either school. This approach had become an easy reflex for me over the years. With my relentless knack for casting myself as second-class in any situation where I really wanted something, ruthlessly tamping down any enthusiasm that might billow expectantly within me, it was no shock when the Goddard rejection letter arrived. I simply saw it as another confirmation of my worthlessness. Or, perhaps they read between the lines and discerned my own ambivalence. Either way, it certainly did not feel good when I read their form letter. Oh, well, I shrugged; I knew I wouldn't impress them. The bigger shock came when Old Westbury invited me to their campus for an interview.

That morning I tried to dress as spiffy as I could, adding a shirt and tie to my slacks, polishing my black loafers. I still didn't have a suit or a sport coat, so I worried the entire time I was travelling if I looked right for this kind of interview. My mother was proud and surprised since other than the brief fantasy of a football scholarship we had never really talked about my being interested in college. She always fell back upon the practical, and relentlessly urged me to find a good, steady job as fast as possible once high school was over. She kissed me good luck as she headed down the stairs and to the bus stop for another day at Woolworth's. I felt lonely and awkward as I began my journey to see if I might be going to college in the fall. Over and over again I had to talk myself into continuing on with what I knew deep inside would be a fool's errand.

It took me a couple of buses and a train ride to get to Old Westbury. When I stepped onto the campus a wave of anxiety swept me crushingly into its arms. Except the few times I hung out at the Bronx campus of New York University, when my cousin Ned was a student there, or cut through the grounds of Lehman College on my way home, I had never before officially stepped foot on a college campus. I didn't know where I was going or even what questions to ask to find my way. Even if I could formulate a question I was too nervous and ashamed to ask. I knew for sure that everyone I passed was looking at me with eyes that scalded, "You don't belong here!"

"Who was I trying to kid," I berated myself mercilessly; this was definitely not my world. With every confused and meandering step closer to the admissions building, I began anticipating the moment when some official would come up from behind and place their hand on my shoulder and escort me off the campus, finally busting me for the imposter everyone knew me to be. It took every fiber of my being to proceed to my interview, rather than turn and run all the way back to the safety of the Bronx.

When I finally made it to my appointment I was immediately engulfed in an air of formality. Throughout the entire interview my body was rigid and my answers were barely beyond monosyllabic. Even though I wasn't thrown out after my first tongue-tied utterance, as I expected myself to be, and the interview lasted 30 minutes, the whole proceeding felt like a huge personal disaster. As I left, I knew that I had only affirmed to these people just what a loser I was. It was terminally clear that I was not now and never would be college material. I was convinced yet again that when it came to school at whatever level, I was simply too stupid to make the grade.

By the time I returned home I felt beaten down and at a loss to find the wherewithal to feel any different. My fate was sealed: while my friends would go off to college next fall, I would remain in the Bronx hoping to find a better paying job than working at the Co-op or, God forbid, Woolworth's. Instead of college, I would probably get married to Shira and have kids, or worse, get drafted and dispatched to Vietnam. As much as I loved and cared about Shira, there was restlessness stirring inside me that did not desire to follow that well-trod path into society's expectations of adulthood. What I could not foresee beneath the demoralization I was immersing myself in over my post-high school future was that my immediate fate would be equally disheartening.

As fall sacrificed it's remaining foliage to winter, and as winter was caressed to melting by sun-heated spring, what remained of my senior year of high school became one non-stop, carefree, do-your-own-thing party. I was shed of any and all thoughts of going to college and that made me feel relieved. I was in love with Shira and she was in love with me, and my working in the Co-op served us well for the time being. I was immersed with my friends, playing basketball with my now mended back, smoking pot and dropping acid, and listening to music. Occasionally we'd even return to drinking beer in the golf course, even though in the growing culture of drugs this previous weekly ritual had become more of a nostalgic novelty. Despite my injury-altered, post-senior-year plans, all continued to feel right in the world. Until suddenly it didn't.

It was the assassination of Martin Luther King, Jr. in April 1968 that truly shocked me beyond my own parochial confines. I was angry and scared as city after city erupted in rebellion, outraged over the murder of a black man who preached peace and nonviolence. It seemed impossible and intolerable that this had happened, but all I could do was wring my hands in shock and outrage.

Then the street fighting between the students and police in Paris erupted that same spring, lifting my eyes to the fact that change was everywhere pressing against the barricades of old paradigms of meaninglessness, conservatism, greed and exploitation all around the globe. When the student takeover of Columbia University occurred right on the heels of Paris, I was glued to WBAI radio's blow-by-blow, on-the-scene coverage. It was almost like I was shoulder to shoulder with the students, literally a mere subway ride away, proud of them as they determined to save Morningside Park from destruction in solidarity with the mostly black residents living in the Morningside Heights section of Harlem.

Further, the nightly news spewed images of the war and the mayhem it was creating right into my living room seven days a week. Anyone who turned on the national newscasts could see American soldiers being shot and shooting Vietnamese people in return. The screams of the wounded G.I.'s, and the tears of their comrades trying to aid and comfort them, was standard fare on the television. Images of U.S. planes carpet bombing rice paddies and the roar of exploding fireballs of Agent Orange defoliating the Vietnamese countryside awed me with their power, while causing me to wonder why our government was enacting such malevolence upon poor peasants halfway around the world. Images of naked children, bodies burnt raw from napalm as they ran down the roads, caught my breath in my throat. Live footage of a Vietnamese policeman putting a bullet through the head of a protestor, assaulted my conscience and turned my stomach. In our neighborhood, a few of the older guys were already contending with being drafted into the Army and attempting to figure out ways to avoid the military altogether or, if they were drafted, praying they'd be sent to Germany instead of Vietnam. As the summer leading to my high school graduation spread before me, and conversations about the war erupted everywhere, I became more determined to understand the whys and the wherefores of our involvement in Vietnam.

Then, shortly before my final year at Clinton was to end, another part of the sky fell in. Bobby Kennedy was assassinated in Los Angeles on June 6, 1968. The whole thing was shown on television, with Bobby lying on the floor dying in the arms of a 17 year-old kitchen staffer, Juan Romero. Mere months prior to his death he had brought his presidential campaign to our neighborhood on a flatbed truck, and I had gotten to shake his hand when the truck stopped near the Little Schoolyard of P.S. 95 so he could briefly address the crowd. For my friends and me he had been a breath of vibrant fresh air. While we were too young to vote (though not too young to go to Vietnam, we constantly reminded ourselves), we saw him as the answer to the stodginess of Democrat Lyndon Baines Johnson and the shadiness of Republican Richard Milhous Nixon, who was once again running for president. It was a crushing feeling to have Bobby Kennedy taken like this from us and, with Martin Luther King, Jr., assassinated only two months previous, the world began to look gloomier and gloomier.

THEN JUNE 1968 ARRIVED, the moment I was supposed to graduate and be done with high school for good. Instead, a new and unexpected reality fell on my head like a ton of bricks. I knew something was off when my homeroom teacher told me to report to the office to pick up my report card. When I arrived, I was handed my report card by one of the administrative personnel behind the counter. I looked at it in stunned disbelief. In the column where the grade was supposed to be entered, huge numerals written in black magic-marker glared back at me. Every class had the exact same notation: 40-D. I tremulously asked the secretary what this meant. "40 is your failing grade and 'D' is for Delinquent, for your truancy," she explained. In a flash it all dawned on me: all the times I chose not to go to home room, all the times I failed to get marked present for the school day, collided in my mind simultaneously like a pile-up of cars at a six-way intersection. My lack of home-room attendance erased all the classes I had attended, all the papers and all the tests I had gotten passing grades on. Simply put, as far as the administration was concerned, I had not been a student at Clinton for nearly the entire year. "What do I do?" I stammered, tears welling up. "Repeat your entire senior year," she replied curtly, "and try to do better."

"Holy shit, holy shit, holy shit," I repeated like a self-denigrating mantra as I left the halls of Clinton for the summer. I was a Super Senior. A *fucking* Super Senior. How was I going to explain this to my mother? How could I face my friends who were going off to college in mere months? It was bad enough that I was not joining them, but up until this moment I had worked hard to soften that reality by reassuring myself that not going to college was *my* choice. While I knew deep inside that I was too dumb to go to college, I was telling my friends that I just wasn't interested, that college just wasn't for me. Now it would become patently clear that I was not joining them because I was going *back* to De Witt Clinton for another whole year of high school. I couldn't fathom what was happening; a whole *fucking* year, I railed in silent rage. All the way home I seriously contemplated dropping out of high school altogether. Why not go find the proverbial good job and avoid the shame of another year at De Witt C? As I awaited my mother's return home from work, I paced restlessly, shooing my sister from my room every time she asked me what was wrong. I had to come up with a story and a plan before my mother got home.

The conversation between my mother and me quickly devolved into shouting and tears. I was trying to blame the school for making a clerical error, claiming that they had made a mistake in marking me absent. She would have none of it, knowing full well that if it was a clerical error then all I had to do was go and correct it. We argued back and forth until I finally told her the truth about cutting homeroom, about going to school when I felt like it and signing her name on the postcards sent from the attendance office. She was appalled and utterly distraught that I had lied and forged her name. When I told her I was going to drop out and find a job she wailed even louder and begged me not to do it, explaining vehemently that neither she nor my father had high school diplomas and look where it had gotten them – a life as a Woolworth's salesgirl cleaning bird shit from parakeet cages, and a broken-down longshoreman who drank himself to death. "You need to be the first in this family to graduate high school," she demanded, pounding the kitchen table. She then went into her typical song-and-dance about how impossible it was to find a good paying job without a high school diploma. As much as I had become tired of that refrain, now it was driven home by a flood of tears as she painted a graphic picture of my ending up just like her, working my whole life and winding up "not having a pot to pee in" when it was all over.

Now I began to cry, partly over my mother's grief-filled anger, the likes of which I had never experienced before, and partly over imagining myself condemned to Woolworth's, or worse. All the while Peggy sat in a chair at the kitchen table, silently taking all of this in for future reference since in the coming fall she was entering her junior year at Walton High School, the year when students were expected to begin making plans for their futures. By the end of the evening my mother and I were both exhausted. I went to my room to ponder all that we had argued about. I fell asleep without any insight as to what to do with my life, now suddenly in complete disarray.

For the next couple of weeks the tension in our house was palpable. My mother and I avoided each other as much as we could and when we did talk it was polite and trite, concerned mostly with the chores that needed to be done. I spent time telling my close friends what had transpired and not a single one of them teased me or shamed me in any way about being left back. Instead, to a person, they advised me to finish and not drop out of high school. When Shira and I sat down together to talk about me being a Super Senior, she also refused to add any more shame to my already overflowing cup. With her heart set on attending college to be a teacher, she reminded me of the importance of getting my diploma and on the value of a good education more generally. She was completely supportive and encouraging. As a result of these many conversations, along with my own moments of introspective wrangling, I decided that I would bite the bullet and commit to finishing my last year of high school . . . again. But this time I vowed to take a different approach.

THE FIRST THING I PROMISED MYSELF was that I would not miss a single day of school in the coming year. Next, I made the commitment that when school started I would clean up my act and not get high as often, reserving that for weekends only. Further, while I wasn't what one would consider an avid reader, I did enjoy it when I made the time. After being left back, I decided to carve out as much reading time over the summer as I could. I outlined my own summer reading program where I set about devouring as many books as I could find. Because of what was going on all across the country and throughout the world, I was strongly drawn to understanding current events, especially the war in Vietnam and the Civil Rights movement. I had already begun to pay more and more attention to the war, especially with mandatory draft registration waiting me upon my18th birthday, just months away. Additionally, the tendrils of my curiosity and my sensitivity about the black protests for civil rights had been growing ever since witnessing my family's reaction of relief, and their "good riddance" attitude, at the news of Malcom X's assassination in February 1965, when I was only 14. After King's assassination, I began to think that maybe Malcom X and the Black Panthers were right – maybe violence was the only way to make social change in America. I determined to spend my summer figuring out this question and more by reading everything I could get my hands on about black history and about the Civil Rights movement. Now that college was no longer an option, I felt the hot breath of military service bearing down more acutely, even with my additional year as a super senior in high school temporarily buffering its arrival. I was too scared to simply oppose the draft by not signing up. Muhammad Ali had already been prosecuted for refusing to serve in the military on the basis of his religious convictions as a member of the Black Muslims, and as a result was stripped of his heavyweight boxing title. If a famous person could be treated like that, I reasoned, there was no way I was going to successfully avoid the draft. Furthermore, I knew that I wasn't quite yet ready to go to jail for my beliefs.

So I turned my attention and all my energy into trying to figure out the world that seemed to be ripping itself apart. With laser-like focus, I set my course to becoming a citizen of the world, and the only way I knew to do that was by acquiring knowledge, and insight, and perspective. The cornerstone of my summer reading was my decision to keep my own journal of newly discovered words. My plan was that whenever I came across a word that I did not know the meaning of, I would immediately look it up in the dictionary. Then, before starting up reading again, I would print the word in my notebook, along with the entire dictionary definition as I found it. At the end of the day I would read through all the words I had written down, sometimes reading them aloud to myself. I was determined to extract the most out of my summer in preparation for returning to high school.

My plan was inadvertently aided by an argument I had with the manager of the Co-op Market, Tony LoBianco. One day I was quite late in returning back from lunch at Shira's house and Tony caught me. I had been scheduled to be on the delivery truck and due to my late arrival orders were beginning to back up. As a result, he lit into me with a fury that felt completely out of proportion to my infraction. In turn, I got mad and the argument rose in decibel level causing a scene right in the front of the store. Finally I yelled, "I quit," and threw my green apron on the floor. As I turned to walk out he replied, "You can't quit; you're fired!"

Fortunately, the job market at the time was such that by simply walking down any commercial area a job-seeker could land a position in five out of five places they visited, even before the ink on the applications was dry. The day after I quit the Co-op, I was on Fordham Road and the Grand Concourse, putting in applications in every store that would take them. Before I walked a full block I was hired on the spot by Bookmasters, a local chain of bookstores in the New York area. It was as if Fate herself had smiled down upon me in my efforts to reform my ways and do better in my Super Senior year of high school. Suddenly I was literally immersed in books, books, and more books. I couldn't have planned it better if I tried and, as a result, I was determined to make the most of my sudden exposure to all these new ideas right at my fingertips.

I had just launched my political studies and social inquiry, when, in August, the Chicago police rioted in response to the thousands of protestors gathered outside the Democratic National Convention. As I watched the police batons rain down with wanton viciousness, then rise up dripping with blood only to descend again and again, all my remaining innocence was crushed into the dirt as disconsolate anger seemed to claim my every waking moment. How much more could I stand? How much more could we as a country stand? Thus it was in the summer of 1968 that I took a radical turn and became more politically aware and active. Like so many other social and political awakenings during the 1960s, mine was also enhanced and deepened by music.

ONE DAY, SHORTLY AFTER HIGH SCHOOL ENDED and summer commenced, Peter Mandel invited me up to his apartment. As I sat on his bed lamenting the fact that I had gotten left back and had another year to serve at Clinton, he began to take out all the albums he had by Bob Dylan. The only Dylan tune that I really knew was what we called the "Everybody Must Get Stoned" song, which was constantly played on the radio and which we had turned into a drinking song as we sloshed back quart bottles of beer in the park on summer nights. In that moment, Peter opened up another world for me as he played song after song, commenting on Dylan's lyrics, noting the brilliance of Dylan's music from the perspective of his own guitar playing, and urging me to see into the depths of Dylan's poetry. I listened with rapt attentiveness as "The Times they are A-Changing" and "With God on Our Side," ripped through my mind and soul, shredding all my previously held ideas and beliefs about America. When he finally played "The Lonesome Death of Hattie Carroll," I was in tears, my heart ripped open by the tragedy of injustices in the segregated South and so many other places. My spirit suddenly felt more determined to right the wrongs taking place in this country of ours.

That entire summer Peter and I would listen to Dylan and drop acid shaped like tiny barrels and dubbed Orange Sunshine. We would take long walks, or sit for hours, using every moment to discuss the need and possibility of revolution in America. We continued to be inspired by Fidel Castro in Cuba, while lamenting the death of Che Guevara in Bolivia. We were energized by the boldness of the Black Panthers in Oakland, California, defending and serving their communities. We saw Vietnam's Ho Chi Minh as even more democratic than America's Founding Fathers, from whom he was modeling his view of a Vietnam free of U.S. colonial oppression.

I was beginning to see that the America I grew up learning about with pride and admiration, was not living up to its ideals. I was bowled over and angry. Like so many other young people, I was stunned by the hypocrisy and disillusioned. I wanted more than anything for my country to be the force for good, for justice. At this point, buoyed by my own growing social awareness, as well as by the virtues of standing up for fairness and justice I had gained simply by osmosis living all these years in this Jewish neighborhood of mine, I felt like it was crucial that I begin fighting to re-find and reestablish America's ideals. I wanted freedom and democracy for everyone, everywhere.

Then one day Bookmasters began selling *Ramparts* magazine and my political sensibilities expanded exponentially. This was an incredible resource for my growing dissident perspective. Published in San Francisco, the epicenter of the antiwar movement and radicalism generally, the magazine began sharply re-shaping my consciousness. Its articles on the war, the Black Panthers, and cultural critique just rocked my parochial view of things. Writings by Jean-Paul Sartre, Che Guevara, Paul Krassner, Eldridge Cleaver, Jack Scott, and Kurt Vonnegut, brought an entire new world to my fingertips. At one point, in response to the magazine's campaign to get *Ramparts* articles in local media around the country, I volunteered to be a point-person in this endeavor and was immediately sent a large envelope of camera-ready copy. Of course, in my exuberance to be a part of the revolution in whatever way presented itself to my 17-year-old imagination, I had failed to think through the fact that I had no idea what to do with these materials and no idea who to talk to in order to find out. Needless to say it was a short-lived moment of zeal. Instead, I returned to my reading and to my own world of imagining.

As a vital bolstering of my imaginative faculties, I nightly dialed my short-wave radio into the music and sultry voice of D. J. Allison Steele, and swooned to her opening poetry: "The flutter of wings, the shadow across the moon, the sounds of the night, as the Nightbird spreads her wings and soars above the earth, into another level of comprehension, where we exist only to feel. Come, fly with me, Alison Steele, the Nightbird, at WNEW-FM, until dawn." With her as my companion-guide, I would allow the music of *The Doors, The Moody Blues, King Crimson, The Chambers Brothers, The Jefferson Airplane,* and a host of others help me find and connect to my true emotions. Sometimes I would turn to the stirring voice of Julius Lester on the airwaves of WBAI, seeding the clouds of my desire for a new way of thinking and being. With one or the other of these voices in the background, I practiced writing political speeches against the war and in support of black liberation. As I finished each one I would read it out loud, imagining myself giving these speeches before hundreds of people. Sometimes I would call Peter and read them to him over the phone and we would launch into a longer conversation about the state of our world and what we could possibly do about it.

IN EVERY FREE MOMENT I HAD THAT SUMMER, I read, and read, and read. I wanted to know what was happening beyond the confines of my life and I wanted to understand why things were happening as they were. For every book I bought at Bookmasters, I stole one, feeling like I was righteously justified since I was educating myself at the expense of "The Man," liberating my mind right under their noses. It was all so heady. I also felt a sense of urgency, like I had to catch up to what was shaking our world, so I did not waste time. One after another I lustfully ingested the books that I knew would change my consciousness for the better: *The Autobiography of Malcom X*; Piri Thomas' *Down These Mean Streets*; *The Invisible Man*, by Ralph Ellison; *Black Rage*, written by two black psychiatrists; Eldridge Cleaver's *Soul on Ice*; *Before the Mayflower* by Lernone Bennett; David Schoenbrun's *Vietnam*; Herman Hesse's *Siddhartha, Demian, Steppenwolf* and *The Glass Bead Game*; Martin Luther King, Jr.'s *Where Do We Go From Here*; *Bury My Heart at Wounded Knee*, by Dee Brown; *The Diaries of Che Guevara*; Jack Scott's *The Athlete Revolution; Steal this Book*, by Abbie Hoffman; *Crazy Horse* by Mari Sandoz, and more and more and more.

I RETURNED TO HIGH SCHOOL ready to rock and roll academically. I was done with my twin nemeses, having just barely passed Spanish and geometry thanks to another round of summer school, so all my classes were English, history, social studies, or general science. I felt I had command of current events and their historical contexts. I wrote well, with boldness and conviction. I spoke in class more often and I finally felt like I knew what I was talking about. In one class, in an unusual turn of events for me, I even became fascinated by earth science and the geologic processes that formed Earth and its various landscapes – a testament to my now insatiable desire for knowing the entire world. Suddenly, exams appeared to me as tiny hurdles, easily surmounted. Like the summer I trained to get in shape for the football team, this summer I got in shape to understand the events stirring the planet and therefore affecting my life.

My world had grown beyond the neighborhood. I felt I had finally come up to par with the intelligence, spirited debate, and depthful inquiry into life that so many of my Jewish neighbors, elders and friends, had exhibited and inspired in me. I never in my life enjoyed school as much as I did in completing my Super Senior year.

Chapter Nineteen
Failure to Launch

Harry Lefkowitz and I planned our getaway from the neighborhood like we were part of the cast of the movie The Great Escape, *and our families were our German captors. I had finally graduated De Witt Clinton High School the previous June. Harry had been busted in his first few weeks at the University of Southern Indiana for smoking pot and was instantly sent packing from college, recently returning to the Bronx. It was autumn 1969 and we were both 18. He was working at the Co-op and I had just landed a job with the New York Public Library in their Bookmobile Division in the South Bronx. Shira and I had broken up in August. The neighborhood was once more feeling empty and excessively confining, with drugs ravaging the social landscape. As a result more than a few people were migrating to Vermont to buy land and get back to nature. Harry and I were restless and couldn't imagine anything better than shedding the Bronx and moving to Vermont, but we couldn't imagine how we could get the money to make that happen. Then we heard about the burgeoning oilfields in Alaska and how jobs building a new pipeline were available simply for the taking. With visions of wheelbarrows full of money and a house in Vermont, we set our sights toward the land of the midnight sun.*

* * * * *

IT WAS GOOD TO FINALLY BE DONE with De Witt Clinton High School, more a boys' reformatory or huge holding cell, than a seat of learning. The month of June 1969 never looked so good, especially since the coming September would, after thirteen straight years, be completely void of any kind of school whatsoever. I had mastered my initial shame about being left back and having to repeat my entire senior year when so many of my friends had moved on to college. I had plunged headlong into being a student again. I had become a voracious reader and as soon as I started being interested in my classes I got good grades, which only motivated me more. Maybe I was not so dumb after all.

My first order of business after school ended was to find a job. I was still working full-time at Bookmasters. It was an okay job with lots of opportunities to purloin books to feed my reading habit. Unfortunately the pay was horrible and I realized that I needed to seek out other employment now that I was done with high school and now smack in a harder, less forgiving world. Meanwhile, the summer progressed slowly, all the routines firmly back in place: hanging out at The Rail, shooting hoops, being with Shira, and getting stoned when Shira wasn't around. When it fully sank in that high school was done and gone forever, I felt like all the air had been let out of my tires, deflated in such a way that I couldn't see any particular path I wanted to traverse into adulthood. I had focused so hard for the past year, determined to graduate, that once it was over a fierce state of fatigue gripped my soul. Wasn't I supposed to be going somewhere after high school? Wasn't I supposed to be out there changing the world that I had spent so much time reading about? As I looked around the neighborhood each day, I wondered if this was now the end of the line. With a lot of my friends back for the summer from their first year at college, I expected the next two and a half months to be a blast before they were gone again. But now I knew for sure that their trajectory was not going to be mine; there would be no saying goodbye to high school and then catapulting into college for me. My realizations that my friends would soon be gone again, and that I would be staying put, tinged my summer with sadness. Mercifully, as summertime claimed us, my despairing thoughts were daily suppressed by friends who offered all manner of distraction. There were regular excursions to Sylvan Lake, Bish-Bash waterfalls, and overnight camping at Ward Poundridge Reservation, all within quick driving distance from the Bronx. Of course, getting high on pot, uppers, downers, methadrine, and LSD, or whatever anyone brought to The Rail that day, was *de rigeur*. Whereas a mere few years ago it was pot and hashish as far as the eye could see, by now the drug scene had spread to include everything under the sun. There were even a few of our neighborhood friends who had begun using heroin.

At the same time, all of us males were faced with the prospect of being drafted into the military, especially me, without the protection of a college deferment. Following our fear and our consciences, we took to the streets to join the protests. We marched in antiwar demonstrations in Manhattan, organized by the Fifth Avenue Peace Parade Committee, with thousands of others to voice how horrible, wrong, and unjust we thought the situation in Vietnam was. We were also drawn to attend "Be-Ins" and "Love-Ins" in Central Park, gathering to listen to music and revel in our freedom and our peaceful care and concern for each other and the entire world. One day at the end of July, a group of us started talking about going to a concert up in Woodstock. It was scheduled for

August 15-18, on a 600-acre farm in White Lake, N.Y. We had all heard that it was going to be the biggest concert of all time, with all of our favorite bands in attendance. A number of people we knew were set on going and already had gotten tickets for all three days for $18. But all I could think of at the moment when I was asked to go was that I could not afford either the tickets or miss work at the bookstore. I reluctantly said no, sealing off my chance to experience what turned out to be the musical-communal event of my lifetime.

THEN SUDDENLY THE WORLD OUT THERE became all too real when one of my closest friends, my surrogate brother, Kevin Hurley, received notice that he was drafted into the army and was ordered to report for duty on July 28, 1969, his twentieth birthday. He was soon to be the property of Uncle Sam.

I was horrified and angry at the prospect. Kevin, on the other hand, had adopted his typical stoic attitude, so often demonstrated by guys with a blue-collar upbringing: that one responds when called, without complaint, without shirking one's duty. Yet all the reading I had done on the Vietnam conflict had me convinced that the war was evil. No matter how many times I heard about the Domino Theory and the possibility of a communist takeover of Southeast Asia, all I saw was an imperialist enterprise that used young men as fodder in order to secure economic gains overseas. The bombing, the napalm, the destruction of villages and the killing of people throughout the country, was monstrous and, as a result, I had begun contemplating refusing to go into the Army if I was drafted. Kevin and I were opposites in this regard.

In early July, just prior to his induction, Jim Lambert, a friend of Kevin's from New Jersey whom he had met during his only year in college at the University of Texas at El Paso, showed up in the neighborhood one day. Along with Jim's sister, Betsy, and another friend, they had heard about Kevin's being drafted and had figured out what to them seemed like a workable alternative. In a spontaneous moment they arrived at The Rail to shanghai Kevin to Canada for his own good. Betsy was head-over-heels in love with Kevin, having met him a number of times through her brother. Although her love remained unrequited, it was her idea to drive to Toronto and investigate the community of draft resisters there as a possible way to save Kevin from Vietnam. Betsy had even talked to someone she knew in Toronto about a possible job for Kevin.

Reluctantly, but overruled by our enthusiasm, Kevin slid into the back seat of the car with Betsy and me. He was pensive, introspective and clearly consumed with a deep moral dilemma: whether to go to Vietnam and fight, or whether to avoid induction by leaving the country and forsaking his right to return to America, possibly forever.

On the way to Toronto we visited Niagara Falls and then walked the beach at Lake Erie, all of us privately reflecting on the utter turmoil this war had created. We were suddenly keenly aware of how fragile our relationships were under this shroud, and how in an instant people we loved could depart us suddenly. It seemed our lives and our friendships could tumble just like the falling dominoes our government kept warning us about in Southeast Asia.

The streets of Toronto were packed solid with bodies. It was like a festival, with hundreds and hundreds of people our age meandering about. Everywhere we looked we saw guys in army fatigues and t-shirts, guys who looked a bit lost, their brows furrowed over their decision to leave America. Side-by-side with these troubled men were many others who were clearly happy to be safe, and elated to have chosen this recourse rather than going to Vietnam. After walking around for a few hours, we all went into a restaurant and began talking about Kevin's options. Before long it was clear that Kevin had no intention of leaving America. He intended to play the hand dealt him without whining and without running away, even if fate landed him in the jungles of Vietnam, even if fate meant he would die there. As we headed to find the car and drive back home we all had tears in our eyes, knowing full well that because of Kevin's determination to not finagle his way out of anything, Vietnam was the likely place for him to end up.

As a last goodbye, just before Kevin was to head off to basic training, he and I decided to spend a weekend up at Lake George. Kevin and I and a few other friends had gone there the previous summer, canoeing to one of the islands and camping there. Each day we would paddle around, exploring the waterways while deftly avoiding being intentionally swamped by the locals in their fast-moving power boats. Whenever we came ashore in the main part of town at Bolton Landing, we would spend our time flirting with the waitresses. That weekend a year ago still held special memories for both of us and it seemed like the perfect place to go before the Army got its clutches on Kevin.

We hitchhiked up to the lake and rented a small cabin in town. We tried hard to recapture the feelings of our last visit, going to the same local restaurant to order the same meals and flirt with the same waitresses, plying the lake waters with canoe and paddles, feeling the open beauty of the area. Yet try as we might, it was beyond our capacity as young men to truly turn and face the fear and grief that had been building ever since Kevin got his induction orders. We knew we loved each other, but within that overarching truth he could not admit his fear of dying and I could not admit my fear of him being killed. Instead we began to snipe at each other, irritated at the tiniest perceived slight or mistake. In our inability to openly reveal our heartsickness we were distancing ourselves from each other in order to distance ourselves from really feeling the anguish that was engulfing us. It was a terrible goodbye.

By the time our friend Phil Pasternak came to pick us up and drive us home, we were both sullen and nearly non-communicative. The only thing that broke the tension on the drive back to the Bronx was the sudden eruption of a torrential summer downpour just as the radio announcer was breaking the news that the first U.S. astronaut, Neil Armstrong, had just walked on the surface of the moon. It was July 21, exactly one week before Kevin was due in Ft. Jackson, South Carolina. As we let this surreal astronomical news sink in we looked at the sheets of rain loudly and unceasingly pelting the windshield of the car, as if we were driving right under Niagara Falls. Then we looked wide-eyes at each other, speculating that these two events, the moonwalk and this thunderous downpour, might somehow be connected and burst out laughing.

When Kevin was inducted into the army everything suddenly went from abstract to vividly concrete. His departure left me heartbroken. I had since registered for the draft the previous November when I turned eighteen; now that I was out of high school with no plans to attend college for a deferment, I began wondering when I would be called up. This Damoclean event hung over everything, pressing in with a disorienting claustrophobia. I desperately had to do something different, go somewhere different, be someone different, and I had to do it before Uncle Sam snatched me. I had watched all summer as an exodus appeared in the making as people began buying land and moving to Vermont. Many of us became quite envious, especially since whenever we would run into one of them visiting the neighborhood they consistently described what felt like an idyllic utopia. Before long, dreams of owning land in Vermont began to seep into my fantasies about the future.

Harry Lefkowitz and I had become increasingly restless being confined to the neighborhood. We talked constantly about how claustrophobic we were becoming. When we found ourselves mutually inspired by this back-to-the-land scenario, we began imagining this as our exit strategy from the Bronx. It was at that moment when we found out about all the jobs awaiting in the Alaskan oilfields on the new pipeline, and all the money we could make there. All we had to do was to save enough cash for us to hitchhike up to Alaska. How difficult could that be, we wondered. We decided that Harry would continue to work at the Co-op Market and I would try to find a better paying job than the one I had at Bookmasters. I was excited, feeling like I had one foot out of the neighborhood already.

WHEN SHIRA AND I BROKE UP IN MID-AUGUST, it was for no apparent reason other than my desiring something different than what the past two and a half years had provided. There was no big fight, or drama; it just seemed to dissolve in our hands, with my hand being the weaker one in trying to hold it together. Shira still loved me intensely, yet my heart was already being claimed by a wanderlust that placed a higher value on my desire for freedom than on our staying together. There was a selfishness uncoiling within me that sought to burst asunder all ties to my life in the Bronx and fly. At the same time there was a growing sense of *fait accompli*, as if we both felt that somehow we had simply arrived at the end of our time together, as if it was all inevitable. She was planning to attend college to become a teacher and I was searching for something in the opposite direction, something out of the neighborhood, something I couldn't quite define but that I knew was just over the horizon. As a result of our separation, of now being single and not obligated to another's plans, a sense of renewed urgency arose as I sought to enact my desire for change and find a job that could usher me into a new chapter, a job that paid more money, a job that could serve as a launching pad.

By September I had parlayed my newfound love of books and my experiences working at Bookmasters into a position with the New York Public Library, in their Bookmobile Division in the South Bronx. I felt especially grown up and respectable in this new job. I had to ride the train nearly to the end of the Grand Concourse, traverse the rough and tumble streets of a mostly black neighborhood, and dress in button-down shirts and slacks, and even bring my own lunch. Everywhere we went with the Bookmobile we were flocked by excited kids and their parents who couldn't wait to return their already read books and checkout new ones. It was a time when everyone knew the importance of reading and education, and gratitude for the bookmobile poured forth everywhere we went. I felt like I was involved in real community service, something that fit into my newfound credo of wanting to serve the people. I was learning things about how a library functioned and I only had to work 9-5, Monday through Friday, with weekends off. Furthermore, it was decent pay.

At the same time I continued to be envious of my friends who were going back to college because they were getting to leave the confines of the Bronx and I wasn't. In a decidedly sharp contrast to how I felt about myself when I was at work or reveling in my dreams of exiting the neighborhood, in reality I was still mired in the tedium of getting high and playing basketball.

HARRY AND I SPENT A LOT OF TIME together imagining how we could find work that would provide us the necessary cash to buy land in Vermont. Once we heard the stories of the Alaskan oilfields and pipeline construction, once we heard about the enormous salaries people were getting just as laborers, we figured that Alaska was the only place for us to go. Of course, our planning consisted in whatever the fevered minds of two Bronx boys could conjure about what we would need to survive on the road and eventually living in Alaska. Our approach was eclectic and naïve. Harry had a plan to surreptitiously borrow a tent and a couple of sleeping bags from Boy Scout Troop 86, so that was one major item out of the way. With every paycheck we began accumulating the items we thought we'd need – a Coleman stove, which we knew nothing about how to operate, huge Bowie-style knives with leather sheaths like we'd seen in the movies, and some of our favorite books to take along, amounting to an additional 25 pounds in one of our duffel bags. We each bought insulated work boots, warm socks, winter jackets, long-johns, and a couple of flannel shirts. Except for our friend, Phil Pasternak, who was going to drive us to a Howard Johnson's on the New Jersey Turnpike where we would begin hitchhiking, we kept all of our preparation secret and to ourselves. We were planning to leave without telling our families until we were well away. We set the date of our departure for November 1, 1969.

It was finally Halloween and we were spending our last night at Phil's house before setting out on our adventure the following morning. Harry and I had left notes for our mothers that they would find sometime the next day. Unbeknownst to us, Phil had invited Betsy Lambert and Jane Minter over to his house as well, to hang out, smoke pot and listen to music and to bid me and Harry farewell. I had just met Betsy a few months ago when we went to Canada with Kevin, and Harry and I had met Jane when we all dropped acid and hung out with her one weekend at Fairleigh Dickinson University, where she was attending college. Now they were both here, materializing on the eve of our departure. It was a weird night. We were mesmerized by a show on the radio claiming that Paul McCartney was dead and that if you played the song "Revolution 9" backwards you could hear the words, "turn me on, dead man." That Paul was clad in black, and shoeless in the crosswalk on the cover of the Abbey Road album, symbolically cinched the deal for millions of fans. Mixed in and adding a sense of gravitas to the weirdness and undermining our initial disbelief, was a lingering tragic sadness that Paul's death could possibly be true; after all, it was being broadcast on the radio. We argued and tried to reassure ourselves that this was a Halloween prank.

As the night wore on and we shifted into talking about our plans to make enough money to buy land in Vermont, Jane and I spontaneously began making out on the floor of Phil's bedroom. I was in heaven, especially since I was already lonely after three months of not being with Shira. As our playfulness and mutual attraction grew, I suddenly became annoyed that something like this could happen the night before I was supposed to leave with Harry.

Eventually Betsy and Jane had to head back to New Jersey. I kissed Jane goodbye, our lips and hands lingering as if we couldn't bear to be parted. When they were gone Harry and Phil kidded me about my new girlfriend. Finally, all three of us turned off the lights and proceeded to get a few hours of sleep. By the break of dawn we were dressed and in Phil's car, heading across the George Washington Bridge to start hitchhiking to Alaska. For a Sunday morning, Howard Johnson's was bustling and it did not take long before we got a ride heading southeast on the New Jersey Turnpike. We were excited to be finally underway, pursuing our dream.

THAT FIRST DAY ON THE ROAD, after a total of about five rides of varying but mostly short distances, we made it to Pennsylvania where we were invited to crash at the house of our latest benefactor. The next morning we were on the road again, duffel bags in tow and thumbs out. It was drizzling and we were cold. After a couple of hours on the side of the road I became lonely and started remembering me and Jane kissing only two nights ago. I told Harry that I wanted to call her, so we agreed to walk to a pay phone nearby. I called collect and she accepted. Before I could say much about how I was feeling about her, she excitedly explained that Betsy had a new plan, that it had something to do with us, and that Harry and I needed to call Betsy as soon as possible to find out what it was all about. She gave me Betsy's number and I hung up and asked the operator to place this call collect as well. Betsy answered immediately and began rattling out her idea. She confirmed out worst fears: Kevin was scheduled to leave Fort Jackson, in Columbia, South Carolina, within the next couple of weeks and then ship out to Vietnam. She said that she wanted to drive down to South Carolina and see Kevin for what might be the last time ever. She wanted Harry and I to come and explained that she would pick us up on the way down. The only caveat was that it would take a week for her and her brother Jim to make arrangements and get off work. She begged us to wait. She spoke about the possibility of Kevin getting killed in Vietnam and, crying, said we should all want to see him one more time, possibly the final time. I told her that Harry and I would talk it over and call her back.

Harry and I went into a small restaurant to get some food and to talk over this change in plans. It didn't take us long to decide to join Betsy, Jim, and Jane on a sojourn to see Kevin before he was shipped to Vietnam. I called Betsy back with our decision and she was elated. We decided that the best place for us to meet would be in Richmond, Virginia. We all agreed that Harry and I would call every couple of days to get a progress report on when they were leaving New Jersey and their likely arrival time in Richmond. Given our very tight money supply Harry and I decided that we should make use of our tent and

Coleman stove and camp out until Betsy and Jim arrived. After looking at a map we chose Shenandoah National Park as our destination since it was in Virginia and not terribly far from Richmond. We headed back to the side of the highway to resume hitchhiking.

It was late afternoon by the time we reached the park. Nighttime would be upon us before long so we set off into the woods to find a place to camp. Sadly, we were, deep down, really city boys. My six months in the Boy Scouts, with our troop meeting in the basement of the Lutheran church, always felt like an alien environment due to my frustrating lack of success in mastering knot-tying and my natural resistance to the whole command-style hierarchy. Furthermore, the absence of any Jewish boys I could relate to immersed me in a bland Protestant world that reminded me too much of home, so I quit. Even the addition of Harry's experiences with scouting still left us not knowing the first thing about spending a week in the woods. We were more adept at stealing a tent than pitching one; more capable of watching our mothers cook than preparing food on a camping stove; more skilled at negotiating the streets of the Bronx at night than the pitch-black woods and the creatures lurking therein.

By the time we settled on a spot it was dark and cold, with November dampness accumulating mistily in the air. With the aid of our flashlights we somehow wrestled the six-man tent into a relatively secure standing position. In the beam of the flashlights we could see our frosty breath as the temperature began to fall. We then used our enormous Bowie knives as hatchets and chopped enough kindling and small pieces of wood to start a fire. We were too tired to try to cook anything so we sat there, warming our hands, acutely alert to all the mysterious sounds the forest was producing. We jumped at every noise. We decided to leave the fire burning and retreated into the tent, unrolling our thin flannel sleeping bags and climbing in with hopes of getting some sleep. Between the sounds emanating out of the surrounding darkness from every direction, and the plummeting temperature, we either startled or shivered ourselves awake just at the very moment when we were finally dozing off. The next morning, as we parted the flaps of the tent, we were greeted by the entire forest floor covered in a couple of inches of snow. We continued to shiver as we tried to rekindle the fire. We were hungry. We were miserable. We were clearly out of our element and we knew it. It was time to surrender.

It took us a mere moment of looking around and assessing our situation, and another moment of telepathic communication, to mutually decide to cut our losses and depart the forest altogether. We were disheartened and demoralized. We decided to leave the tent and the stove but to take our sleeping bags. We kept everything else, all of the clothes and all of the books we had originally brought along. Hefting our duffel bags we headed back the way we came. Once at the road we found a ride out of the park and headed toward the nearest town, Elkton, Virginia, which was only seven miles away and, as it turned out, less than two hour's drive to our upcoming rendezvous in Richmond.

ELKTON WAS A TINY TOWN, with a restaurant, a small grocery store, and an assortment of other shops. At the restaurant we asked about nearby lodging and were told that there was a motel just a mile or so down the road. We grabbed our gear and trudged down the two-lane highway until we found the motel. It was nondescript, a long rectangle of alternating doors with numbers nailed in the center about eyeball level. Colorless curtains covered the inside of the single front window, shielding whatever was going on inside a given room from voyeuristic passersby. It was just like a thousand other motels dotting the American landscape. We explained to the clerk that we would be staying there for a week and he gave us a flat rate, which he claimed, smiling, contained a little bit of a discount compared to charging us for each night of our stay separately. We paid in cash, which seemed to expand his smile considerably. Stretching his arm across the countertop he handed each of us a set of keys. We dragged our duffel bags and walked to the room at the furthest end of the motel, passing only one or two cars in the parking lot. It was well into the first week of November and tourist season was fading rapidly under the press of steel-gray clouds and ever decreasing temperatures.

Our room had a single, queen-sized bed that we would have to share, a bathroom with a shower, a tiny chest of drawers and an even tinier closet, a kitchenette with a sink, stove, and small refrigerator. There was a tiny window just above the sink that looked directly into a stand of trees and bushes, so close that a number of branches pressed and scratched the window pane whenever the wind blew. To us it felt like paradise, especially after our fiasco in the Shenandoah National Forest barely twenty-four hours earlier.

I immediately reached inside my duffel bag and extracted James Fennimore Cooper's *The Deerslayer*, the first of his Leatherstocking Tales featuring Daniel Boone and Chingaghgook. I was determined to finish all five of these books by the time we got to Alaska. Claiming my side of the bed, closest to the front door, I propped up some pillows, stretched out on the top of the comforter, and began reading. Harry busied himself by doing an inventory of the kitchen and all the supplies and implements stored within. When he finished he sat down in a chair near the foot of the bed and said: "Before we leave I will make you my mom's meatloaf for dinner." "Right on," I answered. It was at that very moment when we realized that we hadn't spoken to our mothers since we left four days ago; all they had were the notes we had left them before we disappeared. We looked at each other, eyes wide, and blurted out in unison, "Let's go call them!"

When I got my mother on the phone I was engulfed in an emotional avalanche of her fear about my wellbeing and her anger at being notified with only a note; her curses at me were interspersed with long bouts of crying. She had spoken to Harry's mother and they were both beside themselves with anguish at our sudden and surreptitious departure. It was impossible for me to get a word in edgewise so I had to stand at the pay phone and wait until the storm relented. When she finally calmed down for a minute, I patiently explained that we were safe in Elkton, Virginia and that we would be going to visit Kevin before heading up to Alaska. At the sound of Kevin's name she calmed down a bit more. The idea that we would be seeing our dear friend before he went off to Vietnam made her feel better. I also reminded her that I was nearly 19 years old and reassured her that both Harry and I would be fine. Soon, I promised, we would be working in Alaska making so much money that when we came back I would buy her a brand new color television so she could watch her favorite shows in style. She laughed. She told me she would try not to worry so much and she hoped that everything would work out.

Harry's call home sounded nearly verbatim to mine and I imagined his mother's comments were quite similar to my mother's. How could they not be distraught, after their two sons had simply disappeared from their lives, leaving only vague, handwritten notes? Harry and I had left without a care for what our actions would do to our mothers, so strong had our fantasy become of leaving the Bronx and buying land in Vermont. It all made perfect sense to us to strike out for Alaska, even if it left those who loved us shaking their heads and clutching their breasts in heartache. But at least for now our mothers had been mollified enough so that we could go back to our room and await our rendezvous with Betsy, Jim, and Jane.

For the rest of the week we bided out time, sleeping, reading, eating, walking to town for an ice cream cone. We had eaten one meal at the local restaurant and after that we quickly figured we would be out of money in no time if we continued that lifestyle, so we settled on our once-a-day ice cream treat instead. We stocked up on groceries, mostly oatmeal, bacon, fruit, cereal, milk, and the ingredients that Harry needed for his mother's meatloaf recipe. We spent a lot of time talking long into the night about what we imagined Alaska to be like and how we would feel when we final settled in Vermont. We also tried to imagine what we would do if we were in Kevin's place, facing the prospect of going to war. Harry determined that he was a dedicated pacifist and said he would go to jail rather than kill anyone. I was torn, not knowing what

I would do, seeing my only options as going to Canada or acquiescing to the draft. To me neither choice was a good one.

Our phone calls to Betsy reassured us that things on their end were coming together on schedule; my calls to Jane reassured me that there was a flame being kindled between us even at this distance. I continually had to remind myself of the larger goal of buying land, otherwise I would've fled back home and into Jane's arms. Given the fact that I had just come out of a more than a two-year relationship with Shira, my ability to be alone and feel comfortable was being tested mightily. Toward the end of the week we called Betsy and she said they would be in Richmond in two days. We agreed to meet at the Greyhound bus station.

IT TOOK US ONE RIDE TO GET TO RICHMOND. It took us walking a few meandering blocks to find the bus station. Inside we quickly deposited our duffel bags in two available lockers, pocketing the keys and heading for a phone booth. We called Betsy to let her know that we were here and waiting. She told us that they would be arriving a day late because a couple of other people were also driving down with them and they needed some time to get their schedules in order. We hung up and agreed we would meet them in the bus station on the following day. With our money dwindling we knew we could not just find another hotel. As a result, we were beginning to wonder if we'd even make it to Alaska. We reassured ourselves that we could probably find jobs along the way if we ran out of cash, and we tried to make peace with the idea that getting to the oilfields might take a little longer than we originally anticipated. With our anxiety partially allayed for the moment and our determination restored, we began walking around downtown Richmond. Bus stations are typically on the other side of the tracks in most big cities and, as we wandered around, it became clear that this was also the case here. While the urban environment was nothing new to us as New Yorkers, our unfamiliarity with Richmond began to make us feel on edge. Before long *The Doors* song, "People are Strange," swirled in my head as we passed barred windows and uninviting alleyways. One young man stepped from the shadows and offered us money if we let him give us blowjobs. We declined and hustled quickly away, more determined than ever to find a safer part of town. What were we going to do? We couldn't just walk up and down the streets for the next twenty-four hours, especially since it was overcast, with the cold and damp fingering its way through our winter jackets. We couldn't just camp in the bus station without drawing the attention of the police and possibly being arrested for vagrancy. Finally, on one of the blocks we ventured down, we spied a movie theater playing *Butch Cassidy and the Sundance Kid*, with Paul Newman and Robert Redford.

Neither one of us had seen the movie so we immediately hatched a plan. We would buy tickets and then stay in the movie theater until the last showing, watching the two-hour movie over and over again and resting. We would figure out what to do after they closed and threw us out, but we would be inside and warm at least until around midnight. Harry decided that we needed to smuggle in a small bottle of Thunderbird rot-gut wine to help us unwind and fall asleep. We bought our tickets, got a tub of buttered popcorn and some candy, and planted ourselves in the exact middle of the theater, the huge screen towering in front of us. We loved the movie. When the second show began we filled the empty popcorn tub with the Thunderbird and began swapping it back and forth, grimacing at each sip as it tumbled down our mouths, searing our throats all along the way until it hit like a depth charge inside our stomachs. By the third showing we were in and out of sleep. By the fourth we polished off the wine and we were dead to the world; even the final scene, dominated by endless gunfire from the Bolivian army, could not stir us. When the fifth and final showing ended we were stiff from sitting and, as we marched out of the theater, we were both singing "Raindrops Keep Falling on My Head," so imprinted in our brains had the tune become.

It was now after midnight, the downtown nearly empty of people, so we made our way back to the bus terminal. We asked the porter who was mopping the bathrooms if there was any place to spend the night that was free or cheap. He nodded. "Boys," he beamed, "the place y'all want is The Railroad Y." He gave us detailed instructions on how to get there and we headed in the direction he indicated, leaving our duffel bags in the lockers until we could assess the lay of the land. We arrived at the YMCA, entered the lobby, and positioned ourselves at the front desk. We asked the night manager if we could stay there for the night and he told us the cost. It was more than we were willing or able to part with. We then explained that we were told that a person could stay for free at The Railroad Y. He looked at us and replied that was true; all we needed was a voucher from the police department stating that we were effectively indigent and we would be allowed to sleep there. It seemed that The Railroad Y was reimbursed by the city for the vouchers so it was no skin off their noses if someone slept there for free. The manager took our silence as an indication of our understanding of the rules and directed us to the closest police station. Once there we explained that we had very little money and that friends were coming the next day to pick us up. We asked if we could get a voucher for The Railroad Y for just this one night. Within minutes and without another question, we were each given a white slip of paper and told to present these to the clerk at the Y. We thanked the officer, happy that we would not have to spend the night fending for ourselves on the streets of Richmond, Virginia.

261

Once we turned over our vouchers, the manager directed us further into the building, explaining that there was a common area just down the hall, with the bunks and bathrooms just beyond that. As we began to navigate past the chairs and small round tables in the common area, heading for the sleeping quarters, a voice whispered to us from one of the tables in the far corner. We turned and peered into the shadowy area and saw a gnarled and stubbled face, slightly illuminated by the glow of the humming vending machines that stood at attention against the wall. He was a small, thin man, dressed in mismatched layers against the weather. He must have been well into his 60s, maybe older. He raised a spotted and shaking hand and motioned us to join him. Harry and I looked at each other and then at him, then we walked to his table and sat down. He began to talk; actually, he began to teach. "Where are you boys from?" he rasped. We told him. "What are you doing here?" he inquired further. We explained that we were waiting for friends to pick us up in the morning. "Where are you heading?" came the next question; Alaska, to work in the oilfields, came our proud reply. "Where's your gear?" he asked. At the bus station, we answered. "Well, before you go and retrieve it, I can see that you boys got a lot to learn. So listen up. If you're gonna be on the road you need to know a thing or two, and Roscoe is here to tell you." With that he motioned us to come even closer and began imparting what Harry and I would refer to later as his Hobo Wisdom.

"First off," he began, "there are thieves in places like this, desperate people who will steal whatever they can if you don't protect it. Don't make it easy for them. When you bring your gear back put it under your bed, underneath where your head is resting. Push it way back up in there, up against the wall; make them belly-crawl to get it. This will increase the chances of them making noise and waking you up. Next, keep your wallet in your front pants pocket. Then fold and roll your trousers so the wallet is buried deep in the folds and put them pants right under your pillow. It's hard for people to remove your pants from under your pillow without waking you up. Last, take your shoes and tie the laces together. Stretch the laces behind your neck so that your shoes are on either side of your head as you sleep. It will be impossible for them to untie the laces and if they try to pull one shoe the other will smack you in the face and wake you up. Nobody wants just one shoe, you know. Remember boys, it's all about waking up in time."

We smiled and shook his hand in gratitude. We stood and told him it was time for us to get our duffel bags from the bus station. "When you're out there, can you get Roscoe some cheese and crackers, boys?" he asked guilelessly, knowing full well that in our minds that was the least we could do in exchange for his imparting the wisdom of the road to us. We nodded and turned to go into the night one last time. We returned shortly, our duffel bags in tow and a block of cheddar cheese and a box of Ritz Crackers for Roscoe. While he eagerly opened his treats, Harry and I slipped into the large room filled with beds. The sleeping area was almost empty, with only two or three of the beds filled with bodies. Despite our exhaustion, when we found our bunks we did everything that Joe had taught us, right down to the letter, and we undoubtedly slept more soundly for it.

The next morning Roscoe was long gone, as were the other sleepers who had spent the night. Perhaps, in the spirit of the early bird catches the worm, they had all hit the streets at first light. Coming from our middle-class neighborhood, their kind of early was a far cry from how we typically greeted the day, unless we had to. All of our belongings were exactly where we had placed them. We dressed, packed, and headed over to the bus station to find our friends. It wasn't until mid-afternoon when Betsy and Jim appeared. We leapt up and began hugging each other. As we began quieting down I looked around to see that Jim and Betsy weren't alone. We were first introduced to Mary Ann, Jim's fiancée, and then to Ritchie, a buddy of Jim's who was a car mechanic in New Jersey. I turned my head slightly and spotted the face that needed no introduction whatsoever – Jane. I hugged her for a long time before Betsy began herding everyone toward the car, explaining it was time to get on the road and down to South Carolina. It turned out that Kevin only had a three-day pass good for the upcoming weekend. Once at the car, Harry and I stuffed our duffel bags into the trunk and the seven of us piled into a tiny Chrysler convertible, three of us in the front and four of us in the back. "Fort Jackson here we come," we shouted as we pulled out of the Greyhound terminal and headed deeper into the South.

Columbia, South Carolina, the state capital, had a population of just over 113,000 people. We found our way to what appeared to be the main street. It was a cool and breezy autumn day and it appeared that most folks had chosen to remain indoors. As we parked the car and spilled out like circus clowns, we immediately went in search of a restaurant. Judging by the tranquil look of the surroundings, we all expected the kind of hospitality that at least the literary South was heralded for. We were joyfully boisterous at the prospect of seeing Kevin in a few hours when his off-base pass kicked in, and at the prospect of finally being out of the car and able to stretch our legs a bit. No matter how well we got along, seven of us in that tiny car made for some cramped bodies and cramped attitudes. We must have looked like an odd assortment of humanity: Jim and Mary Ann locked arm-in-arm; Harry and Ritchie arm-in-arm, with Harry wearing Ritchie's English bowler atop his head and Betsy chatting loudly with them; Jane and I dreamily holding hands. When we finally found a restaurant we pushed our way through the doors and came face to face with the owner, glaring at us with his hands on his hips, chest puffed out with belligerence, blocking our way. "No service for your kind, here," he hissed. A downpour of shock and disbelief crashed upon us, instantly flattening our spirits and making us wonder where, in God's green earth, we had landed. Then I realized exactly where we were: below the Mason-Dixon Line in a Southern town where this kind of crap was likely a commonplace occurrence for black people living here. Within the last year and a half Martin Luther King, Jr. and Bobby Kennedy had both been assassinated and here we were, experiencing firsthand just how narrow-minded and dangerous America could be. "I thought this was a free country," I stated, looking away from the owner and silently imploring the waitresses behind the counter to back us up. They all avoided my look, lowering their eyes in embarrassment and perhaps even with some shame. "I don't serve longhairs in my restaurant," he snapped back, indicating Harry and me with our hair curling just below our jacket collars. "That's my right," he drawled proudly. We all looked at each other. "This is bullshit," I said under my breath to no one in particular but loud enough for everyone to hear. It was beginning to feel like a standoff until Betsy said, "Let's get out of here," which broke the stare-down between me and the owner. Once outside we regrouped and decided it was time to go to Fort Jackson and pick up Kevin; maybe he knew of some places around here that would serve longhairs.

When Kevin emerged from the confines of Fort Jackson we were all so incredibly happy. I hadn't seen him in four months, since our troubled trek to Lake George. He looked great, healthy and fit yet still somewhat aloof. I wondered if he was going to continue distancing himself from us as a way to deal with his pending departure into war and the possibility of never coming back. He silently wedged himself into the car and eight of us sped off to find a motel for the weekend. We ended up renting two huge motel rooms in what looked like a grouping of *faux* log cabins. The girls claimed one room and the boys took the other, but all through the weekend we flitted back and forth between the cabins, often creating puppy piles atop one of the queen-sized beds where we lay around and talked, reveling in the feel of each other.

That first night Kevin took us into town to a G.I. coffeehouse, where music was playing and where soldiers periodically stood on the stage to speak out or read poems about how being in the Army and the prospect of fighting in Vietnam made them feel. Sometimes they denounced the war and spoke strongly in favor of peace. Sometimes they talked about wanting to be a good soldier, wondering aloud how they would fare in a war. Sometimes they just wanted to go back home. I was incredibly moved by the poignancy of their expressions of their anger, fear, and alienation from the whole political scene that was mindlessly and mechanically about to hurl them into the jungles of Southeast Asia, my dear brother Kevin along with them.

The next day we decided to get stoned. With drugs being illegal, with us being hippies in the South, and with Kevin being in the military, we didn't want to do anything that might get us all busted and thrown in jail. Kevin suggested we go to the local drugstore and legally buy some codeine-packed cough syrup. After our purchases Kevin took us to an incredible pine forest, the floor of which was covered in the finest white beach sand as far as the eye could see. We sat at a picnic table that was bolted into the ground. We all looked at each other and raised our cough syrup bottles and toasted Kevin good luck. Before long we were all woozy as the codeine flowed sensuously through our bodies. We walked slowly amongst the trees, the bright blue sky arcing over us, the sand giving way to our unsteady footfalls as if we were traversing an entirely different planet.

The next thing I remember was waking up and seeing all of my friends sprawled out on the ground in various states of unconsciousness. It looked like a movie massacre scene; not a body stirred and the world was eerily quiet. I sat up and rubbed the grogginess from my face. As if that was some kind of cue, the others began to find their way into sitting positions, some even attempting to stand, however disorienting that felt. Eventually we made it back to our motel cabins. By the end of tomorrow Kevin would be returning to the fort and, somewhere on our drive back north, Harry and I would be returning to the road and hitchhiking to the west coast and eventually to Alaska. Our hearts were wide open to each other, each chamber filled with a mixture of love for the fact that we were all in each other's' presence, and sadness over the truth that the fabric of our time together would soon be rent in a number of different directions. As the night drew its darkness over us, Kevin and Betsy seemed to disappear to some private space in the other cabin. We gave them their time together and crowded into the remaining cabin: Jim and Mary Ann cooed in each other's arms; Harry and Ritchie sat together talking; I rubbed Jane's back reassuringly. Before we knew it morning came, with its harsh and insistent demands for us to leave this stop-action interlude and return to a world with sharp edges and join the inexorable movement back into the flow of time and responsibility.

With increasing heaviness permeating our hearts, we drove Kevin back to Fort Jackson's main gate. We all stepped out of the car and waited in line to hug him goodbye. I wanted to cry on his shoulder and say something like, "Please don't get killed in Vietnam, man," but that seemed awkward and trite and I didn't want to jinx him by conjuring any images of him not returning. So, I just held him tightly in my arms, feeling so glad that Betsy had come up with this idea, so glad that I had been given one more chance to see my brother. After all the hugging was done and tears shed, we watched Kevin disappear behind the barricades, each of us meandering through our own private thoughts about him, about the Army, about the war, and about how all of this impacted our own lives. As we once again stuffed ourselves into the car, we were all quite subdued. Jim was driving and Betsy had a road atlas open, looking for the best place to drop Harry and I off so we could resume our journey westward. "Interstate 40," Betsy finally said, tapping the page of the atlas with her index finger. "We'll drop you guys off there." With that pronouncement, we pulled out of the Fort Jackson parking lot and headed north.

As the drive proceeded, the atmosphere in the car hung heavy with the dread of separation. Kevin was gone, soon to be on his way to war, and just up ahead Harry and I would be departing. We were all beginning to resist the idea of leaving each other. As we drew nearer the place of our planned parting, Betsy suddenly blurted out, "Let's all go to California!" With electric speed the force of her words spread like a contagion, sweeping aside all rational objections, shutting down the synapses to the frontal lobes where matters of consequence were weighed. We were in, *all* in, and our joy at not having to separate and instead continue our adventure together jolted our systems with extraordinary uplift. Our eyes, our words, our very body language crackled, seven minds melded, seven hearts became as one. When we finally arrived at the junction of Interstate 40 there was not a single question, not a single doubt that we were turning west, all of us. When we were finally sailing along toward our newly agreed-upon destination, the energy in the car settled to a comfortable, warm hum as we snuggled under the arriving nighttime with dreams of California bidding us onward. Yet Odyssey-like, our journey would prove neither straight nor smooth.

SOMETIME LATE THAT FIRST NIGHT we pulled into a gas station in Crossville, Tennessee, to refuel and stretch our legs. We all piled out of the car and while the attendant pumped the gas we broke off into random grouplets and wandered around under the chill, star-filled November sky. Suddenly the air was filled with the sound of shattering glass, as if a brick had been hurled through one of the gas station's windows. Within seconds we all converged at the front of the station only to be confronted with Jim sitting in a pile of glass, his arm bleeding in a steady and ominous flow, and Mary Ann kneeling beside him offering comfort. The attendant was already inside calling for help, while we all circled Jim asking what happened. It turned out that he and Mary Ann were messing around, playing grab-ass, and he slipped on the pebbled area that hugged the building, losing his footing and falling into the plate-glass window. We all stood there looking at him with concern and reassuring him that he would be okay. Someone grabbed a handful of paper towels from the restroom and handed them to Jim, telling him to apply pressure on the gash. I didn't like the way the wound was bleeding so I asked the attendant where the nearest hospital emergency room was. He told me and I bundled Jim in the back seat and joined him there, making sure he kept the paper towels pressed on his arm. Telling the others to wait there, Mary Ann slid behind the wheel and we were off, so focused on getting Jim help that we did not hear the sirens getting increasingly louder and increasingly closer.

It didn't take long for Jim to be stitched up and it took even less for the local Crossville police to arrive at the hospital. At first we thought they were coming to check up on Jim's condition and to get our side of the story as to what happened. Much to our dismay they had come to arrest us, charging us all with disturbing the peace. When Jim was discharged from the emergency room, one police officer placed him, Mary Ann and me in the back of the squad car and headed toward the jail, while the other officer asked for the keys and followed in our car. Once inside we were taken before the chief of police, a heavy-set man with thick, wavy black hair greased and styled in a pompadour that hung across his forehead, dangling imperturbable nearly to his eyes. He had his feet up on his desk, like any self-respecting sheriff of the Wild West, and he was nonchalantly cleaning and oiling a revolver. Needless to say we became very quiet and very still, standing there with our eyes wide and our mouths open in shock. What had we gotten ourselves into? After our experiences with discrimination in Columbia, South Carolina, were we now facing Southern justice?

"Is this the lot of them?" the chief asked, flashing a smarmy reptilian smile at us. "Take 'em upstairs and get 'em settled." With that we were hustled up a flight of rickety wooden steps where four jail cells were located. The first thing the officer did was to place Mary Ann in the far cell on the left where Betsy and Jane were already ensconced. Then he opened the door to the cell on the far right and motioned for Jim and me to join Harry and Ritchie, which we did. No one spoke. We were all in our own private worlds, disparaging that we had landed in this predicament. We couldn't wait to get out of here and for this to be over. We each found a cot and settled in for the night.

We awoke to what we all realized was neither dream nor nightmare but our reality: we were in jail in Crossville, Tennessee. A young man who had been sleeping in the nearby cell when we arrived, who was some kind of trustee, brought us tin plates filled with oatmeal; a single pat of butter floated in the center of each steaming pile of hot watery cereal. While my friends and cellmates could not stomach the idea of eating, I heartily ate all of their food, ravenously spooning down all four tins of oatmeal. The trustee asked us what we were in for and we explained it was for disturbing the peace, and we described what had happened the night before. He shook his head, emitting a long slow whistle from between his lips. "The only thing I can tell y'all is don't get that chief downstairs pissed off; it's all about 'yes, sir' and 'no sir' around here," he said gravely as he began collecting our plates.

Shortly after his departure an officer we hadn't seen during last night's escapade told us to gather our things as he ushered us downstairs and into the chief's office. As we stood there, subdued and fearful of what he was going to do, he began explaining to us the next steps that we would have to follow in order for us to leave his jail. "You've been charged with disturbing the peace, which means you will pay a fine and pay for the broken window at the gas station. We will be taking you to see the judge this morning to get this over and done with." The chief spoke precisely and clearly, like a man used to giving orders to subordinates who never, ever questioned him. "Last night was an accident," Betsy began firmly. "We didn't do anything wrong. And this is a free country. You can't just charge us with a crime we didn't commit. We want a trial!" Perhaps Betsy had missed the look on the chief's face, or perhaps she'd seen it and didn't care, puffed up with democratic, Bill-of-Rights righteousness as she was in that moment. I watched as his face became engulfed by a crimson tide that spread from his neck, upwards across his chin and cheeks, then onto his forehead before disappearing beneath his pompadour. Every single word from Betsy's lips only deepened the shades of red. I could feel the tension claiming the room, from the epicenter of the police chief's eyes and being beamed straight into every one of us standing in front of him; every one of us could feel it, it seemed, except Betsy. As Betsy continued to rant I saw the blood drain from the chief's face, replaced instead by the same reptilian smile from the night before. "Free country!?" the chief exploded, the anger in his voice intercepting Betsy's words like surface-to-air missiles. "Democracy?" he screamed. "*I* will show you democracy. Get these sons-a-bitches back upstairs," he ordered.

We spent the first half of the day chastising Betsy and her freedom-and-democracy speech, and the second half of the day cajoling her to give us her word that she would remain absolutely silent the next time we were in the chief's office. We explained that we agreed with her, but it was wise for her to pick her battles and not go tilting at Tennessee windmills outfitted with guns and badges. For most of the day she was adamant that she was right and we should fight this charge. It wasn't until dinner, when the trustee brought us an anonymous meal in the standard tin plates, that Betsy relented. As we sat there eating we asked the trustee why he was in jail. He explained that he was in for robbing a bank. We were all aghast, having never met a real bank robber before. He shook his head and told us that he didn't do it. Then he dropped the bombshell: the reason he wasn't guilty was that he was in this very same cell, behind these very same bars through which we were now talking to him when the robbery took place. How was that even possible, we all asked at once, our shock and outrage rising. "Because that's the way it is down here," he explained sadly. "They can do whatever they want. The fact that I have a record just makes it worse for me. I'll end up pleading to a lesser charge and they'll clear the case; if I don't they'll just add more years to my sentence." We all turned back to Betsy and began telling her that freedom and democracy isn't the same here as it might be up where we lived. Instead of standing for our rights we needed to do everything and anything that would help us get out of here, which meant that she needed to keep her mouth firmly closed. She eventually agreed and we all collapsed onto our cots for a fitful night.

The next morning, after oatmeal, the routine was repeated and we were hustled downstairs for another audience with the police chief. As he reiterated the protocol that we were to follow, his steely gaze never once left Betsy. With every enunciated word he appeared to be trying to bore holes into Betsy's face with his ever-darkening eyes, testing to see if she would crack. But Betsy remained quiet and when the chief was done we were escorted to appear before the judge. He read us our fines, adding the cost of replacing the window on top of that sum. We all pooled our money and before we knew it we were declared paid in full, packed in our car, heading back to Interstate 40.

OUR SPIRITS WERE IN DISARRAY. We were conflicted between relief and appreciation for our new-found freedom, and the realizations that we were fast running out of money and therefore California, not to mention Alaska, seemed even further away than ever. We wanted desperately to get the hell out of Crossville, Tennessee, but we needed to confer about our next step. With our money supply waning we knew we had to choose whether to go on together or whether Harry and I should be dropped at the side of the highway to continue our trek hitchhiking while the others went back home. Betsy was adamant that we stay together and push on to California. Harry and I were fine with that plan, but Jane, Mary Ann, Jim and Ritchie were wavering, fearful that we didn't have enough money to make it to the coast. The idea of splitting up was completely anathema to the energy that bonded us when we all first decided to head west. We looked into each other's' eyes, feeling a disheartening pall enshrouding us. Finally Jim said, "I have friends in college in El Paso. We can go there and crash for a while, maybe borrow some money from them or work for a few weeks. We can make it to California," he finished, trying to bolster our confidence again. Betsy was ecstatic. "We can do this," she shrilled, and our enthusiasm

269

rekindled, only this time a bit more slowly. Once again we were buoyed by our desire to stay together and the renewed possibility of getting to California. As we returned to the highway, now heading for Texas, I began to sense Alaska fading, but I wasn't about to turn back and make the neighborhood naysayers turn out to be right.

Given our dwindling money we decided to drive straight through, eschewing any idea of lodging. We traversed Arkansas, then the Texas Panhandle, and then directly southwest to El Paso. We sped down the highway, three in the front seat and four in the rear. Those of us not driving slept in the car, or sat up with the driver to keep them awake. Because neither Harry nor I had driver's licenses, and because Jane didn't feel up to it, Ritchie, Jim, Betsy and Mary Ann alternated driving.

It was a long and barren drive and we all felt physically and emotionally drained by the time we made it to Prospect Street, where Jim's friend, Theo Harris, and his roommate Danny Esposito, lived. We were welcomed with open arms and open hearts into their one-bedroom, one-bathroom garden apartment. Even with the addition of seven more bodies crowding into the space, and making it suddenly and intensely communal, it felt like an oasis in the desert of our odyssey.

We spent our first week there hanging out and, in between Theo and Danny's class schedule, playing basketball at the university gym, smoking pot, and drinking bottles of chilled Bali Hai wine in the evening. Each night Theo and Danny retired to their bedroom that was so small the two beds filled the room from wall to wall; the rest of us took places around the living room, on couches under blankets or on the floor in sleeping bags. One morning, I was reminded that El Paso was a desert environment when I killed a scorpion that was attempting to inhabit my sneaker. Even when the crowded conditions began to chafe, especially when we had to coordinate kitchen and bathroom use among the nine of us, we willed it to work by force of our sheer determination not to give up and return home. We received a brief reprieve with the advent of the Thanksgiving holiday, which sent Theo and Danny back to their respective homes on the east coast and gave the remaining seven of us a bit more breathing room. That Thanksgiving I turned 19 years old, surrounded by loving friends, all of us engaged in preparing a wonderful meal bought with our steadily depleting money. As we ate, laughed and listened to music, all of us were clearly saturated with gratitude for each other. I was in love with them all and even though this was Texas and not Alaska, I was ecstatic that I was no longer in the Bronx.

BY THE TIME THEO AND DANNY RETURNED from the Thanksgiving break, the tectonic pressures pulling us apart had already begun to effect changes in our group and, as a result, all bets were suddenly off about ever getting to California or Alaska. The first one to admit that we were stuck here and that we needed to make the best of it was Betsy. She urged us to find jobs so we could get an apartment that would accommodate all of us. She was as clear as ever that going back home was simply not an option and, to my great delight, for the time being so was Jane. As a result of their determination, they immediately got hired as servers at a local bar. It was an encouraging sign to now have an income source. But as the realization of actually living in El Paso, Texas, began to dawn, daily revealing the west coast to be less and less of a reality, even our camaraderie – built upon good times when our dreams still seemed possible – could no longer sustain us. As each of us began to take stock of where our actions at the Interstate 40 turnoff had truly landed us, the cracks and fissures in our group of seven began to take their toll. Jim and Mary Ann were the first to leave, deciding to head to Florida where Mary Ann's family lived and proceed with their plans to get married, plans they had postponed when the wild idea of going to California was hatched. Since it was Jim's car that got us here, their departure meant we were now without wheels. Within days, Ritchie, who in the rush of the moment had abandoned a good job as an auto mechanic, had his family wire him some money and he flew home to New Jersey. My dear friend Harry was next. Realizing that Alaska would never happen, he decided to go visit his sister Roberta, at school in Austin, Texas, before returning to the Bronx. His departure was heartbreaking for me. It not only meant that our plans to get the money to buy land in Vermont were up in smoke, but it also meant that we would not be seeing each other again for how long neither of us really knew. Like Betsy, though, I was willing to do whatever it took to not have to go back to the neighborhood.

In addition to the little remaining money that we had when we arrived, once Betsy and Jane began getting paid and amassing tips we quickly accumulated enough money to rent an apartment. We found a huge, two-bedroom basement apartment on Mesa Street, close to downtown. The front door of our new abode led down to a slightly below street-level space, making all the windows eye-level to the sidewalk; the back door opened onto the rear of the local 7-11 across the alley.

Now that we had rent to pay, it was time for me to get serious about finding a job as well. To that end I borrowed clothes from Theo, who was my height but twenty pounds lighter. Somehow I managed to squeeze into his tan patterned slacks, don one of his white shirts, and foot-bind myself into his brown loafers with gold buckles, and set off to look for work. Every weekday I pounded the pavement, taking the bus to a particular section of town, disembarking, and hoofing it to every factory, store and fast-food outlet in sight. But most places either weren't hiring or, since El Paso shared the Mexican border with Ciudad Juárez, could readily find sources of cheaper labor. When I wasn't looking for work I headed off to the local blood bank to donate plasma in order to be able to contribute some money into our household. Unlike a straight-up blood donation, I could donate plasma twice a week which allowed me to bring home ten dollars. It kept us in bread, peanut butter and jelly, lettuce and cold cuts, beer, and not much else. Yet, Betsy and I were in great spirits, each of us feeling like we were really living on our own, out from under our parents' control, on an adventure of maturity and self-discovery.

Jane, on the other hand, having de facto dropped out of school at Fairleigh Dickinson University was growing more depressed each day. Whenever she called home she was beset with pleas and demands from both her parents that she return immediately. Right before Christmas she told us that she was flying back to her family in Pennsylvania. Despite the weeks we'd all been together in El Paso, even living under the same roof, my relationship with Jane never blossomed. Despite all my nurturing and my promises to love her, she was frightened to give her heart over to me and too timid to buck her parents' wishes. The night before she left, we partied and drank tequila. I was determined that we should make love before she departed and set my mind to somehow convincing her that it should be our farewell moment. By the time I crawled into bed with her, I was drunk and way beyond my capacity to be very loving, emotionally or physiologically. I was inebriated-clumsy and probably shouldn't have even tried, but at some point in the night I found my sexual energy and Jane acquiesced, likely out of guilt or obligation of some sort. It was terrible; I spent myself immediately, rolled off her and passed out. The next day I was horribly hung-over. As the taxi waited to drive her to the airport, I gave her a tired hug and she stood there limp. She left and barely a word passed between us. Betsy and I were now the last of the cohort, trying to make the best of living in El Paso, Texas, she hustling tips in the bar and me a regular client at the blood bank. What the fuck was I doing here, I began to wonder.

BEFORE MY DESPAIR COULD HARDEN into a decision to flee back to the Bronx, Betsy got word from Kevin that he was indeed destined for the battlefields of Vietnam. He had been given a brief period of leave before he had to report for duty, so Betsy invited him to visit us in Texas. Kevin was familiar with El Paso, having spent a semester at University of Texas before getting bored and dropping out. He had met Jim and Theo there, so he had no problem with Betsy's suggestion. His arrival brightened Betsy's spirits and I was delighted to have another chance to spend some time with my dear friend and brother.

Simultaneous with Kevin's arrival in El Paso, Betsy received word that her brother Jim and Mary Ann had spontaneously set their wedding mere days away. They would be having a beach wedding in Naples, Florida, near where Mary Ann's family lived. Before Kevin could even rest for an entire day, we were all standing at the on-ramp to Interstate 10 East, hitchhiking to Florida straight through the Deep South – me with shoulder-length hair and tattered Army jacket, Kevin with his military buzz-cut and pea coat, and Betsy wrapped in a sweater and long coat lined with *faux* fur – our version of *The Mod Squad*. We didn't appear as likely recipients of any Texas driver's largesse, but within an hour a green, somewhat battered station wagon pulled over and we all piled in. The driver's name was Buddy and he was driving from San Diego, California all the way to Pensacola, Florida to visit family. We were thrilled to be getting a single ride all the way into the Florida Panhandle. What we didn't know was that Buddy was an escaped inmate from a naval mental hospital.

We sped along Interstate 10, through the Texas heartland, past the green, tree-studded rolling hills of East Texas, and through New Orleans. As we were leaving the New Orleans area we discovered the Interstate had been re-routed due to some recent storm damage. We pulled into the first restaurant we found, twenty miles north of the gulf coast, in Picayune, Mississippi. As we walked in and were escorted to our table, I could hear the sound of silverware being dropped on plates throughout the restaurant. Then a cacophony of hoots and hollers arose from a couple of tables near the back of the building. "Oh my, lookee here, Jesus Christ just came in," a voice shouted at me. "Look at all that damn hair," another voice added, laughing. I stopped in my tracks, wanting to turn and get the hell out of there. Immediately Buddy placed his hand on the small of my back and said, "Don't worry about these peckerwoods, Tommy. Let's go eat." As he guided me toward our table I saw Buddy give a look to the people who had been involved in the catcalling. It was a look so disturbingly intense that everyone sitting there became instantly mute and looked away.

Just before we arrived in Pensacola, Buddy explained to us that after he visited with his family he would be returning to San Diego. He told us that we should call him when we were on our way back and if he was still in Pensacola he would be happy to give us a return ride to El Paso. He gave Betsy a telephone number.

After a series of rides taking us deeper into the interior of Florida, we found ourselves stuck without a friendly driver in sight for a number of hours. As the sun began setting it began to get colder. We finally got a ride in a pick-up truck. I offered myself up for the bed of the truck, while I made sure Betsy and Kevin got in with the driver. We drove through what seemed like endless miles of orange groves, smudge-pots ablaze and smoking to keep the frost from destroying the crop. This was not the sunny Florida I had come to believe in based on all

273

the Tropicana commercials I had grown up with. I wished I had one of those smudge-pots to wrap myself around in the back of the truck to stave off the cold and to silence my chattering teeth. Nevertheless we made it to Fort Meyers and to the home of Mary Ann's immediate and extended family. They were all busily preparing for the wedding, just two days away, in the gulf coast town of Naples.

The next morning, we were informed that the pre-wedding party was taking place that night. Once again my long hair would be the subject of intense scrutiny and a tense encounter. Whereas in Columbia, South Carolina, it had cost us a meal, and in Picayune, Mississippi, it could've cost us a beating by the local good old boys, this time, in Florida, my hair served to conjure nightmare images that had recently stunned and repulsed the entire country.

IT WAS WELL INTO THE LATTER PART of the evening and the alcohol-induced love-fest was in full swing. People lined up, each one slurring inebriated congratulations to Mary Ann and Jim, all the while clinging to either the bride or groom in order to find steady purchase so they could emote fully without falling over. I had been drinking my share of beer and was sitting in an armchair observing the comings and goings of Mary Ann's family and assorted guests. Two little girls, both under the age of ten, began noticing my hair, pointing and giggling. I pointed at my hair too and smiled back at them. Before long we had a little game going on, where they would point at my hair, laugh, and skip behind their mother's legs whenever I pointed back at them. This went on for a while until their mother caught sight of it. When she did, she suddenly grabbed her daughters and, staring straight at me with fear and anger, whisked them away into another room. When she returned she marched straight to where I was sitting. She was quite drunk and I didn't understand what she was saying at first. I stood up to talk to her. Then a flood of tears poured from her eyes and she wailed in a plaintive voice that everyone in the house could hear: "Don't take my girls away from me; don't take my girls. Please don't take my girls away." I was stunned and a wave of anxious discomfort rose quickly inside me. I suddenly wanted to bolt. "You look just like him," she cried, pointing to my face. "You look just like that Charlie Manson. Please don't take my children," she repeated with even more anguish.

I looked around slowly, feeling every eye in the house on me, knowing full well that each of their brains was culling through all the grisly, macabre images of Manson and the murders of Sharon Tate and her unborn child in godless California's Topanga Canyon, checking to see just how much I really did look like him. And if I looked like him, maybe I would act like him too. I was speechless and my initial discomfort was rapidly changing into fear that I would be thrown out, or beaten up. I was on the verge of becoming a stand-in for Charlie Manson, a lightning rod for these people to vent all their fears about something sick and evil happening to their children, to vent their fears about all the crazy changes that the Sixties were unleashing upon them without their consent, all their fears about pot-smoking, draft-dodging, longhairs wrecking their country. I wanted to leave, but I just stood silently, waiting for whatever Fate had in store for me.

The tension was finally broken when Mary Ann's father swept across the floor and gathered the distraught mother into his arms and gently steered her out of the living room. She never took her eyes off of me until they disappeared around a corner of the house and into another room. Within seconds Mary Ann's father was back, alone, simultaneously reassuring me and all of the still immobile guests that it was her drunken state that had caused the uproar, and it was time we got back to celebrating his daughter's impending wedding. Slowly the party moved back into something resembling its prior energy, as if a briefly frozen clock had been restarted that signaled it was time to drink and dance once again. For the rest of the night I remained on high alert and kept to myself until all the guests had left.

Against the backdrop of beach sand and the lapping waves of the Gulf of Mexico, Mary Ann and Jim's wedding was beautiful and then they drove off for their honeymoon. We had a brief chance to say our private goodbyes and congratulate them. The next morning the three of us were back on the road. After a series of rides we were back on a stretch of highway relatively close to Pensacola and Betsy remembered the slip of paper with the phone number Buddy had given her. She dialed the number in a nearby phone booth. As luck would have it, Buddy was still visiting his family and agreed to drive us back home. Within hours all four of us were back in his green station wagon, heading west along Interstate 10.

IT TOOK WHAT SEEMED LIKE FOREVER to traverse the two time zones that divided up the great Lone Star State, but we finally landed back in El Paso. We thanked Buddy for his generosity and, to return the favor, we invited him to crash at our place for as long as he needed. It was then we discovered that Buddy was suffering from some serious problems. One night I woke up to go to the bathroom. Buddy was asleep on the floor of my room so I had to step over him. As I carefully brought my right foot over his body, Buddy suddenly awoke. Like an uncoiling snake he sat bolt upright, grabbing the neck of my t-shirt with his left hand and with his right thrusting a knife straight at my Adam's apple, stopping just a hair's breadth from slicing open my throat. Even in the limited light I could see Buddy was in strict survival mode, his breath completely paused, waiting, assessing, and his eyes wide and shining like an animal's. "Easy, Buddy," I whispered in the most soothing voice I could muster. "It's only me, it's Tommy," I added in an attempt to reassure him that he was safe and all was well, my hand now holding his wrist just below the knife blade. He looked straight into my eyes, blinked, released my shirt and lay down; within seconds he was sound asleep. I went and sat in the kitchen and waited for the dawn.

When we were all awake and in the kitchen drinking instant coffee, Buddy apologized for what had happened and explained to us that he was running from naval authorities who thought he was crazy. He said it was time for him to make his way back to San Diego and hopefully straighten it out. He thanked us for treating him with kindness and respect, and within hours he was gone, leaving Kevin, Betsy and I completely befuddled as to how someone so kind and gentle on the outside could be so scared and troubled and dangerous on the inside.

Two days later Kevin was gone, flying back to New York to conclude his leave, put his affairs in order, and see his family one last time. Before long he was off to San Francisco, then winging his way across the Pacific to be finally dumped into the middle of the Vietnam War.

NOW IT WAS A NEW YEAR, 1970, and if we were going to make it in El Paso, I still needed to find a job, quickly. Relying on Betsy's meager income was taking its toll on us both. Finally, after over a month of rapidly disintegrating shoe leather, one January day I entered the local Furr's Cafeteria. Located on the far outskirts of Mesa Street, just past the University's Sun Bowl stadium, I applied for a position on the buffet line. I must have pleased the manager, Mr. Jody Ogburn, because he hired me on the spot and immediately took me under his wing with near-parental care.

I was assigned to the drink line, which meant diving glasses into the crushed ice, filling them with the requested beverage, and handing them to the customers as they slid their trays toward the cashier. I was the only Caucasian employee who was not in management and the older Mexican women who ran the kitchen doted over me and helped me find my way in this new environment. In fact, everyone was welcoming and I got to practice my ghastly high school Spanish for the first time in a real-life setting. I worked a split shift; first lunch, then a four-hour break, and then dinner. During those four hours I would walk two miles down Mesa Street to our apartment and hang out and read until I had to be back at work. I was engrossed by Jack London's *Call of the Wild*, with *White Fang* next in line near my bed. Those few hours allowed me plenty of time to daydream about Alaska, and fantasize about someday living off the land, my visions of finding my way to Vermont unrelenting. The best thing about Furr's, though, was that it offered its employees a generous monthly discount card for meals and I was allowed to spend it on food for myself, Betsy, and other hungry friends.

Our lives had once again become routine: Betsy worked nights and I worked midday and evenings. When we got off work we would meet back home and either hang out together or get stoned with friends. Betsy and Theo were beginning to form a relationship and they made themselves scarce at every opportunity. Our apartment became hangout-central, and barely an evening went by without people gathering to smoke pot, drop an assortment of pills, and drink wine and beer, always to the soundtracks of either Led Zeppelin or Iron Butterfly. "Stairway to Heaven" and "In-a-Gadda-da-Vida" became our ritual anthems.

With our hippie creed of never turning anyone away from our door, some heavy characters who worked the edges of the drug trade also passed through our abode. One guy, called simply Claw because of the gnarled enormity of his hands, always kept a sawed-off shotgun in the trunk of his car as protection whenever he made a score. Two guy who visited briefly before disappearing to who knows where, explained to us in matter-of-fact detail how one of them would walk across the border with a backpack full of weed, while the other would station himself in the hills on the American side, cradling a rifle with a scope in case the Border Patrol or bandits tried to intervene. We just took it in stride; it all seemed so normal and run-of-the-mill in El Paso. Drugs were everywhere and because of our open door policy and the sanctuary of our apartment, we made some very good connections. Two soldiers at Fort Bliss, Lefty and Slim, always seemed to be rolling in piles of marijuana; Bat-Man, who was born and raised in El Paso, had a seemingly endless supply of pills, mostly Black Beauties, and occasional hits of LSD; we even had a friend across the border in Juárez, Antonio, the son of one of the nightclub owners, who looked out for us whenever the need for an altered state arose. Most of the time though, a group of us would simply go out into the desert and get high, immersing ourselves in the rugged beauty of the mountainous landscape, watching the sky for shooting stars, singing and talking until the sun rose. For Betsy and I it all felt harmless, even though we knew what we were doing could get us busted. Rather than dwell on the negative possibilities, we spent our time feeling happy to be alive and happy to be on our own, surrendering together to the surreal craziness of El Paso.

ONE NIGHT A HALF-DOZEN OF US decided that we needed a change of pace and we went over the border to Juárez, to the club that Antonio's family owned. Going to Juárez was like entering a liminal zone that wasn't quite Mexico and wasn't quite America. After walking across the bridge, above the trickle of water called the Rio Grande River, we had to navigate scores of raggedly dressed children begging. The most enterprising of them stood beneath the bridge, close to the river, with long poles with wide cones attached to the end. They shook their poles up and down, yelling for people to throw money from the bridge so they could catch it.

Just before stepping off the bridge and into Juárez proper, another set of begging children and their mothers stood or sat stoically. These people were mostly from indigenous groups and both the Americans and the Mexicans looked down on them as a lower caste. Once past them, both sides of the main street were cramped with hundreds of stalls selling all kinds of merchandise, while nearby store windows beckoned with their wares. Bartering and bickering over prices was the name of the game; it was an art form really, with vendors pretending to reluctantly lower their prices while tourists clucked triumphantly at the close of each sale, each side acting as if a great bargain had been finagled from the peasants.

Ceramic artwork, jewelry, rugs, leatherwork, sombreros, colorful ponchos and serapes were on display everywhere you looked. Taking up almost as much space in the stalls as in the stores, were the ubiquitous iconic images painted on black velvet, bordered with flair by lightweight, mass-produced wooden frames. Scenes of desert cactus, huge, colorful sombreros, buxom women overflowing their Mexican peasant blouses, Bruce Lee in fighting stance, John Wayne in mid-swagger, Marilyn Monroe posed seductively against the velvet backdrop, and many more, all vied for attention in every direction. It was a relief when we finally entered the nightclub and made our way to a table to order beers.

Like many nightclubs in Juárez electric music provided the rhythm for a phalanx of strippers who paraded on and off the stage near the bar, gyrating out of their skimpy ensembles with as much enthusiasm as they could muster. Compared to some other establishments that featured live sex shows between women and animals, Antonio's father's club was tame. We all sat unmolested at a table near the bar since Antonio had made it known that we were his guests. As the night wore on and as the beers kept coming, Theo and I got bored at the same time and decided to get some fresh air. We grabbed our half-full bottles and stepped into the street. We meandered for a while until I needed to take a piss. We ducked into a deserted side street and I relieved myself against a telephone pole. As we were about to make our way back to the nightclub we were suddenly stopped by a lone, uniformed city cop. He told us we were under arrest. "What for?" Theo challenged. "Drinking in the streets," he replied in halting English. We burst out laughing. "In Juárez?" we sputtered simultaneously. He nodded. Theo knew this was a shakedown and figured a bribe could likely get us out of this situation, so he asked the cop how much money he wanted. "Cinco dólares," he replied. We each rummaged through our pockets, coming up with four singles between us. I handed my cash to Theo and he said, "Here," extending a fistful of dollars to the policeman. "No," the cop said, shaking his head, clearly insulted. "Not enough. Go to jail now," he finished, rejecting the money. Theo and I had heard stories about Mexican jails and neither one of us were ready for that. "This is bullshit," Theo spat and turned to walk away. As I began to follow him the cop drew his gun and suddenly we were both looking into the barrel of a .45-caliber automatic. I wasn't about to die in Juárez, Mexico, for any reason, much less over drinking beer in public. Immediately I dropped my bottle on the ground and Theo followed suit. We slowly and conspicuously extended our hands and arms skyward.

We were marched off to the local night-court magistrate for a trial. It didn't take long. With our arresting officer piously looking on we were told that the fine for drinking in public was four dollars *each*. Theo and I looked at each other. I quickly told him that it made more sense for him to use the money to get out since he knew Juárez better than me and he could go back and get help from Antonio at the nightclub. We agreed. As Theo was paying his fine I was led to a door and ushered inside. I was maneuvered down a corridor and out into a roofless, open-air holding area. Each of the four walls had strands of razor-wire strung along the top. As I looked closer I noticed what I imagined were bullet holes in some of the walls as well. Dozens of movie images of men facing firing squads ricocheted around my brain; would I get a blindfold, I wondered absently.

As I MADE MY WAY TO AN UNOCCUPIED SPACE along the far wall, a man lying on the floor threw back the blanket he was under and motioned me to lay down beside him, smiling and making smacking sounds with his lips. I ignored him as best I could and finally made it to the furthest wall where I thought I would be far enough away from everyone else and therefore safe. I braced my back up against the cold stone. I could hear the wind swirling above my head and feel it whip down along the wall, grabbing me momentarily in its icy grip, and then relenting briefly until the next gust. I stood shivering, my lips moving in silent prayer that Theo would get back quickly and rescue me. Reluctantly, I looked out into the pen for the first time. What I saw were dozens of Mexican men, in various sitting and standing and leaning poses, all battling the cold, all staring at me. I was the only Anglo in here and this was emphatically their territory. Would the guards even bother if I cried out? To these men I was fresh meat and now I was scared shitless.

The first guy to approach me was about a foot shorter than I, with a mildly protruding belly and a distinct swagger to his gait as he crossed the open yard, smiling every step of the way. He stopped in front of me and looked up into my face. "Give me your jacket," he said matter-of-factly. I shook my head and mumbled "no." "Give me your fucking jacket," he hissed through his smile. "No," I replied, a bit louder. I could sense the rest of the men beginning to pay attention to our interaction. I was wondering if I should just surrender to the fact that I was going to get beaten and robbed and try to dish out some hurt while I was still standing. I knew from watching movies and talking to friends who had been in jail that the worst thing I could do was to show any kind of weakness. Yet, all of a sudden, hoping to delay my fate in hopes of Theo's timely return, I found myself saying to this guy, "I will give you my gloves instead." He immediately agreed and smiled even wider as I took off my gloves and handed them to him. He proudly walked back across the yard, slipping each glove on slowly with a showboat motion of satisfaction. When he reached the other side he was surrounded by a few other guys and they began talking, admiring his new gloves, laughing and looking over their shoulders at me. "Fuck!" I said to myself.

There was no doubt in my mind that now I was going to be these guys' vending machine – insert fist and take whatever you wanted. Before the night was over I saw myself stripped naked, pounded bloody, and maybe even fucked in the ass more than once. I backed up even more, sealing myself to the wall, my eyes flickering from side to side, waiting to see what would happen next. I began to prepare, curling and uncurling my fists, slowing my breathing; I figured I would go down swinging and the next guy who came across the yard to mess with me was going to get nailed. I braced myself for what I knew was going to come sooner or later. It might have been minutes, but it felt like hours before one of the policemen came and escorted me back into the area that served as the courtroom. There was Theo, smiling; Antonio was paying my four-dollar fine. My body nearly collapsed with relief. When Antonio was done he turned toward me and lifted his chin toward the door. "Let's get the fuck out of here, Tommy," he exclaimed, as all three of us stepped into the night and I began to reflexively and eagerly suck down the cool, cleansing, freedom-filled air.

Our lives in El Paso continued on apace into the spring, working, hanging out, getting stoned. Soon our attention was drawn toward the fact that May was only a few months away and that meant the end of the school year at the University and the inevitable departure of Theo and Danny and everyone else back home for the summer. So much of our social life revolved around people we knew from the campus. Betsy and I began asking ourselves if it made any sense to continue living in El Paso over the summer just to prove a point. This city was harsh enough even with all of our friends attending school, and summertime, with most of them gone, would be hot, lonely and excruciatingly boring. Even if I went back home in April, I calculated, I would still have made it six months on my own; was that enough, I wondered, to quiet all the doubting voices externally and, especially, internally?

Betsy and I eventually came to the conclusion that we were done with El Paso. I made my last trip to Juárez and bought a turquoise-blue-and-gold poncho as a reminder of these past months spent growing up on the borderland. I wanted a reminder of all the things I'd seen and experienced as a wet-behind-the-ears nineteen year old. As we were getting everything in order to leave, Theo and Betsy decided to change their plans and take his motorcycle and head to the west coast before going back home. Betsy, at least, would finally get to see California.

I hadn't been in contact with Jane since she left El Paso right before Christmas; I figured she was once more under the control of her parents and we were finished. In my loneliness, and with feelings of sadness and confusion clinging to my decision to go back home, I had recently begun calling Shira. I had started to feel that since Alaska had failed, and along with that my dreams of buying land in Vermont and building a house, perhaps these past six months were really about expunging all the remaining reckless wanderlust from my heart. Perhaps now there would be more room in there for Shira; perhaps it was time to grow up and get real, to find that decent job my mother always talked about and get married.

I decided to purchase an airline ticket and take my first plane ride back to New York City. Betsy and I had tears in our eyes when we hugged goodbye at the airport; we had been through a lot together and had supported each other in those moments when we wanted nothing more than to flee El Paso and hightail it back to the safety of our homes.

The plane ride was uneventful. I spent the entire time looking out the window like a kid on a brand new amusement park ride. Once I was in the terminal, amidst the crowded hustle of New York, a mild shock came over me as I navigated the shifting tides of people on my way to find a taxicab. I was moving and thinking at a very different pace than everyone else around me, slower, more observant, and more sensitive to my surroundings. As I stood on the sidewalk waiting for the next cab, the edges of my poncho lifting in the breeze, I felt like Clint Eastwood in *The Good, The Bad, and The Ugly*, my eyes narrowing in the afternoon sun, my head above the crowds, my mind drifting beyond hum-drum. The fact that I was even wearing a Mexican poncho in New York City told me that I had changed dramatically in the short time I had been away. Maybe I had become more of my own person, I wondered. I wondered as well if the neighborhood had also changed, if I would be welcomed back, if I would even be happy to be back. As the taxi slid up next to me, I folded myself into the rear seat, confident that I would find the answers to all my questions soon enough.

Chapter Twenty
The Game: Glorious Interlude

Dickey Davis had a mouth on him. He also had a laser-like 3-point shot before the 3-point shot was adopted by modern basketball. Lenny Baumann also had a mouth. Dickey was one of our neighborhood's original trash-talkers, with enough basketball savvy to walk his talk. Lenny was also a fine basketball player, shifty with the dribble, able to drive to the bucket, and possessing a skilled bank-shot that he didn't often miss. At the same time, Lenny was prone to debate and argue everything and had the gift of street-corner obfuscation; that, combined with an authoritative, pugnacious attitude, to the uninitiated might make it appear as if Lenny actually won every argument. So all it took for these two to verbally square off on the basketball court one day was for Dickey to hit the winning shot while Lenny was guarding him. As soon as that final basket went in, Dickey crowed and strutted, Lenny vociferously rebutted, and a crowd instantly encircled them, laughing and egging them on. First they went after each other personally, degrading and discounting each other's respective basketball skills. At some point, when Lenny felt the argument slipping away (Dickey's shot had won the game after all), he began denigrating the high school team Dickey played for. Before anyone could say anything, Lenny boldly claimed that a team from our neighborhood could beat Dickey's high school team. The gauntlet was thrown down and Dickey immediately and enthusiastically picked it up, eyes wide with excitement and smiling a Cheshire Cat smile that radiated, "Oh, pity you poor fools, you have no idea what you've just done." In a matter of seconds it was all agreed: Dickey's high school team would come to our neighborhood on a Saturday for a showdown. Instead of the controlled anarchy of our typical street-ball, the game would be organized with timed, eight-minute quarters, a referee, and free throws after fouls were committed. With that settled, a few of us joined Lenny in drowning out Dickey's attempted comebacks, bragging with ever-increasing volume that our team would definitely kick their asses. Others in the crowd were oddly quiet. While we all knew that Dickey was the starting guard for Columbia Grammar prep school, what most of us didn't know – because the world of prep schools was simply not our world – was that Columbia Grammar was undefeated two years running and was the best private school basketball team in New York City.

* * * * *

MY RETURN TO THE BRONX was strange, both in its uneventful nature and in the continued sense of alienation that I couldn't shake. I was not sure what I thought would happen. Perhaps a big welcome-back party celebrating the fact that I had stayed away longer than anyone predicted or, perhaps the opposite – me finally succumbing to my sense of not fitting in anymore and hightailing it back out of there to someplace else, any place else. Instead I was in some kind of listless zone, betwixt and between knowing who I really was and where to call my home. When I walked into my house I was greeted excitedly by my mother, but Peggy was more reserved, unsure how my return would affect the fact that she had, for good and ill, months of my mother's undivided attention for the first time in her life.

Peggy was approaching her senior year at Walton High School, yet her life had barely changed since we first came to the Bronx. She had no real friends, either at school or in the neighborhood, though when people ran into her at the Co-op or EM's, they always said hello and made time for small talk. Whenever I had friends over at the house, everyone was friendly and engaged her in conversation as best they could, before we all convened in my bedroom to get high, closing the door and sending Peggy back to watch television with my mother. When she wasn't in school she mostly hung around the house. Years ago I made it clear that I didn't want her hanging around with me, at Gale Place or at The Rail. As I made less and less effort to extend Peggy any invitations, we became habituated to rarely showing any interest in each other's lives. This approach just seemed easier and less painful.

I had been trained well. I picked up all the cues and attitudes that my mother and grandmother had conveyed with their utter dislike for Peggy, so much so that I unconsciously carried on this family legacy of neglect with my own disinterest. There were times when a flicker of dismay flashed into my awareness over how shitty Peggy had been treated and how tense our relationship always was. But I never felt emotionally equipped to alter what had been set in motion. Now, after fifteen years in the house at 3987 Saxon Avenue, it felt beyond repair

– even if either one of us could imagine what repair would look like at this point in our lives.

Upon my arrival home, Peggy and I remained cordial. Neither one of us seemed capable of dismantling the defenses that all these years of abuse had effectively demanded we construct to protect ourselves . . . even against each other. It was, therefore, quite easy for us to drop into our familiar ships-passing-in-the-night pattern of non-relating. Despite our public stance, which on the surface appeared blasé, we both stewed in our painful histories of hurt feelings, jealousies, and, to Peggy's never-ending heartbreak, competition for my mother's love. As I went upstairs to my room, I felt like I had been re-incarcerated right back to the place where only months ago I was so sure I was leaving forever.

WHAT I FOUND IN MY OLD ROOM TERRIFIED ME. On my bed my mother had placed a handful of official-looking mail. I opened the envelope on top and nearly shit myself as I read the single sheet of paper. It appeared that during my sojourn in El Paso, I had neglected to keep the Selective Service informed of my whereabouts. As a result, not only had I missed a couple of notices to report for a pre-induction physical, I had broken federal law – I had become a draft-dodger. According to the letter that I now held in trembling hands, if I did not contact my local draft board immediately I would be arrested by the FBI. I was stunned, and really pissed at myself. Mere months ago, on December 1, 1969, the draft lottery had been held. A lottery had been instituted in a vain effort to try to make conscription seem fairer, since there was so much resistance to the draft as well as protests decrying it for falling heaviest on poor people and racial minorities. The lottery did nothing to diminish opposition. My number, though, was 281, a relatively high number signifying that I would likely be one of the last called. Now, due to my capriciousness with regards my informing the draft board, I could possibly be arrested or, I imagined, placed at the top of the draft list as my punishment.

Over the next two days I visited my family doctor and obtained copies of the x-rays of my football injury, as well as all the hospitalization and treatment records. The envelope containing all the information about the back injury that had derailed the possibilities of my attending college to play football, and which was now supposed to save my ass from Vietnam, suddenly felt thin and paltry. My mind raced as I talked to any neighborhood friend I met in the street about what I should do. One guy told me to cut off one of my toes; a guaranteed out, he assured me. One of the older guys had taken LSD for a week, didn't bathe, slept in the same clothes, and soiled his pants the morning he was due to report. He was given a psychological evaluation and rejected. Another guy pretended he was gay, put the moves on the interviewing officer, and was punched in the face . . . but also rejected. Another guy showed up in women's clothing; another with track marks up and down both arms and going through heroin withdrawals; another arrived drunk. I was assaulted by these apocryphal tales, hearsay from sources two or three times removed from the actual person being described. The only real human being I knew that had gone to a pre-induction physical was Kevin, and he was sitting somewhere in the jungles around Pleiku.

Clutching my x-rays and medical history tightly to my chest, I took the Number 1 train from Broadway and 231st Street to South Ferry. From there I walked to 39 Whitehall Street, the location of the Military Entrance Processing Station. As soon as I entered into the lobby I felt the tension, the taut faces and coiled demeanors of the personnel standing guard and those bustling about. As I showed my letter-to-report I was directed curtly towards a set of elevators. As I was waiting, I noticed that all of the soldiers were armed. Then it hit me. Barely six months ago, October 1969, the Weather Underground planted a bomb in the fifth-floor women's toilets. The resulting explosion had destroyed the entire floor, sending debris into the streets below and sending induction operations temporarily to the borough of Brooklyn. A no-nonsense atmosphere pervaded every corner of the building and enveloped every encounter. I immediately adopted a passive and submissive demeanor, held onto my x-rays, and prayed I would be allowed to leave when this was all over. Shakily, I sat on a wooden bench and awaited my turn to be interviewed.

Eventually I was ushered into a small room where an officer sat behind a tidy wooden desk. His black plastic nameplate did not register as I slumped into a chair alongside. No introduction, no handshake was forthcoming. With little acknowledgement he stuck out his arm and I preceded to hand him the manila envelope that, with each waning moment, I was sure would not be my ticket out of the Army. He held the x-rays up to the overhead fluorescents, and then placed them on his desk. He removed the medical records, scanned them silently and then replaced all the items back in the envelope. He pulled a pen from the right pocket of his shirt and began making notations on some forms before him. The sound of the scribbling pen filled the room. When he was done he handed me the envelope, shouted, "Next!" and I left.

Towards the middle of the summer I received my draft card. It was a small white rectangle, folded in half. On the front was my name, below that was my Selective Service Number, and below that was my draft status. On the back was a legal reminder about carrying the card at all times, with a stamp from the local draft board at the bottom. Fearing the dreaded "1-A," which meant you were prime meat for the war machine, I was both shocked and relived to see "1-Y," signifying: "Registrant available for military service, but qualified for military only in the event of war or national emergency." By some remarkable act of grace my interviewer had determined that my back injury was enough to place me toward the bottom of the barrel of potential draftees. I was spared having to make the choice of refusing service by going to Canada or following in Kevin's footsteps.

My happiest reunion was with Harry Lefkowitz. When we met in the playground I could not stop hugging him. We had been through a lot together in that single month on the road, our hearts so set on making it to the Alaskan oilfield, as well as during our brief time in El Paso before he left. His big surprise, as he grinningly removed his watch cap, was that he had shaved his entire head down to stubble. I immediately rubbed it back and forth and instantly dubbed him "Zelmo Beatty," after one of the stars of the National Basketball Association who sported the same look. Thus inspired, we immediately headed for the basketball courts and began shooting around, "Zelmo" and I waiting for enough guys to assemble for a full-court game. That was it; I was back . . . at least physically.

My angst over what I still felt was my premature return, was thankfully dwarfed by the fact that the entire city was abuzz due to the fact that the New York Knicks were playing against the Los Angeles Lakers and Wilt Chamberlain for the National Basketball Association Championship. It was early May 1970 and throughout the five boroughs, on basketball courts everywhere, the highest compliments in the form of imitation were being bestowed on the likes of Walt Frazier, Cazzie Russell, Willis Reed, Bill Bradley, Dick Barnett, and Dave DeBusschere. Sadly, our sentimental favorite, gangly 6' 10" Phil Jackson, who we looked upon as the closest thing to a fellow hippie one could find in professional sports, would not be coming off the bench to inflict fouls or grab rebounds due to spinal surgery. With the Lakers and the Knicks representing two of America's biggest cities, one on each coast, there was no doubt that the "city game" was on display and had taken another step into the mainstream to the delight of basketball fans everywhere. I fully joined in the excitement. Thanks to the generosity of Aron Rose, who had bought us both tickets to Game 7 at Madison Square Garden (his personal welcome home to me, he explained), I got to see and feel the inspiring play of Willis Reed, struggling to return after an injury to his leg. I watched with rapidly rising adrenalin as he limped up and down the court and hit his first two jump shots, unleashing a thunderous pandemonium in the Garden that would carry the Knicks past the Lakers that night, 113-99, and onto the pinnacle of the sport with their victory in the final game of the series.

Being mere days back from El Paso, where I had continued to read and study about the Vietnam War and the Civil Rights movement, it was inevitable that I would somehow mix sports and politics, and Game 7 at Madison Square Garden turned out to be the place. I did this by refusing to stand during the national anthem in protest of the continuing war against the Vietnamese people. For the first few seconds it felt like I was going to get my ass beaten and tossed off the upper deck as a few guys began to bluster about me being un-American and ordering me to "stand the fuck up." Instantly Aron quelled all their grumbling by telling them in no uncertain terms that it was my right as an American to not stand. He backed up his words by assuming a Tae Kwan Do stance that evoked an unmistakable readiness to engage anyone who threatened me. By the time the last words of *The Star-Spangled Banner* were drowned in thunderous cheers in preparation for the opening tip, all thoughts about my subversive action had evaporated into the united purpose of cheering the Knicks on.

A FEW DAYS LATER I RAN INTO LENNY BAUMANN AT THE RAIL. He was excited about my return and called me over to ask what El Paso had been like. I told him a few stories about Juárez, got us both laughing, and ended by lying that it felt good to be back. He said he was on his way up to Bronx Science High School to meet a friend and that I had to come along because this guy was definitely someone I needed to know. We walked until we were standing in front of Science, gazing up at the enormous mural that dominated the building's front lobby. The mural was 63-feet tall, made of Venetian glass and crafted by artist Chuck J. Reilly. On it was depicted images some of the world's greatest scientists, with these words inscribed below: "Every great advance in science has issued from a new audacity of imagination." It was always striking to gaze upon the mural and wonder about all that humans had accomplished.

It was after three and barely any students still lingered. Lenny suggested we look for his friend at the rear of the building in the schoolyard. As we went behind the school, a lone figure greeted us, leaning casually against the waist-high concrete retaining wall. Here was a slim, tall, young black man, motionless, writing in a spiral-bound notebook. It turned out that he was not doing homework; he was writing poetry. As Lenny and I approached he looked up unperturbed and nodded to Lenny. By the time we stopped in front of him Lenny was already singing his praises, telling me how incredibly far out this young man's poetry was and what an incredible basketball player he was on top of that. I was instantly intrigued. He remained silent as accolades rained down. I was instantly drawn toward him, feeling a distinct and resonant kinship as well as a respectful curiosity. I felt that something special was about to transpire here and I was suddenly glad that Lenny had insisted that I accompany him. Finally Lenny turned to me and said, "This is James Randolph."

We shook hands, then wrapped thumbs to clasp palms, then shook again. I was already feeling enamored. He had cut school that day to meet a girl who attended Bronx Science but she had stood him up. He had called Lenny and now here we all were. There was something different about this man, something I hadn't experienced in the presence of another person before. James turned to me and asked if I would like to hear some of this poetry. I was both honored and a little scared that I might not understand it and that would become an immediate barrier to what I was rapidly imagining could be a new friendship. He opened his notebook and began reading. What was revealed to me as I heard his poems was the raw and tender heart of another human being, laid bare without shame and without guile. I felt as if these poems were written about my own heart – perhaps to my own heart. His words were about my own struggles as surely as they were about his. We were both young men navigating a complicated and mercurial existence, buffeted by our own exquisite sensitivities, in danger of succumbing at any moment to the pains of the world and numb all feeling, or boldly meet them head-on. I knew and lived these tensions and now, suddenly and unexpectedly, I knew that another person did too. As he finished our eyes met. I knew he felt what I had felt, and I knew he knew I did as well. All I could say, though, was "James, you've got to come to the playground on Saturday and play basketball with us."

Just like that, James Randolph began hanging around the neighborhood. Here was a young black man who played basketball with flashing grace and wrote poetry with heart, and that combination thrilled me to no end. He lived in the East Bronx and went to high school at Evander Childs. Aside from the Simmons brothers, Bobby and Wally, who lived nearly a mile away at Fort Independence and seemed to only show up randomly in the neighborhood, James was the first black person to really join our group of friends.

Playing basketball with James added an entire new dimension to my game since I was the one who most often guarded him. He was the toughest opponent I ever played against. At six-foot-four James was two inches taller than I; he was lean and fast, just as confident slashing to the hoop as he was stopping for a jumper just beyond the top of the key. I was a little bulkier, which helped when I needed to box him out for a rebound. To compensate for his speed I tried to be as tenacious as I could on defense, sticking so close that I could feel when he was about to juke a move. When I had the ball I most often worked my jump shot from about 10-12 feet from the basket or maneuvered around the free-throw line waiting for one of my teammates to pass me the ball; from there my favorite move was a hook shot that I had perfected with a high arc in order to keep James from using his height advantage to block my shot. Our full-court games were fast and our one-on-one battles within the larger game were epic. For both of us it was an incredible bonding as we brought each other to new competitive heights, often leaving the rest of the players as spectators. The day that Lenny challenged Dickey Davis to bring his undefeated high school team to the neighborhood would signal the first game where James and I would play on the same team.

THE GAME WAS SCHEDULED FOR NOON but our neighborhood team was in the playground by 10 a.m., warming up and trying to lose our pre-game jitters. By now all of us knew that Columbia Grammar was undefeated and that their center, Ron Brown, was a force to be reckoned with. It had also begun to dawn on us that they were a *team* that had been playing together for years and, while we had played together for years also, we were still a ragtag bunch of street ballplayers.

Word of this confrontation had been spreading like wildfire for weeks and by 11:30 the playground was filling up with spectators. The benches in the basketball area were reserved for the teams, but every other conceivable space was taken up by onlookers. People of all ages ringed the basketball court, while others hung watching from the fences and kids scrambled up to sit on the branches of nearby trees – it was our neighborhood's mini-version of Harlem's Rucker Tournament. The atmosphere was festive and filled with anticipation.

This was more than just another game. I felt like I had more at stake at some soulful level. From that dimension, this struck me as the culmination of every basketball game I had ever played, a rising crescendo of every dribble, every scrape of my sneakers on the blacktop, every driving lay-up, every blocked shot, every made basket, and every sky-high rebound. This was about every piece of jagged linoleum I stuffed into my sneakers when I wore a hole in them and my mother couldn't afford to buy me another pair. It went far beyond games won and lost and, instead, became a distillation of every time I left it all on the court in a bid for acceptance and recognition and love. This was about heart – having heart and showing heart. If returning to the Bronx was for anything, it surely was for this.

While each one of us felt we could make a serious game of it, and while we clearly had home-court advantage and the assembled throng was decidedly rooting for us, still there were very few in the crowd who actually believed we could even come close to staying with the champion Columbia Grammar squad. This sentiment became even more pronounced when Dickey Davis led his team into the playground and onto the basketball courts. They looked and felt and walked like a team, but not only a team, a team that exuded an expectation of winning every time they stepped on the court. For the past two years this had been exactly what had happened with every foe they faced.

As they pulled off their matching warmups and revealed their matching shorts and jerseys, our team reflexively began to look at what we were wearing. In comparison it looked like we had all been wrestling in a Salvation Army clothing bin and had emerged wearing whatever we could snatch away from the other person. Beyond the look, though, there was their physical prowess itself. Ron Brown was specimen enough, looking more like a football player and outweighing James by at least 30 pounds. As they began warm-ups, it was hard not to just stop and stare at their business-like approach. Their squad was muscular and athletic, giving off the aura of seasoned basketball veterans, eyeing us with looks of bored predation.

We tried to do the same. The contrast, though, could not have been starker. When James dunked the ball on one of his lay-ups, we applauded and hollered, trying to psyche ourselves up. Then, when Ron Brown, slammed down the ball, causing the backboard and pole to sway back and forth, our energy drained quickly right out of our tightening sphincters. As warm-ups came to a close, both teams returned to the benches and selected their starting five. We would play 8-minute quarters. One of the older neighborhood guys had been designated as referee; another guy sat between the two benches at a folding card table, recording stats (points, fouls, rebounds, etc.) and keeping the score using a flip-the-numbers system. Then it was time for the opening tip and we positioned ourselves for the jump ball.

RON BROWN WON THE TIP, his quickness revealing itself despite his bulk. Columbia Grammar moved into offense and began whipping the ball from player to player, looking for an open shot. We had decided to play man-to-man defense, choosing to live or die in the *mano-a-mano* fashion that we typically preferred in our playground. There was a lot of movement, screening and pivoting, as they looked to spring a player free for an open shot or take a pass to the hoop. To the outside observer it must have looked like controlled chaos; in the mix of bodies bouncing off of each other it felt like a relentless effort for us to stay with our assigned man and only switch off when necessary. Finally they slipped the ball into Brown's hands and he turned quickly and scored, deep within the key.

As we took the ball out, I ran down court and suddenly became very aware of the huge crowd that filled the entire playground in every direction. I had never played before a crowd this size. Rather than feel intimidated I felt strangely buoyed by everyone's presence. My old feelings of owning these courts surged within me, as did my feelings of love for this place and for my friends and neighbors, feelings I now wanted to return in kind. I did not want to let them down. At that moment I received the ball on the right flank and immediately released a jump shot. The ball banked in smoothly; game tied, 2-2.

The battle between James and Ron Brown dominated much of the game, with James using his speed and rapier moves to slash through Brown's defensive efforts to score regularly, or else stopping for a smooth jump shot which he hit with unerring accuracy. Brown, for his part, muscled his way up onto the backboards for lay-ups and forcefully rebounded many of his teammates' missed shots for what seemed like easy scores. It was a tough but clean game, with free throws playing a minor role as the ref saw no reason to not let us play hard.

The lead changed hands so many times that we began to forget about the score. We were all immersed, deep in the zone; the only thing of importance was the man you were guarding and the tactical movements of your teammates. It was a see-saw *battle royale* as we raced like thoroughbreds across the blacktop, the urban sun warming and fueling our young bodies. By halftime we were down by eight points. We were holding our own and the crowd let us know by applauding and cheering as both teams filed over to the parkhouse water fountain to get a drink. The Columbia Grammar team was quite a bit animated on their bench, but this time gone was the joking and finger-pointing, replaced by some looks of disbelief and consternation, and voices urging "get it together" and "kick ass"; perhaps they were shocked they weren't dominating us, expecting to be far ahead by double-figures. On our bench we were smiling and laughing, feeling very much in the game and feeling like we could actually win this thing.

On the second-half tip, James won the jump ball this time and we were off and running. We moved the ball around the outside of the key with ease and purpose. Their defense tried to clamp down but James stepped in front of Brown and instantly received a pass. He faked a jump shot and when Brown leapt to block it, he slithered under his outstretched arm and leaned in for an easy lay-up. The neighborhood was on its feet, cheering. I could feel the momentum shifting.

We battled back and forth, the score staying close; no one could get a decisive lead. After we blocked a couple of shots and stole a couple of passes the game was tied. Just before the close of the third quarter the guy I was guarding slipped free for a wide-open shot on the right flank. I was determined not to let that happen. As he adjusted the ball in his hands for the shot, I raced out to where he stood, closing the ground between us quicker than *The Flash*. Just as he released the shot I leapt as high as I could, my right arm outstretched toward the heavens. My hand made contact with the ball and I slapped it as hard as I could and sent it flying through the air all the way to where the Columbia Grammar subs sat on their bench. The third quarter ended with a statement from us while with the neighborhood onlookers went out of their minds.

Score tied, eight minutes to go, eight minutes to see if the street-ballers could topple the mighty city champs. The struggle raged. James and Brown determined to best each other in their game-within-a-game, with the rest of us locked onto whomever we were guarding with laser-like focus. Up and down the court we ran, ten bodies determined not to fail. Every basket we made, every sterling defensive play we executed, caused the gathered crowd to erupt loudly and urge us on. If there ever was a basketball crowd that acted as the "Sixth Man" this was the one. Nothing like this had ever occurred in our neighborhood. It was the David and Goliath story come to life on the asphalt basketball courts of a Jewish neighborhood and everyone was reveling in it all, relishing every play.

Then, just like that, it was over.

The clock expired; the ref blew the final whistle. We all turned to look at the score: 58-54 in favor of Columbia Grammar. Four points separated our team from defeating the unbeaten city champs. Strangely enough, as we walked toward our bench, it didn't even come close to feeling like we lost. We had our heads up, we were laughing and congratulating each other, and we swelled with pride at our unrelenting effort. The members of the Columbia Grammar team looked stunned at how close they came to being defeated. There were no sounds of outright celebration from them. Instead, it seemed more a feeling of relief permeating their ranks as they stood quietly looking over at us. They knew they had been in a battle, perhaps the only real competition they had encountered in the last two years. Dickey Davis was the first to walk over and begin shaking our hands; it appeared that he had developed a new level of respect for his fellow neighborhood basket-ballers.

As the late afternoon sun began its arc westward, the crowd began to thin out and disperse, leaving the basketball courts to the lengthening shadows. The courts stood empty and silent, unsullied by the typical convening of a run-of-the-mill pick-up game. Everyone who'd witnessed today knew full well that they had experienced a once-in-a-lifetime moment. This was especially true for those of us who played.

Finally, I was alone on the bench, sitting there gazing upon the stage where moments before ten of us had been locked in struggle. I sat, recalling each and every move, allowing it all to settle into my heart and into my soul. Basketball had saved my life by allowing me to carve out an identity beyond the emotional lacerations I sustained under my own roof. Here, on these courts, I had been admired, sought after, respected as a player and as a human being. It was never about winning or losing; it was always about freedom – freedom of movement, freedom of expression, and freedom from the familial voices that I had internalized that incessantly told me I was not good enough and never would be. Whenever I was playing basketball I could shut out those voices, silence them during those moments on the court, and sometimes pretend that I had even gotten rid of them for good. I continued to sit there on the bench, the playground nearly deserted now.

Maybe, I thought, coming back to the neighborhood wasn't so terrible after all. As I began walking up Van Cortlandt Park South toward my house, I was feeling so incredible that even if someone told me exactly what the next year-and-a-half would bring, I would've laughed them off. There was just no way that I could fall so fast and so hard from where I stood now; no way that I would succumb to an ugly darkness that would drag me under and away from the sunlight I was, in that moment, joyously basking in. No way.

Chapter Twenty-One
Guardian Angel

I can only imagine what he was thinking as he looked out from his window in the ground-floor apartment directly across Van Cortlandt Park South from The Rail. Most certainly he witnessed the endless stream of drug deals taking place, often in broad daylight, witnessed people carelessly exchanging bags of heroin for cash right in the middle of the street. He must've seen and heard the desperate arguments over who was short-changing who within this nefarious commerce, now ubiquitous. Watching people sitting on The Rail, nodding in an opiate-induced stupor, all equidistant like a flock of stoned-out seagulls while younger children played mere steps away in the playground, undoubtedly stirred a righteous anger within him. It was troubling him to know that the young people his own sons' ages were simply awaiting not only the next drug deal but the next police bust, or worse, the next drug overdose – and it seemed that they could care less. Why he singled me out of this mess I could not fathom. But one day, standing on the steps that formed the entrance to the building that housed his apartment at 92 Van Cortlandt Park South, he motioned for me to come over. I had been sitting on The Rail waiting for someone to show up with some drugs so I could get high. With some trepidation I walked across the street and joined him. He invited me into the apartment and then further back into his office.

* * * * *

THE TURBULENT SHADOWS cast by the saturation of the neighborhood with heroin were growing longer and darker, threatening to swallow all the remaining light. Since my return from El Paso in April 1970, the drug situation had shifted dramatically. From the previous peaceful landscape of pot-smoke daydreams and innocent psychedelic curiosity and exploration, it had now become a world littered with deadly syringes and populated by the daily intrigues and manipulations of addiction. I had been gone just six months and in that short space of time it looked and felt like our neighborhood had tilted precariously on its axis. I, too, had changed and now I walked these familiar streets with unfamiliar steps, hesitant and awkward in my efforts to fit back in, and assaulted with growing alarm that I did not really belong here anymore.

The first indication that all had changed was my effort to return to my relationship with Shira. While I was in Texas we had kept in touch by phone using the popular practice of the day: pirated telephone credit card numbers. Since I was completely unsophisticated in understanding that for this to work you had to call pay phone to pay phone, it lasted a precarious few months until the phone company started demanding payment from the two numbers I most frequently called: my mother's and Shira's. With my mother's tearful voice moaning that she could not afford the bills, or afford her phone being cut off, I immediately desisted and promised my mother that I would pay her back the money I had cost her. I promised Shira that I would do the same. Simultaneously, while I was wondering whether it made sense in my brain and heart to get back together with Shira, I was still imagining the possibility of rekindling some kind of relationship with Jane, now back in school at Fairleigh Dickinson, just across the Hudson River in New Jersey. Our brief connection on our cross-country road trip, and in El Paso, had left me intrigued, with a sense of unfinished business. Needless to say, by the time I was back in the Bronx I was more than a little disoriented about my own life and about where I truly belonged.

Within days of my return, I arrived at Shira's apartment when her aunts were at work, settling back into the clandestine pattern we had adopted in high school. She was attending Lehman College now, in the teaching program, and she looked more beautiful than when I left. It was a clumsy reunion at first, as we sought to recapture the feelings that so bonded us for over two years. We went into her bedroom and unfolded the Castro convertible and made love. We lost ourselves in the hot afternoon, yet as I looked into her eyes I could feel a distinct sensation of being separate, from her, from the lovemaking, even from myself in that moment. With nothing else for either of us to imagine, we decided that we would try to rebuild the relationship we once had. As I walked back home to Saxon Avenue, I wasn't certain whether what I had committed to with Shira, mere moments ago, was really possible any longer.

A few more meetings at her apartment made it clear that too much had changed, both inside me and between us, to be able to resurrect our relationship. Even the passionate lovemaking was not enough

298

to turn the clock backwards. Shira was clear that she was moving distinctly forward in her life, with inspired goals of fulfilling her dream to be a teacher. She was also clear that marriage and a family was a foundational part of her plan. In sharp contrast, I wasn't clear about anything except that the neighborhood was too small and I was growing restive within its confines. With little fanfare or much feeling, we looked hard at what we were trying to reconstitute and realized that it was nothing more than will-o-the-wisps of the past, and with that we moved back into our respective slip-streams and surrendered to the determined pull of our now separate lives.

I had been back less than two months and already I knew I had to get out. Even the momentary ecstasy of the basketball game with Columbia Grammar was not enough, was just too small in comparison to what I felt I was being compelled by, stirred to wake up to. The world was raging with war, anti-colonial movements, and agitations for civil rights and women's rights, struggles for freedom abounding – and I felt they were calling to me in a thousand ways. I wanted to be part of *that*, part of the struggles for peace and justice, not a part of *this*.

Unfortunately, try as I might, I could neither discern nor imagine any exits from the Bronx, or muster the courage to just throw myself into the social activism that I was aching for. The only questions I greeted every day with were when and how could I escape? Little could I guess from this immediate vantage point, just how dark and precarious the journey to discovering those answers would become, or that my very life would depend upon saying no and saying yes at precisely the right moments. At the time, though, feeling like I could barely tolerate facing my growing discomfort and alienation, I chose instead to try to see if I could suppress those feelings and re-fit myself – no matter how tight or uncomfortable the squeeze – back into my old neighborhood.

I was still into drugs but, in my mind, I had drawn an uncompromising line in the sand between what I thought acceptable to me and anything to do with heroin and those addicted to it. Back in the Bronx the spirit of mutuality that permeated me and my friends when marijuana still reigned – which I distinctly felt before I left – was now disturbingly being drained away. It was as if I'd left the planet and returned, without transition, to a lonelier time, a darker, dog-eat-dog future. "What had happened?" I wondered daily. "What's the matter with me?" I asked myself in the mirror every morning, trying to get at my growing agitation over what I saw as decay and decline all around. The answers to these questions, I would discover, would have to be lived rather than hatched inside my mind – a process that would take me places I could not conceive of in that moment.

ONE NIGHT AT DEE-DEE CONFORTI'S APARTMENT, when her younger cousin Connie Steiner was babysitting Dee Dee's two sons, a group of about a dozen people gathered. I began drinking beer and smoking pot. I was sitting off to the side, alone and sullen, looking at the crowd and confirming with every face I scanned just how much things had changed. Half the people in the room were three of four years younger than I, fifteen and sixteen-year-olds who, prior to my time in El Paso, I would not have been caught dead hanging around with, even if I knew they existed. Some of the girls, ignored only recently as the kid sisters of guys my age and older, were now young women. What the hell had happened while I was gone? People were growing up, inserting themselves into places where previously they would not be found, much less invited. In response to my confusion I continued drinking.

Suddenly the effects of the weed and alcohol hit me and I was across the living room threshold and on my way to the bathroom to throw up. I immediately assumed the position so intimately familiar to sick drunks the world over, sitting on the tile floor, my arms wrapped around the toilet, my face gazing at its own reflection in the water that filled the porcelain bowl. As I relieved my sickness I felt cool hands gently stroking the back of my head. I sat back against the bathtub and looked up. There, in white cutoffs and a forest green turtleneck, stood Leah Kirsch. Her eyes stood radiant against her dark skin; her brown hair flowed recklessly down either side of her face and onto her shoulders. Her look, her presence, her hands were all so soothing, so loving, so compelling. I reached both my hands up under her shirt and gently held her naked breasts. I looked into her eyes and she looked wordlessly into mine. Suddenly I shook my head and said, "This isn't right; you're Mark Kirsch's little sister." As I began to release her and remove my hands, Leah pressed her hands onto mine, holding them in place wrapped around her breasts. "It's okay," she whispered.

The next day we were boyfriend and girlfriend. And we were inseparable.

Leah was an elemental ball of energy, straining upon an inner battlefield possessed of roiling, freedom-seeking desires that ceaselessly percolated, while chafing under an onslaught of restraints she deemed patently unfair. She was sixteen and bored in high school at Music and Art; her parents had a painful divorce and she lived at home with her mother and younger brother; and she was a girl child with all the incumbent discriminations and proscriptions based on her gender. She felt a deep connection to nature and loved spending time in the golf course, or Upstate at Ward Poundridge campgrounds.

She was emotionally expressive, raw at times, no matter whether the feeling was happiness or sadness, ecstasy or anger. Her sheer vitality enlivened me to the point that I didn't care anymore about the state of the neighborhood; I was suddenly lifted above all of that. All I cared about was being around her.

As the summer approached it seemed that everyone who wasn't strung out on heroin (and a few who were and wanted to kick the habit) shared a collective desire to drive cross-country to California, specifically to Berkeley. It was as if a contagion had swept over The Rail, compelling people to find some way to make it out to the West Coast in what was taking on the airs of a holy pilgrimage. Neither Leah nor I were working at the time but we were determined to join the planned migration and get to the coast somehow. My first step was to handwrite a letter to Leah's mother, Jan, vowing that I would protect Leah along the way and requesting that she, in turn, pen a letter giving us her permission for her underage daughter to accompany me on these travels. Leah's mother was very impressed with my eloquent articulations and my pronouncements that I would love and care for Leah while we were on the road. We thanked her profusely when she gave us her letter and we set about trying to figure out how we could drum up the money to fund our trip.

One day the news spread that the U.S. government was looking for Census takers and they were paying good money. Instantly, about a half-dozen of us marched to the Census office. We signed up, were trained as Enumerators, given official name badges, and a plastic red, white, and mainly blue shoulder bag with pens, pencils, Census forms, and the addresses for a specifically designated neighborhood. We were given a certain number of short forms (paid less) and long forms (paid significantly more), and sent on our way. Each address was tagged to a specific form and it was our task to work the neighborhood until we found people at home and had gotten all the necessary information. We were to work the entire month of June. That was it; easy money. Or so we thought.

Without fail, every time we canvassed an apartment building people were either not home, or not interested, or were eating dinner. Sometimes people were polite in their refusal, other times angry curses about "government bullshit" followed us as we hastily retreated down the staircases. It was a bit easier to get folks to fill out the short forms since they took much less time. As the days wore on fruitlessly, Leah and I could sense our cross-country trek evaporating like a highway heat mirage. Then one of our friends had the bright idea of faking the long forms for the apartments we could not get a response from, filling them out however we wanted in order to get our wages bumped up. We were all instantly re-energized and the last two weeks of June flew by as we raced around various Bronx neighborhoods taking the Census where we could, and making the Census where we had to. Needless to say the 1970 Census, at least in a few tiny pockets of the Bronx, was a dicey tally.

By the beginning of July, Leah and I had more money but still not enough. So in an act both bold and humble, we turned to our community. We went to The Rail one day and began soliciting donations for our cross-country adventure. Somehow we tapped into a generosity of spirit, of helping one another which momentarily transcended the selfish pall that heroin had cast upon the landscape of late. Perhaps it was Leah's innocence and youthful determination; perhaps it was how people responded to our own excitement, to the loving energy we emanated together. Perhaps in this reciprocal act of asking and giving, there appeared a brief flash of the strong, deeply ingrained communal values that so characterized our neighborhood. Whatever it was, by the end of that day we had enough money to securely hitchhike across the country together.

We set about preparing. We were two urban kids with no serious experience regarding camping out for a prolonged period, the weekend trips to Poundridge with barely a sleeping bag in hand and my single night in Shenandoah National Park with Harry Lefkowitz, notwithstanding. Everyone we knew who was going cross-country was buying new Kelty backpacks so we followed suit, using some of the money we made from the Census. We packed clothes, figuring we needed only the basics since once in California we would have access to a laundromat. Then we packed cooking utensils and strapped borrowed sleeping bags to the lower part of the backpack frames. Then we packed food, figuring that whenever we camped we'd just build a fire and make our own meals. Since George Asawa's macrobiotic diet was gaining popularity, Leah had us pack pounds of rice, beans, noodles, dried vegetables, dried fruit, dehydrated milk, oatmeal, and other foodstuffs that went into my backpack; I'd be lucky if I didn't topple over from the weight the first time I tried to walk. However, in our minds, we felt completely ready.

FINALLY IT WAS TIME TO SET OUT. Our first destination was Buffalo, New York, where we had promised to visit Adam Sokol before heading to California, and because from there we could catch Interstate 90 West. Early one morning we met at The Rail. From there we hiked up Van Cortlandt Park South and went to the entrance ramp to the Major Deegan Expressway heading north. We quickly got a ride from someone heading quite a ways upstate. After the driver deposited us upon reaching his destination, and as we were making our way across the road to the on-ramp for the next leg of our journey, a New York State Police car pulled up in front of us, coming to an ominous halt. Out stepped a State Trooper in full regalia, hat brim pulled low, almost touching the tops of his mirrored sunglasses. He was not happy. He began explaining to us that it was strictly illegal for us to be hitchhiking on *his* throughway. He further explained that he was going to have to write us a ticket. Just as he was reaching for his ticket book the sound of shrieking tires caused him to look up and over our heads, and caused Leah and me to turn around in unison.

Barreling down the road toward where we stood was a car whose driver was clearly out of control, swerving this way and that as the car rocketed forward. We all stood there watching. Suddenly the car moved onto the shoulder of the road, directly in line with the police car and still coming on strong. Leah and I stepped further away from the roadside; the Trooper stood there unflinchingly waiting for what he clearly knew was going to happen next. And it did. The car plowed headlong into the rear of the Trooper's vehicle with such force that the impact lifted the rear of the car off the ground and up into the air. The brief silence that followed the initial crash was broken by the two rear ties of the police car returning loudly to earth in a cloud of dust and gravel. When all had become still again the door opened and a clearly drunk driver stumbled out, grinning or grimacing in response to his transgressions it was hard to tell. The Trooper turned to us and said, menacingly, "Get the fuck out of here. Now!" We quickly headed toward the direction of the on-ramp and almost immediately got our next ride. Within hours we were in Buffalo, crashing at Adam's apartment on Pauline Street.

The next morning Adam drove us from his house and let us out at the on-ramp of Interstate 90 West. It was overcast and drizzling. We were immersed in grey, the grey of the clouds and the grey of the industrial area that surrounded us on all sides. Nothing looked promising at first as we stood there, faces wet and eyes attempting to offer reassurance to each other. Our thumbs were out as traffic trickled by. Approaching us slowly was a Volkswagen van, which everyone knew was always a sure ride. When it actually did pull over we were elated, just to get out of the rain and to really be getting on our way. We raced to the passenger side, where the driver – a woman along with two kids sitting in the back seat – had already rolled down the window. Excitedly we asked, "Can you give us a ride?" "Where are you going?" she responded. "Berkeley," we exclaimed in unison. "So am I," she said as she pushed the sliding side door open. With that single ride, we all headed toward Berkeley, California.

What Leah didn't know at the time, and what was causing me increased restiveness, was that just prior to our departure I had received a phone call from Jane, the woman I had been wondering about since returning from El Paso. During that call she professed that she had made up her mind and that she was now in love with me. I was shaken and stirred. She said all the words I had wanted to hear from her and yet I had just been swept up in a relationship with Leah that was exhilarating and fresh and I was head-over-heels – until that phone call. Now my heart was completely confused. It was a confusion to which I would find resolution in the most unexpected way, and it would leave lasting wounds that Leah and I would never recover from.

OUR FIRST STOP WAS YELLOW SPRINGS, OHIO, home of Antioch College. When we first entered the van, our driver told us her name was Wendy and explained that she had some stops that she would be making along the way to California, the first one being in Ohio. Since we weren't in a rush and since we didn't want to forsake this single ride straight to Berkeley, Leah and I happily went along with her itinerary. Upon our arrival in Yellow Springs, we all disembarked and walked into the local head shop, figuring if anyone knew the lay of the land they would be found here. All manner of paraphernalia, fabric from India, and spiritual icons and trinkets filled every corner of the store. Incense wafted throughout, filling our every pore with scents of patchouli. We instantly made friends with the owner, Kristoph, and his amazing dog, Govinda. Govinda was all white, some kind of mix of German shepherd and wolf. As we told Kristoph of our travel plans, he asked Wendy if he could get a ride with us to Aspen, Colorado, so he could visit his wholesalers and place orders to replenish his inventory before the start of school. She agreed, saying that she also had friends in Aspen that she would like to see. Kristoph then told Leah and I we could crash in the bedroom in the back of his store until we all left for Colorado.

Yellow Springs was famous for being a stop on the Underground Railroad that ferried escaped slaves to the north, and our few days spent in this very liberal, very hip college town were mellow and a wonderful way to ease into our cross-country journey. Antioch had a free bicycle policy, making all the bikes on campus available to whoever needed one, so we rode around campus and the town daily. Thanks to our host, Kristoph, we also had access to the campus gym (where Leah and I played some basketball) and to the campus pool where we swam naked at night. It was all so idyllic. After a few days we all piled back into the van and headed west once more, leaving Govinda with one of his owner's friends. Now we were on Interstate 70,

304

our minds fired with imaginings of the counter-culture mecca known as Berkeley.

Our next stop was in a public park in Kansas, right next to a lake. My images of Kansas had all been of flat land covered in corn stalks, but this scene, while definitely pastoral, was touchingly beautiful. There were no cornfields here, only rolling hills bathed in the softest green, dotted periodically with stands of trees. The sky was big and blue, with huge puffs of white clouds, and the lake reflected all of this on its placid surface in such a way that from certain angles you could not tell lake from sky, disorienting, almost like an Escher drawing. We set up the camper and Leah and I shared our food supplies which we cooked using our driver's Coleman stove. We sat and ate and talked long into the summer night.

LEAH AND I HAD NEVER SEEN ANYTHING LIKE the Rocky Mountains. We were in complete awe at their majestic sweep, angling right into the heavens. As we made our way up to Aspen we were silent, spellbound beyond any and all previous experiences with nature. When we arrived at our destination, Leah, Kristoph, and I disembarked and Wendy headed into town with her kids to visit people she knew. The house we were staying at was in the mouth of a canyon, all wood and glass the better to see out onto the ruggedly beautiful terrain. We were invited to crash in the living room and we proceed to set up our sleeping bags and make ourselves at home. The businessmen got down to business and Leah and I were left to fend for ourselves.

The second day we were there I got sick, a combination of fatigue, altitude and the stress of Jane's voice in the recesses of my mind demanding some kind of reply. Leah decided to accompany the guys on a trip into Aspen while I stayed at the house resting. While they were gone I wrestled and wrestled over what to do, who to choose to be in a relationship with. I finally decided and began writing Jane a letter. In the letter I said that I had committed to Leah and her mother that I would get us both safely to Berkeley. I explained to Jane that once we arrived there, I would make sure Leah hooked up with some of our neighborhood friends and I would hitchhike back home. I planned to mail this letter once we arrived in Berkeley. As I heard everyone returning to the house I folded the letter and placed it in the breast pocket of my flannel shirt.

Early the next morning Leah and I decided we would explore the canyon behind the house. We set off with the two Irish setters that lived there. It was chilly so I grabbed my flannel shirt and pulled it on. We hiked up the canyon until we came to a confluence of boulders that made further access a bit tricky, especially for the dogs. Leah and I scrambled atop the biggest boulder, the canyon beckoning once more on the other side. We ascended further; I was mesmerized and wanted to climb higher and higher. Leah suggested I continue exploring on my own and said she would wait for me there. I unbuttoned my shirt and dropped it on the rock next to her and turned to begin my skyward trek.

I climbed and climbed, compelled by some magnetism within the mountains themselves, pulling me further into the back country. At one point I came to an impasse. The only way to continue was to move laterally across an apron of shale and rocky debris to firmer terrain about fifty feet away. Once on the other side, I knew I could continue my ascent. Being completely ignorant of anything having to do with mountains or climbing safety, I leaned my body close to the sharply angled ground and began inching my way across, the shale bunching up under my feet allowing me to keep purchase. Suddenly, upon my next step, the shale under both my feet gave way and I began sliding down toward the lip of the cliff, over which lay the floor of the canyon hundreds of feet below. Miraculously, through no effort of my own, the shale recollected under my feet in such a way as to halt my slide into oblivion. I lay there, my heart thumping, sweat leaking from my pores in what felt like sheets. As I regained my equilibrium I began to carefully look around and assess my situation. Slowly, with baby-steps, and finding tentative handholds on the stems of some of the tenacious mountain plants, I inched back the way I had come until I was once again on solid ground. Visions of my own death lingered close by as I made my way back to Leah. As I reached the spot just feet above the boulder where I had left her, she was standing up looking at me. Her face was stricken with pain, distorted in tear-streaked anguish as she accusingly held the letter I had written to Jane, shaking it skyward for me to see.

For the next few hours we tried to find our way back to the house. The dogs had long since returned and we were on our own. As we walked we argued fiercely with each other, me attempting to defend my choice of returning to Jane, Leah fighting for me to recognize the love that she and I had discovered together. We tried many different ways to get back, to the house and to each other, but we were lost, literally and within our relationship. Finally, as the sun was beginning to set, we sat eye-to-eye and cried. We admitted that we did really love each other, and wanted to remain together; as Leah graphically put it, it was time for me to let go of the fucking ghosts and step into this relationship with her, right here, right now. I tearfully agreed. As if this was the signal the mountain spirits needed, we instantly found our way back to the house, returning exhausted and shaken on so many levels. What we did not know then was that while we had won the immediate battle of staying together, we had lost the war of ever having a trusting, committed relationship again; this would play itself out over the next two years in unpredictable and mutually hurtful ways.

We arrived at a house in the Berkeley hills as night was falling. It was surrounded by trees and the air smelled so different from New York City. It was peaceful and from the windows we could see the Bay Bridge and the lights of San Francisco beyond. The next day we parted from Wendy and her children and made our way down to Shattuck Avenue. We had an address where some of our Bronx friends were crashing. Upon arriving there we found Ezra Baum and Aidan Cleary, both smiling from ear to ear, both feeling and looking incredibly happy. Aidan, especially, was in such a loving groove, something that I had never seen him manifest before. It was as if he had achieved some kind of personal homecoming, some real inner peace, with his arrival in Berkeley. Perhaps there *was* magic here. They welcomed us joyfully and told us that there was another house on Shattuck where more of our friends were hanging out and where there was room for us to stay. We all headed over there and found Aron Rose and Barry Roth, who had driven an old Renault sedan across the country together. We also found Sam Prinz and Sherrie Bieber there. Leah and I took over a vacant room, dropped our backpacks in the corner, and rolled out our sleeping bags immediately. We then set out to explore Berkeley.

IN THE SUMMER OF 1970, Berkeley was emblematic of the counterculture I felt strongly could remake the country. Shattuck Avenue was always crowded, oftentimes shoulder to shoulder, the sidewalks populated with every image I had read about come to life. Beautiful black men and women sported bold afros, berets and black leather jackets, who I took to be none other than members of the romantically infamous Black Panthers. White guys in army surplus shirts and jackets, maybe veterans of the Vietnam War, women in long flowing skirts with peasant blouses, everyone looking like they were glowing with life, with freedom, with a commitment to living differently than how society relentlessly ordained.

On nearby Telegraph Avenue vendors lined both sides of the street in a most dynamic and colorful bazaar, soliciting buyers for tie-dyed clothing, incense and incense holders, polished stones containing various healing, auric energies, musical instruments galore, hand-carved Native American-style flutes, abstract artful images, photographs, glassware, and handmade jewelry fashioned

307

from household cutlery. The streets were abuzz with smiling faces, unafraid and casting loving looks to each person they passed.

At Sather Gate and Sproul Plaza, one of the main entrances to the University of California's Berkeley campus, hundreds more gathered. Some had joined in drum circles, congas and *djembes* held between their knees, giving off pulsing, primitive rhythms that sent people swaying and dancing unabashedly. We watched the orange-robed Hare Krishnas playing their instruments and singing and chanting, proselytizing in their own unique way among the throngs of searching youth. Myriad people passed out leaflets and flyers announcing a cavalcade of events going on throughout the Bay Area: an antiwar protest; a women-only consciousness-raising meeting; a fundraising dinner to support Vietnamese students and educate people about the true nature of the war going on in Indochina, and much more.

Socialists, communists, and Trotskyites stood behind tables covered with books by Marx and Engels, Lenin, Stalin, and Mao Tse-tung; they all vied for attention, cajoling people to take a stand against U.S. imperialism while doing their best to explain to those who would listen why their particular way to the new world was really revolutionary and therefore the better way. I felt I had reached nirvana, like I had been transported right through the pages of *Ramparts*, the magazine that had so buoyed me in New York, and spit out the other side into Berkeley, smack into the heart of people truly living in ways I had only dreamed possible. Right then I considered never going back to the Bronx, but I had committed to Leah in the mountains, and to her mother in a heartfelt letter, that I would see this journey through from beginning to end. I was determined to not let Leah down ever again.

WITHIN DAYS OF OUR ARRIVAL we headed over to People's Park Annex, where, according to a flyer we were handed while walking down Shattuck Avenue, a pig roast was going to take place – the pig symbolizing the police and those in power in the American government and corporations. The original People's Park, so named because the year before, in May 1969, Berkeley students, local business people, residents and their supporters had taken over a small piece of derelict land owned by the University of California's Board of Regents and turned it into a park. When Governor Ronald Reagan staged a pre-dawn raid by California Highway Patrol and Berkeley Police forces on May 15, clearing the park and cordoning it off with an eight-foot chain-link fence, the fuse was lit for a direct confrontation. In response, a determined protest of over 3,000 people erupted the same afternoon the park was fenced off. The police resisted with tear-gas and batons.

308

When the protest swelled to over 6,000 people the police responded with lethal-force buckshot in an effort to disperse the crowd. In the mayhem that followed, one bystander, James Rector, was shot and killed, one man was blinded, and more than one hundred people were sent to local hospitals. As a result, Reagan declared a State of Emergency and 2,700 National Guard troops were sent to occupy Berkeley that evening. Over the next days and nights, protestors taunted the troops, offering them drinks they claimed were spiked with LSD, along with plates of marijuana brownies to mellow them out. In response, Berkeley police often covered over their badges with tape, or wore masks, in order to beat suspected protestors with impunity. Five days after the initial confrontation, with the protests and skirmishes continuing unabated, National Guard helicopters dispersed airborne tear-gas over the entire Berkeley campus. Things eventually subsided but the park remained surrounded by chain-link and off limits. An air of tension ran through Berkeley like a steadily humming electric current.

It was a year after the original attempted liberation of People's Park when we arrived in Berkeley, and a mere two months after the murder of four students at Kent State University by Ohio National Guard troops on May 4. After nationwide school strikes at high schools, colleges and universities involving more than four million students to protest the National Guard's lethal actions. As a result, the stalemate with the park had once more risen in peoples' consciousnesses since the area remained fenced off to community access, with no progress being made toward making it an athletic field or returning it to the people. In the face of this frustration, a People's Park Annex was established in the flats of northwest Berkeley on Hearst Avenue to provide an alternative place for political activity and tribal gatherings, like the one Leah and I were heading to.

It was indeed tribal and it smelled to me of a kind of freedom I'd never experienced before.

Everywhere, people in various altered states, various states of clothed and partially clothed presentation, and various states of peacefulness or agitation, thronged within the park. Music was everywhere, drums, guitars, flutes, and whatever makeshift instrument that could be wielded. While people were literally in every corner of the park, the main focus was a fire-pit, over which sat a metal spit skewering a very large, intact pig being slowly rotated by a few self-designated rotisserie-men. Leah and I were blown away. She was a bit overwhelmed and I was galvanized; I had found more of my political-activist tribe. When, finally, the pig was done pieces of its flesh were cut away from the carcass and handed out as people pressed hungrily toward the fire-pit. The meat was delicious in a transgressive way, making me feel like I was partaking in something much larger than myself and my immediate hunger. The pig's head was eventually severed and hoisted on a pole. A parade began to snake around the park to symbolically announce that the people had overcome the pig, the image of which had become synonymous with the forces of law and order, the governmental powers-that-be, and the deadening status-quo. It was like *Lord of the Flies* on acid, drawn and colored by Peter Max. I was delirious by the time we made it back to the house on Shattuck Avenue, thinking that maybe I really did need to join the revolution and stay here in Berkeley. But other distractions were on their way.

The following day we found out that Sam and Sherrie had gotten a puppy from the Berkeley animal shelter. Instantly Leah was enamored and determined. That afternoon we headed to the animal shelter where we found the most beautiful puppy, part Australian shepherd with white, black and grey fur and a loving disposition. I had been reading Alexander Dumas' *The Three Musketeers* before we left the Bronx and I suggested the name "Athos," after one of the musketeers. Immediately Leah agreed and she and Athos began an intense love affair.

A couple of days later I found Leah consulting a California road atlas, Athos happily by her side. Not being as politically oriented as me, and making this trip to primarily get as far away from any kind of urban environment even remotely like New York, after two days in Berkeley Leah had had it. She was determined to lose herself in the woods. As she perused the maps of northern California she pointed to Lassen Volcanic Park, 237 miles northeast of Berkeley, one of the many national parks dotting the state in every direction. It was settled. Early the next morning, we packed up our belongings and headed over to the on-ramp of Interstate 80 heading east, located at the bottom of University Avenue, closer to the bay. There was always a long line of hitchhikers at this spot, cardboard signs in hopeful hands, scrawled with their desired destination. On the advice of one of our friends we had created a sign that said simply "Lassen," in order to attract the attention of only those drivers going as close to our destination as possible. While the hitchhiking line was always long it also always moved fast. Within minutes we were in the back of a car driven by two young men about my age, also heading to Lassen Park to do some backpacking.

Four hours later we were at our campground, tent erected, sleeping bags in place and Leah, Athos and I cuddling together. We spent nearly a week there, exploring every volcanic configuration we could find, traversing the cinder cone, navigating the bubbling mud pots, even hiking to the top of Lassen Peak. For two of those days I went backpacking with the two guys who drove us to the park, while Leah and Athos stayed at the main campsite. They were on a quest to find what had been designated on the map as Lemonade Springs. After traversing some of the most exquisite terrain I'd ever seen, we eventually found it and, amazingly, it did taste just like lemonade. As a result of this immersion in the sheer beauty of Lassen, I began to wonder once again about buying land in Vermont. Maybe that was where I needed to be, rather than in the politically charged urban world where I imagined myself a dedicated revolutionary. Owning land and a home in Vermont would certainly bring Leah and me closer together. Leah and I left Lassen Park reluctantly and returned to the crash pad in Berkeley. We were filled with wonder and excitement over the beauty we had experienced, which very quickly became tempered by the need to turn our attention to hitchhiking 3,000 miles back to the Bronx.

LEAH HAD A VERY SPECIFIC TIMETABLE for our return trip: stopping to visit her old sleep-away camp, Camp Lindenmere, before it closed for the season. Camp Lindenmere was a predominantly Jewish camp in Pennsylvania's Pocono Mountains, and this was Leah's first summer not attending since she was a little girl. Despite our intense adventure together, she clearly ached to have just one more moment's experience there. We were already into early August and Leah wanted me to see the camp she loved before the summer session ended. It was a place where she blossomed from a girl into a young woman, a place she escaped to every summer from the stresses of family dynamics, and a place which she cherished dearly; she wanted me to share some of what she experienced there. So once again we tramped down University Avenue and took a spot at the on-ramp to Interstate 80 East, this time holding a new cardboard sign: New York City.

It wasn't quite as easy as when we left Buffalo just over a month ago; no archetypal VW van came out of the misty rain to our rescue with a single ride back home. Our first ride took us to the outskirts of Sacramento, some 90 miles away from Berkeley, where we wound up waiting on the roadside for seventeen hours before we got our next ride in a huge tractor-trailer truck. The driver took us from there all the way to Chicago before he had to veer south to Indiana and beyond. A few more rides and before long Leah, Athos and I were walking up the roadway to Camp Lindenmere. Once there it was like old home week for Leah as she hugged her friends, the camp's owners, her former counselors, and her younger brother Samuel. I was introduced to everyone and we shared some of our road-trip exploits around the evening campfire. They let us spend a couple of days there and we hiked by ourselves during the day and joined the larger group only at mealtimes. It was a beautiful transition point for Leah and me. Perhaps, intuitively, we wanted to linger in the innocence of Camp Lindenmere, to try to forget or at least soothe some of the damage that Leah's finding my note to Jane had wrought. But the tension between us never fully subsided. Without wanting to openly admit it, we both realized that whatever love we began this relationship with, whatever trust had been extended by each of us to the other in order to undertake this cross-country journey together, had been severely damaged. As we hitchhiked out of Camp Lindenmere we were both quite shaky as to whether there was a future for us back home, or anywhere else for that matter.

It was the middle of August when we arrived back in the Bronx. Because we now had Athos, and dogs were not allowed into the Amalgamated apartments, we surreptitiously juggled and smuggled Athos between our two houses. After seeing so many beautiful natural landscapes during our cross-country adventure, it was suddenly apparent that our neighborhood, despite it being about as un-urban as a Bronx neighborhood could possibly be, was just too crowded and too built-up for our new sensibilities. And we were not alone. We discovered upon our return that what only a few months ago had been a faint migratory trickle northward to buy acreage in Vermont – the first wave of which had motivated Harry and I to head for the Alaskan oilfields – had now become an open spigot of people wanting to get back to the land. What we were also confronted with after barely two months on the road, and what seemed to serve as both impetus and impediment to turning toward the Green Mountain State for refuge and solace, was that the heroin deluge had swept even more people into its whirlpool of addiction and hustle.

THE EUPHORIA OF BEING IN CALIFORNIA dissipated quickly upon the hard rocks of Bronx reality. For starters, I had no job and no prospects for one, relying once more on my mother doling out money from her already paltry Woolworth's paycheck. At nearly 20 years old I was back to getting an allowance. Instead of becoming either a political activist or finding ways to get land in Vermont, I was back playing basketball, smoking pot and aimlessly inhabiting The Rail. I grew increasingly dejected and depressed; it was just a matter of time before the seductive waters of heroin were lapping at my toes, despite my professed determinations to never walk upon those shores. Soon, with hardly a ripple of resistance, or even much fanfare, I was sniffing bags of heroin along with the rest of the neighborhood junkies. And just like the rest of them, I continually told myself that I would never get addicted. When I finally did, when I finally slipped below the waterline, I rationalized the truth away by reassuring myself that I could quit the stuff any time I wanted to. I just didn't want to.

Now that I had crossed over to a world I had sworn I would never inhabit, my new last line of defense against shredding my self-respect completely, was that I would never, ever shoot up heroin. Amidst the tedious days of increasingly aimless boredom, succumbing to this new drug happened so fast that I barely noticed. I found myself just going along, saying yes to the drug more often than I said no. I wanted to believe that since so many of my friends were now populating the world of heroin, it too could be a place of caring and sharing, just like the previous world of smoking pot and tripping on acid had once been. I was in for a very rude awakening.

By mid-September, I was hooked and my life began to more and more revolve around sniffing dope and getting high. Initially there was a moment in the heroin scene that did resemble the kind of sharing that took place whenever someone used to buy a bag of marijuana, a sort of camaraderie indicating that there was always enough to go around, that no one would be left out. Sadly, this was only the briefest instant, especially as more and more people turned from snorting to shooting heroin. Attitudes hardened and a dog-eat-dog meanness set in.

DAILY LIFE NOW THAT I WAS A HEROIN ADDICT was utterly predictable. Immediately upon awakening I would first rummage through my pockets to see if I had any stash left from the night before. Failing to find that morning hope, I would start to call around to see if anyone was selling, a slow panic building whenever I received negative answers. If I found someone who had some smack, sometimes I would invite them to my house, especially if I had no money and could only offer a safe place to get high in exchange. If I had some cash, I would go to their house and we would get stoned together. Once high, the day was beautiful; I had avoided getting sick and I was now functional.

On other days there would be no dope to be found at all. When this occurred everyone headed either to The Rail or to the front of EM's candy store, responding to some inner collective alarm to gather in tribulation. The same greetings would be exchanged over and over again: "You holding?" the question was uttered perfunctorily as we gave each other "skin" – palms touching then sliding slowly apart. "No man, you know who is?" would come the flat response and another sharing of skin. Without options, there we would stand, huddled, shifting our weight from one foot to the other in a dance that signaled growing agitation and worry about slipping over the red line into real withdrawal. In the parlance of the times, we were all on the verge of getting "sick" and longed with every fiber of our being only to find the drug that would make us "well."

Eventually, someone would drive up and say that they had a connection over in the 225th Street housing projects, or in the East Bronx, or in Harlem. We would pool our money and one or two of us would jump in the car and ride along; the others would wait, trusting that a quick return with the goods was in the offing. When the car came back to the neighborhood, explosions of anticipated relief would go off deep in the quivering solar plexus of every junkie, and each person would take their drugs and disappear back into the shadows to get high. Heroin for us was like the One Ring was to Golem in Tolkien's *Lord of the Rings* trilogy: essential to our own wellbeing and precious beyond caring about anything or anyone else, yet equally mercurial as it instantly disappeared up our noses or into our arms, leaving us strung-out Golems with the frantic need to find more, ever more, all the time.

Without a steady supply of money I had to find alternative ways to get my drugs, so I bartered my house so people could safely get high in exchange for some of their stash. That worked well for a while but, as is heroin's way, I needed a certain amount just to maintain equilibrium and not get sick and go into withdrawals. And before long, I needed increasingly more in order to actually feel stoned. I was lost in a bad predicament, all my pretentions about being above it all, about being more politically conscious, about being stronger than everyone else were now buried in an avalanche of crystalline powder. I was hopelessly flailing around, increasingly caught in an addiction-driven vortex and I knew it, yet I felt powerless to do anything about it.

Then one day, out of the blue, one of my friend's fathers stood on the steps of his apartment building directly across Van Cortlandt Park South from The Rail. He motioned me to come over. Because his son Adam and I were friends since junior high school, over the years Adam's father and I had brief interactions whenever I was over at the house, so we knew each other slightly. But I was confused at first, since we did not really have any relationship to speak of. We all knew Adam's father was a gifted watchmaker and an official with the Toymakers Union, and that in the back of his apartment he had his office workspace, chock-full with an assortment of tools and toy parts. Because of his position, his kids always got the latest toys first. He was short and compact, with a quiet demeanor covering a stern union-made toughness that told you he wasn't to be trifled with. There was no real reason for him and me to talk, much less for him to invite me across the street to do so. I was sure that he was going to lecture me on wasting my life by messing with drugs.

I crossed the street and he took me into the apartment and led me back to his office. He reached for an envelope and withdrew a piece of paper. It was a letter, on union letterhead, neatly typed and signed by him. Without offering me an opportunity to read it, he simply explained that it was a letter of introduction and that I should take it to the address in Brooklyn written on the front of the envelope. Once there I was to ask to see the man whose name was also on the front. Without another word he folded the letter into the envelope, sealed it, and handed it to me. While I did not realize it at the time, simple as that, Mr. Allen Sokol saved my life.

Chapter Twenty-Two
Turbulent Seas

I had never been on the ocean before, much less in a storm. This was my first ship. It was our third day out of the Sea-Land docks at their Port Elizabeth Terminal in New Jersey, and my third day of looking green and feeling sick as a dog. I was not used to an environment that rolled and pitched like this, making every movement a study in balance. I had already broken the big toe on my right foot by dropping an acetylene tank on it as I wrestled against the bucking of the ship to move it into place on orders of the First Engineer. The ocean had become so rough that one night we had to secure ourselves into our bunks; I did this by lacing rope back and forth through the bed frame from my mid-chest down to my thighs. This way, if the movement of the ship tried to eject me while I was sleeping, the rope would act as preventative webbing and keep me from flying out of my top bunk onto the steel deck. This being an old vintage World War Two Liberty ship our quarters were at the fantail; officers slept at midship, as did the galley crew, both closer to the mess hall. The weather got so bad the captain restricted us from using the deck to make our way from our quarters to the mess hall, and commanded that we traverse the shaft alley instead.

The shaft alley was a cramped passageway that allowed seamen access to the propeller shaft in order to check oil levels and temperature gauges to see if all was well, and for general maintenance and repair. It led from the engine room aft, to a ladder that led upwards into our quarters. Because of the severity of the weather we now had to use this cramped and circuitous route each and every mealtime. One evening as I lay nauseous and moaning in my bed, I decided I had to try to eat something. I stood up unsteadily, left my foc's'le and instead of climbing down into the shaft alley I confusedly stepped out onto the deck instead. The air was instantly refreshing; I felt immediately exhilarated. To hell with the shaft alley, I thought; I can make it. I grabbed the deck railing with one hand and stretched my other toward the bulkhead for balance and slowly made my way toward midship and the hatch that led to the mess hall. Holding on for dear life, the waves undulating wildly and dashing water onto the deck and across my feet with every roll of the ship, I inched my way forward. Just as I was reaching to open the hatch, the ship rolled violently starboard, slamming me up against the deck railing at hip height. I knew I was about to go overboard. All I could see as I looked down was the outstretched arms of the ocean reaching for me.

* * * * *

I WAS SITTING ON MY SECOND TRAIN OF THE MORNING, heading to the Seafarer's International Union (SIU) located in Brooklyn. In preparation I had determined to clean up my act and go cold turkey and detox the heroin out of my system. Since my addiction was recent and as a result much easier to break, I experienced three days of only minor hell. As a result of cleaning up, I was ready and determined to follow Mr. Sokol's instructions. I was holding the letter he had given me, wondering where all this was going to take me. What I thought I had been given was the possibility of a steady union job, with decent pay, and maybe the ticket for Leah and I to finally be able to buy land in Vermont and get away from drugs forever. It was a vision that I would learn over the next year was way too small and, in that very smallness, my dreams would arrive stillborn, aborted by much pain and suffering. But for the moment I was riding above the houses of Brooklyn, feeling only the sky was the limit, thinking of the Green Mountain State as the elevated train pulled into the station.

I entered the union hall and went past rows of benches to the first desk I saw. I felt like I was back in a version of Bradley's Bar, with rough and tough laborers of every shape, size, and race milling about, checking the job board or waiting to bid on the next job call. Instantly I felt like a child among men, inserting myself into their world, a world I knew absolutely nothing about. I asked the person standing as a wooden podium where I could find the man Mr. Sokol told me to present his letter to. I was directed upstairs. I knocked on the door and was told to come in. In a tiny, cluttered office, stood a man with glasses, a balding head, and a smoldering cigar clenched in his teeth. He was one of the Seafarer's union officials, holding a similar position as Mr. Sokol did in the Toymakers Union. It was clear to me in a flash that I was in the presence of a powerful man. It was also clear that I was now a favor that Mr. Sokol would have to reciprocate at some future time and, further, whatever I did in this setting would reflect on Mr. Sokol as well. I became very alert, my people-pleasing antennae stirring as I wordlessly handed him the envelope and watched him tear it open and read over the letter. As he finished he laid the letter on his desk, looked me up and down as if appraising livestock, and muttered, "Good."

I barely had time to thank him when he sent me down the hall to get my head shaved, military style, and have a picture taken. The next stop was to donate blood, a procedure that was topped off with an offer of either a shot of whiskey or a cup of orange juice; I chose orange juice. Then I was sent across the street to a three-story dorm and given two work shirts, two pair of dungarees, socks and a pair of work boots, and a baseball cap with Seafarer's International Union embossed on the front. I was assigned a dorm room and a bunk. I sat there stunned as the sun began to set. I had imagined an initial meeting and then me going home to wait the union's reply. Instead, I had been as good as Shanghaied. It turned out that I had been accepted into the SIU's Harry Lundeberg School of Seamanship for training in the arts of being a qualified merchant mariner. The two other guys who were already living in the dorm explained that we would be waiting until enough people were recruited to form the new incoming class at the school, and then we would be bussed to Maryland. In the meantime we would begin acting like seamen and spend our days in the Brooklyn dorm sweeping, cleaning, and polishing everything in sight, over and over again until it was time to leave. I called Leah and told her what had happened; she was surprised but happy that I had been accepted. I called my mother and she was ecstatic that I finally had a good union job and I was going to make something of myself. About a week later, as the requisite bodies filled the dorm and we became the newest batch of seamanship trainees, I was allowed to go home to the Bronx for a weekend to say my goodbyes and gather personal effects. Within two weeks of arriving at the SIU headquarters, just as the calendar was turning October, twenty-two of us were shipped by charter bus to Piney Point, Maryland, where for the next three months we would be known as "Life Boat Class No. 57."

PINEY POINT, MARYLAND, was exactly as its name implied, a flat, pine-tree covered stretch of land that jutted into the Chesapeake Bay. It was a training facility comprised of an administration building, a large mess hall and galley, three free-standing dormitory barracks, a red-painted medium-sized ship where the incoming class was housed for the first two weeks and where lifeboat classes and other trainings were held. Moored not too far from this ship was an elegant two-masted schooner that was used as part of the ceremony for each graduating class. It was a beautiful location, idyllic with its combination of woodland and waterway, even with the ominous jelly-fish floating across the surface close to the docks. Underneath the apparent tranquility though, everything and everyone was dedicated to a single mission: produce competent seamen to replenish and expand the ranks of the Seafarer's International Union.

There was a lot at stake for the young men who came through this training. Not only were they automatically in the union, they graduated with their first ship assignment guaranteed, no waiting at the union hall behind senior union members. Further, each Piney Point graduate was granted a "B-Book," with a green cover that signified to everyone that you were a product of the Harry Lundeberg School and therefore had gotten a bit of a leg up in your career. The radar among a given ship's crew was continually on the alert to any B-Book'er who was too cocky or had airs. By virtue of obtaining a B-Book fresh out of school, we leap-frogged one wrung up the seniority ladder ahead of guys who only possessed their Seaman's Papers (the identification card issued by the U.S. Coast Guard), designating them eligible and qualified to work on ships. The only higher designation in the union was those members who, by virtue of their longevity in the industry, held the prized "A-Book," with its stylish black-leather cover. While it was true that A-Book members always got first dibs during job call, for a kid just out of high school or in his early 20s, a B-Book was a damn good start into the world of unionized work, especially this particular world of being a merchant seaman.

Life at Piney Point had a definite rhythm and structure. We were first housed in the red ship, moored right at the dock near the parade grounds. It was designed to give us the feel of being at sea. The gentle rocking of the bay waters gave me the finest and deepest sleeps I had ever had. Bunks were fitted into the design of the ship, with random placements and at curious angles; more than once I cracked my head on the bulkhead trying to alight too quickly from my upper bunk. This was where I learned to make hospital corners with my sheets when making my bed. This was mandated by one of the mid-level administrators who found joy in riding the new arrivals every chance he got. He would come around each morning as we stood at attention near our freshly made bunks and try to bounce a quarter on each mattress. If it bounced your hospital corners did the trick and you were dismissed to go to breakfast; if it did not bounce he pulled the bedding from your bunk, tossed it on the floor, and commanded you to re-make the bed. At every turn we were being fashioned into seamen who would proudly represent the SIU.

For the first two weeks, each day was divided into learning about ship safety in the morning, especially the life boats, with afternoons devoted to close order drill on the small concrete parade ground nearby.

My two closest friends were Cadet Thomas from Hawaii and Cadet Christian, from St. James, Virgin Islands. We all bonded immediately; we sat next to each other in each of our classes and always shared meals together. Among ourselves we mocked the rigid discipline of marching and standing at attention for bed-check and inspections, while inside we remained grateful for this opportunity, imagining how our lives would dramatically change when we became seamen and the dreams this job could make real for us. Daily, we buoyed each other's spirits as the autumn days progressed toward winter.

Life boat training was a mandatory class and one that we all had to pass in order to continue the training. It amounted to learning about every part of the life boat and the davit mechanism that lowered it to the water in case of emergency. We spent hours going over and over the parts, how they worked, and how to lower and raise the life boat. At the end of the two weeks we took a written test and staged our very own life boat drill. We finished up by breaking into teams and having life boat races – complete with coxswains keeping our rowing rhythm steady and our competitive spirits high. We raced from the ship, around a buoy that seemed like it was miles out in the bay, and back again. We all were relatively uncoordinated, a comedy of errors if ever there was one, but it was our first taste of fun since we arrived and we laughingly soaked up every minute of it.

After life boat training was complete, we moved from the red ship over to one of the barracks, which was one huge room with rows of bunks evenly aligned between the front doors and the toilets in the rear. Once there we were issued a set of dress khakis that we had to wear on Sundays and at any official function. We also had two of our original classmates, Mike Dennis of Wyoming and Barry Hicks of Tennessee, designated as our boatswains (or "Bo'suns" in the vernacular). They both had been in the military and were the perfect choices for keeping us relatively in line. Their immediate supervisor and our lifeboat instructor was Mr. Matthews, a tall, lean, no-nonsense black man who was easy to get along with unless someone stepped out of line and broke a rule. Then he would be nose-to-nose with the offender, drill-instructor style, delivering a dressing down that was painful to receive and almost as painful to witness.

In our limited spare time, fenced in as we were, guys mostly hung out, talked, smoked cigarettes, and played half-court basketball near the barracks. Cadet Christian and I were often on the same basketball team, him jabbering distractingly in his Virgin Island accent while on defense, me gathering rebounds whenever he missed a shot. Here in my familiar environment of hoops I began to make friends beyond my immediate classmates, as I garnered respect for my on-court skills as well as for my fair and friendly, supportive temperament. Because of these attributes, after about a month at Piney Point, I was promoted to being an Assistant Bo'sun and moved into the adjoining quarters with Mike and Barry. I was eager to do a good job and in my zeal I became a hyper-vigilant shrew, ever on the lookout for infractions. I was on everybody's case. People couldn't figure out the changes that were taking place in me, nor could I. I felt like I was under a powerful spell, or the spell of power. I was tense all the time and making everyone else uptight as well.

One Sunday afternoon my classmate, Cadet Romano from Brooklyn, came into my quarters and explained the situation in no uncertain terms. "Here's the deal, Donovan," he began quietly, with a seriousness that riveted me to my chair. "If your bullshit doesn't stop, I will have a few of my guys meet with you when we return to Brooklyn, *capische*?" Instantly the message was transmitted. I nodded. As he left the room the spell I was under dissolved in an onslaught of images of three or four of Cadet Romano's menacing Italian buddies waiting for me, all of whom I was certain would be intensely muscular and "made guys" connected to the Mafia. I felt that I had learned an important lesson about the seduction of power and, from that day on, the rest of my time at Piney Point was mellow. I did what my job as Assistant Bo'sun required, but I did it fairly and with conversation, humor, and respect.

As late-October rolled around I was beginning to forget about the whole heroin scene in the Bronx, replacing those images with images of buying land in Vermont, and Leah and I getting the hell out of New York for good. But in short order I was reminded of all that I wanted to move beyond and just how entwined I was, even at this distance, by the threads still tethering me to the neighborhood. The school's one and only visiting day was fast approaching, when family and friends would arrive to spend a Saturday with loved ones, including enjoying a barbecue lunch. Leah was taking the bus down and as much as I wanted to see her, I was a bundle of confused and troubled emotions at the prospect. I wondered what she had been doing these past weeks up in the neighborhood without me there; was she still getting high, was she sleeping with someone else? I shuddered and tried to dismiss the images before they gained purchase in my psyche.

When she arrived we hugged stiffly. As I showed her around the school, it was clear just how alien an environment it was to her, and I kept wondering if my newfound excitement at being a merchant seaman was strange to her as well. After lunch we walked back into the pine forest and sat together. She produced a couple of bags of heroin, one for each of us. Despite my reluctance to getting high, but at the same time fearful of increasing the strain and distance between us, in an awkward bid for togetherness I inhaled it all. I quickly felt stoned since I hadn't had any drugs since back in September. For Leah it was just a matter of using the heroin to take the sickly edges off, since it was clear that her need was beginning to show after the long bus ride and I wondered how many bags she had that she wasn't about to share given the hours it would take to get back home. Now I knew for certain that she was still addicted. There was friendliness but little warmth between us, almost as if she had come here just to get high and not to see me. Then it was time for her to go. As I watched her board the bus I worried that even more changes had occurred in the neighborhood since I had been gone.

I WAS GETTING CLOSE TO GRADUATING the Harry Lundeberg School of Seamanship and it was time to choose a specific department to sail under. Right after completing our lifeboat training and certification, the rest of the program was structured to introduce us to each of the three divisions that comprised a ship's complement: mess hall cooks, deckhands, and engine room crew. We each spent three weeks training in one department and then rotating to the next for another three weeks. For mess hall training the three weeks were spent in the school's cafeteria and galley learning the ropes of dishwashing, table set-up, and shadowing the cooks as their assistant – which meant slicing and prepping food and generally being their go-fer. While I actually enjoyed the meditative solitude of scrubbing pots and pans, I hated working in the galley. When one of my classmates described how working in the galley was one of the most dangerous places on the ship, especially in high seas when scalding liquids could be splashing everywhere, I quickly crossed this department off my list.

The next stop was the deck department. This brought us back to our original home, the red ship. For weeks we learned about chipping and painting, the seamen's Sisyphean struggle to stay ahead of the corrosive powers of wind and saltwater. We learned how to rig a Bo'sun's Chair, essentially a tiny wooden slat-seat that would allow you to dangle from smokestacks or over the side in order to chip and paint those hard-to-reach places. We also returned to safety training, revisiting the launching of the lifeboats as well as practicing our assigned tasks in case we ever had to abandon ship. As much fun as it was to be on deck in the open air, and as romantic an image as it was to picture myself leaning on the railings as the ship slid into foreign ports-of-call, I knew that there was another season called winter – filled with storms and rough seas – that capped my decision to forego a career as a deckhand. Besides, I simply hated tying knots ever since my abject failure as a Boy Scout.

My final option was choosing the engine room, becoming a part of the "Black Gang" as it was historically called. Due to the filthy work the men in the engine room engaged in when coal-powered ships ruled the seas, the black dust and soot they carried on their clothes and on their faces marked them instantly as dwellers of the ship's underworld, members of the Black Gang. This training took us into the engine room of the red ship for hands-on instruction. We also got the privilege to train in the engine room of the school's schooner. While I was equally incompetent with tools as I was with knots, I was still drawn to the Black Gang. Even when we were told to beware of leaks of superheated steam which could cut a man in half, and which remained dangerously invisible for a number of feet before condensing, I was still favoring working down in the engine room. Even after our instructor demonstrated how to find one of those invisible leaks by methodically and carefully waving a broom through the air until the handle was severed by the super-heated steam, thereby revealing the location of the leak, I remained undaunted. I felt safe down inside the ship, almost as if it was a separate reality, almost as if I was still on land. When we were finally asked to select our department, the engine room was definitely for me.

Our last hurrah before leaving Piney Point was our graduation, the first part of which culminated in our class manning the schooner for a trip up the Chesapeake Bay to Washington D.C. All of us were in our chosen departments, either in the galley, in the engine room, or on deck. We even broke up into four-hour shifts to stand watch, exactly like it would be at sea. This was our version of a shakedown cruise, where we could safely put what we learned into practice under the watchful eyes of our teachers.

The other reason for the voyage was our serving as a lobbying force in D.C. to demonstrate to politicians the need for legislation to ensure that cargoes be carried by American ships and not under foreign flags. To this end we were feted at a luncheon, listened to speeches by various representatives promising to do everything they could to strengthen America's merchant fleet, and toured around our nation's capital. We felt like dignitaries. Standing alone on the deck of the schooner on the way back to Piney Point, I was beginning to feel like I was stepping into something that was going to bring me a whole new life. But I was also worried about the life I was returning to back in the Bronx and whether it would snatch me and drag me under again.

The formal graduation ceremony back at the Harry Lundeberg School of Seamanship was short and sweet, with our instructors proudly watching as we filed across the front of the mess hall to receive our diplomas from high-ranking union officials. We packed quickly the next day, said our goodbyes to the friends we made who still had time to serve at Piney Point, and thanked some of the instructors we had come to like and respect. As we were loaded onto the bus bound for Brooklyn and the SIU headquarters, an incoming bus pulled onto the campus and another lifeboat class tumbled out into the waiting hands of Mr. Matthews and a cohort of other instructors gathered to greet them at the front entrance of the administration building. I could see the eagerness in the instructors' faces, the expectant energy causing them to shift restlessly from one foot to another; they were ready to get their hands on these unsuspecting trainees and whip them into shape, just as they had done with my class. As I glanced back at the unfolding mayhem, as Mr. Matthews and the others attempted to fashion them into marching formation, I smiled. I had made it through and I felt stronger and clearer than I had in years. I had been whipped into shape and I realized what a damn good thing that had been. As the bus emerged from the canopy of pine trees and onto the highway heading north, I closed my eyes and thanked Mr. Sokol once again.

IN THE UNION'S MIND the post-Harry Lundeberg School of Seamanship plan was crystal clear. Upon arriving in Brooklyn we would not have to go through the regular union hall waiting-based-on-seniority, but instead we would immediately be assigned a ship to begin our careers as merchant seamen. This was one of the benefits of attending the training school and it made perfect sense: we had our training, we had our clothes, we had spent three months being imprinted as mariners, and this was a way for the union to both obtain a return on their investment and impress American shipping companies regarding the quality of young seamen readily available to fill the open positions. But the four-hour bus ride was enough to gnaw at my self-confidence regarding how quickly I could embrace this new path. A wave of insecurity engulfed me as I began to wonder what Leah was doing, if she was sleeping with other people, and what other havoc the heroin scene was creating for her and, as a result, for me. As the skyline of New York City came into view, I had decided that I could not ship out right away and I began formulating a different plan.

As we disembarked the bus, we were herded into union headquarters where some half-dozen union officials were sitting at desks waiting to process us formally into the union and immediately onto a ship. As I sat down I was handed my coveted B-Book that signified that I was officially in the Seafarer's International Union. Its green cover had "T. Donovan – 41904" embossed in gold stamped right below the official union logo. As I held it a surge of pride pulsed upwards into my chest and I almost forgot about getting back to the Bronx and to Leah. The rustle of papers being pushed across the desk for me to sign snapped me back into focus. I hastily lied that my mother was very sick and I needed to go home first before shipping out. The union official looked quizzically at me for a moment. He explained that if I chose not to ship out now, I would be just another guy in the union hall trying to catch a ship at the mercy of the seniority system, even with my B-Book. I told him I understood but this was a family emergency. He paused, as if to reassure himself that what he was hearing from me made sense. Then he gathered the papers back toward his side of the desk and handed me my B-Book, saying, "Okay, see you in the hall." As I stood and began heading toward the door I heard him yell, "Next," and I was wracked by uncertainty. As I hefted my duffel bag, left the building and headed toward the subway, it dawned on me that I was responding to a darker, more unpredictable "Next," and I was suddenly very nervous.

It was the latter half of December when I arrived back in the Bronx and my worst fears barely did justice to the situation in the neighborhood. In the space of three months it seemed everyone was either selling heroin or using it, and more often than not doing both. I was appalled. Despite that brief interlude of sniffing heroin with Leah under the trees at Piney Point, I had returned to reading books about oppression and how heroin was being used to keep down communities of color. Throughout my time at seamanship school, I continued to be avidly interested in the social struggles currently raging, especially the Vietnam War, where Kevin was still fighting, and the burgeoning Women's Movement which was causing me to reevaluate the whole paradigm of masculinity. I even turned in the direction of spirituality while at school, daily reading the *Tao De Ching*, which helped my determination to stay clean and off drugs. I had even begun using positive affirmations while standing before the mirror each morning in my dormitory room. As I repeated aloud to myself, "Every day, in every way, it's getting better and better," I felt like I was getting my head together again, reminding myself that joining the Merchant Marine was first and foremost about getting land in Vermont and leaving all the drugs behind once and for all. I thought I had gotten stronger as a result of my time in Piney Point. But the seductions were strong as well, and once back in the neighborhood my resistance was tested daily, hourly, within what had become a thoroughly drug-infested milieu. After a couple of frustrating weeks of making little headway getting Leah and my other friends to quit heroin, I decided that since I was the one who had a job where it was possible to make the kind of money necessary to realize our vision, it was time to finally take the steps to achieve the dream of owning our own land. It was time for me to lead by example; it was time shape up and to ship out.

I walked into the union hall and immediately perused the various postings of upcoming jobs. The way it worked was that when a ship was organizing a crew, two union officials would stand behind the main desk and read aloud the job openings off of 3x5 index cards. Anyone who was interested in that particular run would then bid on it by approaching the desk with their A-Book, B-Book, or Seaman's Papers in hand. The union official would then select the guy with the most seniority for the job, leaving the others to wait around the hall until the next position came open. It took me less than a week of commuting back and forth from the Bronx to Brooklyn by subway before my B-Book was selected. As the unlucky union members turned away from the desk, the union official handed me some papers to sign and another piece of paper listing what my position was, what ship I was assigned to, and when and where I was to join as a new crewmember. I had to be there the very next day so I hustled back home to grab my barely unpacked duffel bag. I was excited to finally begin this new chapter of my life. I read the paper I received at the union hall as the subway train clacked rhythmically over the tracks on its way back to the Bronx. I had the entry-level engine room position of Wiper, as part of the crew on the container ship *S. S. Azalea City*. The ship was moored at the Port Elizabeth Terminal in New Jersey, at the Sea-Land Services docks.

On January 7, 1971, I walked up the gangway and onto the fantail of the *Azalea City* feeling proud, satisfied, and a bit nervous. On one side of the ship's berth a concrete and glass office building stretched inland away from the ship, a huge Sea-Land sign beaming from the nearby rooftop across the harbor toward Manhattan. Massive cranes that moved along tracks in the dock to accommodate wherever a ship was moored, hovered over everything, mantis-like in their concentrated stillness. I thought of my father and felt a wave of kinship between us, him a longshoreman and now me a merchant seaman, following him into the world of ships and docks and rough and tumble blue-collar workers. As my foot hit the deck all my romantic notions of going to sea dissipated. On the fantail was a five-foot-high pile of metal scraps, paint cans, dirt and rust, and pieces of rubber gasket, pipes, and hose. Atop the debris stood a white and grey seagull, completely unperturbed by my arrival. The next rude awakening was the fact that everywhere I looked or touched was solid steel: the deck, the railings, the bulkheads, the ladders, everything. There was not a single soft or forgiving spot on the entire ship. I was entering a hard world populated by hard men. It seemed I had lost sight of this in the sheltered environment of Piney Point. Now, the truth that this was a real ship about to cross the Atlantic Ocean, and I was part of its crew, suddenly clanged home.

THE *AZALEA CITY* WAS A CONVERTED LIBERTY SHIP, used extensively for transporting cargo during World War II. As such the officers' quarters were amidships, close to the mess hall and galley, one deck above the main deck and right beneath the bridge. Engineers had only to drop two decks below into the engine room and Mates had only to traverse one deck upward to their stations on the bridge. The men staffing the galley were also quartered in the same area but on the level of the main deck. The rest of the deckhands and engine room crew were quartered aft, near the fantail and right above the propeller. As I stepped through the nearest hatch I found my foc'sle immediately on my right, at deck level. Nearby, a ladder descended to a larger area housing a series of small rooms with bunks, an open common area with tables and chairs for playing cards or sitting around talking, and a bathroom with toilets and shower stalls. My quarters were tiny, with a set of bunk beds pressed against the starboard bulkhead, just under two portholes. Two tall, thin, metal lockers were attached to the bulkhead nearby. A grey metal desk with a matching metal chair was across the room, a solitary light bulb protruded from the ceiling. Gritty linoleum, scuffed indelibly by the comings and goings of endless streams of work boots, covered the deck. Alone, and the first to arrive, I immediately claimed the upper bunk.

The rest of the crew arrived throughout the day. My roommate and fellow Wiper, Cedric, was a black man from Jamaica, about four or five years older than me, in his mid-20s. He was friendly and quite happy to have the lower bunk (why he was so happy I was to find out within mere days of our departure). We hit it off nicely. Hours into our first day at sea, once the ship passed the 12-mile limit, we were told to dump the mountain of debris on the fantail overboard. As our shovels bit into the pile, and as we flung empty paint cans over the side, I was appalled at what we were doing. My heart went out to the ocean and its inhabitants that we were willfully and mindlessly polluting. I had read Rachel Carson's *Silent Spring* and was aware of the growing environmental movement attempting to wake people up to what humans were doing to the planet and its ecosystems.

I began to wonder if the problem was the very immensity of the ocean itself and how easily we could be lulled into thinking that the ocean was so big and vast that it could handle anything we did to it. Was it possible that all the junk we were throwing overboard was just being absorbed and causing no harm at all? Was the ocean really a self-cleansing ecosystem? As I watched pieces of rusted metal sink beneath the waves, and oily paint congealed and floating on the surface, along with pieces of wood and linoleum, I became quite certain that this was not the case, and what we were doing was hardly benign. I imagined how many other ships were doing something similar, every day, all around the world. I felt anger and sadness rise up in my throat; sadness at what we were doing to our planet and anger that raising my voice here, on this ship, would have no effect whatsoever and only alienate me from the crew and likely get me fired. I was frustrated and decided to stuff my feelings down deep, until each shovelful tossed over the railing became but a mechanical action, devoid of further thought and feeling.

Despite the hard, dirty and destructive nature of the work, I felt paradoxically good, like I was coming of age in the world of men and men's labor. When the ship lost sight of the Manhattan skyline, and all around us there was nothing but water, I realized just how tiny our ship was, a mere speck bobbing on a watery vastness. At the same time, the elemental power of the ocean, the mystery of what lurked beneath its waves, and the horizon stretching 360-degrees to kiss the dome of the sky was arrestingly beautiful and nearly overwhelming in its magnificence. I was in about as natural an environment as one could possibly ask for. As I basked in the awe and magnitude of where I was standing, I thought for certain that this was going to be a great experience.

Then the seas got rough.

BY NIGHTFALL ON THE FIRST DAY I was already feeling quite seasick and was the brunt of more than a few jokes about how green I was looking, especially as a novice Piney Point graduate struggling to get his sea-legs under him. When the cooks served gumbo and all I could fixate on were the pieces of green, slimy okra floating around in my bowl, I hastily retreated to my foc'sle and onto my bunk where I lay nauseous and moaning until morning. On the second day the ocean swells were really taking their toll on my equilibrium. I stumbled through my workday, barely eating. In the afternoon, the First Engineer told me to bring him an acetylene tank so he could do some burning in order to complete a job he was working on. As I began muscling the tank across the engine room deck the ship rolled and it slipped out of my hands and fell onto my right foot. Somehow it hit perfectly, just behind the steel toe of my work boot, breaking the metatarsal of my big toe. Now I had excruciating pain to go along with my nausea. I hobbled through the rest of the day as best I could, tight-lipped and determined not to show any pain or ask for the rest of the shift off.

The seas got rougher still, heaving the ship up and then crashing it down onto the roiling ocean. It became too rough to work. It was suggested by one of the more experienced crew that we might want to take some rope and lash ourselves into our bunks in order to get a halfway decent night's sleep and to not be flung around the foc'sle. By dinner time I was too sick and in too much pain to eat so I went straight to my rack and to sleep, threading the rope zig-zag across the metal frame of my bunk to serve as a webbing to keep me from being tossed bodily out of my bed. It was a fitful night; I could hear the wind blowing and the waves heaving. I could also hear my shipmate sleeping soundly right below me, without any need for ropes to keep him in bed due to its low center of gravity. I could feel the ship being lifted by the waves; then the waves would drop away from beneath the stern and I could hear the propeller grinding in the open air right before the ship crashed back onto the water. It was eerie and deeply disconcerting. I nervously began to wonder how ships really stay afloat rather than being swallowed by the turbulent seas. I wondered if my first ship would be my last.

Come the morning of the third day the seas had yet to subside, so all work except for standing watch (which Wipers did not do) was called off. The crew was ordered to use the shaft alley during mealtimes since it was safer than going on deck to get to the hatch at midship that accessed the galley and mess area. I remained in my foc'sle nursing my throbbing toe and trying to find my equilibrium. Slowly the green color drained from my face and my nausea ratcheted back significantly. I was still a bit unsteady but by dinner time I was ready for nourishment. I got down from my bunk slowly and carefully. I opened the door and instead of going down the ladder to the shaft alley, I pushed open the hatch leading out onto the stern. The fresh air tasted salty and I suddenly felt revitalized after three days of pain and lethargy and sickness.

With the ocean continuing to have its way with us, I knew it wasn't a good idea to walk along the deck to the galley but I was suddenly feeling exhilarated. I grabbed the starboard railing, while bracing my other hand against the bulkhead, and proceeded step-by-step toward midship. The ship was pitching and rolling with the fierceness of a rodeo bull determined to unseat whatever foolish rider had arrogantly dared to attempt to master pure instinct. In this moment I was that fool and the sea was ferocious in her elemental undulations. As I reached toward the handle of the hatch that led into the galley area, the ship rolled starboard and I was slammed up against the railing at waist height. I looked down and saw the sea open its dark and white-flecked mouth. I was certain that I was about to tumble overboard and be swallowed by the cold and indifferent ocean. Suddenly the ship rolled violently leeward and I was thrown from the railing and forcefully onto the deck, sliding into the bulkhead where I reflexively reached up and grabbed onto the hatch handle and held on tightly, gasping the air and realizing that my death sentence had been pardoned by some miracle or an intervening act of grace. I struggled to catch my breath and get my legs under me. After what seemed an eternity paralyzed in fear, and shuddering with relief that I was still on board, I scraped myself to a standing position and entered the galley. The beef stew that night tasted exceptionally good and I savored every mouthful, remaining quiet regarding my escapades on deck. When it was time to return to my foc'sle I made my way into the shaft alley and walked happily aft, glad to be alive. For the rest of my time on the *Azalea City* I tried to listen, pay attention to my surroundings, and not fall overboard.

As Wipers, we worked an 8 a.m. to 5 p.m. shift every day, with work assigned after those hours designated as overtime. Overtime was hungrily sought by nearly every crew member because while the basic monthly wages were okay, it was the hours of overtime that ballooned paychecks exponentially and made the days and weeks at sea away from family more bearable. Given that the ship ran 24 hours, subjected to all the elements of sea and salt and wind, all the stresses and strains of plying the ocean, there was plenty of overtime to be had. For us Wipers, this meant getting two to three hours of overtime each evening. Wipers, as the name implies, are the janitors of the engine room. For the first two hours of each day our task was to clean the engine room crew's quarters. This consisted of wiping down furniture, emptying waste cans, and mopping the decks. After that, we were subject to the whims of our immediate supervisor, the First Engineer, who gave us our assignments on the basis of what was required to maintain a well-functioning engine room. Often our job would be to assist him in one of his maintenance projects. Whenever he did not require our help we were at the beck-and-call of the Second and Third Engineers, as well as the rest of the more senior members of the Black Gang whenever something needed to be wiped up, cleaned, painted, or whenever anything needed to be moved, hauled, or tossed overboard. Our most despised task, though, was "blowing tubes."

Blowing tubes was the way that the boilers that powered the ship had the built-up combustion residue removed in order to ensure the smooth functioning of the system. Every day at 4:30 p.m. the tubes on the *Azalea City* were blown. What it meant for this lowly Wiper was squeezing my entire body in behind the boiler and locating the sets of pulley chains that dangled there. These chains hung down from the smoke stacks on the upper deck all the way into the engine room. The chains were often hot to the touch so I would don either a pair of work gloves or grab two of our standard red cotton shop-rags (one for either hand) before commencing. Then I would grab the chains and begin pulling. Somewhere aloft the tubes would open, spewing all manner of ash, debris, and scalding droplets of water down upon my head and shoulders. Even wearing a watch cap and safety glasses was no guarantee of getting away without some searing pain from the water or a face full of soot. This was our final daily task at the end of each shift. Fortunately, as a result of our getting good and dirty after blowing the tubes, we got to quit about 20 minutes early to go and clean up before dinner. After we ate it was back to the engine room for overtime work.

CROSSING THE ATLANTIC OCEAN for the first time had me mesmerized. The sheer vastness of the sea, the fact that everywhere I looked all I could see was water, gave me a perspective about our human relationship to this immense natural world that I never was able to imagine by simply reading books. Every free moment I had I was on the fantail, gazing at the horizon, watching the clouds, listening to the sound of the engine and the lapping waves. At night I would stare down into the churning wake, watching the propeller send phosphorous to the surface of the water, mirror images in the ocean of the stars in the black sky above. As a result of my recent turn toward spirituality, and the use of positive affirmations when I was training in Piney Point, I was now reading *The Baghavagita* in another effort to make sense of my place in the cosmos. I was fascinated by the entire story, but especially the scene on the battlefield where Arjuna refuses to enter the battle, and he and the god Krishna have a deeply moving conversation about Arjuna's struggle whether to fight in the war or not. As I read Krishna's response about Arjuna's duty to karma, I sat on the stern and I began thinking about Kevin's decision to accept his fate and not resist the draft. I began to wonder if that was not the more noble and heroic thing to do, even as I hated this war and saw it as a criminal action by the United States against the out-gunned nation of Vietnam, and as much as I feared for Kevin's life in the war zone.

What about our tiny human decisions? Peering over the railing, I wondered do we really have choices in our lives? Are we merely tiny parts of a gigantic whole that miraculously comes into existence and just as miraculously moves out of existence, similar to the seemingly endless churning of phosphorous brought to the surface by the invisible propeller to just as quickly fade into the black waves as the ship moves on? I felt like the sea was opening my mind as I read this book, was somehow encouraging me to imagine and entertain thoughts that not so long ago would've been prohibitively foreign to my sensibilities; I would've pushed them immediately from my consciousness, if I even let them get that far. As a result I began to wonder anew how I should confront the scourge of heroin in the neighborhood, what was my karmic role in this great battle?

One night, after some crewmen were swapping stories at dinner about ships they'd been on where guys had simply and inexplicably jumped overboard, I found myself alone at my usual place on the stern gazing intently into the sea. They'd all described these deaths as acts of suicide, carried out by men who had been at sea too damn long and just went nuts. Shaking their heads in troubled bemusement they stopped short of speculating further on what could possibly cause someone to take their own life in this way. Yet somehow I knew that suicide wasn't the case, couldn't be the case – at least not for all of them – for I, too, had felt the compelling urge to jump into the ocean and I knew I was not suicidal. There was something else going on, something that *The Baghavagita* made so very clear to me: there is Oneness that we humans all long to return to.

During my nights on deck, alongside the magnificence of the ocean, when an ache so great welled up inside me that I physically and mentally had to restrain myself from leaping over the railing, these were not moments when I desired to die – no, quite far from that. On the contrary, every fiber of my being desired to live and to live fully in the embrace of the totality of existence, a totality that the undulating sea promised. If there ever was a Siren song to be heard, this was mine. But I was young, still stuck in the warring dichotomy of life and death and I wanted to live my life, see my friends, and make love to Leah. So, I resisted the magnetic pull. But as a result I felt like a changed person, like someone who had glimpsed previously hidden realms that now informed my very being, my very soul, in ways I knew would make them available to me throughout my life. Within days my trips to the stern became exercises in wonderment over the majesty and beauty of our natural world and the vast mystery of the universe.

THE FIRST PORT THE *AZALEA CITY* DOCKED WAS GENOA, in northern Italy, built into the hills overlooking the Mediterranean Sea. As I stood on deck as we approached the mooring, so many emotions bombarded me. I couldn't believe I was about to enter another country. Besides that trip to Toronto, I had never left the boundaries of the U.S. before and I was struck by how small our planet really is. It was completely surreal to me to be standing on this part of the globe and looking back across the ocean at the country I called home. The bustle of the port refocused my attention as I watched our deck crew secure the thick rope lines round the bits on deck and the evenly spaced cleats on the dock. Simultaneously with the docking of the ship, cranes had already removed the hatch covers and had begun off-loading the containers onto waiting semi-trucks; no wasting time in the automated world of international shipping. Fortunately for Cedric and me, our shift was virtually over so we got to head ashore.

As we roamed the streets together, I let him take the lead since he was more experienced. Cedric' sole mission was to buy some sharp new Italian clothes at the cheapest price possible, so we navigated through the streets around the port, upward into the shopping district. For hours we went from store to store, Cedric trying on clothes and me quiet and wide-eyed at this new world bustling around me, the music of the Italian language everywhere. Eventually he found enough deals to make him feel like he'd gotten some really snazzy threads at prices he was happy with and could brag about back home. Next stop was a meal.

I had no idea that we were in store for a *seven*-course meal, Italian-style. More and more food just kept coming to our table, everyone on the restaurant staff encouraging us to *"mangia, mangia,"* everyone laughing and friendly. When we were finally finished we just sat back, engorged with soup, bread, fish, antipasto, pasta, salad, and dessert. As a 20-year-old from the Bronx, it was the most incredible culinary experience I had ever had in one sitting, making the Jewish delis, Chinese restaurants, and pizza parlors back home – and even the Italian restaurants on Arthur Avenue – seem paltry.

As we made our way back to the ship, Cedric said we should find some women and get laid. I stopped in my tracks, oddly taken aback since the concept was hardly foreign. On the contrary, it seemed to be part of every guy's fantasy. From the dormitories of Piney Point, while we were imagining life as lusty mariners, to the lecherous winks from some of the guys at The Rail who knew I was in the Merchant Marine, it appeared to be part of the mythic folklore and mission of what every seaman was expected to do when visiting exotic ports-of-call. But as I stood there, I knew deep in my heart that this was not my expectation of myself – far from it. I was determined to honor my relationship with Leah; as confusing and up and down as it was I still felt like I was committed to her. Furthermore, even if I was single, I knew it was absolutely against my growing feminist sensibilities to seek out a prostitute. As Cedric and I parted company, him disappearing into a dimly lit bar and me turning toward the ship, I felt good and righteous that I was sticking to my principles. What I couldn't know at the time was that in the ensuing months my principles and a whole lot more would be threatened by moral dilemmas I could not even imagine.

At the next port of Livorno, Italy, I remained on board the ship rather than venture into town.

ON THE WAY BACK TO THE U.S., the Third Engineer, Tom Bishop, and I befriended each other. Tom was a virtual hippie among the engine room officers. He had longish blond hair that barely touched the back of his collar, but was still dangerously close to being long enough to cause some raised eyebrows among the old-timers on the crew. Tom was from North Haven, Connecticut and had attended King's Point Merchant Marine Academy. He was two years older than I and, compared to the other members of the crew who were mostly middle-aged, we instantly recognized a kinship between us. We had been working together on a variety of engine room projects and it was clear that we had similar temperaments and outlooks on the world. Before long I was going up to his foc'sle after dinner or after working overtime, and there we would listen to *The Moody Blues* on his reel-to-reel tape player and talk late into the night. We would spend hours, laughing and philosophizing. The power and mystical beauty of *The Moody Blues'* songs was perfect for my contemplative state of mind. Whether it was "Question," or "Melancholy Man," or "Tuesday Afternoon," or "Nights in White Satin," I was consistently transported beyond time and space, beyond the confines of the ship, and beyond my very limited mind into a realm of imagination and reverie.

Eventually we stumbled upon the fact that we both had dreams of buying land in Vermont. Tom had a more worked-out plan that he now wanted me to be a part of. In his vision we could buy land together, and ship out for only six months over the winter and early spring months when Vermont was snow-covered; this way we could earn enough money for us to live in Vermont during the summer and autumn months before having to ship out again. It was brilliant. I was immediately smitten with this scenario and the idea of being partners with Tom. The dream that Harry and I failed to manifest just two years ago now felt within my reach. I silently thanked Mr. Allen Sokol again, and busily filled my mind with images of Leah and I finally living in Vermont. It was these vivid fantasies that helped get me through the dangerous and dirty workaday world of the Black Gang.

I RETURNED TO THE U.S. ON FEBRUARY 10, 1971, after four weeks at sea. The highly automated nature of the merchant shipping world gave me 24 hours with which to get home from Port Elizabeth to the Bronx, see Leah, and repack my duffel bag for a return trip to Italy on the *Azalea City*. It felt a bit grueling, yet I was dedicated to working as hard as I could and taking as many ships as I needed to in order to get the money to realize our dream. This quick turnaround, hard as it was to not spend any real time with Leah, I took in stride as part of a larger necessity. What I discovered during my brief visit to the neighborhood was so disheartening that I felt like boarding the *Azalea City* and never coming back.

Incredibly, within the single month of my absence, a fundamental alteration in what I perceived as the moral fabric of everyone still hanging out at The Rail had taken place. On the one hand, heroin was so firmly entrenched in the neighborhood that it was now the single-minded focus of every human interaction among my friends, the *lingua franca* that imbued all conversations, coordinated all comings and goings. People had become willing to say, do, or be anything at all if it put them in possession of their precious drug. If heroin was plentiful, then there was celebration and sometimes even a rare moment of sharing took place. If the supply dwindled and ran low, it was everyone for themselves as people jockeyed for a position closest to whoever had the goods that particular day. Each morning began as a hunt to get high, which meant being able to sniff out who had drugs or who could get access quickly. These desperate, self-serving machinations made the phrase "fair-weather friend" appear as a compliment.

Simultaneous with the stultifying power of heroin, a wave of sexual promiscuity swept the neighborhood, flipping the previously followed script of going-steady exclusively in favor of having sex with whomever you felt drawn to. It was a strange alchemy, combining a drug-induced free-love free-for-all with the winds of women's liberation that posited monogamy and marriage as indentured sexual servitude. Aswirl within the *zeitgeist* of the adult "key parties" infecting the middle class, where sexual inhibition was forcefully stripped away as people our parents' ages randomly exchanged house keys and slept with the person whose keys they chose, the social stage was set for a militant rejection of what was deemed oppressive ways of relating. Our neighborhood would not be immune to this "Love the One You're With," boundaryless approach to sex under the banner of finding personal liberation.

Addiction and promiscuity – these commingling factors created a fog that shrouded the streets of the neighborhood and darkened the alleys of my heart. I was having plenty of trouble just battling my feelings about the enslaving nature of heroin. I also knew deep inside that non-monogamy was anathema to my romantic sensibilities, and the idea that my girlfriend Leah would willingly and eagerly sleep around with anyone – even as a testament to her own agency and ultimate freedom – was too much for me to handle. In the single day of being home I felt like many of my previously stable reference points were teetering toward collapse.

That night, as I waited for a taxi to take me back to the ship in Port Elizabeth, Leah and I lay side by side, fully clothed, on the cot in the sun parlor in my house on Saxon Avenue. I wanted so much to make love with her. Since I stepped off the ship the previous day, all I could think of was the romantic image of me as seafarer being welcomed into the sexual embrace of my waiting lover. After all, I was at sea in order to make our dream of buying land in Vermont come true. But there was too much distance between us. It was as if I represented a different, more conservative life, one she had recently jettisoned. I felt like she could barely wait for me to leave again so she could get back to the drugs and back to some other lover. We lay there, barely speaking; confusion, alternating with anger, buffeting my brain and body. When the taxi honked its horn we got up and walked downstairs to the street. We hugged and kissed perfunctorily. Within minutes I was alone, on my way back to the *Azalea City* for another month at sea. I wasn't sure if I could bear it. I kept trying to reassure myself that once Leah and I left the neighborhood and made it to Vermont, we could start afresh and all would be well between us. Even before the taxi crossed the George Washington Bridge to New Jersey, waves of doubt were already undermining what would shortly prove to be mere sandcastles of my mind, vastly unfit as reassuring bulwarks against the erosive force of what was to transpire over the coming year.

Chapter Twenty-Three
The Year of Darkness

I woke up one morning in a fog. I had no idea how much heroin I had snorted into my nose the night before. My head felt thick and I was unsteady on my feet. My sinuses felt blocked and irritated. I walked into the little pink and white bathroom and stared into the mirror. I looked and felt unrecognizable. I reached out and pulled a wad of toilet paper off the roller and readied to clear my nose. I inhaled and then blew out. I was immediately seized with a burning sensation that fired its way through my nasal passages, up into the front of my head, and through my eye sockets before landing like a ball-peen hammer right between my eyes. The whole inside of my face felt seared. I pulled the tissue away from my nose and looked down. What I saw scared the shit out of me. There, covering the entire wad of toilet paper was blood and chunks of mucous membrane from the inside of my nose. It looked like the entire lining of my nasal passages lay before me. I was shocked and my nose continued to throb and burn and bleed. This time I'd gone too far; sniffing bags of heroin day after day, month after month, had completely wrecked the inside of my nostrils. I knew I was in deep shit. I also knew that if I didn't get high soon I was going to go into withdrawals, and that would be pain beyond what my nose was feeling.

I jumped into the shower and dressed quickly, still trembling from what had just happened. I made it down to The Rail and walked toward a group of guys who were already into a mid-morning high. I skinned palms with one of them and asked, "You holding?" They nodded and, after looking around to check if the coast was clear, we exchanged money for goods. I took the bag to the back of the handball courts and sat against the concrete wall. I tore the top off and inserted a tiny, shortened plastic stir-straw and inhaled. Instantly my nose and head seemed to ignite and blow apart again. The pain was even more excruciating, as the dope, and whatever was used to cut it, wreaked havoc on the raw tissue. Tears filled my eyes. Immediately I knew that I could no longer get high simply by sniffing; I had to find another way of getting off, and soon.

* * * * *

Throughout my second tour on the *Azalea City*, February to March 1971, I was fixated on what I now knew was going on in the neighborhood and what I knew was going on with Leah. My fevered imagination, coupled with what I had seen and heard during my 24-hour visit between ships, had me manically crazed and overwhelmed with anxiety. Images of Leah having sex with someone else, male or female or both at once, and everyone getting stoned together pummeled me relentlessly. I swung between vowing to forsake Leah and the Bronx altogether and be my own person, or redoubling my efforts to get us both to Vermont and safely away from New York for good. In a strange way, despite my isolation from the entire goings on back home, and all the stress my imagination conjured, life aboard ship was mercifully routine, and I immersed myself in the daily routines in a bid to maintain my sanity.

Tom Bishop and I continued our conversations about buying land in Vermont, though now my visits to his room were less regular due to the First Engineer's views about his officers fraternizing with lowly crew members. I spent my time diligently performing my regular Wiper duties, saying yes to all offers of overtime and, in whatever spare time was left, sitting on the fantail mesmerized by the undulating ocean or reading. Despite all the *tzuris* that was roiling both in my head and back home, I decided to try to enjoy this trip as much as possible.

Our first port was Cadiz, Spain, just east of Gibraltar, the gateway to the Mediterranean Sea. It was a lively place, the streets filled with people. All that I had read about Spain under the repressive Franco regime had not prepared me for the vibrance I found everywhere. I was so smitten by the city and the people that I convinced my foc'sle-mate, Cedric, to take a horse-drawn carriage ride with me through the narrow cobblestoned streets. Afterwards, we ate dinner, drank wine, and eventually stumbled back to the ship, arm in arm, laughing.

Our second stop was a return to Genoa, Italy, for more eating and drinking and laughing. Next the ship moved down the boot of Italy to Livorno, where Tom and I took a taxi inland to the Leaning Tower of Pisa. It was so eye-opening to finally depart the one-dimensionality of the port cities, with their incessant presentation of shops, restaurants, bars and prostitutes. In Pisa I got to see architecture that exuded history. We immediately climbed the Leaning Tower, spiraling upwards eight stories, past the plaque honoring Galileo, to finally look out upon the city. One of my biggest surprises was upon entering a huge Catholic cathedral nearby in the Piazza del Duomo, and actually feeling the awe that a house of worship is supposed to inspire – the stain-glass filtering the light in myriad hues, the ceilings disappearing heavenward into the shadows, the altar grand and commanding. Gazing at the crucifix I was overwhelmed with the figure of Jesus and understood as never before the immensity of his suffering and dying for the sins of humanity. In this church, whether one believed or didn't hardly mattered; I could feel and experience the power and majesty of this religion in ways that made the churches back in New York – especially stolid Kingsbridge Lutheran – seem bland and paltry in their spiritual presentation. I thought about my father and how he always crossed himself whenever he passed by or entered a Catholic church. I felt the chasm between him and me regarding our differing attitudes toward the Catholic Church, him holding a sense of awe and me – bordering on atheism – simply not caring one way or the other. I was at a loss as to how in one generation things could change so dramatically. I wondered for a moment, as I took in the awe-inspiring splendor within and without the cathedral, if I was missing out on something important. But my religious musings were short-lived. As we left the Leaning Tower of Pisa, Tom hustled us excitedly into a store with large wheels of cheese protruding from every nook and cranny. We purchased a kilo of Swiss cheese and hailed a taxi for the ride back to the ship.

Our final stop was Bremerhaven, Germany, near the North Sea. This time a whole group of the Black Gang went ashore together, straight to the bars. Around a large table we ate, drank, sang, and applauded the dancing girls. I was having a blast until, in response to the inevitable below-the-belt instinct – that for some reason I wasn't able to feel – it was once again time for my shipmates to find prostitutes. Within what seemed like seconds I was alone at the table; everyone else had disappeared into the arms of a woman. I watched one of the remaining dancers. I stared at her face and saw her middle-aged lines and wrinkles through the crust of her pinkish make-up. Her breasts were pushed up by her costume and her waist was matronly thick. Her legs moved slowly against the music, as if they were drained of energy after being on stage for so long. We caught each other's eyes and I was suddenly sad and lonely and feeling her loneliness. I was also aware of how easily it could be for two lonelinesses to grasp onto each other, to shed their clothes as a way of shedding the skins that demarcate people as separate entities and desperately go at it, the commerce of the anonymous transaction but a thin veneer barely disguising the more primal need for basic human contact. I finished my beer, shook my head, and meandered back to the ship, keeping my loneliness intact as well as my continued commitment to Leah. A few nights before we were to dock back at the Sea-Land terminal in Port Elizabeth, I went to Tom's room after dinner. As usual, we turned on *The Moody Blues*. As the song, "Nights in White Satin" began filling the tiny space we began munching on hunks of what was left of the Swiss cheese. By the end of the night we had solidified our commitment to buy land together in Vermont.

I HAD ANOTHER 24-HOUR LAYOVER before the *Azalea City* would be heading back to Europe. Once again there was distance between Leah and me and therefore no sex. The neighborhood scene had only intensified, with heroin and promiscuity abounding *en flagrante*. I felt confused and left out. I didn't know whether to run or whether to join in. I ached in my loneliness, struck paralyzed by my alienation. As the deadline for returning to the ship drew closer, Leah decided to drive me to the Sea-Land terminal. We were quiet on the drive. As I left her car and ascended the gangway onto the ship my heart was at its breaking point, stretched between my fear of losing Leah and my possessiveness toward her, and my commitment to get the money so we could leave the Bronx – which meant being gone more unbearable months at sea. As I reached the deck I turned to wave but she was already gone. Nothing but night inhabited the parking lot. As I contemplated this next month in the middle of the Atlantic, I had a very bad feeling.

Before heading across the ocean the *Azalea City* was scheduled for a one-day stop in Newport News, Virginia, to offload some cargo and pick up containers bound for Italy. It was here that I made the decision to leave the ship and go home. I just couldn't stand it anymore; I had to know what was really going on in the neighborhood, what was true between me and Leah. As I was packing up my gear, I explained my decision to Tom. Out of the blue, he began reciting maritime folklore to me. He told me a mythical story about how an angry seaman once took all his belongings off a vessel and got charged with jumping ship, while another, more reluctant seaman left some belongings behind and was simply fined by the union for missing his ship – the lesser and more forgivable behavior, the likes of which many a drunken or lovesick sailor the world over had succumbed to at one time or another. As he finished his parable, he explained that the next part of his plan was to come to the Bronx in the summer, pick me up, and off we would go to find a piece of property in Vermont. I perked up slightly. We shook hands and embraced. I left with a half-full duffel bag and a half-empty heart. Slowly and with effort I made my way to the downtown bus station.

For the entire bus ride I reiterated to myself my understanding about the slavery inherent in heroin, both the personal addiction and the crime of selling it to get other people hooked. I knew from all my readings that heroin particularly oppressed black people in the ghettoes of America and this was another part of the injustice that I could no longer abide. I was determined to heroically clean up the heroin in my neighborhood for good. I wanted it out of mine and Leah's lives. I felt self-righteously clear about how I wanted us to live together. All the way from the Virginia docks to the Bronx, first by bus to the Port Authority then by subway to the Mosholu Parkway stop, I rehearsed the speech I would give to Leah and anyone else who would listen. I was donning my White Knight armor, ready for battle

When I got home on February 12, 1971, I found out that Kevin had been discharged from the U.S. Army and had returned home from Vietnam eight days earlier, on February 4. All my speeches could wait until I saw my dear brother. The very next day I met Kevin in front of EM's. There he stood, decked out in a dark suit and nonchalantly smoking a cigarette, with a semi-smirk that seemed to say, "That wasn't so bad. Did you miss me?" "Fucking-ay, I missed you," I silently answered his look with my own. Seeing him there, right back in the neighborhood, drove home to me just how much I loved this man and how wonderful it felt to have him back unharmed. I wrapped my arms around him and refused to let go until it became uncomfortable for us both. Together we started walking down Gouverneur Avenue toward The Rail. One of the first things he said to me was how he could not continue living at his parents' house; too much had gone down since he was in Vietnam and it just wasn't a good scene anymore. He explained that he was already looking for an apartment to rent. I grabbed his arm and stopped us in our tracks. "You should move into my house," I exclaimed. "We could live upstairs on the top floor and you wouldn't have to pay rent, just buy your own groceries." Kevin looked back at me and smiled. "Good deal," he said matter-of-factly.

Within the week we were roommates, to the delight of my mother who thought Kevin walked on water and to the palpitating heart of my sister Peggy, who maintained a crush on Kevin since the moment she met him over seven years earlier when she was eleven. Kevin moved into the room closest to the bathroom and toward the rear of the house, the room my cousins had used for their bedroom and which had recently been mine. I relocated to the room at the front of the house, the room that once served as my aunt and uncle's bedroom. I was elated.

In less than a month Kevin moved out.

What precipitated Kevin's departure was my abject neediness regarding my relationship with Leah and how my desperation took precedence over everything, over every other relationship in my life. The minute Kevin moved in, Leah wanted to move in also, mostly to get away from her family and to be close to Athos full-time. On top of that, Leah wanted her best friend, Aviva Fayman, to live with us as well. With the prospect of having Leah that close, I rationalized that we could now really work to get back together and I acquiesced to all of it. What

I didn't realize in my weakness and haste to please Leah was that the heroin and promiscuity that I had been fitfully trying to keep at bay, I had instead invited right under my very roof. It took an instant for Kevin to recognize what was going on, to realize that it would not be just him and me living together, and to see how unrecognizable I had become. Perhaps my self-degradation was too much for him to bear, or perhaps he didn't want to have a daily reminder of how far I had tumbled. Within hours after making his decision to move he was gone.

THE NEXT FOUR MONTHS, between March and June, were like living in the clutches of a slowly ratcheting vise-grip. At first I tried to keep away from heroin. Hanging out at The Rail, I still smoked pot and hash, and popped a few uppers and downers when they were available. With Kevin gone it was now Leah, Aviva, and me along with two dogs, Athos and Zephyr, a puppy that Aviva adopted and brought into the house. If that wasn't bad enough, people came and went at all hours of the day and night, either to get high or maybe even hoping they could get laid. My mother and sister watched this parade with increasing agitation, since hardly anyone who showed up actually said hello or interacted with them anymore. It was a free-for-all that was driving me insane yet I was too afraid to extricate myself because I knew it would mean losing Leah. I tried so hard to adapt to the promiscuous lifestyle that was so repugnant to my temperament and all my sensibilities, old fashioned as they were increasingly perceived.

One day as I lay in bed having sex with Aviva, and Leah lay in the bed alongside having sex with another guy, Leah's and my eyes met. I knew that I was supposed to be okay with all this, that I was supposed to be accepting this as freedom and liberation. Instead it was my anguished confusion that I was trying to convey to her with my urgent looks. I wanted Leah to feel that I loved her, and her alone, and I didn't want to keep doing this. I had no idea if she understood. In the tangle of bodies and failed communication, it was one of the worst moments of my relationship with Leah.

She and I were locked in a cycle of continuing the damage first sustained in Colorado, of making each other hurt over and over again, as if trapped in a hamster wheel of mutual affliction. In our daily actions and interactions we seemed to be saying: if the trust is broken let's not try to repair it, instead let's keep picking the scab beyond healing. We were hooked together as a perfect sadistic and masochistic pairing. Yet neither one of us were able to jettison our hearts completely and flee. Instead we just lived in this pained limbo, wondering every so often – when we surfaced long enough from the drug-induced stupors to think about our lives at all – whether there was anything that could break us free. In the neighborhood, life continued to revolve around procuring heroin. Even the arrival of spring could not penetrate the darkness that refused to relinquish its hold.

I was still practicing my anti-heroin speech in my head, though by now it was mostly for my own benefit in attempting to keep intact an ever-fraying lifeline I prayed would stop me from returning to snorting dope. One night, for whatever myriad reasons that had accrued like barnacles on my heart, I had enough. I was determined to call Leah out and demand that she either choose heroin or me. When I got home that evening the perfect scene greeted me. There before me was a table covered with heroin, with a pile of glassine bags and a roll of tape at one end. Around the table sat Leah, Aviva, and James. James, who I hadn't seen much of since I went to merchant marine school, was genuinely happy to see me, though his focus immediately shifted to explaining the intricacies of how much money we could all make, depending on how many times we cut the product before us. I was stunned. I had thought James was more sensitive and nobler than to resort to selling drugs. Yet, here it all was. Here we were about to graduate from using the drug to selling it, and the organizer of the plan was the black man who I loved as a brother. We had dozens of deep, heart-to-heart conversations about poetry, about racism, about colonialism, about the slavery that heroin always brings with it. Out of our conversations, despite our own continued use of other drugs, I thought we had forged a basic agreement about heroin in particular. I was outraged and distraught, my love for James falling in fragments onto the floor of my heart. I immediately launched into my speech.

It poured out of me in torrents. I was like a combination end-of-the-world zealot and carney barker, preaching and testifying, cajoling and selling my point of view like our lives depended on it. I did not miss a single political or social fine-point in my fiery diatribe. I incriminated the system, the dealers, and each of us in the room at that moment. I was righteously indignant, as if somewhere inside I knew that this was my one and only chance to break the chains we were continuing to acquiesce being shackled to by continuing to get high. And now we were turning a blind eye to selling dope. It was powerful; I was powerful. They were stunned, and so was I. I watched as James wordlessly gathered up the drugs and left. Leah and Aviva moved to the bed and sat huddled together without uttering a word. I could not determine what the impact of my words had been, as all my pleas and condemnations had been met with silence. I sprawled on the other bed with my heart racing towards exhaustion, and soon fell asleep.

For the next two days Leah walked around me tip-toeing on eggshells. Aviva made her presence scarce. James had disappeared back to the East Bronx. I was flying pretty high, self-propelled into a rarified atmosphere by my new vantage point from atop my self-righteous political soapbox. But even I, like Icarus, could see the ground approaching fast. For the truth of the matter was that we weren't about to leave the neighborhood; we had no money and even less imagination with which to create something better. And as every junkie knew, if you don't exit the drug-infested environment, sheer willpower alone is no match for both the drugs and the human need to be part of some kind of group or community – even if that group was eventually going to cause your demise.

Therefore, the shelf-life of my speech that I thought would rally everyone to turn their backs and reject heroin, was painfully short.

When my fire subsided I had nothing left to say, nothing to offer that was more appealing than our current reality. As a result of my failure of imagination, we all drifted back into the comforting embrace of smack. Leah, Aviva and I soon set about the daily routine of finding drugs, getting high, and pretending we liked what we were doing and pretending we liked each other. I was completely demoralized.

SPRING ARRIVED, but despite the lovely weather unfolding all around me it had no revivifying affect. Life was about one thing: getting high. I was back in the whole scene again, with only one thing on my mind. The days repeated themselves with little or no variation as heroin became our central organizing principle, our *raison d'etre*, without which there seemed little reason for anything else. Then, as if in answer to a long-forgotten prayer, Tom Bishop called me and said he was off the ship and was ready for us to go find a house in Vermont. It was a Saturday when Tom arrived at my house in the Bronx, and Leah, Aviva, and I loaded into his car and off we went to finally create our dream. Tom had no idea that Lady Heroin was also a silent passenger in the car that day, with dreams and plans of her own.

It took us a single day to find the place that delighted us all. It was located within the town limits of Hardwick and was being sold by a local dairy farmer. It was 12 acres of land, seven comprising a timbered hillside and five made up of pasture, complete with a stream. A gravel driveway (snowplowed, we happily discovered, by the town of Hardwick in winter) led from the road to an eight-room farmhouse. The house had an attached barn on one side and a three-story concrete chicken coop directly behind it. The cost was $17,500. For us city kids it was the paradise we had all imagined when the Vermont migrations out of the Bronx had first begun. Once decided upon, we drove to the farmer's house. As we sat around the kitchen table drinking fresh milk, getting the details of the property, Tom pulled out $1,000 dollars, setting the stack of ten 100-dollar bills on the table in front of the farmer as a sign of our commitment and good will. "This is until the bank opens on Monday," Tom explained. The farmer smiled and stood, prompting us all to stand. With a simple handshake the deal was done. We drove back to the house and began imagining what it would be like for us to live there.

By July we were all moved in. Tom had expected it would be only him and me, but did not seem too put out that I was inviting Leah and Aviva to join us. We moved a minimal amount of items, mostly kitchenware, our mattresses and bedding, our clothing, a record player and some albums. The bedrooms were on the top floor; Tom took the master, Leah and I the next largest, and Aviva took the smallest.

Throughout the month of July we tried to acclimate ourselves to being out of New York, struggling to find our balance in a very new and different environment. Aviva took to the change immediately, enjoying planting vegetables and wearing overalls. She and I spent a couple of days building a fence around a wild strawberry patch, feeling like real homesteaders. Leah and I were uptight, with each other and with the fact that we were not done with heroin, physically or psychologically. In fact, Leah seemed to be driving to the Bronx nearly every week to buy drugs. Tom was also gone a lot, back and forth, tending to matters in North Haven, Connecticut, and bringing furnishings to our new home in Hardwick; he had no real idea of the tensions we were wrestling with. One afternoon when he returned, Tom and I began mapping out our plans to ship out in the winter months and live in Vermont during the summer and autumn. I was getting excited about this new life, even as I knew there was still so much to resolve between Leah and me. In August, Tom and I decided that we should have an open house and invite our Vermont friends and neighbors. It was an evening that started off with so much promise, but by nightfall all would be betrayed.

I hoped and prayed and imagined Vermont would be different, that now that our dream was at hand Leah and I could begin anew. But between the chasms of our own making, and drugs and sexual experimentation, so much had conspired to severely weaken the bonds of a love that a year previous had looked and felt so effortless. As the house became populated with neighbors and some of our Bronx friends who had made the pilgrimage to Vermont years earlier, Leah conspicuously disappeared into the crowd. My solar plexus intuitively sagged and tightened simultaneously, as the minutes of her absence accumulated. In my anxiety and fright I began to search the house, my sense of ominous foreboding rising with every room I passed through without finding her.

When, later that night, I found Leah behind the house hidden in the grass and in the throes of fucking another man, everything that tethered me to reality ruptured there on the spot. I crumpled onto the ground right next to their now-still bodies, balling myself into a fetal position, howling and wailing my heart out. The man instantly scuttled off, clutching clumsily at his pants while picking up his shoes as he ran. Leah was unperturbed and actually annoyed with me for the interruption. I was dissociating rapidly, my wrenching sobs now drawing the attention of the revelers. Tom came to my rescue. Telling everyone to continue partying, he helped me upstairs to his bedroom where he tried to calm me down. All I wanted to do was leave – leave the house, leave Leah, and leave Vermont for good. I knew the man Leah had just been with, and he lived just down the road in another town. Suddenly, Vermont was just too damn small for me. I knew that after this episode, I would be obsessively jealous and afraid every time Leah left the house if we continued living here, or anywhere else for that matter.

Tom tried to convince me to stay, reminding me that this was *our* house, *our* plan to live in Vermont, and that Leah and Aviva should be the ones leaving. I could not hear it. I was done with it all, with Leah, Vermont, and most especially with my pathetic self. By morning it was decided. Leah, Aviva, and I were going back to the Bronx and both of them back to their families' apartments. Leah and I were no longer a couple. Twice the dream of buying land in Vermont had withered; once due to simply immature and naïve planning on the part of Harry and I, and now due to my immature approach to matters of the heart, all devilishly compounded by drug addiction. After the first Vermont debacle I met and fell in love with Leah; this second time, losing Vermont meant I was losing Leah too. Both times I wound up back in the neighborhood facing a future of getting high and hanging out at The Rail. As we drove back to the city, I thought I had reached my lowest point. I was dead wrong.

IT SEEMED THAT IN THE FEW WEEKS we were trying to transform ourselves from urban dwellers into Vermont pioneers, things had changed yet again in the neighborhood. The incessant need for drugs did two things: it sent junkies scouring the landscape throughout the Bronx and into Manhattan, and it also brought drug dealers into the neighborhood, where they soon discovered The Rail and its heroin-hungry flock, among whom I was now dejectedly perched. It was doubly disconcerting to the neighborhood families and elders that these new arrivals were both drug dealers and black. The tension between the Amalgamated board members, the drug dealers, the police, and the drug addicts, many of whom were themselves residents of the neighborhood, was about to ratchet up to unbearable.

Norman and Boo were first to arrive. They were a two-man operation, Norman posing as the brains and Boo taking on the role of the ever-present sidekick and the muscle. Norman was thick and round and probably could take care of himself, but seemed to prefer the negotiating aspect of this shadowy commerce. Boo was tall and athletically built, possessed an ever-present smile, and constantly radiated a "don't-fuck-with-me" attitude no matter what was transpiring. They both dressed in pressed and sharply creased slacks and Banlon shirts. Somehow, Kevin had made the first connection with these two and would often go to their apartment in Manhattan to score. Their presence in the neighborhood, though, was short-lived. Norman and Boo quickly felt the unwelcoming vibe from the neighborhood parents and grandparents who demanded and got increased police patrols. Despite the lucrative potential of selling drugs, Norman and Boo stopped coming around; instead they designated Kevin as liaison between them and the rest of the desperate customers populating The Rail. What this meant was that if we wanted drugs from them we would have to send Kevin, and only Kevin, with our money. Oddly, and without warning or provocation, this apparently mutually beneficial business arrangement was jettisoned forcefully and emphatically.

One night, we all pooled our cash and sent Kevin to score, as we had so many times in the past. When he arrived Norman took the money while Boo punched Kevin in the face, pushing him out of the apartment and nearly down a flight of stairs. When Kevin returned and told his story of how he had gotten ripped off, we were all up in arms and it was only his reluctance to retaliate that kept us from going there *en masse* with baseball bats and pipes to get our money back. Instead we just wrote them off the list of potential drug connections and turned our attention to figuring out how to get our drugs from someone else.

Another black dealer who appeared on the scene shortly thereafter was a lone wolf who brought not only attitude but an entire well-crafted persona to The Rail. His name was Hassan. Hassan was wiry and intense. The thing about Hassan that was radically different than Norman and Boo was that Hassan was determined to never show his fear about being a one-black-man operation in an entirely white neighborhood. To this end, Hassan compensated for the unwelcoming atmosphere and police presence that Amalgamated management tried to use as a deterrent, by openly prowling the streets with a bullwhip coiled around his left shoulder. Hassan would uncoil his bullwhip and periodically demonstrate his mastery of it by stripping a tree branch of its leaves, repeatedly propelling an empty soda can across the street, or snapping cigarette butts off the sidewalk. He was a black version of *chutzpah* and I was instantly drawn to him, partly because of his edginess but mostly because he agreed to front me bags of heroin to sell on commission. Under this arrangement he would not have to deal openly and I would keep a percentage for my own use and return him the money from the drugs I sold. At that point I would get another consignment. Given that Vermont had completely fallen apart and I wasn't in any emotional shape to get on a ship, and I was, as a result, devoid of any real cash flow, this seemed the perfect alternative. Besides, becoming a drug dealer seemed eminently befitting my dispirited breakdown and abject capitulation into the ugly grip of heroin.

It was bad enough in the eyes of the adults that heroin was being sold and used in the neighborhood, but now that outsiders – blacks no less – were coming around, their removal became a line drawn in the sand. The trustees of the Amalgamated, with the backing of just about every family, had made it clear to the police that they wanted the neighborhood purged of heroin and purged of black drug dealers. This was a complex proposition since many of the sons and daughters of the people up in arms were also caught up in the drug scene. In a tactical compromise the trustees figured that coming down really hard on the black dealers would send the appropriate message and perhaps scare some of the neighborhood druggies back into their right minds. In any case police, both uniformed and undercover, began swarming more intensely than ever.

As a Wanna-Be drug dealer I was painfully naïve and dangerously stupid. I would carry drugs around with me and make deals whenever someone wanted to, often exchanging drugs for cash right out in the open. How I never got busted in the act was beyond my comprehension. More fatally, I was a classic example of why it never works for addicts to be drug dealers – their need eventually eats past their own percentage and into the drugs they were obligated to sell to keep the accounting balanced, thus falling further and further into debt to their connection. Hassan was increasingly unhappy about this and warned me, fingering his bullwhip with menace. Every time I picked up drugs to sell and gave him less and less money he demanded that I make it right with the next consignment and come even with what I owed him. But I was in another zone, demoralized about my future, reckless, and adopting a devil-take-the-hindmost attitude to my life as long as I was getting high. One day Charlie Baumann and I were leaving my house after getting high, on our way back to The Rail. As we were crossing Van Cortlandt Park South an unmarked police car suddenly cut us off and two plainclothes detectives grabbed us and began pushing us up the path that led toward The Plateau and Ghost Town, out of sight of any passersby. The cop in charge was Detective Donleavy, out of our very own neighborhood 50th Precinct. Once back behind the trees and bushes and out of the public eye, they stopped and began frisking us. Fortunately, this time I had left

Hassan's entire heroin supply back in my house. They began telling us that they were on to me selling dope. They explained that they weren't interested in busting me and only wanted the name of my supplier; if I gave it up I was free to go. I refused. Suddenly, the other cop hauled off and punched Charlie square in the middle of his chest, sending him to the ground doubled over and gasping for breath. Pain welled up in Charlie's eyes. Instantly he was pleading innocence, begging them to let him go, telling them with tears streaming down his face that it was Hassan who was dealing.

Next, Donleavy turned to me and asked me to confirm the name Charlie had just given them. Again I refused. Without warning Donleavy swung for the fences, his right fist connecting with my jaw. My head snapped back in an explosion of light and before I knew it I was flat on my back in the grass, the whole world spinning. He reached down and pulled me by the collar into a sitting position. "A name," he ordered. I remained silent. From his back pocket he pulled out a knife. He snapped it open and a six-inch gleaming blade appeared before my eyes. Slowly he pressed the tip of the knife against my throat. "The name, motherfucker," he demanded. I kept mute. The knife pressed harder. I was determined; even if he sliced my jugular vein open right there, I was not going to be a snitch. So I just sat there, desperately trying to hold onto some remnant of principle no matter how confused.

For so long now I had been studying how the police were part of the system that keeps people in line. While heroin was certainly an oppressive force in the lives of black people, I had read that cops were also. In my mind I had to choose between standing up against two forms of oppression; I chose not helping the cops bust Hassan. Fury built in Donleavy's eyes. Finally he relented, removing the knife from my Adam's apple and putting it back into his pocket. "You dumb fucks," he shouted. "Don't fucking worry, we're gonna get him. And we're gonna get your asses too. Now get the fuck out of here," he ordered. Charlie and I stood and took off running, him to The Rail and me back to my house. Once home I panicked. I thought the cops would be there any minute and I was afraid about them finding drugs and what it would do to my mother and sister. Suddenly all the dark dimensions and consequences of addiction and dealing were painfully clear. I raced upstairs to my room and gathered over $200 worth of heroin and flushed it down the toilet. I was so terrified, the thought of getting high so far removed from my mind, that I didn't even consider taking a few bags just for myself.

By the time I got back to The Rail, Charlie had spread the word about how I refused to give Hassan up to the cops. From the gathered crowd, Whitey, a particularly noxious junkie and imitation tough guy whose bright, colorless hair earned him his nickname, immediately went after me. "Why'd you protect that nigger for, man? Now the cops are gonna come down harder on us," he yelled in my face. Hearing the word "nigger" was too much for me. With what could only be described as a roar from the depths of my being, I grabbed Whitey around the throat with both my hands and lifted him off the ground. His face instantly reddened and his mouth sputtered unintelligibly, his feet kicking as they frantically searched for terra firma. I was ready to choke him to death right there. Instead, I threw him over some shrubs where he went sprawling onto the ground. I leapt onto him and began wildly punching him in the face and head. Once the stunned crowd had gathered their wits, I was finally pulled off of him. He stood slowly, wobbling a bit, blood oozing at the corner of his lip, and pointed a finger at me. "You're fucking dead, man," he spat as his girlfriend helped him walk away.

My world was disintegrating rapidly; the cops were breathing down my back, and now Whitey's bad-boy buddies would be looking for me. I had to get off the streets for a while; I had to have some time to think. I walked to Leah's house, which was the closest place I could think of going. She immediately took me in and I found what would turn out to be but a brief moment of sanctuary.

ONCE NIGHT HAD FALLEN I began to feel safe about making my way back home. It was after 10 o'clock when I left Leah's apartment. As I scurried to cross Gouverneur Avenue and duck into the shadows of the Seventh Building, I ran right into the living embodiment of Whitey's death threat. Sitting in a convertible waiting for me were two of Whitey's pals, Billy Lurie and his lapdog, Eric. How long they had been there I had no idea, but they were clearly pissed about what I had done to Whitey. They left the car, Billy from the driver's side and Eric bounding over the passenger door. They both confronted me, pushing me up against a parked car. Billy stood directly in front of me, sunglasses adding to his menace; Eric stood just behind Billy's shoulder, shifting from foot to foot. For years Billy had the reputation of being one of the Bronx's toughest guys, someone you'd never want to mess with, ever. Yet, there I was, eyeball to eyeball with him as he seemed to be measuring in his mind what the appropriate revenge would be for what I did to Whitey. In a surprisingly quiet voice he explained that I shouldn't have done what I did and it was only right that I should get my ass kicked in return. Eric bobbed and nodded behind Billy, hissing "Yeah, yeah," as if to punctuate Billy's comments. "Kick his ass, Billy," he seethed. I didn't want to fight Billy Lurie; few people in their right mind would. Even if he had been alone, and I was not standing in front of two people wanting to kick my ass, it would've been an impossibly bad scene. In hopes of staving off what was shaping up to be my bloody demise, I quickly launched into my side of the story, explaining my run-in with the narcs and how I would never rat out anyone, even Hassan, and how Whitey's bullshit remarks sent me over the edge.

To my surprise Billy was actually listening, weighing what I was saying against some hidden calculus regarding the strength and importance of his connection with Whitey. When I was done I looked intently through Billy's sunglasses and implored, "C'mon Billy, I don't think we should fight over this." Perhaps sensing something shifting in Billy's silence, Eric began hissing again, "Let's kick his ass; let's kick his ass." Billy continued being silent for another minute and then raised his hand. The hissing behind his back stopped. Without a word Billy turned and walked over to his car, followed by his clearly disappointed crony. As they slid into the convertible and drove off, I sagged against the parked car for a moment and then quietly made my way slowly home. Despite being spent beyond exhaustion all I could think of was what I would say to Hassan about his heroin, now dissolving somewhere in the New York City sewer system.

When I told Hassan what had happened he was very matter-of-fact, very businesslike, but with a coldness that expressed to me just how unhappy he was at this turn of events. "You *owe* me," he seethed. "You owe me a lot of fucking money, man. I best be getting that money soon; until then, no dope from me, motherfucker." These were the last words I ever heard directly from Hassan as he turned and strutted away, bullwhip coiled in place.

Within a couple of weeks the police finally busted Hassan. The last time I saw him in the neighborhood he had a patch over one eye. He was telling the assembled crowd of druggies that he lost the eye as a result of a beating the cops had given him after they threw him down a flight of stairs. He was unrepentant and determined to not let the cops intimidate him. Without one mention of the money I owed him, or even a look in my direction, he simply vanished after that day. A couple of months later the word got around the street that Hassan was now dead, a story circulating that he had been shot by police in an arrest gone bad. The grim realities of life under the dictates of heroin were driven home ever more forcefully.

Autumn was approaching and the money I had made from my last ship back in March had dwindled, spent mostly on drugs; even my brief foray into being Hassan's heroin emissary did not slow the outpouring of cash – quite the opposite. Even though I was emotionally screwed up after the nightmare in Vermont, I was even more screwed up being physically strung out. I wasn't in any shape to get on another ship to make a quick payday, so I began looking for a shore-side job. My friend, Reggie King, was working at Pathmark Supermarket. With Reggie's good word, and my experiences working at the Co-op Market, I was made the assistant dairy manager on the midnight to 8:00 a.m. shift. The store was closed during these hours, so my job was to re-stock the dairy cases in preparation for the start of each shopping day. It was the perfect gig. I worked alone, I had enough privacy to take a blow of heroin when I wanted to, and I got a decent wage – and, most importantly, I was either working or sleeping, which left me little time to hang out at The Rail.

The neighborhood was still patrolled regularly by the police but with the black drug dealers gone the overt heroin scene had diminished slightly, drifting away from The Rail and relatively out of sight. Things were feeling pretty mellow for a change, even though we all knew that the plainclothes narcs were still itching for a big bust. I spent my days laying low, getting high in friends' houses, continuing to do the attraction/repulsion dance with Leah, and pondering where the hell my life was going. After a couple of months of nightshift at Pathmark, I got bored and realized once again that with my Merchant Marine credentials I could just ship out every so often when I needed to and make three times the money in a single month as I could as a dairy manager. I quit abruptly and returned to trekking daily to the SIU headquarters in search of some coastal runs, which were of shorter duration.

IN EARLY NOVEMBER, I joined the crew of the *S.S. Connecticut*, a tanker that was on its way to Texas City, Texas, with one brief stop in Florida. It was a nondescript ship with a crew I barely spoke to, even my fellow Wiper and roommate. I was sullen, there for very practical reasons and, if I had conversations at all, they were about the job at hand. After two weeks of work, during which time I snorted the minimal amount of heroin to keep me from being sick, we arrived in Texas where I was paid in cash, as usual, and given a ticket to fly back to New York. With my money replenished I was back at The Rail and ready to get high again. Nine days later, on December 2, I was boarding the *Anchorage*, another Sea-Land container ship bound for Puerto Rico and a quick turnaround. I began thinking that this kind of lifestyle just might work.

My roommate on the *Anchorage* was, for some unknown reason, very different and I was immediately attracted to him. Perhaps it was his gregarious nature and his smile; perhaps I just needed a dose of human connection after months of hustling heroin in a world that lost sight of the person and only saw humans as either customers or a means to get high. Whatever it was, my fellow Wiper and I, a black man about my age from Brooklyn, hit it off. He went by the name of Junior. We discovered that we both loved basketball, which he referred to as "balling." This always made me laugh because, as I explained to him, in my neighborhood "balling" meant getting laid. This made him laugh even louder.

We were also a bit rebellious in poking fun at the standard seafaring terms the older guys used to describe the ship's environment. Instead of bow, we said "up front"; for aft we said "in the back"; we referred to bulkheads as "walls," the deck as the "floor," the overhead as the "ceiling." When we went to the engine room, instead of saying going below we said we were "going downstairs" or "going to the basement" and, similarly, we used "upstairs" as a substitute for topside. No matter how hard the job, or how dirty, or how hot the water drops that splashed on our heads from blowing tubes, we laughed at everything. I even cut back dramatically on sniffing dope and I never did it in Junior's presence.

We were so boisterous, reveling in our companionship, that some of the crew thought we must be homosexuals and the rumors began to spread. We didn't care. Since nobody openly accused us, or tried to hassle us in any way, we continued in our merriment even louder, goofing on all the mariner lifers. What made it all the more funny to us was that together we could see the surreal situation we were immersed in, while it appeared to us that everyone else in the crew thought that this was reality. And perhaps that was the real problem some of the crew had with us – we were young and capricious in our commitment to the vocation of seafaring. But for them this was their whole life, for the rest of their lives, and they did not need reminding of that fact by a couple of kids who didn't take their plight as life-long laborers respectfully, and would probably be moving onto some other job a few years down the road. As a result, there developed an odd, unspoken tension between some of the crew and us whenever Junior and I appeared together.

During our first day in Puerto Rico, after our watch was completed, Junior and I decided to explore the Old San Juan section. It was early evening and we took a taxi from the docks into the heart of the tourist area and began walking around. The area was alive and bustling. We headed to a bar for some food and something to drink. At the end of the meal Junior turned to me and said he was going to get laid and asked me to come with him. I declined, once again shaking my head slowly, my spirit sinking as my friend prepared to leave. I had no reason to believe or expect that Junior would be different than any other mariner I had worked with regarding the need for sex and the use of prostitutes. But once again it hurt to be left alone like that, even though I was choosing to stand on my own principles. As soon as he was gone I ordered more rum and Coke.

I began walking along the crowded streets. Suddenly I was struck by a sight straight out of a pirate movie, as right before me the walls of a stone fortress loomed. Castillo San Cristobal the placard read. I was mesmerized. I walked up to the main doors and pulled. They were locked, a nearby sign explaining that it was after hours. I didn't have tomorrow, so I began circling the building looking for a way in. Everything was locked. Finally I noticed that the construction of the corners of the fort was built in such a way that part of the wall was designed in a ramp-like fashion that ended at a ledge just below the parapet. I went toward one of the corners in the rear, away from the main street. I backed away from the wall and prepared to scale the heights. I took a running start, building up my speed with each stride. When I hit the wall I just kept running up the stone ramp and at the very peak of my climb launched myself high enough to grab onto the ledge. I dangled there for a minute, catching my breath, and then I pulled my body over the wall and the fortress was mine.

I spent hours exploring the fort. I raced up stairs to where the cannons sat pointing out to sea, pyramids of now-immovable cannonballs at the ready. I looked down on the white sand-beaches and the ocean sparkling in the moonlight. I imagined sailing ships exchanging fire with the fortress and hand-to-hand, sword-flashing skirmishes everywhere. I pretended I was the commander of the fort as I raced from wall to wall directing my imaginary troops. Tiring, I made my way down into the interior.

Before I had much chance to examine this part of the fortress I was startled by the night watchman. We both shrieked in surprise. He began yelling at me in Spanish, asking me to explain what I was doing there, threatening to call the police. I tried to tell him in my broken, high-school Spanish that I was drunk and had fallen asleep and had gotten locked in when they closed. He must have believed me, or feared for his job, for instead of calling the cops he grabbed me by the scruff of my jacket and pushed me out of the front door, quickly locking it behind me. I was laughing out loud as I hailed a taxi to take me back to the ship.

On our way back to New York we hit some heavy seas that sent the ship pitching and rolling. Typically this was a signal to limit work in the engine room to standing watches, and doing only what was absolutely necessary so no one was put in harm's way. It seemed our First Engineer thought differently about the level of inclemency the weather was presenting. Instead of following the standard procedures he decided that he wanted the engine room to be spotless before arriving back at the Sea-Land docks in Port Elizabeth. He told me to begin cleaning one of the compressors. I took my bucket of soap and water, and some rags, and began wiping down the machinery. As I worked my way around one of the compressors, careful to get every spot of grease and grime off, the ship rolled suddenly. I was thrown toward the spinning armature of the compressor. As I sought to regain my balance the rag snagged on the armature and my right hand was pulled into the machinery. As fate would have it, instead of my hand being sucked into the compressor and mangled, possibly lost, I hit the armature in such a way that the spin bounced my hand back out. Pain shot through my entire arm as I clutched my hand to my chest. I was bleeding from two spots, one on my thumb and one on the knuckle of the nearby index finger. I couldn't bend my wrist or make a fist without serious pain. I was immediately sent to one of the deck officers, who doubled as the first-aid dispenser. He had no way of telling if it was broken or not, so I was simply given the standard aspirin and ordered not to work. He consigned me to remain in my foc'sle until we got back to port. For the next three days, after each meal, I sat on my bunk or slept, trying to keep my hand from being further damaged by the sea-determined movements of the ship. It was a long, painful return. Once docked, Junior and I parted company, him to the union hall for another ship, me heading back to the Bronx where I knew it would be easy to find some real painkillers.

The day after I returned I was on the ferry heading to Staten Island where the Public Health Hospital was located, the hospital where members of the military and the merchant marine were sent. After a very long wait and some x-rays, I was diagnosed with a broken wrist and a broken thumb. I was placed in a cast that ran almost to my elbow but still allowed me to wiggle my fingers slightly.

There must have been some paperwork sent between the hospital, the Sea-Land company, and the Seafarer's International Union because at the start of the new year I was contacted by a union attorney asking me to come to his office in Manhattan to discuss what happened and to determine if I had a possible lawsuit against the First Engineer and Sea-Land. During the meeting, when the attorney heard the circumstances of the bad weather and high seas, it was decided that I did indeed have a case to pursue. He had me sign some papers and explained to me that while the case was being prepared, I would have access to money in the form of a draw against whatever my final settlement would be. All I had to do was to come to his office, sign off, and he would give me the cash I needed. I was elated. Now, even without working, I could get cash for drugs.

As the pressure from the cops continued, as drug sources dried up, got arrested or simply disappeared due to the extra police scrutiny, and as the pressures of our addictions built, we had to once more look beyond our neighborhood confines in our search for drugs. As it is with street networks, word spreads fast and ubiquitously and before long we were made aware of a dealer over near East Tremont Avenue, a Bronx neighborhood that was mostly Puerto Rican. One day me, Michael Katz, and a few other guys piled into Kevin's car and headed there to score. We parked and immediately became the focus of dozens of curious and menacing looks from people trying to determine if we were undercover cops, stupid white guys lost in their neighborhood and therefore easy prey, or potential customers. Three of us got out and three stayed in the car. When I explained who we were there to see, some kind of silent signal was communicated and the neighborhood went on with its business – which now appeared to include us.

We were escorted into an apartment building and immediately began climbing the stairs. At the top floor our escort pounded on a door, speaking something in Spanish. The door opened and we were led into the kitchen where, behind a grey-topped Formica table, with stainless steel legs, sat a guy in a wife-beater t-shirt and boxer shorts bagging heroin into small glassine envelopes. He looked up briefly and then continued with his work. As he closed each bag, folding it into a very thin package, he sealed it with a tiny piece of black tape. When he was done he uttered ominously, "Black for death, man. This shit is a killer." We nodded impatiently, jaded as we'd become by all the advertising that went along with every drug sale in order to justify the price, or to seduce new clientele. We exchanged our money for the bags of heroin. I put them all in my pocket and we turned to leave. As we piled out of the apartment his voice warned, "This shit is death, man." The door closed behind us.

We were excited as we walked toward the car. We got back in and I ended up in the rear seat. But before we could even start the engine a police car, with lights flashing, blocked our exit. We all froze. "Shit," was the collective sentiment that rippled silently throughout the car. Maybe a disgruntled neighbor called, fed up with the endless stream of junkies coming and going, just like the families in our neighborhood had become. Whatever the case, we were about to be busted for possession of heroin.

As the cops walked toward our car, motioning us all to get out, I began inserting the six bags of heroin in between my fingers in a desperate attempt to hide them from the inevitable search. As I exited the car I immediately put my hands up in the air as a sign of submission and in an effort to keep my hands from the cops' consideration. They searched each of us one by one, with one cop doing the pat-down while the other stood watch over the rest of us in case anyone was stupid enough to try to bolt. When he got to me my hands were still in the air, which he seemed pleased about. As the officer patted my shirt pocket he pulled out my merchant seaman's I.D., issued by the Coast Guard. I immediately became more submissive, explaining that I had a ship waiting for me, that I didn't want to jeopardize my livelihood, and reiterating that we were not drug users. He placed my I.D. back in my pocket as we continued to stand. Two other cops arrived and began searching the front seat, the back seat, and the trunk of Kevin's car. They found nothing. All the cops looked at each other, knowing full well that there was no other reason than drugs for a carload of white guys to be in this East Tremont neighborhood. But without finding any evidence they told us to get our asses back to wherever we came from and that they better not see us there again. We all thanked them as our bodies relaxed noticeably.

As we pulled away everyone in the car wanted to know where the drugs were, did I swallow them or successfully throw them away? I held up my hands, fingers rigid and close together. They looked puzzled. Then I spread my fingers wide and the bags floated onto my lap. Bedlam erupted. "No fucking way!" seemed to be the consensus as we all began laughing. We immediately drove to a friend's apartment. Once there we all began sharing our spoils, sniffing the contents contentedly through tiny plastic stir-stick straws. When I came to, after what felt like a comatose-like nodding out, I saw everyone else strewn about the apartment still out cold. As people began to regain some semblance of consciousness we looked at each other in befuddlement, with rising trepidation over the unusually powerful effect the drugs had on us. We all registered the same thought: given what a few snorts had done, we realized that if anyone had actually shot that stuff up they would be dead. That dealer was right – that shit *was* killer. The next look that crossed our smiling faces was – when can we get some more?

It took us about a week to return to the East Tremont neighborhood. This time our reception was quite different. As we got out of the car, two guys came over and explained that the dealer we saw last time was no longer selling. If we wanted to score then two of us had to come with them. We agreed. When I was handed all of the money we'd collected, Paulie and I turned to follow them. We walked about two blocks and then entered an apartment building. As we headed for the stairs I suddenly knew that everything was wrong, that we were going to get ripped off. But the power of even the slightest possibility of getting heroin overruled all the intuition howling in my head and screaming around my gut. As we went up the first flight of steps, the staircase split, one set of stairs going to the right, the other to the left. They started to lead us up the left-hand stairwell then suddenly changed their minds, as if remembering that the apartment was up the right staircase. As we turned to follow their instructions we were now in front of them and they were behind us.

All my alarm systems went off but it was too late. An arm snaked around my neck, pulling my head violently backward, while the other hand pressed a knife blade across my throat. Paulie was in the same position. "Give us the money," the voice hissed into my left ear as the knife edge sat menacingly against my Adam's apple. I fished into my pocket and drew out a wad of bills. The hand that had been pulling my head back released and he reached around and grabbed the money. "I should cut your throat," he spat through clenched teeth. "One of your boys from your neighborhood stabbed one of us last night, motherfucker." I desperately tried to explain that I had nothing to do with that, didn't even know about it. He applied more pressure to the blade as if vengeance was definitely on his mind. I winced as I felt the fine edge of the blade move closer to splitting the skin open. I imagined my blood gushing out. "Don't do this, please," I begged. But there was only silence, the coolness of the blade, and my racing heart.

Suddenly, as if breaking a spell, but without withdrawing their arms from around our necks, we were told to take off our shoes and our pants. Once they were off we handed them to our assailants. They told us to count to 100 and to not follow them before we were done counting. We nodded numbly as they took off down the stairs with our money, our sneakers, and our pants. We looked at each other for a split second then raced after them, now in our socks and underwear. We found our pants and sneakers on the floor in the lobby. As we got dressed we knew they were long gone. We slunk back to the car, defeated. Someone lifted my chin as we were explaining what had happened. There for all to see was a long red scratch where the knife had come so close to biting deeply into my neck. It was all they needed to see to make my story real.

When we got back to Kevin's apartment in University Heights we were all dejected. Like in the aftermath of any trauma we all began second-guessing what we could've done to avoid getting ripped off, or ways we should've turned the tables and disarmed them. I had a knife at my throat and I knew it was all a fantasy, but my mind conjured up different endings at will, endings where I made a slick martial-arts-style maneuver and triumphed. Eventually we all made peace with the fact that we had gotten ripped off, except for Kevin's roommate, Nicky. Perhaps it was the fact that he didn't get his drugs and was jonesin', or perhaps it was his typical bravado personality talking, but for some reason Nicky would not accept that we had returned empty handed. He kept badgering me about why I gave up the money so quickly, about why I didn't fight back. "I would've kicked their asses," he strutted. He accused me of being scared, of giving up too easily.

I finally had enough and started telling him to back off. We were in each other's faces, nose to nose, yelling. Everyone else was watching, tense from our recent altercation; they began telling us to cool it. I thought about hitting Nicky but realized I still had a cast on my right wrist. Suddenly, as if in a dream, a scene from a John Wayne movie took over. "You know what, Nicky," I began. "I won't hit you, not this time,"

I spoke, recalling the script. Then, as I started to turn away, out came John Wayne's culminating words: "The hell I won't." With that utterance I spun fast and backhanded Nicky in the jaw as hard as I could with my casted arm. His head snapped back, but he regrouped quickly and immediately jumped on me. Then the others all jumped on us, pulling us apart. Nicky was fuming; I was laughing, mostly about how John Wayne had possessed me for a moment. The altercation was just one more example of the havoc heroin was creating in all of our lives, and how our friendships with each other were devolving and imploding whenever the drug was scarce or unavailable.

ON THE CALENDAR IT WAS JANUARY 1972, a new year, but in my life it was just 31 days without any recognizable endings to celebrate or beginnings to set goals for. Every day was consumed by the insipid hustling for drugs from the minute I woke up to the minute I went to sleep. Snorting heroin was all I did, all I looked forward to, if looking forward was even possible for an addict who was compelled beyond any kind of willful looking, or thinking, or choosing.

The morning I blew the insides of my nose into a tissue, I also blew some of my brains into the mess as well. Later, when I tried to snort some heroin in an effort to get straight and not be sick, my nose erupted with an interior fire that doubled me over in pain. In the face of trying to get high, despite the agonizing pain ripping through my nostrils, it became clear to me beyond a doubt that my level of addiction was now beyond any rational control. Tellingly, my first thought was not "I have to stop doing this and clean up my act"; on the contrary, it was, "Since my nose is gone, I guess the only way to get high now is to shoot up."

I was about to cross a threshold that I had kept my distance from for over a year. The last remnant of my self-respect, tattered as it was by my becoming an addict in the first place, now lay completely shredded at my feet, dissipated and dispersed by the chill winds of utter dependency on heroin. For a minute, as my decision hovered in the air before me and the slight possibility of rescinding this dangerous step still lingered, I watched as if I was floating right over my own body, watched as my spirit stepped shakily into the land of the desperate and the lost. Instantly all doubt receded, as if this was indeed my next rational move. I headed down Gouverneur Avenue to find the one person I knew would agree to share his needle and get me off.

I found him standing in front of EM's candy store. He was wearing a pea coat, collar turned up against the cold. Charlie Baumann leaned against the brick façade; his wavy blondish hair tousled by the breeze, moving from one foot to another as if he was sick and needing to get high himself. But I knew he was fine, that this had simply become his standard junkie body language. More importantly, though, I knew that he had a stash of heroin in his apartment because, mere days ago, I had watched him tie off and shoot up while I sat nearby and inhaled a bag of dope. I motioned Charlie over and told him what I wanted to do, what I wanted him to do for me. He stepped back and looked at me incredulously, a devilish smile stretching across his mouth as he contemplated a new convert. "Let's go to my house."

Charlie was the youngest of my old friend Lenny's siblings. He was short, handsome in a boyish way, and possessed some of Lenny's skill with words. But whereas Lenny *always* managed to verbally extricate himself from serious confrontation, Charlie had just enough of an arsenal of verbal putdowns and comebacks to make him dangerous only to himself. In other words, he had a big mouth without the mental dexterity or physical fire-power to back it up. He always seemed on the verge of getting his ass kicked by someone.

Once inside Charlie's apartment he asked me if I was sure I wanted to go ahead with this. I nodded silently, the pain in my nose reassuring me that I had no other choice. Charlie looked at me, wondering. It had been barely a few weeks ago since he had asked me in this very room if I wanted to shoot up. I had steadfastly and self-righteously declined, holding firm to my convoluted holier-than-thou position, as if there were really gradations of junkies. Now here I was asking him. Yet even in this situation I still clung to the idea that he was more fucked up than I was, lower on the addiction totem pole, holding fast to my belief that I wasn't really like him.

"Let's go into the bathroom," he said as he grabbed his works and a couple bags of dope. He lowered the seat and the lid in one motion and sat me down on the toilet. I began rolling up the sleeve of my shirt and bared my left arm for his inspection. He rubbed the inner crook of my elbow with his palm, suddenly slapping his hand hard across the area, reddening my skin and causing the veins to rise up slightly. "Look at those veins," he remarked, noticing their pristine condition – a junkie's wet-dream compared to the hard-to-find collapsed condition that inevitably accompanies prolonged shooting up. Charlie tied off my arm just below my bicep, causing my veins to bulge even more. He then picked up a metal spoon and emptied the contents of one glassine envelop of heroin into it. Taking up a homemade syringe, comprised of an eye-dropper with the business end of a needle attached to it, he drew up some water from a glass and squirted it onto the spoon where it began mixing slowly with the drug. Charlie then produced a cigarette lighter and flicked it until the flame held steady. He began moving the flame just beneath the spoon, the heat facilitating the mixing of the water and the heroin into an opaque solution. I watched intently as the water and heroin bubbled briefly and became one. Charlie closed the lighter and laid it on the sink nearby. He then placed the nose of the syringe into the pool of liquid in the spoon and pressed the black rubber bulb at the other end, sucking it all into the glass cylinder. He held it up near his face and began flicking it with his index finger to make sure there were no air pockets in the liquid. He then lowered it toward my waiting forearm, looking at me one more time to see if I was going to back out. I simply looked back at him, impassively. I felt the needle and looked down just as it nosed under my skin and into my waiting vein.

As I felt the warmth flooding into my body I looked at Charlie. He was intent on taking care of business. Suddenly the day I first smoked pot with Bob Glesser filled my mind. How radically the world had changed in less than six short years. That summer day in the golf course, I knew in my heart that my drug transgressions were going to lead me to new worlds, new insights, new beginnings and mind-expanding experiences. Now, here in Charlie's bathroom, my transgressions felt like the end of the line, a place where beauty was absent, where my eyes were closed rather than wide open, where my heart was sealed and selfishly concerned only about my needs, which were now running the show. Rather than the force of life that led to my explorations in the world of marijuana and psychedelics, it was my desire to deaden any and all feeling other than the rush of getting high, which I sought from my constant dance with heroin. But a sudden, overwhelming sense of peace quickly put a stop to all my comparisons. I was now feeling good rather than on the verge of being sick, rescued by what felt like the soothing hand of God from further withdrawal. All was now made right in my world as the drug made its way throughout my body and brain, with its distinctive sensual rush suddenly made exponentially more powerful and seductive by virtue of my mainlining. Charlie explained that since this was my first time we would only use one bag, just enough to get me straight, un-sick, maybe a little high.

That's the dangerous thing about heroin: in order for addicts to really get stoned, to really go into a deep, dreamy nod, a junkie needs a greater and greater amount, thus increasing the risk of an overdose, especially when shooting up. In my case, one bag was plenty to stave off withdrawal and get me feeling incredibly good. I could suddenly see and feel the exquisite appeal of shooting up heroin. My entire body surrendered to the high, aswirl in a dreamlike free-fall, tumbling gently onto clouds. As Charlie withdrew the syringe he smiled knowingly. "Come see me when you need another boost, Tommy," he offered, as he began readying for his own shot. As I left his apartment and headed toward home, snow had started to fall. In my mild haze, I walked with my face turned skyward, feeling the flakes land on my cheeks and melt.

I dreamily decided to focus on the sparkling beauty of the snow and bury any and all trepidations that were trying to get me to wake me up to what I had just done.

Two days later I was back in Charlie's bathroom. This time there was little chatter between us; instead it was the mechanical fulfillment of need, very businesslike. Afterwards, walking through the cold January air toward EM's, I felt like I had finally reached the bottom of my life. Was I now my father, I wondered, my spirit broken and me drowning my pain with heroin instead of alcohol? What was the point of my life? As I was waiting for the light to change so I could cross Van Cortlandt Avenue West, images of my deteriorating life and my dead father flashed rapidly across my anxious mind. I abruptly changed my mind and turned instantly left and began walking past P.S. 95 back to my house. I knew I had to figure some shit out; continuing to shoot up was only going to get me dead.

Once home I went upstairs to my room and lay down on my bed, staring at the ceiling. I tried to muster the energy, the courage, the heart to disable my current trajectory, to pull myself up before I finally crashed headlong as a corpse into junkie abyss. The best I could come up with was to go cold turkey right then and get straight; maybe then a clear idea, a way out, might become available to me. I felt I needed the type of flagellation that kicking heroin would provide, a punitive and self-punishing physically painful reminder of what I had just done by twice breaking my own sacred vow to never shoot up.

UNLIKE ALCOHOL WITHDRAWAL, kicking heroin is not life threatening, but it is hellishly painful both physically and psychologically. Fortunately, I was not kicking a $200 per day habit, so I hoped that my discomfort would be short-lived and therefore more manageable. I could feel the drugs from my visit to Charlie's house still very much in my system as I got undressed and buried myself under the blankets. I was determined to ride it out. I slept fitfully that first night and by morning my body had its antennae alert and sending me messages that it was time to get high. I tried to ignore them and pulled the covers over my head in an effort to ward off the demons that were arriving with each passing minute, beckoning me, expecting me to conform to the familiar pattern. I refused. Within hours I was sweating and trembling, but it was my mind that was the worst part, screaming inside my head that I needed to get high, that whatever I was doing, for whatever reason, was a bullshit lie. I walked over to the winding staircase and yelled for my mother. She opened the door and turned her head up to face where I was standing. I told her that I was sick and that I just wanted to sleep, asking her to please not disturb me. She responded, like most mothers do, by asking if she could bring me anything. I emphatically told her no and she turned back into the main part of the house, closing the door behind her. Trembling, I went back to my bed.

The first day without drugs felt like a really bad flu, my body sweating and shaking incessantly.

But it was the second day that nearly drove me out of my house and down to The Rail to find anyone who had drugs. It began in my legs. It was like every single muscle, every single muscle fiber, was on fire. I was burning up and had no heroin to soothe it. Then the flames swept up to my stomach, chest, neck, and shoulders, each muscle agonizing in withdrawal. I'd never felt anything like this. Every single square inch of my body ached and throbbed and screamed its unrelenting demand for relief, and that meant heroin. I couldn't lie down or sit still without pain; I couldn't walk without pain. My body became the focus of an all-encompassing torture by a red-hot laser I could neither shut off nor get away from. Throughout the entire day, my body knotted, and knotted, and knotted further, twisting me into the deepest despair I had ever experienced. I begged God for this to end. I promised, on my mother's life, that if I made it through I would never shoot up again, never do heroin again. I don't remember falling asleep; perhaps I passed out, my body wisely succumbing to the pain by simply checking out.

On the third day I felt maximally spent. The pain had significantly subsided and the thoughts in my mind were less about heroin and more about food. I still ached but nowhere near the dark nadir I had reached the previous day. Once again, I spent the entire day in my bed, listlessly going in and out of superficial sleep.

When the morning of the fourth day arrived I knew I was through the worst. I congratulated myself on not throwing up. I donned a pair of sweatpants and, bare-chested, stepped onto the front porch into a brisk, sunny January day. I took a deep breath and exhaled, the steam from my mouth dissipating slowly. The cold air felt so good, so enervating and enlivening on my body. I looked out on nothing in particular, gazing more inward than outward. I was clean now, but outside my house heroin's Sirens were everywhere, singing seductively. I took another deep breath. I had no idea if I could maintain my present determination to keep off drugs; all I really knew was the truth of the line from the Rolling Stones' song: "It's just a shot a way." I returned inside and headed for the shower. I turned on the water as hot as I could stand it. Before immersing myself, I turned my face to the mirror above the sink. As I watched the billowing steam obliterate my reflection, I muttered to myself: "One day at a time, Tommy, one day at a time." I stepped into the tub, slid the shower curtain closed, and began my ablutions.

Chapter Twenty-Four
The Invitation

When Michael Katz finished reading aloud the letter he had received from Harvey Bender, my mouth fell open, my eyes widened, and my imagination exploded. Harvey's letter was imploring Michael to flee the drug scene of New York and join him in California. Harvey was using everything he could think of to paint a picture of an entirely different life: a life filled with political activism, marching and protesting against the war, people living together in a collective household and attending weekly study groups debating political theory. Most importantly to me, though, was their determination to see drug use as reactionary and enslaving, ideals I had once tried to live and preach without any lasting success. Harvey was describing his life in San Francisco and every word he wrote reawakened my sense of justice, fairness, and my desire to do something good in the world. All the virtues I dreamt of embodying, my perspectives on equality, of standing up for what's right, my vision of helping create a different world that I had fashioned between my father's heroics and living 17 years in this Jewish neighborhood in the Bronx was suddenly re-blossoming – virtues that had lain too long dormant under the sleep-inducing shroud of drug addiction. I was galvanized.

Even though Harvey's letter made no mention of inviting me, the images that were forming like a movie in my head captured me in every frame. I could see myself in San Francisco. I saw myself studying and discussing progressive politics, protesting the Vietnam War, marching with Black Panthers, veterans, students, and women, all of us demanding peace and social justice. I sat there on Michael's bed and was momentarily lost in my dream. I looked over at Michael and said, "We have to get out of the neighborhood." He knew immediately that I meant we had to somehow find a way to get to San Francisco.

* * * * *

As January 1972 moved to a close, any and all thoughts of a happy new year were nowhere to be found. My staying clean of heroin lasted all of two weeks. Once again I returned to The Rail, snorting dope whenever I had the money or the opportunity. My only solace, my last shred of partially restored self-respect, was my renewed refusal to ever shoot up again. I had re-crossed the Rubicon in the other direction. Still, the walls were closing in and the pressure from the cops was ratcheting up in intensity. After a brief respite in the aftermath of the black drug dealers being purged, the police were at us with renewed determination. Under pressure from the Amalgamated board members – who were in turn pressured by concerned families – the police were once again charged with putting an end to the scourge of heroin and restoring the neighborhood to its formerly pristine, drug-free and dealer-free environment. Unmarked cars with plainclothes narcotics detectives snaked through the neighborhood hourly, the detectives staring menacingly at us as we gathered at The Rail. They were silently reminding us by their constant presence that eventually they would prevail, just like they prevailed in removing Hassan from the neighborhood and, shortly thereafter it appeared, from life itself. The previous summer I had already felt their wrath in a frightening altercation in the park with a knife-wielding detective that left me feeling like a marked man with time running out. Regular cop cars continued their patrols as well. Yet there we were, gathered at The Rail every day. With no options we could imagine, the habitual was clearly more comforting and familiar than trying something new; plus, it took courage and conviction for anyone to turn their back and leave the herd.

I knew addiction to be the truth of my every day; I could feel my slow disintegration. After my brief foray into shooting up earlier in the month, I had come partially to my senses and returned to only snorting heroin. It was my distorted way to pretend that I wasn't really falling fully into drug-induced narcissism and complete indifference. Yet every day, I would nonetheless make my way to The Rail and sit, waiting for the *faux* camaraderie and connection of heroin. I would often be joined by Leah, our relationship in tatters, no longer a couple. Yet I was still emotionally hooked, despondently hoping we could somehow get back together while at the same time vowing not to subject myself to the inevitable pain that our idea of relationship continually spawned. A dozen other zombies would populate The Rail by midday, all in various states of disarray. Some were sick and needing a fix immediately, others were just maintaining after having gotten off that morning. The ones we envied were those most recently stoned and into a deep nod, their chins sagging to their chests, eyes closed, oblivious, like old men done before their time.

Everything, every conversation, every facial expression, every gesture was about heroin. Where can I get some? Do you have some? Can I have some? If you didn't have money you could trade your house as a safe place to get high. If you had a set of works, you could offer to share in exchange for a fix. Then, after everyone had gotten high, sweet sensual warmth would envelope us into a cocoon of togetherness. Through half smiles and hooded eyes we would look at each other lovingly, briefly forgetting that only moments ago we would've stepped on each other's faces if it meant being able to get high.

Internally, I was desperately trying to hold it together. At the completion of my last two-week stint on the *Anchorage* back in December, I had reached my cumulative three months of being at sea and was now eligible to upgrade my seamanship job classification – which meant more job opportunities and an increase in pay. With that in mind – and a casted wrist that prevented much other activity – I figured I would utilize my time somewhat productively while I continued to get high and wait for my wrist to heal. I enrolled in a Coast Guard training class to upgrade my seamanship papers to the designation Fireman/Oiler. The training was to be held in Manhattan, business hours Monday through Friday, for one month beginning in February.

The funny thing about shipping out as a Fireman/Oiler is that it involved very little actual work; that was reserved for the overtime clause in the union contract. Instead, during the two four-hour shifts (broken up by eight hours off, but dedicated to as much overtime as possible), the Fireman watched steam pressure gauges in the boiler room and the Oiler checked oil pressure gauges throughout the rest of the engine room. But they had to know how things worked in order to recognize when they weren't and to troubleshoot the possible fixes; hence the class. It was fairly interesting and I was glad to be moving beyond the Wiper classification; if I never had to blow tubes again it would be too soon.

Within the first week of class I met J.J., a young black man who lived in Harlem. The strange thing about junkies is that they think they are keeping it cool even when they are high, like the rest of the world is clueless. But all it takes is the practiced eye of a cop, another junkie, or someone who's been around junkies to bust through the façade. In Harlem, J.J., who was clearly not strung-out but a middleman, had definitely been around other junkies. Halfway into our first conversation, which began by comparing ships we had sailed on, he moved the talk seamlessly to heroin. There was nothing left to say after that; J.J. became an instant connection to a regular supply of drugs.

THE FIRST TIME I WENT TO HARLEM to score, I met J.J. at the 125th Street subway exit. We walked over to 127th Street and turned toward his apartment. Once we crossed Amsterdam Avenue and headed east the street was less populated and I was the only white person to be found. Suddenly our progress was halted when five or six guys surrounded us. "Everything cool, J.J.?" one of them asked, indicating me with a movement of his chin. As usual, they thought I was an undercover cop. "Everything is cool, my brothers. My man here is cool," J.J. replied, smiling. I felt a distinct wave of relief sweep over me as they parted and when we finally arrived at J.J.'s apartment. There I met his mother, who was in the process of getting ready for night-shift work. She was a tall, full-bodied woman, with a welcoming smile, very happy to meet any friend of J.J.'s. He told me to hang out and reassured me he would be back shortly.

I sat quietly in their living room, looking around at the furniture, the knick-knacks, and the pictures. On one wall, just to the side of a hutch, were pictures of John F. Kennedy and Martin Luther King, Jr., side by side. I was struck immediately by the dissonance between these two men who fought for freedom in their own particular ways, and my buying heroin in Harlem – heroin, one of the most enslaving drugs available. Fortunately, J.J.'s arrival and my own needs rescued me from having to ponder the depths of this contradiction for very long. In J.J.'s bedroom he handed me a flat, tin-foil package filled with white powder, the sight of which made my junkie eyes widen and my heartbeat quicken. I handed him some money and I stuffed the heroin down into the front of my pants, into my underwear. I said goodnight to J.J.'s mother and he escorted me back to the subway station.

This went on for the entire month we were in our training class together. I soon began copping drugs for my friends in the neighborhood. Yet even with this regular connection I was not at peace; I was still a strung-out junkie always on the lookout for how to get more for myself, regardless of who might be in the way. One time I collected a couple hundred dollars and went to J.J.'s to score. I returned home with the drugs but told everyone that I had gotten ripped off and both the drugs and money were gone. Instead I kept the all heroin for myself. I was never fully trusted after that, but junkies are somewhat forgiving if they think another score might be in the offing. And so it went.

Then, by the beginning of March, it was over as quick as it began. Our training course ended and J.J. found another ship to work on. Just like that he was gone and so was the drug connection. As a result, I became so desperate for drugs that I would do almost anything, say anything, in order to get a fix. I would guiltlessly walk my friends home at night in the hopes of discovering where they stashed their drugs. One time I did steal someone's stash they had hidden in the golf course and immediately called Leah and a bunch of friends over to my house to indulge. When the people whose drugs it was came to my house asking if we were all getting high on their stuff, I told them, with the straightest face and feigning insult, that this was heroin I had bought myself, and they were welcome to join us if they wanted . . . which they unhesitatingly did.

Before long I could not look at myself in the mirror without a feeling of entrapment gripping me. Staring at my reflection I could not face all the times I had stolen and lied and manipulated. Strangulating shame at how far I'd fallen from my own noble self-image engulfed me. All my inflated plans about how I was going to rid the neighborhood of heroin lay punctured by the same syringes I had plunged into my own arms. As winter melted toward spring, I felt like I would never, ever get out. My life appeared like a single series of repetitive acts, the same day after day: get up and head down to The Rail; find out who had some smack or who had the connections to get some; get high in someone's house; repeat the next morning, *ad infinitum.*

Periodically, when I became desperately low on money, I would take the train to Times Square and judiciously ask for a small advance from my union attorney. Smilingly, he would hand over a check, no questions asked. Then, with my supply of cash restored, getting heroin was no problem. Back in the neighborhood, I would see guys playing basketball in the playground or in the Big Schoolyard. The cast on my wrist had been off for a while, but basketball no longer possessed any allure. Even if it had, these guys, who would've unhesitatingly invited me to join in the past, now hardly gave me any notice.

Pressed hard between the police and the compulsions of addiction, my life felt increasingly circumscribed and shrinking daily. Not only that, but I was feeling the inner collapse of whatever morality I still possessed. Who had I become? What had I become? As I stood on the back porch of my house one evening, with Harvey's letter of invitation swirling in my mind, I looked out over the neighborhood and realized there were only three options left: one, start shooting up again and eventually die of an overdose; two, get busted and go to jail; or three, escape the Bronx and make a bold bid for freedom.

ONE BITTERLY COLD NIGHT in early March, as Michael Katz and I were getting high in my bedroom, he suggested we get out of town for a couple of weeks and make ourselves scarce until the intensifying police crackdown subsided and things returned to relative normalcy. He suggested we take some Methadone and go to Florida for a couple of weeks to kick. I argued that this wasn't far enough, or for long enough, and adamantly stated that if we go anywhere it should be to see Harvey in San Francisco. He shook his head and began describing the warmth and beauty of two or three weeks in Florida, reiterating that this was the perfect place to get clean again. Yet I knew this brief reprieve would not be enough; I had kicked cold turkey just months ago and here I was back in the hamster wheel again. Florida was still too close for my liking and, more disastrously, after Florida we had no other plan but to return to The Rail – which meant eventually returning to heroin. Besides, even if things went back to normal, even if the police made themselves scarce and the heroin scene returned to the shadows rather than flagrantly parading itself in front of the playground, what kind of life would that be? I only had to look around the neighborhood to find the answer to my question. Heroin ruled; the debris of people's lives lay strewn around The Rail for all to see. Even the good options of the straight life felt too confining – get married, raise a family, get a membership in a beach club on Long Island, and spend 30 years taking the subway to Manhattan hoping retirement would arrive before my heart attack. It was all too grey, too bland. I wanted none of it. I wanted to be in California, actively resisting the war and fighting for real social equality and justice. Instead I was medicating my shame and frustrations away each day only to have them return the next, demanding more solace and numbing.

ONE DAY AS I WAS WALKING DOWN GOUVERNEUR AVENUE, returning from EM's candy store to the playground, I froze in my tracks as image after image assaulted my mind, unbeckoned and definitely unwanted. I stood across the street, gazing fixedly at The Rail, when suddenly I felt the ghosts of the *Shoah* all around me. I could see them reaching out from railway boxcars, see them gaunt and emaciated in striped uniforms. I could see their faces and bodies superimposed on the faces and bodies of my friends sitting mere yards from me on The Rail. It all crashed in on me in that moment; it all made unbearable sense.

In similar ways that the rail lines in Europe had taken the Jewish populations and other undesirables to concentration camps and to their death, our stationary Rail had now become the site of hourly drug deals and the silent witness to our slow demise under the squealing, crushing wheels of heroin addiction. No longer was The Rail a place of ice cream trucks, a-cappella singing under the lamppost, or innocently sharing a joint together. No longer was it the spot to wait until someone with a car pulled up to offer a break in the boredom by driving to Nathan's for the best hotdogs and fries, or up to Poundridge to camp, or over to the Botanical Gardens and the Bronx Zoo. No, the laidback potheads, the psychedelic seekers of mind expansion, and even the goofy, harmless alkies were now figures of the past, replaced by skin-and-bone wraiths, junkies that smelled of death. And I was one of them.

Somehow we had broken a vital connection with life and I was reeling under the sudden realization of the spirit-crushing weight and inertia brought on by living within this severance and dissociation. I could see all my noble ideals lying in a rusting metal casket, jumbled in with all the despicable things I had done, all the ugliness I had become. Daily I was laboring to carry this heavy load while longing to put it down somewhere, somehow. I had become a pallbearer at my own ongoing funeral, the slow, heroin-shrouded procession to oblivion ending here at The Rail. I shook my head and prayed for a miracle to get me out of the Bronx.

Then, one day in mid-March, the air brisk and the sky sunny, Michael Katz pulled up in front of The Rail in a car that I'd never seen before. I was sitting there with a bunch of other guys in the usual junkie posture, slouched over, nodding in a half-dream state. Michael rolled down the window and yelled, "Who wants to go to California?" My head snapped up, suddenly keenly awake, the drugs scattering and fleeing from my body and mind. No one else moved or batted an eye in response to Michael's question. As I sat there, now wide awake and shed of the drugged dullness that only moments ago engulfed me, all of our conversations about Harvey's letter instantly crystallized and replayed in my head. Had Michael gotten my message that we had to get as far from the neighborhood as possible? Here he was, ready to go, with a drive-away car that all we had to do was deliver on time to its owner waiting on the west coast. Whatever wildness this was, whatever motivated this turn of events, there was no way in hell that I was going to blow it this time. Somewhere inside I knew that if I did not respond right here, right now, that I would never, ever leave The Rail, except, perhaps, handcuffed in the back of a police car or in an ambulance as an overdosed junkie. "Give me an hour," I shouted, already lifting myself from The Rail and heading up Van Cortlandt Park South to my house.

I PACKED MY DUFFEL BAG with the necessary essentials (including work clothes for my next ship). I picked up my Merchant Marine I.D. card from the dresser and stared at it with a renewed sense of the possibilities. I held it in both of my hands, cradling it as if it was a sacred talisman. Before putting it back in my wallet, I recalled to mind that day in Mr. Sokol's apartment when he handed me his letter of introduction that I was to present to his friend at Seafarer's International Union. What I couldn't see at the time of our conversation, I could now see so vividly. I had successfully upgraded to a Fireman/Oiler; I had a clear and solid career path directly in front of me. I could find a job pretty much whenever I wanted one. I had my ticket out of the neighborhood because I could go anywhere in the country there was a Seafarers International union hall – and San Francisco was one of those cities. All I needed was transportation (which was right now awaiting me at The Rail), and a place to stay until I got a ship (Harvey's invitation), and I was set. For the first time in over two years I felt the taste of freedom and the possibilities that Mr. Sokol had originally offered me, alive upon my tongue.

I grabbed my gear and went downstairs to the kitchen. I sat at the table and explained what was going on to my mother and sister. I told them that I was heading to California to get a job on a ship. They were shocked at first by the suddenness of my announcement, but my mother understood this time. She knew that I was now a working man and working men went where the jobs were. She was proud of me. Peggy, too, was happy at my announcement. We all hugged together and then I hugged my mother, looking into her eyes and telling her that I loved her. And then it was time to leave.

I hefted my duffel bag and made my way through the kitchen toward the landing and the staircase to the front door. I stopped and looked around, a wave of emotion drenching me as memories flooded from every room, memories of all the joy and beauty, hardship and trauma that took place under this roof over the past seventeen years. I made my way down the steep stairway, every creak a reminder of how many times I traversed these steps. I opened the heavy yellow door and stared out onto Saxon Avenue. I looked right, down the line of private houses stretching toward Sedgwick Avenue and the Reservoir. Then I looked left, toward the Sixth Building and The Bushes in the park beyond. With a glance I recalled my near fatal moment during the construction of an addition on St. Patrick's Home for the Aged and Infirm across the street, along with images of black-clad nuns gliding across the grounds. I spent the most time looking at the two modern towers that had sprung up from the destruction of the original First Building, my mind's eye visualizing every entrance, A to Z, in the old ivy-covered Tudor structure: the flower beds, the fountains and the fish, the red slate tiles we leapt upon as we scrambled over the walkways. This was the flagship building that seeded the soil for the Amalgamated to take root, built in 1927, the same year that my father came to America and the same year my immigrant grandfather purchased this house I was now readying to depart. Hopes and dreams for a better life swirled everywhere I looked, in everything I remembered.

Now it was my turn.

When I closed the front door behind me I turned and glanced at the tarnished metal numbers, 3987, that signified the place I called home, for better and for worse, all these years. As I walked down the five stone steps of the stoop, I felt weightless. I looked up at the tree my

Uncle Chuck always imagined as a giant pistachio ice cream cone and smiled. I turned reflexively left, as I did thousands of times before, when I would race headlong for sanctuary in the embrace of my neighborhood friends, race straight to the playground or to Gale Place and into their welcoming arms and loving hearts.

Now, cutting through the Sixth Building, across the colorful slate walkway, I stepped from red tile to red tile one final time. Then down the stairs and through the arch and I was on Van Cortlandt Park South and walking toward The Rail. Michael, noticing me approaching, stepped behind the car and opened the trunk. I tossed my duffel bag inside and slammed the lid. Michael slid in behind the wheel and I stood on the passenger side. A couple of guys stood near the car on the other side, talking to him through the open window, no one else able or willing to fathom the opportunity this idling engine offered.

From this vantage point I looked down toward Gale Place, site of our coming of age as young Panthers. Then I looked down Gouverneur Avenue and recalled all the journeys between the playground basketball courts and EM's candy store, all the trips to the Co-op Market, where I worked my first real, fulltime job. Finally, I turned and looked over the roof of the car in the direction of the playground. It was all there, all the images alive and emanating from every corner: my first scuffle in the sandbox at age 6, to my basketball exploits, to making out with Shira in the golf course in the grace of a humid summer night. I could hear the voices and see the faces, like the whole neighborhood was there to say goodbye. I nodded my head, humbly and in honor of everyone who I'd rubbed up against in any way, everyone who'd helped fashion me into the complex person I was in that moment.

Then I looked at The Rail. For generations it had served as a gathering spot, an anchoring point for different groups of kids and young adults. As one generation moved on, another took its place and claimed The Rail as theirs. The upcoming generation was always poised patiently, knowing they would eventually dwell at The Rail as people got jobs, went to college, got married and had kids of their own. It was just the way it was in our part of the Bronx, a natural fact of neighborhood evolution.

Yet in the swirling energy of the Sixties the old world changed and us along with it. Through music and the social tremors vibrating the very fabric of the planet, touched deeply by emanations of love, peace, tolerance, acceptance and understanding, The Rail became a kind of commons, where generations began to mix together regardless of age. This was a significant change, an adaptation that was profoundly beautiful as The Rail turned more inclusive.

But then our world changed yet again, with the arrival of heroin. Now The Rail felt like an anchor wrapped around my legs, dragging me down, dragging down all of us who chose to remain there.

But maybe not, I wondered as I stood there, my thoughts forming anew. Maybe it was us who were now dragging down the true spirit of The Rail by burdening it with our lifelessness, our jaded ennui with the world we had inherited, our sad conclusion that the only thing left to do was to numb out. Maybe *I* owed The Rail, and owed the neighborhood that nurtured me. Maybe I owed more than I'd given, a lot more. Maybe the way to repay that debt was to somehow live up to the obligation passed to me by generations now gone, by men and women – my Irish father among them – who dreamt about and labored for a freer, more just life. Maybe the way of honoring them was for me to leave and strike out into that world with the same *chutzpah* that went into creating this neighborhood in the first place, brought my father to these shores, and enabled people to survive the *Shoah*.

With these thoughts aswirl in my mind, I joined Michael in the front seat. Images of arriving in San Francisco, kicking drugs for good, becoming active and engaged in changing the world danced compellingly in my mind, beckoning me onward. He put the car in drive and we pulled away from The Rail, heading up the hill.

As we moved slowly under the sun dappled trees that arched above Van Cortlandt Park South, the dancing light and shadows conjured my memories of that first drive down Saxon Avenue when I arrived in the Bronx in 1956. Only this time instead of arriving, I was departing, leaving the neighborhood for good but carrying the true spirit of The Rail within my heart forever.

Epilogue

It took us three hours to navigate our way out of a snow storm in Pittsburgh before we finally found our bearings and headed west. When, after over 30 hours of straight driving, Michael began hallucinating that we were in the Macy's Thanksgiving Day parade, complete with floats and balloon figures all around us, we figured it was time to pull over for a while. Thick snowfall in the Rockies forced us to take a more southern route through the Four Corners area, where we immediately fell in love with a Navajo checkout girl, the most beautiful human we'd even seen. When we finally crossed into California we were exhausted, him from doing all the driving and me from staying awake to keep him awake. We decided to skirt Los Angeles and not become ensnared in its nightmarish traffic jams. We headed north, then west, and eventually made our way to Highway 1, eager to drive up the legendary coast road to San Francisco.

As soon as the ocean came into view I asked Michael to pull over. He found a parking area near a beach and cruised to a stop. We exited the car and slowly walked down a set of concrete steps onto the sand. I was wearing my white Converse high-top sneakers, a pair of black dungarees with my Garrison belt buckle rakishly shifted toward my left hip. I was wearing a white t-shirt, over which hung the Army jacket I had gotten at a surplus store, its right-side pockets singed from the brushfire Michael and I had extinguished in a time and a place that now seemed so incredibly long ago and far away.

The beach sand shifted awkwardly under my weight, each step feeling like I was walking on a different planet, a planet with heavier gravity and unsure footing. I saluted my two hands just above my eyebrows, fingertips touching, in an effort to provide a shield against the bright sun. I took a deep breath. The air smelled different than in the Bronx. A smattering of palm trees dotted the sidewalks above the beach and near the highway. Directly in front of me the Pacific Ocean sparkled, its waves incessant against the shore, an image I had only glimpsed through television shows and movies. I felt like the first human to ever set eyes upon this ocean. I can only imagine the look on my face as I tried to comprehend where I now stood. Between my astonished visage and my clothes, which were hardly beachcombing chic, I was certain that I cut a rather alien figure standing there. I sat down, back against a concrete retaining wall, somewhat self-conscious but mostly in shock that I was no longer in the Bronx.

It had all finally come to pass.

I looked up at Michael, extending my hand. He clasped it firmly and pulled me to my feet. We stood facing the glistening ocean one more time and then we turned toward the car. In a matter of hours we would be in San Francisco.

I had arrived and I was ready to take everything my Bronx neighborhood had gifted me with – and all of it was a gift I now realized – and become part of changing a fast changing world.

I had already started my new life.